CROWN ASSETS

The Architecture of the Department of Public Works, 1867–1967

Crown Assets recounts the history of the building program of the Department of Public Works from 1867 to 1967. One hundred years of government construction generated a broad and diverse network of post offices, federal office buildings, customs houses, drill halls, quarantine stations, hospitals, experimental farms, research institutions, and many other types of architecture. Janet Wright interprets these buildings through the forces that shaped their design and construction. Federal buildings mirrored the evolution of Canadian architecture in terms of changing styles and building technologies. They were also the product of a political and bureaucratic process and were shaped by policies, programs, and priorities. It was the interaction of these two forces – external architectural influences and the internal requirements and expectations of federal government – that defined the unique character and scope of federal building in Canada.

Crown Assets is lavishly illustrated with 194 black and white illustrations and 8 colour plates, richly depicting the federal government's profound impact on the character of the built environment in Canada.

JANET WRIGHT is an architectural historian with Parks Canada, in Calgary, Alberta.

CROWN ASSETS

The Architecture of the Department of Public Works, 1867–1967

Janet Wright

UNIVERSITY OF TORONTO PRESS
Toronto Buffalo London

Copublished by University of Toronto Press Incorporated, the Department of Canadian Heritage, Parks Canada and the Canada Communication Group – Publishing, Supply & Services Canada

Catalogue Number: R62-286-1995E

Printed in Canada

ISBN 0-8020-0912-3 (cloth)
ISBN 0-8020-7892-3 (paper)

Printed on acid-free paper

Canadian Cataloguing in Publication Data

Wright, Janet, 1951–
  Crown assets : the architecture of the Department of
  Public Works, 1867–1967

  Issued also in French under title: Les biens de la
  Couronne.
  Includes bibliographical references and index.
  ISBN 0-8020-0912-3 (bound) ISBN 0-8020-7892-3 (pbk.)

  1. Public buildings – Canada. 2. Architecture and state –
  Canada – History. 3. Canada. Dept. of Public Works.
  I. Title.

  NA4229.W75 1997   725'.1'0971   C96-931745-X

University of Toronto Press acknowledges the financial assistance to its publishing program of the Canada Council and the Ontario Arts Council.

Contents

Acknowledgments

In 1982 the Federal Heritage Building Review Office (FHBRO) was established within the National Historic Sites Directorate of Parks Canada. Its mandate is to identify and evaluate federal buildings that are of heritage value and to assist custodial departments in the management and maintenance of these buildings in a manner that will respect their historic character while continuing to serve the changing needs of government. Over the past fourteen years the FHBRO office has evaluated 4,900 buildings across Canada resulting in almost 1,200 designations. Of those designated, 226 have been identified as 'classified' buildings, the highest level of designation under the policy. A valuable by-product of this process has been the thousands of evaluation reports and the many thematic studies generated by the staff of the Architectural History Branch of National Historic Sites Directorate to assess the historical, architectural, and local significance of these structures. This body of unpublished research represents a rich source of information on the architecture and history of Canada as viewed through the lens of the federal building inventory. *Crown Assets: The Architecture of the Department of Public Works, 1867–1967* has relied extensively on this material, but it has only scratched the surface in terms of the wealth of information that the branch holds.

This book was made possible through the support of Parks Canada. In particular I would like to thank Christina Cameron, director-general of National Historic Sites Directorate, Susan Buggey, director, Historical Services, and Mary Cullen, chief of architectural analysis, who saw the project as a means of making our research more accessible to the public and of increasing public awareness of the importance of federal buildings to the Canadian landscape. I also wish to acknowledge the support provided for this publication by the Department of Public Works and Government Services Canada. In particular I wish to thank Susan Hum-Hartley, director of the Heritage Conservation Program, Real Property Services, Canadian Heritage, who recognized in this book the important contribution of her department to our history.

During the course of my research I also benefited from the advice and assistance of many people across the country. In particular I would like to acknowledge the following: Margaret Archibald, Ottawa; John Bland, Ste-Anne-de-Bellevue; Kelly Crossman, Ottawa; Derek Draper, William Head Correctional Institution in British Columbia; Neil Einarson, Winnipeg; Christopher Hives, Vancouver; Jacqueline Hucker, Ottawa; Frank Korvemaker, Saskatoon; Ted Mills, Victoria; Anna O'Neill, Yellowknife; Pierre du Prey, Queen's University; Geoffrey Simmins, Calgary; Douglas Stewart, Kingston; Christopher Thomas, Victoria; Jim Taylor, Calgary; Rhodri Windsor-Liscombe, Vancouver; and Harold Wright, Saint John, N.B. I am grateful to Nathalie Clerk at Parks Canada, who used her own extensive knowledge of Canadian architecture to ensure that the French translation accurately captured the meaning and content of the original text. I would also like to thank Monique Trépanier, who organized the illustrations, verified the captions against the text, and proved to be an able architectural photographer when required.

Finally, I would like to thank the late Mr E.A. Gardner and Mr James A. Langford. As former chief architects of the Department of Public Works their personal accounts of their careers in the department provided valuable insight into the nature of government architecture.

CROWN ASSETS

The Architecture of the Department of Public Works, 1867–1967

Introduction

In 1867 the federal Department of Public Works inherited a small building inventory from the colonial government of the United Canadas. The transfer of administration also included one staff architect who established the beginnings of the Chief Architect's Branch, which was formally set up in 1871. One hundred years later the branch, renamed the Building Construction Branch in 1953, had expanded to hundreds of employees operating out of headquarters in Ottawa and ten district offices. By then the original inventory had expanded into a vast and far-flung network of government buildings and institutions. No other part of government, institution, or corporation has had such a powerful impact on the character of the built environment in Canada. Its post offices, customs houses, government office buildings, drill halls, penitentiaries, immigration halls, quarantine stations, military hospitals, hospitals and schools for Native people, experimental farms, and federal research institutions firmly established the federal presence across the country and provided individual communities with some of their most important and most familiar architectural landmarks.

The scope of this study is defined by the buildings that were designed and constructed by or for the Chief Architect's Branch. The study covers a hundred-year period, from 1867 and the establishment of the federal Department of Public Works, to 1967, a date coinciding with a period of departmental restructuring that turned the branch into a highly decentralized organization in terms of both geography and function. It embraces a broad and diverse group of buildings which ranged from the Parliament Buildings in Ottawa to small Royal Canadian Mounted Police detachments in the High Arctic. Not all that was constructed with federal dollars during this period is examined, however. The Department of Public Works was set up in 1867 as the government's central construction agency, but its exclusive mandate was constantly being eroded and redefined. The administrative ideal, which consolidated a government function in one department, was in constant conflict with the inherent tendency for individual departments to seek operational self-sufficiency. The departments and services that generated large building inventories, such as the Department of National Defence, the Department of Transport, and the Canadian Parks Service, and the agencies with specialized building needs, such as the Penitentiary Services, the Experimental Farm Service, and the National Research Council, often felt that their building needs could be better served by creating their own departmental construction agencies. At a low point in the department's mandate, the Chief Architect's Branch controlled only 40 per cent of the federal construction budget.

This study is not intended as an administrative or political history of the Department of Public Works or the Chief Architect's Branch. Two excellent studies have already covered much of this territory.[1] Douglas Owram's *Building for Canadians: A History of the Department of Public*

Works, 1840–1960 provides a comprehensive overview of the department and of the broader political and organizational issues that shaped its history from the establishment of the Board of Works under the government of the United Canadas to 1960 and the Glassco Commission on Government Organization, which marked the beginning of the period of extensive reorganization. Margaret Archibald's *By Federal Design: The Chief Architect's Branch of the Department of Public Works, 1881–1914* examines the evolution of the branch in terms of its organizational structure, roles and responsibilities, staffing, training and supervision, contracting out, and processes for project initiation and management. Both of these studies discuss buildings, but only as by-products or as the physical evidence of the political forces and administrative procedures that created them.

I am deeply indebted in this study to both these works but I approach the same subject area from an object-oriented perspective. The buildings – not the organization – are the centre and the starting point for this study. The federal building inventory that was produced over the course of a century constitutes a visual history of the evolution of federal architecture. From this body of work one can ascertain predominant stylistic influences at any given period and the emergence of distinctive patterns or groupings of buildings defined in terms of design, function, structural types, or geographical distribution. It can be used to identify periods of high productivity, of relative dormancy, of change, and of resistance to change. It can also point to such changes in policies and practice, within the program as the constant shift between a reliance on staff architects and the use of private architects on commission.

The building inventory provides the basis for identifying and describing the character and characteristics of federal architecture in Canada, but the buildings cannot be understood in isolation from their political and cultural context. Federal buildings in Canada were products of a creative process that was carried out by architects and engineers, and they reflect the evolution of Canadian architecture – its changing styles and the emergence of new building technologies and approaches to design and planning. Building for government was also a political, economic, and social act that was carried out within the administrative culture of a federal

bureaucracy, and it was shaped by that bureaucracy's policies, programs, and priorities. The interaction and interrelationship between the two forces – external architectural influences and internal requirements and expectations of government – defined the unique character and scope of federal building in Canada.

The evolution of federal architecture traces a path of development that parallels the history of Canadian architecture in general. The stylistic progression of government building – from the Second Empire style of the post-Confederation era to the eclectic medievalism of the late nineteenth century, the Edwardian Baroque and the Beaux-Arts classicism of the early twentieth century, the modern classical and Art Deco influences of the 1930s, and the modernism of the postwar era – mirror the stylistic progression of Canadian architecture. The Chief Architect's Branch was also responsive to new building technologies and materials. For larger government buildings, traditional masonry structures (some with cast-iron supports) gave way to steel and reinforced concrete framing in the early 1900s. At the other end of the building scale, the development of prefabricated buildings also provided an economical and efficient solution to some of the government's basic building needs on the Prairies during the early settlement period and later with the opening up of the North in the 1950s. Government buildings were also quick to respond and adapt to changing approaches to facility planning, particularly with respect to such specialized building types as penitentiaries, hospitals, and quarantine stations.

The changing face of federal building corresponds with the evolution of Canadian architecture but, within that general framework, the buildings adhered to their own distinctive pattern of development, which was determined by internal factors and considerations. As a rule, government architecture placed itself comfortably within the mainstream of established architectural tastes and it rarely assumed a leadership role. Architecturally its evolution also tended to follow an irregular, halting path of development. Much of what was built for the government conformed to standard requirements, and the most efficient and economical approach was to design buildings that stayed within established design precedents. For this reason, each distinct period of building was dominated by a few basic design types which were developed either on contract or by the staff of the Chief Architect's Branch. Once these prototypes were established and shown to be successful, they proved to be extremely resistant to change. At times federal design did deviate from the architectural mainstream, however. During the first half of the twentieth century, the Department of Public Works was preoccupied with the concept of a national capital and with the need to define a distinctive architectural image for federal buildings in Ottawa. The identification of the Château style as the most appropriate theme sent government building in Ottawa on its own architectural tangent from which it did not return until the 1950s.

Federal buildings are also the by-products of the changing politics, priorities, and policies of the government. These factors determined the type of buildings that were constructed, where they were constructed, and how much money was spent. For example, the building program of the 1880s and 1890s can be interpreted as the built expression of Sir John A. Macdonald's National Policy, particularly with respect to the annexation of western Canada. Within a decade, the Chief Architect's Branch had constructed there the basic administrative infrastructure of the Dominion government in the form of a network of public buildings, courthouses, and North-West Mounted Police posts. The series of experimental farms established across the country to improve agricultural productivity and to develop crop varieties suited to Prairie and other regional conditions, and the construction of industrial schools across the West were the product of the government's policy to assimilate the Native population into an agricultural economy. In the 1930s federal public building became an instrument of economic policy, providing jobs and economic benefits. In the 1950s the rapid growth in government – brought on by economic prosperity and the implementation of many new social, technological, and cultural programs – generated a demand for a new type of multi-purpose office building in Ottawa and across Canada.

The relationship between the buildings and government programs and policies is central to this study and defines its organizational structure. The study is divided into eight chapters that correspond to eight distinctive periods of building. For almost every period the time frame is determined by political, economic, or administrative factors. Events such as war, changes in government, changes in the pattern of government spending, and changes in administration mark the beginning and the end of each period. The fact that each period often coincided with the introduction of new styles, new design types, and, sometimes, a new chief architect is an indication that changes in government had a direct impact on the character of federal architecture and on the activities of the Chief Architect's Branch.

Politics and patronage also played an important part in the history of government building. Politicians regarded public works as a useful political tool that should serve political goals. It is not the purpose of this study to detail the intricate web of relationships between the federal government, other levels of government, local riding associations, special interest groups, and all those who had vested interest in government buildings. However, it must be acknowledged that political patronage was an ever-present factor in the federal building program. Questions as to where money would be spent, whose property would be purchased as the site of the new building, which materials would be used, which architect would be appointed to design or supervise the construction, and who would serve as the clerk of works were influenced by political considerations. Overt corruption was rare in the history of the department. Strategic spending on government buildings was a basic tool for gaining or holding political power. The Public Works Construction Act of 1934, which formed an important plank in the Conservative government's re-election campaign of 1935, allocated approximately 75 per cent of the money to be spent on public buildings to government-held ridings. The single largest allocation went to the riding of Calgary West, which was held by Prime Minister R.B. Bennett.

The role of the Chief Architect's Branch in defining the evolution of the federal building program has been subject to much misinterpretation. On the surface, it resembled a large architectural firm with a complex hierarchy consisting of architects, engineers, draughtsmen, and support staff. Within this organizational model it was assumed that the chief architect would act as the senior and principal designer of the firm. Although he may not have had a direct hand in the design of every building that came out of the office, the history and evolution of federal building can be interpreted as an expression of his creative imagination and architectural sensibilities.

This notion that the chief architect served as 'architect to the nation' was a constant source of friction between the federal bureaucracy and the architectural profession. Throughout the history of the branch it was argued that the position should be held by the best architect in the country. On occasion the sentiment was also expressed from within government circles. In 1914 Adam Shortt, who chaired the Public Service Commission, questioned the decision to appoint E.L. Horwood, a little-known Ottawa architect, as the new chief architect. He wrote:

> In towns and cities in which these buildings are to be erected, they will naturally occupy some of the most prominent sites. They will also involve such an expenditure of public funds as will of necessity, render them very conspicuous architectural features in the various urban centres. To all Canadians, who appreciate the opportunities which such a situation provides for the elevation of the artistic standards of the general public and for the reputation of our country in the estimation of cultured visitors, the importance of the selection to be made for the position of Chief Architect for the Dominion Government cannot be estimated.[2]

His letter was a passionate appeal for excellence in public architecture, but it also demonstrated a fundamental misunderstanding of the role of the chief architect and of his office.

In practice there was only superficial resemblance between the Chief Architect's Branch and a private architectural office. The branch was responsible for new construction but it was also responsible for the ongoing management, maintenance, and repair of most of what it built. This property constituted a vast real estate empire and its management accounted for the largest share of the branch's operating budget and most of the personnel resources. The fact that the Department of Public Works owned the buildings that were constructed radically altered the traditional client/architect relationship which was central to the design and construction process in private practice. Government buildings were constructed according to basic requirements identified by the departments that were to occupy the buildings but that would not pay the cost of construction. The Department of Public Works, and through it the Chief Architect's Branch, was both client and architect. It provided architectural services to the government, but it also served as a financial comptroller of the federal construction dollar. It was its job to see that the money was spent wisely and efficiently. There was also a certain amount of pressure to ensure that the money was divided up among as many projects as possible in order to satisfy the constant demands for new buildings from government departments, individual communities, and the politicians who represented them.

The Chief Architect's Branch operated as part of a larger government bureaucracy, and it was expected to serve and to be subservient to its goals, priorities, and performance standards. The goals and priorities are well illustrated by the men who were hired to head the office. The position of chief architect has always been filled by skilled and competent professionals, but from the beginning national design credentials was never a requirement of the job. A good chief architect understood that his primary role was to manage federal properties, avoid public embarrassment to the government of the day, and administer a national building program in a responsible manner while maintaining acceptable standards of design and construction. Senior management within the Department of Public Works always believed that these qualities were nurtured within their own organization. Thomas Fuller (chief architect from 1881 to 1897) was the only one to come to the job with an international reputation as a leading North American architect. Of the remaining nine chief architects included in this study, seven were career federal civil servants, many with little or no professional life outside the confines of the federal bureaucracy. Two were drawn from small private practices, and one, James A. Langford (appointed chief architect in 1963), was recruited from the Saskatchewan public service, where he had been deputy minister of public works.

The changing role of the Chief Architect's Branch also reflected the priorities and values embedded in the federal bureaucracy. When an architect's branch was first established, its primary function was to manage the federal buildings stock and to carry out minor construction projects.

New construction was to be contracted out to architects in private practice. The outside architectural community would continue to play a key role by designing some of the best and most innovative works of architecture as well as hundreds of lesser-known buildings across the country, but the Department of Public Works quickly recognized the advantages of maintaining a resident architectural staff. Despite constant lobbying on the part of the architectural profession to contract the work out to private architects, the department always defended the use of its own staff. It argued that the members of its staff were more efficient because they were familiar with the requirements of the various client/tenant departments, they maintained consistent standards, and, most importantly, they understood the need of keeping within initial budget allocations. In the words of one chief architect, government architecture was shaped by three basic considerations: time, money and quality.[3] It was the job of the Chief Architect's Branch to achieve an acceptable balance between the three factors, with the third generally being subordinate to the first two.

From a critical perspective it was not a climate that invited architectural innovation or the highest standards of design excellence. The demand for careful cost control and efficiency tended to encourage standardization and repetition in design. It also made the branch resistant to new ideas and new technologies that could potentially take a project into unknown and unpredictable architectural territory. Throughout the history of the program, the Department of Public Works and the Chief Architect's Branch were severely criticized by the architectural community. In 1911 the journal *Construction* published an editorial with the self-explanatory title, 'A Competent Chief Architect and Representative Government Building the Most Pressing Need in Canada's Advancement.'[4] Similarly, in 1962 Sandra Gwyn, writing in *Canadian Art*, analysed with considerable insight the creative constraints within which government architects worked: 'Government is more interested in the finished product, in showing the public its money's worth . . . Government involvement in art is subject to public and political pressures . . . and these pressures tend to result in an inevitable timidity and restraint.'[5] In both cases the solution was an open competitive system for major architectural projects and direct contracting to independent architects for other works.

While there is justification for criticisms, the sense of dissatisfaction with the quality of federal architecture was not shared by all. Government buildings were designed to meet the needs of three basic client groups – politicians, the government, and the public – and each group viewed public buildings from its own standards and expectations. For politicians buildings were tools of political power to be used to dispense federal benefits to deserving towns, cities, and regions. Politicians were interested in the federal building program, but judging from the substance of the debates in the House of Commons they were primarily concerned with where the money was being spent and whether it was being spent responsibly. As experience has shown from the construction of the original Parliament Buildings in the 1850s and 1860s, the Langevin Building in the 1880s, and the National Arts Centre in the 1960s, charges of cost overruns and financial mismanagement are vulnerable points for any government. Accusations of architectural conservatism or artistic timidity are not.

For the government, federal buildings had two principal functions. They were built to provide the necessary accommodation for government institutions, but they also had an important role to play as symbols representing the federal presence in towns and cities across the country. In some case these symbols were expected to take the form of imposing architectural landmarks. New government buildings that were constructed for important national institutions or that were prominently located structures in Ottawa or other major urban centres had to be monumental and demonstrate the highest standards of design and construction. Although federal government architecture was generally not known as an innovative force in Canadian architecture, the buildings provided an opportunity to showcase the work of many of the country's best architects working within the mainstream of the current architectural standards.

The majority of federal buildings were erected on a modest and economical scale but they too were built to project a suitably dignified architectural image that would reflect creditably on the state. The typical federal buildings – Government of Canada Buildings, post offices, customs houses, drill halls, as well as other buildings for the whole range of government functions – were solidly constructed and competently designed structures that assumed an important place within communities by virtue of their scale and central location. Most were not outstanding works of architecture, but they were invariably welcomed with enthusiasm and regarded as valuable and pleasing assets to the community. Federal architecture was the product of government and bureaucracy but it was also an expression of public tastes and standards. From the experience of one hundred years of government architecture, it would appear that the public expectation of federal architecture was, in most instances, satisfied by good, competently designed buildings that found a comfortable balance between architectural dignity and sensible economy.

The architecture of the Department of Public Works evolved within the limitations and restrictions imposed by government, and critics could be justified in arguing that federal government architecture fell short of its full potential. From a historical perspective – from a consideration of what was built rather than what might have been built – the achievements of the Chief Architect's Branch over the course of the century have been substantial. It has overseen the construction of many of the country's most notable works of architecture. In Ottawa its buildings and many attempts at comprehensive urban planning have transformed a small provincial centre of the lumber trade into a dignified national capital that has come to stand as a symbol of the nation as a whole. The most important contribution of the Department of Public Works and of the Chief Architect's Branch lies not in the few award-winning designs, but in the thousands of smaller government buildings that can be found in cities, towns, and rural communities across the country. The buildings designed by and for the Department of Public Works often conform to standard patterns and types of design, but together they define a consistent and recognizable image of the federal government, one which has woven a common visual thread into the culturally diverse fabric of this country.

CHAPTER ONE

Building a New Nation, 1867–1881

Between 1867 and 1881 Canada's Department of Public Works laid the foundations of what would become a vast network of federal buildings and institutions. It also established the basic structures of an administration that would define the process of public building within the federal government for the next hundred years. During these first fifteen years the department was responsible for the construction of a wide variety of building types, including drill halls, federal penitentiaries, quarantine stations, immigration buildings, and marine hospitals. The most visible components of the post-Confederation building program, however, were the twenty-five new post offices, customs houses, and urban public buildings designed in the rich and ostentatious Second Empire style. These buildings were intended to provide the necessary accommodation for federal services, but they also fulfilled an important symbolic function. Confederation had been built upon an uneasy union between disparate regions, each with its own and often conflicting goals and identities. New federal buildings, particularly those large and expensive structures strategically located in major urban centres, firmly established the presence of the new federal government in the community, and created an impressive and recognizable symbol of government that projected an image of prosperity, stability, and confidence.

The Colonial Legacy, 1867–1869

The two years following Confederation marked a transition for the Department of Public Works. The roles and responsibilities of the new federal department were officially defined by an act of Parliament passed in December 1867,[1] but it was formed out of the Department of Public Works of the colonial government of the United Canadas.[2] The old organization and staff were simply absorbed into the new level of government and bureaucracy. Most government construction remained under the control of the Engineering Branch, which was headed by the chief engineer, John Page. Public buildings, which formed a relatively small part of this program, were nominally administered by the assistant chief engineer, F.P. Rubidge, who had been on staff since 1841.[3]

During the early years of Confederation very few new projects were initiated by the department. The business of taking inventory and sorting out federal and provincial property and responsibility fully occupied the staff. The new department also inherited a sizeable building inventory, which included six post offices and ten customs houses, as well as such other specialized buildings as quarantine stations, immigrant sheds, and marine hospitals.[4] Most were located in Montreal, Toronto, Kingston, and Quebec and were designed in the classical or Italian Renaissance style that was characteristic of public buildings in British colonies around the world. The federal government also assumed responsibility for the Parliament Buildings in Ottawa, which had been built to house the government of the United Canadas (Figure 1.1). From an architectural perspective, these buildings represented one of the finest examples of High Victorian Gothic architecture in North America. The decorative vocabulary was inspired by the Venetian Gothic style; the composition and treatment of materials reflected the picturesque eclecticism that characterized British architectural aesthetics of the mid-nineteenth century.[5] Dramatically situated on a high promontory overlooking the Ottawa River, the original complex consisted of three separate buildings symmetrically grouped around large, open grounds. The Centre Block, which was designed by Thomas Fuller and Chilion Jones, housed the House of Commons, the Senate, the Library, and the offices of the members of both houses. The two flanking buildings, designed by F.W. Stent and Augustus Laver, contained the various government departments. Construction had begun in 1859 and the buildings were occupied in 1865 but, because of cost overruns and general mismanagement, construction continued for another decade.[6] As discussed later in this chapter, the Parliament Buildings – the completion of the Library, the development of a landscape plan and the construction of a large addition to the West Block – remained a preoccupation of the department throughout the 1870s.

The significance of this complex transcends the aesthetic merits of the architecture. Although the product of a colonial government, it would emerge as an evocative symbol of Canada. The eclectic historicism of the group of buildings freely interpreted European and British architectural traditions, and seemed to express Canada's distinct national identity, which, in itself, was defined as an eclectic mix of British and French cultural roots transplanted in a northern climate. Throughout the history of federal building, the visual and symbolic imagery of the Parliament Buildings exerted a powerful influence on the architectural and cultural identity of the federal government in the national capital.

Redefining the Department of Public Works, 1869–1871

The period of transition ended with the appointment of Hector-Louis Langevin (1826–1906) as minister of the Department of Public Works in December 1869.[7] At the age of forty-two, Langevin was a relatively young but rising figure in the Quebec Conservative caucus who would eventually assume the role of senior Quebec minister to Sir John A. Macdonald. Langevin was well suited to the job and his skill as an administrator was noticed early in his career. In 1872 the prime minister wrote to the governor general, Lord Monck, that Langevin 'has turned out to be a first rate administrator, prompt, decided and of good judgment. He is the best minister of public works that I have ever seen in Canada.'[8] Throughout his career Langevin would exploit his portfolio to dispense patronage to his friends and supporters, but one could argue that Macdonald's assessment of Langevin as the country's best minister of public works still applies today.[9]

Langevin viewed public works as an important component of any federal initiative in a community, and, under his direction, public building was given a much higher profile. Impressive public buildings stood as tangible proof that the government was an agent of civic improvement. In 1885 Langevin, still minister of public works, defended the charge that too much money was being spent on buildings. He argued forcefully that the government required 'public offices on a scale commensurate with the wealth and the extent of the city. It is hardly dignified for the Dominion to have its public offices in a rented or poor building in large cities.'[10] Though he was absent as minister from 1873 to 1879, Langevin's power and enthusiasm energized the department for twenty-one years. His administration, particularly in the later years, was regarded as the golden age of federal architecture in Canada.

Within a year of Langevin's arrival, three major building projects were in early planning stages and four more were under discussion. To carry out such a large program of public building, Langevin decided that an architect's branch independent of the Engineering Branch would be required. Rubidge was the logical person to head the new section – he clearly wanted the job – but it was equally evident that Langevin wanted to bring in new people. In 1871 Rubidge reluctantly retired from the civil service, and in the spring of that year Thomas Seaton Scott, a private architect working out of Montreal, was hired to head the new branch. He was initially identified simply as architect. In February 1872 Scott successfully

1.1. Lithograph by J.W. Winham and W.R. Berry of the buildings on Parliament Hill in Ottawa, Ontario, in the 1870s. Architects for the Centre Block: Thomas Fuller and Chilion Jones; architects for the East and West Blocks: Augustus Laver and F.W. Stent; landscape plan by Calvert Vaux, 1873. (NA, C-947)

petitioned senior officials within the department to grant him the more impressive title of chief architect.[11]

The title chief architect has always conjured up the image of an 'architect laureate,' an architectural mastermind who exerts overall design control and puts the stamp of his own personality and aesthetic sensibilities on all buildings constructed by the department. The apparent importance of the position was reinforced by the fact that it controlled the largest public building construction budget in the country. Throughout the history of the Chief Architect's Branch, the architectural community would argue that this position should be given only to the country's best architects. The government's persistent refusal to hire according to this criterion was a constant source of friction between the two groups.

The difference of opinion stemmed from the government's definition of the nature of the job and the skills required to perform it. While the Chief Architect's Branch was often regarded as the government's in-house architectural firm, in practice its role was considerably more complex and more diverse. By the early 1870s the branch had assumed responsibility not only for the design and construction of public buildings but also for their ongoing maintenance and repairs.[12] It was a dual function that required an architect who would function as the senior architect on staff as well as the chief administrator of an extensive property management program.

In fact, in these early years the principal function of the chief architect was to manage rather than to design. In 1871 the minister of public works wrote to the Privy Council recommending that the staff of the engineering and architecture branches be kept to a minimum. Whenever work was required a contract would be awarded to an architect or engineer in private practice. As outlined by Langevin, a staff architect would be retained in Ottawa 'to direct the architectural works authorized by the [G]overnment of Canada and to control and regulate the progress and expenditures upon such works.'[13] Because no major design work was required of the Chief Architect's Branch, Langevin specified only that the department hire an architect 'with some draughting experience.'[14]

The selection of Thomas Seaton Scott was indicative of the profile that the senior staff architect or chief architect was to assume. At the time of his appointment, Scott had established a moderately successful practice in Montreal, but he would not have been considered a leading figure on the Canadian architectural scene.[15] Born in England in 1826, he had immigrated to Montreal in the 1850s, supposedly to work in some unspecified capacity on the construction of the Victoria Bridge. He was subsequently hired to supervise the construction of Christ Church Cathedral in Montreal, which had been designed by the English architect Frank Wills. Scott's association with this building – one of the most outstanding examples of the Gothic Revival style of the period – enabled him to set up his own architectural practice, but he was never to achieve anything of its scale or quality in his own right.[16] Scott had not shown himself to be a brilliant designer, but he had proved himself to be an able architectural manager in his competent supervision of building projects such as Christ Church Cathedral. This was exactly the skill required of the federal government architect as defined in the 1870s.[17]

Defining an Architectural Image for the New Dominion

The organization of the branch coincided with a conscious decision to redefine the architectural image of government buildings. The picturesque medievalism of the Parliament Buildings, which would emerge in the early twentieth century as an evocative and recognizable symbol of the government of Canada, did not seem appropriate for the 1870s. Although much admired for their excellence in design and construction, the Parliament Buildings were still the product of the old system of government and were associated with the old colonial ties. The new government clearly wanted to create a fresh architectural image that was distinct from the past.

A suitable model was found in the United States in a group of post–Civil War federal buildings that had been designed in the late 1860s and early 1870s in the ostentatious Second Empire style.[18] In March 1870 John Drewe, inspector for the Toronto Division of the Post Office, offered the Department of Public Works a set of plans for a post office that had been drawn by Alfred B. Mullett.[19] Mullett was the supervising architect of the Treasury Department in Washington and had been responsible for federal buildings in the United States. The Mullett plans, first suggested for the new post office in Quebec City and for some reason ignored, re-emerged in the planning of the new post office in Toronto. In November 1870 Toronto architect Henry Langley was hired to prepare the plans but he was also given clear instructions that his design was to conform generally to plans provided by the department (Figure 1.2).[20]

The design of the Toronto Post Office epitomized the Second Empire style as it had evolved in North America, and in many respects it represented the architectural antithesis of the Parliament Buildings.[21] Although both styles were manifestations of High Victorian eclecticism, one was European and secular in its associations, while the other was British and ecclesiastic. The Second Empire style was spiritually rooted in the grandiose monuments of the French court of Louis-Napoléon, such as the new Palace of the Louvre (1852–7) by L.T.J. Visconti and Hector-Martin Lefuel. Features such as the steeply pitched mansard roof and the horizontal ordering of the façade into tiers defined by the classical orders were inspired by the architecture of the French and Italian Renaissance, but these sources were freely interpreted. The ornamentation was rich and sculptural. The complex massing, which was symmetrical in plan but broken by projecting pavilions, created an ostentatious and exuberant architecture. The ornate roof treatment, defined by a raised tower, iron cresting, and ornate dormers, reflected Victorian tastes for varied and picturesque effects.

The layout and interior of the Toronto Post Office also defined a pattern that would reappear in subsequent buildings of this type.[22] The entire ground floor of the main block housed the large postal lobby. As was the case in all federal post offices, this public space was decorated in a grand and opulent manner. Corinthian pilasters supported an ornate cornice that surrounded the room. In order to create a sense of openness and to allow for internal flexibility, light cast-iron columns were used for internal supports on the ground level. A screen and counter that separated the public lobby area from the working space behind was kept low to enhance the sense of space. Because of the size and volume of mail to be handled in the building, a large, one-storey wing was constructed to the

1.2. Toronto Post Office, Toronto, Ontario, 1871–4. Architect; Henry Langley. The building was demolished in 1960 to make way for a new federal building, the William Lyon Mackenzie Building, which was started in 1961. (NA, PA-149200)

rear to provide a work area for sorting mail. Typically, this area was lit from above by a skylight. The upper floors contained office space, some of which was to be left undeveloped in order to accommodate future expansion. These latter areas were more modestly detailed.

The Toronto Post Office represented one of the most expensive and sophisticated buildings erected by the federal government during this fifteen-year period. A major building in a major urban centre, it incorporated materials and construction technologies to create a public monument that would endure and that would project an appearance of solidity and permanence. The main elevation was faced with sandstone imported from Ohio. By the early 1900s political pressure dictated the use of local or Canadian materials, but in the 1870s the government remained fairly flexible on this issue. Architects could request the use of imported stone if local materials did not have the desired colour or sculptural potential. As the various Canadian stonecutting lobbies became stronger, the use of foreign stone became less common in federal building. Only the main or street elevations of the Toronto building were faced with stone: for the side and rear walls the local buff brick typical of Toronto was used. The highly ornate cornice was made of galvanized iron, and the steep slope of the mansard roof was covered in slate shingles from Richmond, Quebec. Construction techniques and materials were also chosen for durability and resistance to fire. While the exterior walls were of solid masonry construction, the internal structure consisted of a grid of cast-iron columns and imported wrought-iron girders. Interior walls were built of brick.[23]

The setting was also an important consideration in the development of a new public building. Many factors influenced the selection of a particular site. A public building, by its size and function, constituted an important focal point in a community, and the purchase of a lot by the federal government brought economic gain not only to the owner of that site but also to those who owned land around it. It was inevitable, therefore, that the government should try to direct the benefit toward its supporters. But within the framework of politics and patronage, the Department of Public Works also sought locations that would be central and convenient to the public and that would firmly establish the building as

a central landmark within its urban setting. The Toronto Post Office illustrates well this conscious and effective use of setting. Although corner locations were generally preferred, this building stood at the top of a T-junction formed by Toronto and Adelaide streets, where it created an impressive conclusion to the vista from the bottom of Toronto Street (Figure 1.3).

In the Toronto Post Office the federal government established a prototype for federal buildings that would endure for the next ten years. When Scott assumed office in Ottawa, he was expected to accept the new architectural image for public buildings. In his previous work Scott had, in fact, shown almost no inclination towards the Second Empire style, having established himself as a designer of Gothic Revival churches. Perhaps for this reason, one of his first activities as a government architect was to indoctrinate himself in the approved mode by touring the cities of Portland, Boston, and New York, all sites of new Alfred Mullett buildings.[24] On his return to Ottawa in 1871, Scott enthusiastically adopted the Second Empire style as architectural policy.

Over the next three years, a boost in building activity produced some of the finest examples of the Second Empire style in the country. The Montreal Post Office, designed by H.-M. Perrault (1872–6), and the Toronto Customs House, by R.C. Windeyer (1873–6), illustrate well the richness that characterized this period of public architecture (Figures 1.4 and 1.5). The Montreal building drew upon a more formal classical vocabulary, with monumental Corinthian columns and an abundance of stone and cast-iron detail that demonstrated the skill of local stonemasons. The Toronto Customs House adopted a more flamboyant interpretation of the Second Empire style. The exterior was articulated by a vertical sequence of rusticated piers, panelled pilasters, and paired pilasters. The light, delicate quality of the detailing contrasted with the heavier, more robust character of the Montreal building. Like the Toronto building, its ground floor was defined by a large, open space supported by cast-iron columns that housed the postal lobby and mail room.

The Toronto Customs House was exceptional for its elaborate and unusual interior design. Although the building was demolished in 1919, the surviving detailed architectural drawings reveal a sumptuous interior that surpassed most other federal buildings in its grand scale and lavish detail (Figure 1.6). The main entrance and vestibule opened into a grand hall that rose up three storeys to a lantern at the top. It contained a wide central staircase that led up to the customs long room on the second level. This room, which served as the main public reception and working space, provided the focus of the design and its central function was clearly expressed in the quality of its interior detail. Measuring 60 feet by 40 feet, the room extended through two storeys and was enclosed by a high, coved ceiling. Tall, semicircular windows on three sides of the room provided a brightly lit interior. The cornice, windows, and door surrounds and the two fireplaces were elaborately decorated with richly carved and moulded wood and plaster detail.

These new government buildings were welcomed with enthusiasm by their communities, and their symbolic meaning was clearly understood by the public. A published account of Toronto written in 1884 described the recent contributions of the federal government to the local environment:

> The Customs House is one of those among our public buildings which, like the General Post Office, illustrates most vividly the vast advance made by our city in the last ten years . . . As in the case of the Post Office, the architectural beauty of the Customs House is enhanced by its central and commanding situation. It is a palace not unworthy of the commercial interests of a great and progressive city.[25]

In smaller towns, customs offices were usually located above the post office, but in large cities the customs house often overshadowed the post office. Up until 1917, with the introduction of a federal income tax, customs revenue provided the principal source of income for the federal government, and therefore the customs house represented an important source of the nation's wealth.[26] Such a building required a palatial public space to mark its importance to local trade and commerce. Generally the customs house of the nineteenth century housed the administrative and

1.3. Toronto Post Office, Adelaide Street, as seen from the bottom of Toronto Street in the 1890s. (NA, RD-348)

1.4. Post Office, Rue Saint-Jacques, Montreal, Quebec, 1872–6. Architect: H.-M. Perrault. Now demolished. (NA, PA-53140)

public services; a separate storage depot, or 'customs examining warehouse,' was often located adjacent to the building. In the 1870s two major customs examining warehouses were constructed, one in Toronto and the other in Montreal.[27] Adopting a typical warehouse formula, these buildings featured open plans and fire-resistant construction consisting of cast-iron columns, wrought-iron girders, and concrete flooring. By the early twentieth century customs houses would incorporate public offices and the examining warehouse into one building.

Buildings such as the Montreal Post Office and the Toronto Customs House represented the most notable products of the federal building program in the period up to 1881. Because they were located within major urban centres, lavish buildings with generous budgets could be justified. In smaller communities, more modest buildings were designed and constructed by Scott's own staff. The Victoria Customs House, designed in 1873, typified this scale of building (Figure 1.7). The retention of the mansard roof placed this building within the federal architectural family, but the architecture was reduced to its most economical terms. Constructed of solid brick instead of the more expensive stone, it employed a simple block plan modestly detailed with a bracketed wood cornice, stone quoins at the corners, and cut-stone trim around the windows and entrance. This building represented the earliest example of a typical in-house design that would become increasingly prevalent as the decade wore on.

The Emergence of a Self-Sufficient Chief Architect's Branch

In November 1873 the Conservative government of Sir John A. Macdonald was defeated in the House of Commons and a new federal government under the leadership of Alexander Mackenzie took over. Changes in government do not necessarily affect the day-to-day workings of a government department, but in this case the transfer of power marked a noticeable shift in policy. As leader of the Opposition, Mackenzie had vigorously attacked the Department of Public Works for its extravagance, waste, and corruption. His party had come to power on a platform of fiscal responsibility and efficient government. To ensure that his election promise was fulfilled, Mackenzie, who had been trained as a stonemason, decided to take on the public works portfolio himself.[28] The arrival of his Liberal government coincided with an economic recession and declining federal revenues. These two factors created a new climate of frugality which was clearly reflected in the buildings.

More significantly, the process of designing buildings within the federal government changed. Under Langevin, the branch had functioned primarily as an administrative and coordinating office for contracts awarded to private architects, but after 1873 few commissions were granted and most new plans were prepared by Scott and his staff. By internalizing the design process in the federal bureaucracy, the government was able to maintain much tighter control over expenditures. This new policy marked the beginning of a process of expansion and growing self-sufficiency within the federal government's building bureaucracy that would continue unabated until the 1930s.[29]

The new policy would also trigger the recurring debate over who should design government buildings. Throughout the history of the branch, the architectural lobby argued that the use of private architects would result in higher standards of design, but this would only be true if the best architects were hired. In government, the selection of an architect was made by politicians and, as a result, political as well as professional credentials had to be taken into account. The appointment of the Toronto architect R.C. Windeyer to design the Toronto Customs House illustrates well the nature of the process. In 1872 Langevin wrote to the prime minister: 'If you have no objections, I shall appoint Mr. Windhier [sic] and his partner, architects of the Toronto Customs House work. Windhier is strongly recommended by Beatty and Harrison and backed by a real gentleman his nephew who is a great friend of yours. It is a pressing matter. What do you say?'[30] The selection of an architect was one of a number of ways that a politician could repay a political favour, reward political loyalty, or simply demonstrate to his constituents his political influence and his ability to act in their interests.

For the politicians and the bureaucracy, however, these small patronage

1.5. Customs House, Yonge at Front Street, Toronto, Ontario, 1873–6. Architect: R.C. Windeyer. The building was demolished in the 1910s to make way for the new customs house, which was not started until 1929. (NA, PA-46479)

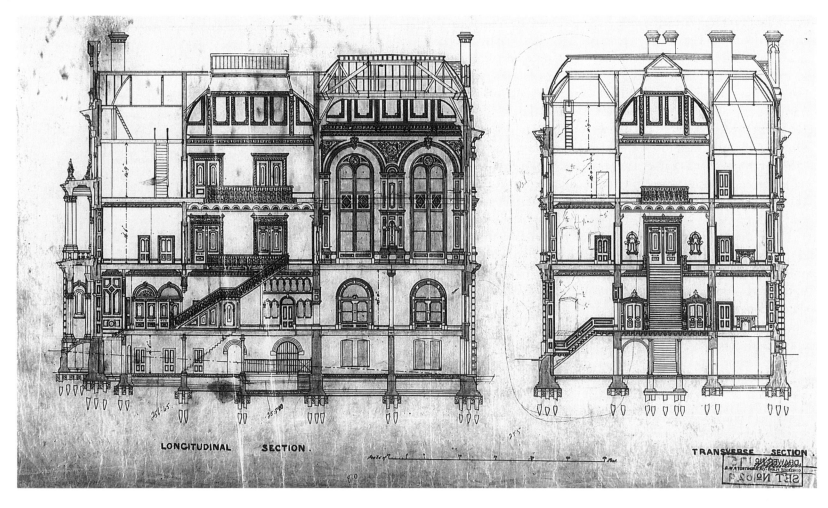

LONGITUDINAL   SECTION.

TRANSVERSE   SECTION

1.6. Architectural section, Toronto Customs House. The two-storey long room can be seen in the longitudinal section. (NA, NMC 39532)

appointments were, for the most part, an administrative nuisance that brought few political rewards.[31] The government was always under irresistible and understandable pressure to hire a local person when possible, which did not always result in the best or most competent architect being hired. It was easier to maintain consistent design standards and tight budget controls by carrying out the initial planning and design work within the federal bureaucracy. Staff tended to be more familiar with the specialized needs of the client departments and more willing to accept the constraints imposed by the government. Politicians were spared the petitions of architects for contracts, and they were relieved of the sensitive business of appointing one architect while overlooking another.

The impact of the new policy was evident in the character of the buildings constructed under the Liberal administration. Whereas the buildings of the early 1870s had demonstrated a lavishness of expenditure and individuality of design, under the Mackenzie regime they became increasingly economical in their execution. Public buildings continued to stand as symbols of the state, but they were now symbols of a state that was ruled by a strong sense of economy and fiscal responsibility.

During this period, fewer buildings were constructed and those that were built tended to be small, compact buildings, similar in design to the Victoria Customs House.[32] The post office in Fredericton, New Brunswick, designed in the last days of the Mackenzie government, provides a good example of this level of building. Although modest in scale and detail when compared to a building like the Toronto Post Office, it nevertheless demonstrates a growing maturity in the quality of the designs by the Chief Architect's Branch. The lively contrasts of brick and stone and the central emphasis, created by the imposing entrance architrave and the raised tower, set the design, at little cost, above the purely functional level to make it an important government building (Figure 1.8).

Even larger buildings, such as the Mackenzie Building (1876–8), which formed the nucleus of the newly established Royal Military College in Kingston, demonstrates this spirit of economy (Figure 1.9).[33] The mansard roof with iron cresting and the symmetrical pavilion massing places this building well within the Second Empire style, but the quality of its detail contrasts sharply with a building like the Toronto Customs

1.7. Customs House, Victoria, British Columbia, 1873–5. Plans prepared by the Chief Architect's Branch. (Public Works and Government Services Canada, Heritage Recording and Technical Data Services, 1980)

1.8. Post Office, Fredericton, New Brunswick, 1878–9. Plans prepared by the Chief Architect's Branch. (Public Works and Government Services Canada, Heritage Recording and Technical Data Services, 1987)

House or the Montreal Post Office. Constructed in the intractable limestone of Kingston, the façade is severely articulated with simple, cut-stone trim.

The Mackenzie Building is also one of the few federal buildings of the 1870s to survive with its interior intact. The main entrance opens into a vestibule featuring a cross-ribbed vault supported on four plaster columns. From here, a short flight of stairs leads to a larger entrance foyer dominated by a wide central staircase that rises up through the centre of the space to a landing lit by tall, semicircular stained-glass windows (Figure 1.10). The staircase is finished with paired octagonal newel posts with inlaid wood decoration, two richly turned free-standing colonnettes, and intricate fretwork design decorating the staircase stringers. The principal hallways, which extend on either side of the entrance hall, are finished with pine wainscoting and finely crafted pine mouldings and doors. The economy of design referred to in the mid-1870s should not be equated with the spare, minimalist interiors that today's economies can bring to public building. While certainly not lavishly finished by the standards of the period, the Mackenzie Building illustrates the high quality of the craftsmanship and materials that were generally brought to all important federal buildings during this period.

There were a few notable exceptions to this pattern of restraint. The largest and most complex project undertaken by Scott and his staff during the Mackenzie administration was the completion and expansion of the Parliament Buildings (see Figure 1.1). Here the climate of restraint was not as evident. The Library wing, which is defined by the octagonal structure at the rear of the Centre Block, was modelled after a medieval chapter house. The exterior was designed by Fuller and Jones but no plans were prepared for the interior. This task was left to the staff of the Chief Architect's Branch, who developed a Gothic decorative theme in the form of richly carved shelving and galleries that harmonized well with the massive ribbed-vault structure of the interior dome.[34]

Between 1875 and 1879 the staff also carried out a landscape plan for Parliament Hill, which had been designed in 1873 by Calvert Vaux, a well-known Anglo-American landscape designer. To complement the symmetrical arrangement of the Parliament Hill grouping, Vaux devel-

1.9. Mackenzie Building, Royal Military College, Kingston, Ontario, 1876–8. Plans prepared by the Chief Architect's Branch. (Public Works and Government Services Canada, Heritage Recording and Technical Data Services, 1990)

1.10. Main entrance foyer, Mackenzie Building, Royal Military College, Kingston, Ontario. (J. Wright, Parks Canada, 1993)

oped a formal layout with a wide central avenue and two diagonal walkways that cut across the grounds (see Figure 1.1). At the front of the Centre Block, Vaux introduced a substantial retaining wall, which was broken by a wide central staircase leading to the main entrance. This element served to create a smooth transition between the lower ground of the two departmental buildings and the higher ground of the Centre Block. Visually, it also gave added emphasis and prominence to the building that represented the seat of government.[35]

In 1874 work began on a large addition to the West Block (Figure 1.11). The entry of British Columbia, Prince Edward Island, and Manitoba into Confederation and the acquisition of the North-West Territories from the Hudson's Bay Company had resulted in an increase in the size of government and bureaucracy in Ottawa. The West Block addition demonstrated the ability of the Chief Architect's Branch to tackle with competence a demanding and sophisticated design problem. The new addition harmonized well with the existing building in its use of similar materials and Gothic detail. The Mackenzie Tower, its dominant feature, provided a central focus to the elevation, and masked, to some extent, the transition between the original building and the new construction. The eavesline was raised and the mansard roof suppressed in order to provide a more spacious and functional third storey. The resulting design created a new, secondary focus to Parliament Hill. The principal elevation was still defined by the three buildings grouped around the central square facing onto Wellington Street, but the West Block addition and the Mackenzie Tower dominated the view of the hill from the west end of the city and the Chaudière Falls area of Hull. As will be seen, the Mackenzie Tower would become an important feature in the development of a comprehensive plan for a government precinct to the west of Parliament Hill in the early twentieth century.

The second major undertaking initiated under the Mackenzie government was a new customs house in Saint John, New Brunswick (Figure 1.12).[36] Built to replace a structure that was destroyed in the fire of 1877, it was a massive E-shaped building that measured 200 feet across the front. The two end pavilions, housing the Department of Marine and

1.11. Mackenzie Tower, West Block, Parliament Buildings, Ottawa, Ontario, 1874–8. Designed by Thomas Seaton Scott and the Chief Architect's Branch. (NA, PA-46492)

1.12. Customs House, Saint John, New Brunswick, 1878–81. Designed by J.T.C. McKean and G.E. Fairweather and the Chief Architect's Branch. Demolished in 1961. (NA, C-3087)

Fisheries (on the left) and the offices of the Department of Customs and Inland Revenue and of the Department of Public Works (on the right), formed discrete units with no internal access to the middle section, which housed the customs long room. The decision to build on such a grand scale may have been influenced by the fact that the Liberal government was heading into an election and that two of the three ministries to be housed in the building were, at the time, headed by New Brunswick representatives.

Although the design of the building has been attributed to the local firm of J.T.C. McKean and G.E. Fairweather, the documentation is not conclusive on the issue. In the annual reports of the Department of Public Works, McKean and Fairweather are generally referred to as 'local' or 'superintending' architects, terms that usually denote a supervisory rather than a designing function; however, departmental correspondence relating to the project indicates that McKean and Fairweather played an active role in the design of the building. In this case the design was probably a cooperative effort between the branch and the local architects; the attribution of a design to an individual architect or firm was not usually clear-cut. Throughout the history of the branch, the relationship between the Chief Architect's Branch in Ottawa and local contractors was complex and shifting. Some architects were allowed a great deal of independence, while others were expected to execute a set of working drawings that had been prepared by the branch. As the Second Empire design of the Saint John Customs House indicates, however, all contract architects worked with a clear understanding not only of the functional requirements and the allocated budget, but also of the approved style for federal architecture in a given period.

The return of a Conservative government in 1878 marked a return to the old policy of hiring more private architects on commission and of relying less on the branch staff. Between 1878 and 1881 new public buildings were planned for Saint John in New Brunswick and for Belleville and St Catharines in Ontario, and all were designed under contract to private architects. Both of the Ontario contracts were given to R.C. Windeyer, indicating that he had kept up his useful contacts with members of the Conservative Party.

Outside central Canada and the Maritimes there did not appear to be as much pressure to hire local architects. Instead, the Chief Architect's Branch initiated the practice of relying either upon the services of district engineers to oversee projects or upon resident staff architects in areas where there was a concentration of work.[37] For example, in 1873 the branch dispatched J.P.M. Lecourt, originally from Quebec, to serve as resident architect in Winnipeg and to oversee the construction of three small public buildings and a federal penitentiary.[38] Around 1880, in the midst of the building boom in Winnipeg created by the impending arrival of the Canadian Pacific Railway, he reappeared to supervise several new building projects. Private architects were practising in Winnipeg at this time, but clearly they lacked the necessary influence and political connections required to secure government contracts.

Establishing a Client Base

The Chief Architect's Branch always regarded the design and construction of post offices, customs houses, and other urban public buildings as its first priority. For this reason, the branch was always able to maintain a close and effective working relationship with such departments as the Post Office and Customs and Inland Revenue that occupied these buildings. But the Chief Architect's Branch also provided architectural and engineering services to many other departments. It built immigration buildings and quarantine stations for the Department of Agriculture, marine hospitals for the Department of Marine and Fisheries, penitentiaries for the Department of Justice, and drill halls and armouries for the Department of Militia and Defence. With many of these departments, particularly those with specialized needs, such as the Penitentiaries Branch of the Department of Justice and the Department of Militia and Defence, the architect-client relationship was not always easy. During the 1870s and 1880s the Chief Architect's Branch would retain control over most public buildings, but there were clear signs of the beginnings of tension between the branch and some departments that felt they should have control over their own construction programs.

Penitentiary Architecture

During the 1870s the Chief Architect's Branch was asked to design several federal penitentiaries for the Department of Justice. The first was located at Stony Mountain near Winnipeg (1873), and it was followed by two more at New Westminster in British Columbia (1874) and at Dorchester in New Brunswick (1876).[39] The influence of the Chief Architect's Branch can be seen in their exterior design. All three featured a central administration block designed in an austere version of the Second Empire style. The Dorchester Penitentiary, which was the most elaborate of the three, featured a symmetrical plan that was accented by three projecting pavilions and a high mansard roof (Figure 1.13). The exterior massing resembled to some extent the nearly contemporary design for the Mackenzie Building at the Royal Military College in Kingston, but it was given an even more severe interpretation. Detailing of the façade was restricted to patterns of stone quoining around the doors and windows; even the iron cresting, originally evident at the Royal Military College building, had been eliminated as too frivolous.

The Second Empire elements of the Dorchester Penitentiary were a superficial mask to a building whose layout and organization reflected principles of prison design that had originated in the prison reform movement of the late eighteenth and early nineteenth centuries. In the early nineteenth century the prison was transformed from a place of detention into an instrument of reform. New prisons were built based on the assumption that to confine and control was to correct. By placing criminals in a controlled and structured environment that combined individual confinement with a program of work and moral training, deviant behaviour could be corrected. In the nineteenth century Canadian penitentiaries adopted the 'Auburn' plan, which had been developed in the United States early in the century. The plan combined individual cells with congregate work areas. The typical Auburn-type block consisted of two freestanding rows of cells set back-to-back and stacked in tiers. Open galleries around the outer perimeter of the block provided access to the cells (Figure 1.14). The Kingston Penitentiary, established in the 1830s, was the first and largest example of the Auburn plan in Canada and it was also the first to employ a Greek cross plan, consisting of a central rotunda with four radiating wings. One wing housed the administrative services and the remaining three incorporated banks of cells, all of which could be observed from the central point in the rotunda.

The plan and spatial organization of federal prisons designed by the Chief Architect's Branch adhered to the Kingston model. The Dorchester Penitentiary featured a front administration block containing offices, an apartment for the warden, and a chapel. A large, open rotunda, forming the central observation point, separated the administration block from the cell block, which was made up of tiers of cells laid out in the typical Auburn pattern. By the 1870s prison conditions had become a little more humane, although prisoners were still held for most of the day in cells that only measured 4 feet by 6 feet. The elongated windows on the exterior of the cell block at Dorchester were characteristic of the penitentiary designs of the 1870s and had the advantage of bringing more light to the interior. Although the Greek cross plan was not evident in the building as constructed, it was designed to accommodate two more wings that would project from the centre guard room when the need arose.

According to the annual reports of the department, all three penitentiaries – Stony Mountain, New Westminster, and Dorchester – were designed by the staff of the Chief Architect's Branch. Internal correspondence suggests that the Penitentiaries Branch exerted considerable control over the design and construction process. In the early years of Confederation the Penitentiaries Branch had managed its own buildings, and in 1872 it appointed Thomas Painter and James Adams, both trades instructors at the Kingston Penitentiary, as architects for the penitentiaries at Kingston and St-Vincent-de-Paul. In 1874 responsibility for all buildings within the branch was transferred to the Department of Public Works, but both Painter and Adams appear to have been closely involved in developing the plans for the prisons at Stony Mountain and New Westminster.[40] After 1874 a compromise arrangement was worked out with the appointment of John Bowes as the designated penitentiary architect. Although Bowes was nominally on the chief architect's staff, he appears to have worked exclusively for the Penitentiaries Branch until his retirement in 1892.[41] This arrangement was, however, a constant irritant to

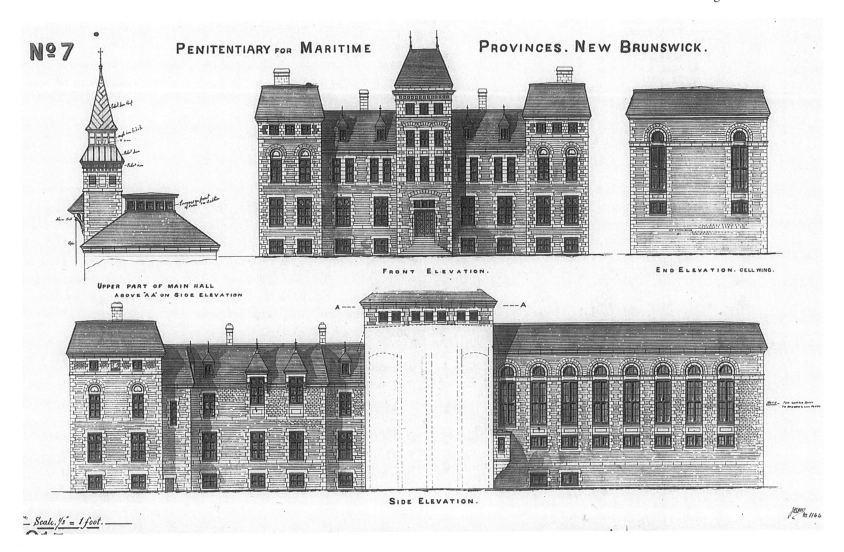

1.13. Drawing of front, side, and rear elevations, Dorchester Penitentiary, New Brunswick, 1876–9. Plans prepared by the Chief Architect's Branch. (NA, NMC 57901)

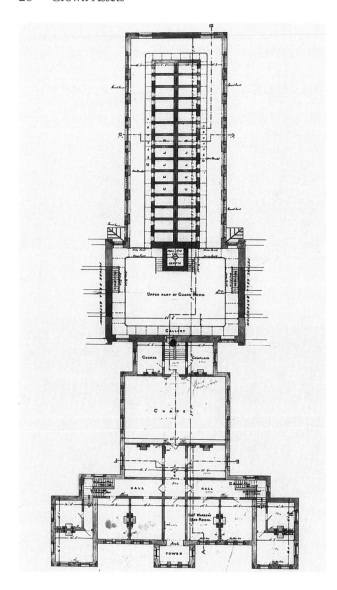

1.14. Floor plan, Dorchester Penitentiary, New Brunswick. (NA, NMC 57904)

the Penitentiaries Branch, which felt that the Department of Public Works was too slow in responding to its needs. By the late 1890s it had taken charge of its own construction and only called upon the services of the Chief Architect's Branch when needed. These services would be transferred back to the Department of Public Works only in the 1960s.

Drill Halls and Armouries

Another important client for the Chief Architect's Branch was the Department of Militia and Defence. In the nineteenth and early twentieth centuries Canada had no standing permanent army and relied instead on an active volunteer militia for its military and civil defence. To maintain and train these volunteer militia units, a network of armouries and drill halls had to be provided in communities across the country.[42] Training took the form of regular drill exercise and target practice. The provision of an indoor parade ground with lighting enabled training to continue in the evenings and year-round. Facilities were also required for the safe storage of arms and equipment.

As with the Penitentiaries Branch, there was always a certain amount of tension between the Department of Militia and Defence and the Department of Public Works, and for fifty years the two departments would battle each other over jurisdiction. The militia wanted to maintain control over its own building programs; it did not think that the civilian architects in the Chief Architect's Branch were capable of designing buildings according to military standards. In 1867 Walter Moberley, an engineer then working for the Northern Railway of Canada, was asked by the Department of Militia and Defence to prepare three standard plans for drill sheds of varying sizes.[43] The plans called for simple, inexpensive wood-frame buildings, and over the next five years more than 110 of these structures were erected across Ontario and Quebec. By the late 1870s, however, plans were being developed to replace some of these temporary sheds with permanent drill halls of brick and stone. By this time the Chief Architect's Branch had built up a permanent staff of experienced architects, and it felt that these buildings, which would form important landmarks in the community, should fall within its mandate.

In the 1870s three brick drill halls were constructed in Ontario, but only one, the Cartier Square Drill Hall in Ottawa, was designed by the Chief Architect's Branch (Figures 1.15 and 1.16).[44] Built in 1879 to house the Governor General's Foot Guards and the 43rd Battalion, it is the oldest extant city drill hall in the country. The plan was typical of the new drill halls. A large, open drill area measuring 178 feet by 75 feet was flanked on two sides by two floors of smaller rooms and armouries. The upper level was reserved for mess rooms and band rooms for officers and non-commissioned officers. A lean-to gun shed ran across the back of the building. Structurally, it was quite conservative, incorporating stone foundations, brick-bearing walls, and a fairly conventional timber queen-post truss system instead of one of iron or of iron and wood. According to the branch's annual report, the cost of the building was modest, and like many of the low-budget departmental designs the exterior design relied on the combination of red brick with white brick detail in the window and door surrounds for decorative effect.[45] The design was vaguely Italianate in style, with its tall, round-headed windows, although the stamp of the Chief Architect's Branch can be seen in the use of mansard roofs, originally ornamented with iron that crested on the two corner towers.

The Department of Agriculture and the Immigration Service

The Department of Agriculture, which operated immigration depots and quarantine stations, was one of the Chief Architect's Branch's most important and least troublesome clients. In 1867 the federal government had inherited a few immigration sheds at Quebec and Montreal and two quarantine stations, at Grosse Île, downstream from Quebec, and at Partridge Island, at the entrance to Saint John harbour.[46] Although the building activities of the Department of Agriculture were fairly modest in this period compared to the large-scale expansion that took place between 1890 and 1914, the department quickly set to work in upgrading and expanding its building inventory. The department needed to create a network of facilities that could efficiently process new immigrants from their port of entry to their final destination. It was motivated less by

a deep concern for the comfort and welfare of the immigrants than by the realization that, if left to their own resources, poorer immigrants would become destitute in major cities and ports.

The quarantine station represented the first step in the immigration process. Quarantine stations had been established in the 1830s at Grosse Île and Partridge Island in reaction to a series of cholera epidemics.[47] Quebec was the most important port of entry, and Grosse Île was, therefore, the largest facility, consisting in 1867 of about twenty hospital sheds, several staff residences, Catholic and Protestant chapels, and various service buildings.[48] Partridge Island was much smaller, consisting of a few hospital sheds and a residence for the medical inspector. In 1872 and 1873 the system was expanded with the development of a station at Lawlor's Island, near Halifax, and of another minor station near Chatham in New Brunswick.

In the 1870s the quarantine system was much more rigorous than it would become by the 1930s. In general, it reflected a virtually nonexistent science of epidemiology and a consequent problem of identifying illnesses quickly and accurately. All ships entering Canada were inspected by resident medical officers. If a contagious disease was suspected, the ship and all its passengers would be held in quarantine for approximately two weeks. Quarantine stations in Canada typically consisted of a landing wharf, hospital facilities for the sick, and residential barracks for the convalescent or healthy. There were also a number of residential and service buildings for the resident medical and support staff.

During these early years, a very basic standard of construction was adopted for the buildings. Quarantine stations tended to expand and contract in reaction to immediate needs, and generally the buildings were regarded as temporary. Many of the structures were referred to as sheds and most were constructed from a wooden frame set on stone foundations or piers. Exteriors were sheathed in clapboard, or occasionally in board and batten siding; roofs were usually covered with wood shingles. The buildings were not meant to last and, as a result, very few survive from this period.

At Lawlor's Island, the Department of Public Works constructed two small hospital sheds and one convalescent shed, but most new building

1.15. Cartier Square Drill Hall, Ottawa, Ontario, 1879. Plans prepared by the Chief Architect's Branch. (M. Trépanier, Parks Canada, 1989)

took place at Grosse Île.[49] Around 1873 an immigrant shed, some stables, and other service buildings were constructed. One of the few surviving buildings of this period at Grosse Île is the Protestant Chapel built in 1877–8 (Figure 1.17).[50] Its board and batten siding, Gothic windows, and decorative wooden buttresses represent a toy-like example of the Carpenter Gothic style. The original plans, prepared in Ottawa by the Chief Architect's Branch, were for a much simpler structure featuring rectangular windows. It would appear that the local builders or staff took it upon themselves to dress up the building with the added detailing. Throughout the history of quarantine stations, the local staffs maintained a certain degree of self-sufficiency from the public works office in Ottawa, often initiating and carrying out some smaller projects on their own.

In the early 1880s the network of immigration facilities began to expand and the Chief Architect's Branch began to use a more solid and permanent type of construction for some projects. In 1881 work began on a two-storey hospital at Grosse Île (Figure 1.18). Built of load-bearing brick on stone foundations, it conformed, for the most part, to standard hospital conventions of the period. The centre block contained administrative offices, waiting- and day-rooms, kitchen facilities, and staff bedrooms. The two outer wings contained the wards. They measured 60 feet by 25 feet, accommodated twenty beds, and had windows on three sides. This was a typical ward design of the period.[51] The form was determined by the number of beds that could be supervised by one nurse and by the need to allow light and fresh air to enter. The louvred shutters were a standard feature of hospital design; they let in air but the staff was able to control the amount of light.

Immigration stations formed the other major component of the network. Prior to Confederation, immigration sheds had been built in Montreal and Quebec. They were very simple structures that provided rudimentary crude shelter for the new arrivals. In the 1870s, the Department of Agriculture called upon the Department of Public Works to expand this network with a series of new buildings in major transportation centres across the country. These later buildings tended to be more solidly built of wood or brick with stone foundations. Most were two storeys in height

1.16. Interior view, Cartier Square Drill Hall. (M. Trépanier, Parks Canada, 1993)

1.17. Protestant Chapel, Grosse Île, Quebec, 1877–8. Plans prepared by the Chief Architect's Branch. The plans show flat-headed windows and doors; the pointed windows and door were modifications made on the site. (J. Beardsell, Parks Canada, 1990, S-181-1)

and were located along railway tracks. Intended to provide shelter for only a short time while the new arrivals were being processed by immigration agents and transferred onto another train, they were equipped with offices for the immigration agent, a dining hall, a kitchen, and sleeping areas on the second floor. Between 1870 and 1873 immigration stations were built in Toronto, Kingston, Quebec, Montreal, Sherbrooke, and London.[52] In 1881 the Canadian Pacific Railway reached Winnipeg, bringing with it immigrants planning to settle on the Prairies. Between 1880 and 1882 an immigrant hospital and a large immigration shed were constructed in Winnipeg and another immigration building was constructed at Brandon. Again, these buildings tended to be fairly cheaply constructed, and within twenty years they would all be replaced by larger buildings.

Marine Hospitals

The Chief Architect's Branch was also responsible for the construction of a number of marine hospitals. These buildings, which were located in or near significant centres of shipping throughout the Maritimes and Quebec, provided hospital accommodation for Canadian and foreign sailors. Administered by the Department of Marine and Fisheries and paid for out of a special tax levied on shipping tonnage, they were intended to relieve local hospital facilities of the responsibility of caring for non-resident sailors. At Confederation the department inherited approximately seven marine hospitals from the various colonial governments.[53] This service remained intact until the 1930s, but very few specialized marine hospitals were built after the 1880s.

The 1870s represented a brief period of expansion for marine hospitals. New buildings were constructed at Victoria, British Columbia (1872), St Andrews, New Brunswick (1873), Souris, Prince Edward Island (1875), Sydney, Nova Scotia (1876), Pictou, Nova Scotia (1878), and Lunenburg, Nova Scotia (1879).[54] Unlike the large immigration hospital at Grosse Île, these buildings were generally small cottage hospitals designed to accommodate eight to twelve patients. Surviving architectural plans for these buildings reveal considerable variety in design, but the Marine Hospital at Lunenburg provides a good illustration of the scale

1.18. Hospital, Grosse Île, Quebec, 1881–2. Plans prepared by the Chief Architect's Branch in consultation with Frederick Montizambert, medical superintendent, Grosse Île. Destroyed by fire in 1968. (NA, PA-46800)

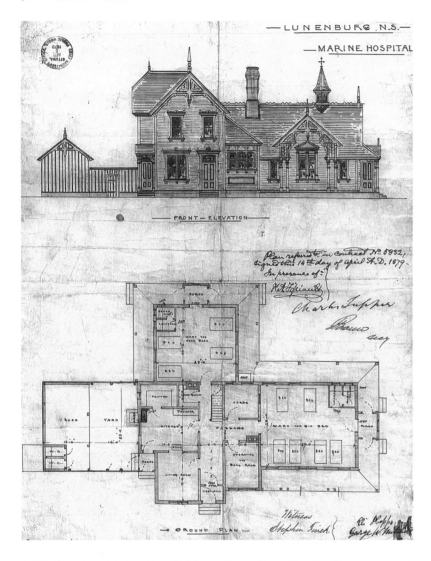

1.19. Drawing, Marine Hospital, Lunenburg, Nova Scotia. Plans prepared by the Chief Architect's Branch in 1879. (NA, NMC 23403)

of building and the residential appearance of the design (Figure 1.19). It was a two-and-a-half-storey wood-frame and clapboard building, with one-storey wings to the side and rear. The main part of the building contained offices and living accommodation for the resident steward and the wings housed the wards. The design was typical of High Victorian domestic architecture in North America. Features such as the asymmetrical L-shaped plan, decorative bargeboard and finials along the eaves, and the elaborate and richly turned millwork of the porch were typical of the period. Only elements such as the ventilator on the roof, to bring fresh air into the wards, provided a clue to its hospital function.

Planting the Flag: Building on the Prairies

In 1870 the federal government purchased from the Hudson's Bay Company a vast tract of land that included present-day Manitoba, Saskatchewan, and Alberta. The small area around the Red River settlement, where a thriving agricultural community had been established in the early part of the century, was carved out of the old Hudson's Bay territory to form the province of Manitoba. The remaining land, populated by Native people and Métis living a nomadic way of life based on the buffalo hunt, was placed under a territorial government controlled by Ottawa. The annexation of the territories constituted a key piece in fulfilling the Canadian vision of a nation from sea to sea. Federal policy during the post-Confederation era was shaped by the government's intent to Canadianize the Northwest.[55]

Federal building in Manitoba took on a scale unique to the Prairies. By the 1870s Winnipeg was already an established community with a population of close to 4,000 inhabitants, and the type of federal building it required did not differ substantially from other mid-sized towns elsewhere in the country. In the mid-1870s the government constructed a post office and land titles offices in Winnipeg and a federal penitentiary at Stony Mountain. All were solid, brick structures with the emblematic mansard roof.

The Department of Public Works was also responsible for the construction of the provincial legislative building. Manitoba had been given

1.20. Manitoba Legislative Building, Winnipeg, Manitoba, 1881–3. Plans prepared by the Chief Architect's Branch. (NA, PA-31611)

1.21. Superintendent's Residence, Fort Battleford, Saskatchewan, 1876. Plans prepared by the Chief Architect's Branch. Fort Battleford is now a national historic site. (J. de Jonge, Parks Canada, 1989)

limited provincial status in 1870, but it was still dependent on federal grants for about 80 per cent of its revenue.[56] The provincial legislative assembly represented an integral part of the federal system of government, and the government in Ottawa clearly felt that it was in its interest to visually and symbolically confirm that system by generously financing a building.

That the design of the buildings bore the characteristic stamp of the Ottawa office was a clear expression of the close relationship between the federal and provincial levels of government (Figure 1.20). The configuration of the façade, a wide central pavilion flanked by two end pavilions, resembled, to some extent, the newly completed customs house in Saint John, but the detailing on the Manitoba Legislative Building was much more restrained. Decorative definition was limited to the use of cut-stone trim on the string-course, quoins, and moulding around the semicircular and segmental windows. As was typical of a design by staff, the building demonstrated an economy and simplicity in materials and execution, but its tight, compact composition and its effective massing also demonstrated the ability of the Chief Architect's Branch to produce good, competent design in spite of these restrictions.

Outside Winnipeg the building activities of the branch were of a much more rudimentary nature. In 1873 the North-West Mounted Police (NWMP) was organized to guard the territories and to impose British law and order on the resident population. A number of posts were established throughout the territories, including at Fort Walsh in 1875 and Fort Macleod in 1876. Given the remote locations, these buildings were usually constructed by the NWMP using local labour and resources. The relationship between the NWMP and the Chief Architect's Branch was always rather informal, with the branch taking on contracts or helping out with projects when requested, with very little design work being done in Ottawa.

Most of the branch's activities in the North-West Territories focused on the development of the new territorial capital at Battleford. Between 1876 and 1878 the branch constructed a government house, various residences for government staff, and a land titles office. It also designed the buildings at the NWMP post, which was part of the federal establishment at Battleford.[57] The only building of the period to survive unaltered is the superintendent's residence at the fort; its design and construction is characteristic of the period (Figure 1.21).[58] The absence of milled lumber necessitated the use of a squared-timber Red River frame, which was the traditional construction method for the buildings of the Hudson's Bay Company. The exterior was originally sheathed in rough clapboard and pine shingles.

Despite this adaptation to local materials, the outward appearance of the building is one of English domesticity and civility. An L-shaped building with an off-centre gable decorated under the eaves with a Gothic trefoil motif, its design was a type familiar to North American house pattern books and to popular journals, such as *Rural Farmer*, that were dedicated to agricultural and domestic improvement. By eastern Canadian standards they were modest, functional buildings, but they were conceived in terms of central Canadian and European values that were transported to the Prairies, thereby clearly identifying the fledgling settlement as an outpost of the British Empire.

Conclusion

During the 1870s the Chief Architect's Branch was transformed from a small administrative office to a small but competent design and construction team. The original staff of five grew to around fourteen employees by 1880. The annual budget for new construction increased fivefold over the same period,[59] and the branch also established itself as the principal architectural service for the federal government. It showed itself capable of erecting a wide range of building types, from grand public buildings to modest immigrant sheds and such specialized building types as penitentiaries and drill halls.

Compared to later periods of building, the volume of construction during the 1870s was relatively small, but many outstanding works of architecture were produced. The new federal government clearly wanted to establish a firm presence in the community, and its post-Confederation building program focused on the construction of large public buildings in major urban centres. By consciously adopting the Second Empire style as the approved 'federal' style, the Department of Public Works established an architectural image that became synonymous with the institutions of government. These buildings represented some of the most outstanding examples of Canadian public architecture during this period, and they played an important part in the dissemination of the Second Empire style across the country.

Unfortunately, very few of these buildings have survived. By the turn of the century the ostentation and eclecticism of the Second Empire style was considered the epitome of bad design, and their demolition was sometimes seen as an act of civic improvement. Of the twenty-four post offices, customs houses, and public buildings that were built during Thomas Scott's tenure, only a few stand today. The Mackenzie Building at the Royal Military College in Kingston, the post office in Fredericton, and the customs house in Victoria are the most notable survivors. Some of the finest buildings constructed during this period, such as the Toronto Customs House and the Montreal Post Office, have long since disappeared. Until recently the survival of federal buildings depended on external factors rather than on conscious efforts to preserve the best that were built.

CHAPTER TWO

The Golden Age of Federal Architecture, 1881–1896

The period between 1881 and 1896 has often been regarded as the golden age of federal architecture. This perception is owed primarily to the presence of Thomas Fuller (1823–98) as chief architect to the Department of Public Works. For the first and last time the office was held by an architect with an established international reputation, and he would leave an indelible mark on the nature of federal building in Canada. As chief architect, Fuller brought the branch to maturity. Although the emergence of the Chief Architect's Branch as a self-sufficient architectural service had begun in the 1870s, Fuller gave it professional credibility, thereby firmly establishing its place within the federal bureaucracy. He inherited his staff from his predecessor, but under his guidance the branch was able to achieve a level of excellence in design that surpassed its previous efforts. The influence of Fuller on the architecture of the Department of Public Works continued to be felt far into the future. Two of the next four chief architects had served under Fuller, and the impact of his work could still be detected into the 1930s.[1]

Federal buildings of the late nineteenth century reflected the richness and range of Fuller's architectural skills. Large public buildings were often designed in a late-Victorian reinterpretation of the Second Empire style, but Fuller's best work and his most significant contributions were the smaller federal buildings that were erected in dozens of communities across the country. In these he experimented with a variety of architectural themes that were rooted in the picturesque eclecticism of the late Victorian design. Good materials and good craftsmanship were applied to designs where the simplicity and economy of plans were masked by rich textural surfaces and varied rhythms and outlines. The picturesque quality of the designs were often enhanced by the effective adaptation of the designs to the site. Between 1881 and 1896 over seventy-eight small urban public buildings were constructed.[2] As a group, they created a language of architecture that came to define the public image of the federal government in Canada.

Fuller's tenure also coincided with the gradual and inevitable transformation and expansion of the Chief Architect's Branch, which would irreversibly change the nature of the office. When he assumed the position in 1881, the federal building stock under the department's control was relatively small, but during the course of his tenure the volume of building rose steadily. Between 1878 and its peak in 1888–9, spending on public buildings increased by 300 per cent.[3] At the same time, the branch was asked to design a whole new range of building types to meet the needs of new programs and the expanded responsibilities of the federal government in the administration of the North-West Territories. Court-houses, new immigration facilities, schools, and agricultural buildings were added to the building inventory. During his early years as chief architect, Fuller was actively involved in the development of most of the new designs, and he and his staff had the time to explore and experiment with new architectural solutions. This spirit of innovation would soon be suppressed: by the late 1880s a climate of restraint had been imposed on the Department of Public Works. Budgets were cut even though the demand for new public buildings continued unabated. Fuller and the branch coped with the increased workload, limited staff, and restricted budgets by reducing the amount of money spent on each project and by adopting a greater standardization of design. The spirit of invention gave way to demands of economy and efficiency.

Reorganizing the Department of Public Works

The appointment of Thomas Fuller as chief architect was only one of a number of significant changes within the Department of Public Works. In 1879 the Railways and Canals Branch became a separate department.[4] As a result of this restructuring, the Department of Public Works lost 90 per cent of its overall budget and suffered a significant loss of power and status within the federal bureaucracy.[5] But these changes also raised the profile of the Chief Architect's Branch within the department. Previously, railways and canals had dominated the affairs of the department; after 1879 public building emerged as the largest program, controlling approximately 40 per cent of its annual expenditure.[6]

Hector-Louis Langevin, who served as postmaster general after his re-election in 1878, took over the reconstituted department in 1879.[7] His return brought a repeat of the pattern of 1869 and marked the beginning of an energetic building program that was financed, to a large extent, by a new tariff imposed in 1879.[8] At the same time it was decided that the department was once again in need of new architectural leadership. In September 1881 Langevin asked the Privy Council to agree to the retirement of Thomas Scott, even though he was only fifty-five years old.[9] It was later suggested that Scott was forced out by Langevin because he had refused to approve some extra payments to a contractor who had made a generous donation to Langevin's campaign fund.[10]

Scott was replaced on an acting basis by the assistant chief architect, David Ewart, who had been on staff since 1871. Although Ewart had

considerable experience in managing the program, he had no professional profile outside the government.[11] By the end of the 1870s the advantages of a self-sufficient architectural service within the government were clearly recognized by the new administration, but Langevin also regarded federal buildings as important expressions of the state, and he insisted on high standards of design that would reflect positively on the national presence. Langevin obviously did not think that these standards could be met by a relatively unknown government architect. Instead, he wanted a person with an established reputation to take over the Chief Architect's Branch.

On 5 October 1881 Thomas Fuller wrote to Samuel Keefer, with whom he had worked on the Parliament Buildings and who was also an influential member of the Conservative Party:[12] 'I have just heard that it is very probable that the position of Architect to the Dominion of Canada will shortly be vacant. If so, I should like the appointment and think I have some claim but I would not in any way or on any count do anything to the prejudice of the Incumbent. I would be much obliged if you will kindly interest yourself on my behalf.'[13] This was a fairly typical letter from the files of the Department of Public Works, in which a potential candidate for an appointment solicits the support of influential friends in the government. In this case, however, it may well be that someone within the government had prompted Fuller to write. It was unlikely that knowledge of Scott's retirement, which was not yet official, would have been available to the public, certainly not to Fuller who was then residing in New York State. Fuller clearly had influential friends in Ottawa who were looking out for him, and he did not hesitate to use these connections to get the job. Keefer immediately forwarded the letter to the prime minister with this recommendation: 'if it is the intention to fill Mr. Scott's place, you have here a rare opportunity of securing, on your own terms, the services of the best architect I know of in America.'[14] John A. Macdonald then wrote to Langevin recommending Fuller for the appointment, and it was done.

Thomas Fuller was born in England in 1823 and received his professional training in the office of James Wilson of Bath, with whom he later formed a partnership.[15] In 1857 he immigrated to Toronto, where he quickly established himself as a designer of churches in the Gothic Revival style. In 1859 his firm of Fuller and Jones won the competition for the design of the new Centre Block of the Parliament Buildings in Ottawa. Although the project was fraught with scandal and mismanagement, the commission firmly established Fuller's reputation throughout North America. In 1867 he won another major competition, this time for the state capitol in Albany, New York. By 1876 the project was in disarray: not only was the budget out of control, but also architectural fashions had changed. The Romanesque Revival style was now in vogue for public buildings, and Fuller's vaguely Second Empire design was severely criticized by some American architectural critics. In 1876 Fuller was dismissed from the project and he retreated to temporary professional obscurity in upstate New York.[16]

At this low point in his career, the position of chief architect was understandably appealing to Fuller, and in turn the department was prepared to overlook certain facts – Fuller was three years older than Scott, and his credentials as a responsible manager had been badly tarnished. Political influence played an important part in Fuller's appointment, but his renown as an architect had been built on the solid foundation of his design for the Parliament Buildings. Mishaps in the United States did not seriously undermine his reputation.

The Early Years: Explorations in Style

Fuller was at work in Ottawa by December 1881. He inherited his staff from his predecessor, and apparently he made no attempt or was unable to bring in new people when he took charge. Over the next fifteen years a few young men would be recruited into the office as the workload increased, but the core of Fuller's staff remained relatively stable from the 1870s.[17] This consistency in personnel did not, however, carry over into the architecture. His influence on buildings can be detected almost at once. The most remarkable feature of his tenure was his success at imposing his own aesthetic values on a staff that had been occupied for almost a decade with designing federal buildings according to a fairly rigid stylistic mode. No other chief architect would have such a powerful personal impact on the work of the branch.

The work of the Chief Architect's Branch under Fuller's influence bore the mark of all the complexities and inconsistencies inherent in the architectural aesthetics of the late nineteenth century.[18] It was a period that owed much to the writings of British architectural theorist John Ruskin, who stressed the visual and decorative qualities of design and advocated an architecture exploiting the rich effects of colour and texture found in natural materials. Ruskin also promoted the development of a new vocabulary of ornamentation that was inspired by the forms of nature. He felt that the Italian Gothic architecture of the fourteenth and fifteenth centuries best exemplified these qualities. (In fact, it was the architecture of this period that had inspired Fuller's design for the Centre Block.) But Fuller was never limited to one style. By the 1860s and 1870s architects of the Victorian period had begun to broaden their explorations into the architecture of the past in order to discover new forms and vocabularies that could be freely incorporated into their buildings. Fuller's work for the federal government reflected the free picturesque eclecticism of the period. Gothic, Romanesque, Flemish, British vernacular, and classical elements were incorporated into his buildings but always with his own sensitivity and command of complex rhythms and with the varied massing and fine detail that defined his style. This eclecticism was most apparent in the early years of Fuller's term as chief architect.

The Langevin Building in Ottawa was the earliest and most expensive project undertaken by the branch during Fuller's tenure (Figures 2.1 and 2.2).[19] Begun in 1883, it demonstrated Fuller's ability to draw upon a variety of historical sources to create a design that was rooted in the past but that was contemporary in spirit.[20] It is a massive three-and-a-half-storey building which extends 280 feet along the south side of Wellington Street facing the Parliament Buildings. The pavilion massing and the use of a high mansard roof suggests the influence of the Second Empire style, although the building's overall design bears only superficial resemblance to that style. The ornate Renaissance detailing associated with federal buildings of the 1870s had been abandoned in favour of a heavier, more robust vocabulary that was derived from a variety of sources. The round-arched windows that were accented by squat, round columns were drawn from early Italian or Romanesque sources. The two-storey, shaped dor-

2.1. Langevin Building, Wellington Street, Ottawa, Ontario, 1883–9, Plans prepared by the Chief Architect's Branch. The Langevin Block was refurbished in 1975–7 and now houses the offices of the prime minister and of the Privy Council. (M. Trépanier, Parks Canada, 1993)

2.2. Main entrance foyer, Langevin Building. (M. Trépanier, Parks Canada, 1993)

mers suggest Flemish or Queen Anne influences. The simple grid pattern, characteristic of the Second Empire style, was not evident here. The façade was divided horizontally into three distinct levels, and each level was defined by a different pattern or grouping of windows. This complex articulation of the façade was also evident in Fuller's design for the Centre Block of the Parliament Buildings, although it was expressed there in a Gothic vocabulary.

A very generous budget for the Langevin Building allowed for a level of skill and construction that was not possible on smaller projects.[21] For its façade, ochre-coloured sandstone was imported from New Brunswick, and the columns were made of a polished red granite. A local sandstone was used for rear walls. The interior structural frame, which consists of cast-iron columns, wrought-iron girders, steel joists, and concrete-slab floors, was fairly sophisticated in its building technology, and it illustrates well the complexity of structural framing systems before the advent of mass-produced steel and skeletal steel frames. The roof frame was also built of iron, and this was probably the first federal building designed to accommodate an elevator. The high level of skill of the workers for the masonry is evident in finishing details such as the rounded corners and the deeply channelled stonework at the ground level. The rich, naturalistic carving in the frieze and in the medallion motifs below the second-storey windows fully exploits the decorative and sculptural potential of the soft sandstone.

The Langevin Building provided Fuller with one of his few opportunities to design an interior space that rose above the more functional standards applied to most government buildings.[22] The focus of the interior is a spacious entrance foyer, which features four polished granite columns and a wide staircase that is accented by a finely wrought iron railing. One of the most notable features of the interior was the office layout. An early manifestation of the emerging science of office planning and administration, the plan consisted of small private offices for senior managers and of a number of larger open spaces for clerical staff. Presented to the House of Commons as a model of modern planning, this open arrangement permitted close supervision of a group of employees.[23]

The Langevin Building represented the first major expansion of the federal government off Parliament Hill. It was also significant for the part it played in revealing the blatant patronage, corruption, and irresponsible management within the Department of Public Works that sometimes marred Langevin's administration. In 1883 a contract was signed with the firm of A. Charlebois for $295,000 for a building to be completed in 1886; it was finished two years later than scheduled at an additional cost of $214,000. The department might have survived the ensuing accusations of delays and cost overruns, but the scandal was intensified by complaints from subcontractors that they were forced to pay kickbacks to the general contractor. They claimed that Langevin knew about the kickbacks but that he took no action. This scandal was followed by even more damaging revelations of patronage and corruption in relation to the Quebec construction firm of Larkin, Connolly and Company. Briefly, one of the firm's silent partners, Thomas McGreevy, was a Conservative member of Parliament who was related to Langevin by marriage and had provided financial assistance for Langevin's campaign fund for the 1878 election. Larkin Connolly and Company received approximately $3.1 million in government contracts between 1878 and 1891, and it was suggested that their successful bidding was owed to inside knowledge of the competing tenders.[24]

The resulting scandal forced Langevin's resignation as minister of public works in 1891, and the chief engineer in the department was also dismissed for accepting a small 'gift' for his part in the process. Again, Fuller emerged from the scandal with his reputation relatively intact, but that of the department was badly damaged. Partly as a result of these scandals, a royal commission was established in 1892 to examine issues of patronage, staffing, and administration in the civil service.[25] Although no concrete reforms resulted from this investigation, it marked a turning point in the history of the department and of its relationship with the rest of the government. Patronage would always play a part in federal public works, but the predisposition of ministers for managing the department as their private domains for personal and political gain was on the decline. After 1892 a clearer separation of powers between the government and the civil service developed and would lead to the emergence of a modern federal bureaucracy in the early twentieth century.

The Hamilton Public Building was under construction at the same time as the Langevin Building, but it was very different in its interpretation (Figure 2.3). Built in 1882–7, its design, with a rusticated base supporting a row of Corinthian pilasters, drew upon a fairly traditional Italian Renaissance vocabulary. Although it bore some resemblance to the federal buildings constructed by Thomas Scott, it cannot be interpreted as a transitional design between two administrations. Rather, it represented a development from Fuller's own work of the 1870s, which was dominated by the Second Empire and Italian classical styles.[26] The handling of the detail was characteristic of Fuller. He delighted in rich and varied textures created by a complex build-up of decorative forms. The first layer consisted of the heavy moulded door and window surrounds, onto which were superimposed panelled pilasters and a richly decorated frieze and cornice. The main block of the building represented a fairly conventional essay in Italian Renaissance forms, but the treatment of the roofline introduced a new, non-classical element into the design. Although less ornate than the mansard roof of the 1870s, the roofline assumed a new picturesque irregularity in the steeply pitched pyramidal roofs of the clock tower and of two smaller corner towers.

Between 1882 and 1885 four medium-sized public buildings were designed in an eclectic style that blended Flemish, Queen Anne, and classical elements. The Brockville Public Building reflects this broader, more eclectic decorative vocabulary (Figure 2.4).[27] The main façade is symmetrically arranged with two flanking pavilions that are accented by shaped Flemish gables. A raised pediment, which extends through the second floor and is supported by massive stone consoles or brackets, gives a central focus to the design. The flanking doorways provided separate entrances to the post office on the ground level and to the customs office and caretaker's quarters on the second and attic levels. Although the design incorporated classical elements, it was still rooted in High Victorian aesthetics. The smooth-dressed stone detail and trim is set against the rusti-

2.3. Public Building, Hamilton, Ontario, 1882–7, in 1927. Plans prepared by the Chief Architect's Branch. Now demolished. (NA, PA-57440)

cated stone walls, creating rich textured surfaces. The round-arched entrances and the window treatment, with large panes of glass in the lower sash and a multi-paned sash above, are typical features of a federal building by Fuller. The organic quality of the carved stone panels, composed of entwined maple leaves, conformed to John Ruskin's call for a new decorative language that was inspired by the forms of nature.

Variations of this style were applied to new federal buildings at New Glasgow in Nova Scotia, Newcastle in New Brunswick, and Charlottetown in Prince Edward Island.[28] The stylistic type then disappeared from the repertoire of the Chief Architect's Branch. The Brockville building was one of Fuller's most finely crafted buildings, and the rejection of the type was probably the result of the cost of construction rather than of a dissatisfaction with the design. Buildings of this type invited a high degree of ornamentation, and all four buildings in the group were among the most expensive small post offices of the period. The cost could amount to as much as double that of other federal buildings of equivalent size.[29]

The post office in Baddeck, Nova Scotia, built in 1885–7, represented a slight departure from Fuller's High Victorian eclecticism. The simple, informal quality of the design reflects the influence of the Arts and Crafts aesthetic that had emerged in Britain in the 1870s and 1880s (Figure 2.5).[30] A development resulting from High Victorian Gothic and the writings of John Ruskin, the Arts and Crafts movement advocated a new architecture that was rooted in the vernacular buildings of Britain. It asserted the necessity for architects to re-establish the link between the craft of building and architectural design. The Baddeck Post Office reflects these new aesthetic values. A simple stone block, it features a modest, hipped roof that is accented by an asymmetrical arrangement of dormers and a gable detailed in a half-timber motif. In contrast to the decorative richness of the Brockville building, the exterior is devoid of any applied decoration. The windows and doors are placed on the façade in an irregular and random manner. Despite this lack of architectural pretence, the building maintains a commanding presence on the street by means of the sense of weight and mass that is created by the roughly textured stone walls.[31]

The Galt Public Building: A Prototype of the 'Federal Style'

The Public Building in Galt (now Cambridge), Ontario, is an early example of a design that would be most closely associated with Fuller's work at the Department of Public Works (Figure 2.6).[32] The building was one of many variations on a plan developed in the early 1880s, but by the mid- and late 1880s the formula emerged as the dominant model for small public buildings. Begun in 1884, the Galt building was constructed to house the post office and the customs department. A two-and-a-half-storey stone block with an attached clock tower, it demonstrates well Fuller's ability to bring architectural sophistication to a small urban federal building. The distinctive articulation of the main façade was to become a trademark of Fuller's public buildings. The ground floor is punctuated by three bays that feature a large central segmental window flanked by two narrow, flat-headed windows. On the second level, the pattern is varied by the insertion of two small windows above the central window below. The roofline is dominated by a heavy parapeted gable with two semicircular windows. Executed in local limestone, the surfaces are richly textured with rusticated walls that are contrasted by smoothly dressed trim. The heavy corbelling under the eaves and the diamond pattern of the stonework under the peak of the gable were medieval motifs favoured by Fuller. The central entrance of a typical Scott design was replaced by a side entrance, accessed through a heavy, round-arched porch that is vaguely Romanesque in style.

In plan and interior design, the Galt building is typical of its period. It is composed of standard features that were adapted to the individual peculiarities and constraints of the site. The main floor housed the post office, which was divided into a public lobby at the front and a working area. The two areas were divided by a counter. Four cast-iron columns support the floor above; interior finishes were simple and functional, consisting of a tongue-in-groove wainscoting on the ground floor, with heavy moulded trim around the doors and windows. The upstairs areas, containing the customs offices, were more plainly finished. The attic housed the caretaker's apartment.

2.4. Public Building, Brockville, Ontario, 1882–6. Plans prepared by the Chief Architect's Branch. The building now houses the Catholic Cultural Centre. (Public Works and Government Services Canada, Heritage Recording and Technical Data Services, 1982)

2.5. Post Office, Baddeck, Nova Scotia, 1885–7. Plans prepared by the Chief Architect's Branch. (Public Works and Government Services Canada, Heritage Recording and Technical Data Services, 1982)

The Galt building also demonstrates a sensitivity to setting and an ability to adapt a design to the unique qualities of a site.[33] The building was situated on a narrow lot sandwiched between the main business street and the river. To adapt to the compressed site and to take advantage of its frontage on two sides, the one-storey wing containing an examining warehouse, which was usually attached to the rear, was shifted to the side elevation. As a result, the building features two principal elevations, one facing onto the street and the other overlooking the river, and makes an imposing statement from two different standpoints.

The Galt Public Building represents the most common design type associated with Fuller's term as chief architect. Throughout the 1880s and 1890s dozens of buildings based on this model were produced across the country. The most elaborate examples date from the 1880s, when the branch appears to have had more time to develop individual variations. The early buildings were also noted for their richness and diversity of detail and for the high polish and refinement of the materials. The public building at Windsor, Nova Scotia (1883–6) (Figures 2.7 and 2.8), and the public building at Summerside, Prince Edward Island (1883–6) (Figure 2.9), provide two of the most sophisticated examples of the type.[34] The use of red-brick walls with dressed-stone trim provided a common alternative to the rusticated and dressed stone found on the Galt building. The Windsor building was notable for its rich and varied decorative vocabulary. The diamond-patterned stonework under the main gable, the chequer-board pattern under the second-storey windows, the complex corbelling under the eaves and string-course, and the fan motif in the lunettes over the second-storey window were recurring features in Fuller's decorative vocabulary. The Summerside building is more modestly detailed, but it features a clock perched on top of the roof, a common alternative to an attached tower.

Economy and Restraint: Transformations in the Federal Style

The first five years of Fuller's term was one of the most creative and dynamic periods in the history of federal building. Fuller seems to have stepped into the job with energy and enthusiasm, assuming the role of master architect to the nation. He experimented with a wide variety of architectural ideas, demonstrating both a knowledge of current architectural trends and an ability to develop the ideas in ways that were fresh and inventive. Each project was treated as a separate problem demanding a unique design solution that gave individual attention to the particular conditions of a site. By the late 1880s, however, this spirit of innovation became less evident.

Throughout the decade of the 1880s the inventory of federal buildings had grown steadily. Moreover, the scope of federal building had expanded with the early settlement of the Prairies and the establishment of new programs such as the Experimental Farm Service and the Indian school system. The increased administrative load of the chief architect demanded that Fuller delegate more of the design work to his staff.[35] At the same time, the government entered into a period of fiscal restraint. Economic depression in the 1890s brought a sharp reduction in the levels of expenditure, which would not be restored until the early 1900s. After 1888–9 fewer public buildings were being constructed but, more significantly, less money was also being spent on each project. Between 1889 and 1896 the average cost for the construction of a small federal building decreased by almost 40 per cent.

The departure of Langevin in 1891 and the tarnished reputation of the department in the wake of the McGreevy scandal may also have had an effect. Langevin had played a key role in shaping the building program of the Department of Public Works for over twenty years; during this period he had approved lavish spending on buildings that were intended to be 'a credit to the Dominion.' After Langevin, the public buildings were still expected to reflect credit on the government, but the idea of government buildings as monuments of the state became increasingly tempered by a growing concern for economy and efficiency.

The impact of an increased workload and of restricted budgets can be detected in the character of the work at the end of the 1880s. The range of designs became increasingly narrow as federal buildings began to fall into a few set patterns. While many buildings were well designed and solidly constructed, they became simpler and more economical in exe-

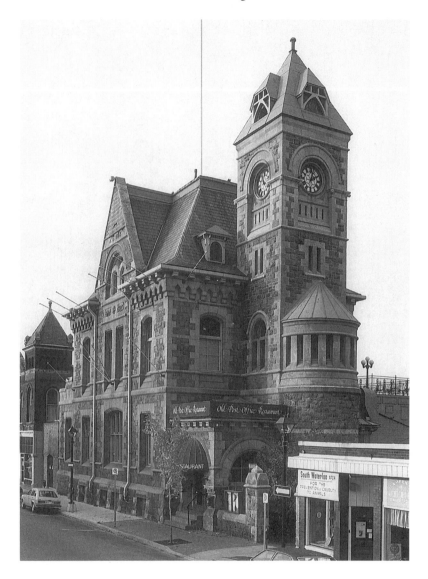

2.6. Public Building, Galt (now Cambridge), Ontario, 1884–7. Plans prepared by the Chief Architect's Branch. The building now houses a restaurant. (Public Works and Government Services Canada, Heritage Recording and Technical Data Sources, 1982)

2.7. Public Building, Windsor, Nova Scotia, 1883–6. Plans prepared by the Chief Architect's Branch, *ca.* 1884. Now demolished. (NA, PA-135532)

cution. The public building at Portage la Prairie embodied one fairly typical solution to government design in the latter part of Fuller's tenure (Figure 2.10). Although the basic components – rectangular plan, parapeted gable, and the characteristic disposition of windows – remained fundamentally unaltered, much of the detailing evident in such earlier buildings as the Galt and Windsor federal buildings was eliminated. Decorative stonework was restricted to the diamond pattern applied to the central gables. The walls are composed entirely of a heavy, rusticated stone, giving the building a massive, rugged quality characteristic of the Romanesque Revival style and the work of the American architect Henry Hobson Richardson. Another common cost-saving measure was the substitution of rolled-metal roofing for the more expensive slate shingle.

The public building of 1889–91 at Strathroy, Ontario, was constructed of brick, but the stone trim was now rusticated rather than smooth dressed as had been the case in the building at Windsor (Figure 2.11). The rusticated texture compensated for the lack of decorative detail, which had become increasingly subdued and restrictive. Ornamentation was limited to the gable and the entrance porches. The public building (1888–91) at Almonte, Ontario, provides a comparable design but it was executed in rusticated stone (Figure 2.12). This building also illustrates the trend toward greater simplicity, although the architect's sensitivity to site is still very evident. Situated on a triangular lot near the top of the slope of Mill Street, the design exploits the irregularities of the site in an effective but unconventional manner. Rather than turn the building to overlook the town, which would have been the logical solution, the main façade was turned to face onto the narrow streetscape. This tends to lessen the visual importance of the main entrance but, as seen from the side elevation, it highlights the complex massing of the building that is created by the receding planes of the projecting gable, main building block, and one-storey rear wing. The result was a dynamic and picturesque composition that dominated the town and provided one of the clearest images of the central role of these federal public buildings in a small town.

Another fairly common variation on the theme is illustrated by the public building in St-Hyacinthe, Quebec, of 1889–94 (Figure 2.13). Like the Galt building it featured a corner clock tower, but the large central gable was replaced by a smaller parapet dormer set flush with the main façade. The flanking side entrances and the complex rhythm of the window arrangement, with a wide central window at the ground level, paired, round-headed windows on the second level, and a set of three small windows in the gable, are characteristic of federal design of the period. Many similar buildings were constructed in the 1880s and 1890s. Some were of brick and some of stone, and in scaled-down versions the clock tower was often eliminated.

In western Canadian cities it would appear that different standards of design were often applied to federal buildings. In the older, more established centres, such as Winnipeg and Victoria, fairly sophisticated buildings were built, whereas in other communities the Chief Architect's Branch tended to erect large but architecturally undistinguished buildings.[36] The public building in Brandon, Manitoba, was a large three-storey block, finished in an extremely modest and economical manner (Figure 2.14).[37] The central parapet gable seemed to be an architectural afterthought that was intended to raise the design above a basic industrial level. This double standard was a recurring theme for government building in the West during the 1880s and 1890s. It may reflect a lack of interest on the part of the Chief Architect's Branch for these distant projects, or it may reflect a lack of local skilled craftsmen and contractors to carry out complex, intricately detailed designs. Whatever the reason, by the early twentieth century this distinction between eastern and western Canada ceased to be a significant factor.

Armouries and Drill Halls: A Battle of Jurisdiction

The network of drill halls and armouries continued to expand in the 1880s.[38] In 1881 a new minister of militia and defence, Adolphe Caron, prepared a report on the condition of militia structures in Canada. It revealed that of the 127 buildings owned by the department, only four were constructed of brick or stone, and that the remaining wooden structures were in a dilapidated condition. Caron called for the construction of new facilities across the country. At the time, the construction of drill halls was still a responsibility of the Department of Public Works, and in

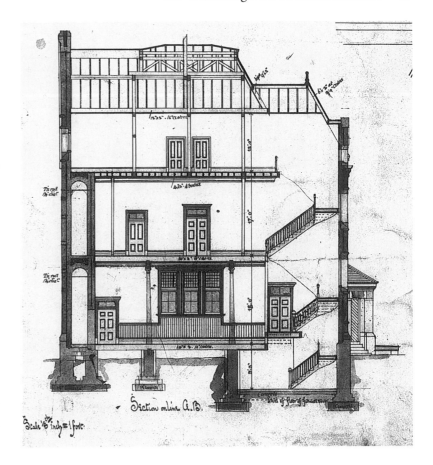

2.8. Longitudinal section, Public Building, Windsor, (NA, NMC 60460)

2.9. Public Building, Summerside, Prince Edward Island, 1883–6. Plans prepared by the Chief Architect's Branch; construction supervised by David Stirling. (Public Works and Government Services Canada, 1982)

1883 the Chief Architect's Branch began work on the design for a new one in Quebec. Unfortunately Caron and Langevin were bitter rivals, and Caron resented the large government contracts for drill halls being under Langevin's control. He fought for, and won, control of this area of construction in 1884. Over the next ten years, a number of large drill halls were constructed by the Department of Militia and Defence under the direction of Henry James.[39] James had previously been employed in the Chief Architect's Branch, but in 1884 he transferred to Militia and Defence as the head of the Engineering Branch.[40]

In 1891 Langevin resigned as minister, in 1892 Caron left the Department of Militia and Defence, and the following year Henry James died. At that point, responsibility for the construction of drill halls was transferred back to the Department of Public Works. In the next few years, only three were constructed, but two of them, an armoury in Toronto and another in Halifax, were to have a far-reaching impact on the design of drill hall in Canada. They were the first to employ a modern, metal truss system that permitted far greater spans than had previously been possible.[41] They also clearly marked a transition in the role of drill halls and armouries. No longer simply places to store weapons and to provide a sheltered parade square, these buildings became important military and social institutions within the communities. The Halifax and the Toronto armouries both provided an expanded range of facilities, including lecture halls, a library, a billiard room, and a bowling alley, as well as the prerequisite drill hall and space for the storage of weapons.

The Toronto Armoury of 1893 was a massive brick building with rusticated stone trim designed in a castellated Romanesque style (Figure 2.15). The general plan and massing did not differ significantly from the earlier generation of buildings. The high, pitched roof with a large central entrance into the hall, flanked by two pavilions, resembled the Cartier Square Drill Hall in Ottawa of 1878. The Toronto building introduced a new architectural language to armoury design. Crenellated corner towers and massive round-arched windows weighed down by heavy rusticated stone voussoirs evoked romantic associations of medieval castles and fearless warriors. This design type would establish a standard of design, en-

2.10. Public Building, Portage la Prairie, Manitoba, 1896–8. Plans prepared by the Chief Architect's Branch. Like many early federal buildings in the West, it now serves as a city hall. (Public Works and Government Services Canada, Heritage Recording and Technical Data Services, 1982)

2.11. Public Building, Strathroy, Ontario, 1889–91. Plans prepared by the Chief Architect's Branch. Shops now occupy the ground floor. (Public Works and Government Services Canada, Heritage Recording and Technical Data Services, 1982)

gineering, and planning that would shape the character of armouries for the next thirty years.

The North-West Territories: New Demands on the Branch, 1881–1896

During the 1880s and 1890s the activities of the Chief Architect's Branch became increasingly complex and wide-ranging. Nowhere was this expansion more evident than in the North-West Territories. The Macdonald government had regained power in 1878 with a promise to build a strong national economy. Protective tariffs that would reinforce the economic link between East and West constituted a key element of the National Policy. Within this economic framework, the settlement and the agricultural development of the Northwest were essential components. The Prairies would produce crops for export and provide a new consumer market for eastern manufactured goods. Although the federal government had established a basic administrative framework for the development of the West, during the 1870s settlement remained sporadic. The government would not be successful at attracting significant numbers of immigrants to the Prairies until the early twentieth century, but with the completion of the transcontinental railway in 1885 the role of the federal government in the Northwest became more pervasive.[42]

Government buildings represented a small but highly visible component in the process of the Canadianization of the Prairies. The range of buildings constructed by the Department of Public Works clearly mirrored the goals and programs associated with the National Policy. The establishment of basic administrative and judicial structures was manifested in the construction of territorial government buildings and a network of court-houses. To enforce laws, North-West Mounted Police posts were established and expanded. The provision of basic federal services to new communities – postal delivery, the levying of customs duties, and the registration of land titles – called for the construction of new public buildings and land titles offices. The proposed assimilation of the Native population required industrial schools. Buildings to house and process new immigrants and for the establishment of a system of experimental farms were products of the government's policy to encourage and assist agricultural settlement on the Prairies.

Regina: The New Capital

When the Canadian Pacific Railway (CPR) was re-routed through the southern Prairies, the territorial capital was moved from Battleford to a new site located near the banks of the Wascana River and adjacent to the railway line. The site was named Regina after Queen Victoria. In 1882 approximately forty wood-frame buildings that had been prefabricated in the East were shipped by rail and assembled over the course of the winter. These early buildings included a residence for the lieutenant-governor and a building to house the territorial council chambers. By the late 1880s, however, these early buildings were gradually replaced by more permanent structures.[43] A new Government House was built in 1888–91, and in 1891 an Administration Building to house government offices was erected near the original legislative buildings (Figures 2.16 and 2.17).

Both buildings reflected the new sense of permanence in government buildings on the Prairies that was fostered by the arrival of the CPR; at the same time, they also illustrated the functional type of design that was considered appropriate to the territories. The Administration Building is a long, rectangular brick building punctuated by paired segmental windows, and its mansard roof refers back to a formula for designs that was associated with the tenure of Thomas Scott. The Government House, although finely finished in the interior with grand public rooms, is very plain in its exterior design. It is impossible to detect the influence of Thomas Fuller in either of these buildings. Nevertheless, both buildings served their functional and symbolic purposes well. As described by one member of Parliament, Government House was 'a solid structure, and a structure, that while a handsome one, is not one that has any extravagance as to ornamentation. It is such a structure as a person representing the Government of Canada, and representing Her Majesty, and who is the head of society as well as political life in the North-West should have.'[44]

Government House and the Administration Building were both located about one and a quarter miles west of the commercial centre of the

2.12. Public Building, Almonte, Ontario, 1888–91. Plans prepared by the Chief Architect's Branch. (Public Works and Government Services Canada, Heritage Recording and Technical Data Services, 1982)

2.13. Public Building, St-Hyacinthe, Quebec, 1889–94. Plans prepared by the Chief Architect's Branch. The building now houses offices and apartments. (Public Works and Government Services Canada, Heritage Recording and Technical Data Services, 1982)

town. The decision to build on such an inconvenient site was the result of conflicting interests between the CPR and Edgar Dewdney, the lieutenant-governor of the North-West Territories. The process also provides an unusually transparent illustration of the political and economic significance attached to the location of a public building, particularly in Prairie towns where the impending arrival of the CPR generated intense land speculation. Originally, Dewdney proposed that the townsite be located near the government buildings, which had been built adjacent to land he and some associates had recently purchased from the Hudson's Bay Company. If the plans had gone ahead, Dewdney and his associates would have owned much of what would have become downtown Regina. However, the CPR thwarted these plans of huge profits by building the railway station further east. The town naturally developed around the station, but Dewdney was able to recoup some of his losses by convincing his friends in government to locate some of the government buildings, including the new headquarters of the NWMP, near his land. As a result, the new town was spread out over two miles, with a commercial centre at one end, where the post office, immigration buildings, and territorial court-house were located, and an administrative centre at the other.[45]

Building for the North-West Mounted Police

By 1883 the CPR had reached the foothills of the Rocky Mountains, thereby establishing an efficient supply route for goods and materials. For the Department of Public Works, this meant that many of the problems encountered in building on the Prairies, particularly for the NWMP, were eliminated or at least alleviated. When the new headquarters, which would become known as 'the Depot,' was moved from Fort Walsh to Regina in 1882, the department was able to assemble quickly a number of prefabricated buildings that had been shipped by rail from the East.[46] Eight more buildings were constructed by a local contractor the following year. A long, one-storey, wood-frame, gable-roofed building, which originally housed the mess hall, survives today in a much altered form as the chapel. Although all other nineteenth century remnants of the Depot have disappeared, the organization and location of the buildings around a main

2.14. Public Building, Brandon, Manitoba, 1889–92. Plans prepared by the Chief Architect's Branch. Now demolished. (NA, PA-32849)

2.15. Toronto Armoury and Drill Hall, Toronto, Ontario, 1893, as seen in 1922. Plans prepared by the Chief Architect's Branch. Now demolished. (NA, PA-97252)

2.16. Government House, Regina, Saskatchewan, 1888–91. Plans prepared by the Chief Architect's Branch. (J. Wright, Parks Canada, 1991)

2.17. North-West Territorial Government Administration Building, Regina, Saskatchewan, 1891. Plans prepared by the Chief Architect's Branch. The building, now owned by the province of Saskatchewan, was restored in 1979. (J. Wright, Parks Canada, 1991)

barrack square and a subsidiary stable compound is still evident in the present-day plan.

Over the next few years, the Department of Public Works and the Chief Architect's Branch constructed many new buildings for the NWMP at Regina, Battleford, Lethbridge, and Prince Albert. At Lethbridge and Prince Albert, posts containing officers' quarters, a men's barracks, a stable, a storehouse, a blacksmith's shop, and a guardhouse were established (Figure 2.18).

The NWMP and the Department of Public Works had good working relations during this period, and the post at Prince Albert was described by the police as their 'best finished and best laid out post' and a 'credit to the clerk of works and the Superintendent of the post.'[47] At the same time the NWMP, like the Department of Militia and Defence and the Penitentiaries Branch, wanted to move towards greater control of its own building requirements. The Chief Architect's Branch in Ottawa prepared plans for many of the buildings, but it appears to have had very little to do with their construction. Generally, the branch gave responsibility for project management to a clerk of works, whom the NWMP would claim was not able to fully understand their needs. In 1888, although the police commended the efforts of the Department of Public Works, they also identified the need to appoint 'a competent architect to take charge of the North-West Mounted Police improvements.'[48] In many cases, the NWMP simply avoided the issue by by-passing the Department of Public Works and hiring local contractors and architects to construct new buildings. The police were thus able to maintain an informal working relationship with the Department of Public Works, calling upon its services when required but initiating and funding projects independently. In fact, most of the construction begun during this period may have involved the services of a clerk of works who was generally paid by Public Works, but the buildings were not designed by the Chief Architect's Branch. In contrast with the territorial struggles it entered into with the Department of Militia and Defence, the Department of Public Works seems to have been quite willing to let the NWMP take over many of its own projects in remote parts of the country.

The Territorial Court-house

The absence of a provincial level of government in the Prairies outside the very limited boundaries of the newly created province of Manitoba meant that the federal government had to take on a whole range of building responsibilities. The construction of court-houses usually came under provincial jurisdiction, but in the North-West Territories this became a first priority of the federal government. The presence of court-houses would clearly symbolize the establishment of the new social order that was being imposed on the Prairies. Although the administration of law had been the responsibility of Ottawa since 1870, up to 1885 it was undertaken in a rather makeshift manner, primarily by the NWMP and a few appointed magistrates. Courts were generally housed in buildings constructed for other purposes.[49]

In 1886 the federal government implemented a major overhaul of the system of justice in the territories in preparation of an anticipated increase in immigration. The territories were divided into four judicial districts in 1882, and in 1886 provision was made for the appointment of judges, clerks of court, and sheriffs for each district. An independent Supreme Court of the North-West Territories was also established, thereby creating an autonomous court system within the federal structure. The construction of court-houses constituted an important component of this overhaul.

Between 1886 and 1905 ten new court-houses were built across the Prairies.[50] Some of the early ones were very modest wood-frame buildings, but by the late 1880s they were taking on a new air of permanence. The first of the new generation was the court-house in Calgary, built in 1888. A solid, two-storey sandstone structure, it featured a low, hipped roof with a central parapeted gable and deep arcaded front porch. Typical of court-house design, the ground floor contained offices. A large courtroom was located on the second floor. One of the last examples and the only one that survives of these territorial court-houses is the Fort Macleod Court-house. Built in 1902–5 and designed under the direction of Fuller's successor, the building maintained the essential character and quality characteristic of these territorial court-houses (Figures 2.19 and 2.20). A

2.18. North-West Mounted Police Post, Lethbridge, Alberta, in 1888. Designed by the Chief Architect's Branch. (Glenbow Archives, Calgary, Alberta, NA 635-10)

two-storey brick structure with stone dressing and a cross-gabled roof, it clearly identifies itself as a public building in its solidity of construction, in the formal symmetry of the façade, and in the use of datestone and heavy brick for the entrance porch, but, at the same time, those affectations to 'style' that were so evident in the federal buildings of central and eastern Canada were dispensed with. The building now serves as the Fort Macleod Town Hall, and the second-storey courtroom is used as the town council chamber.

The Assimilation of Native People and the Industrial School

The successful transformation of the Prairies into an agricultural hinterland depended on the peaceful settlement of the Native population. During the 1870s a series of treaties were negotiated with the Plains Indians through which they ceded established claims to the land in general in exchange for rights to reserve lands. To the Native population, the reserve system may have been seen as a means of permitting the peaceful co-existence of two conflicting societies; to the government, the reserves were an interim solution to the Indian problem. The function of the reserve was to place the Native population under protective custody until it could be successfully assimilated into the white community. The idea was to transform these nomadic peoples, with their tribal way of life, into independent cash-crop farmers, agricultural workers, or domestic servants. In this way they would become productive participants in the National Policy.

Education was regarded as the most effective and efficient tool of assimilation.[51] Previously, this work had been left to the various churches and missionary groups working in the Prairies; under the 1880 Indian Act the federal government assumed responsibility for Native education. Although the government maintained a close working relationship with religious groups, which often administered and provided the staff for schools, the federal government attempted to initiate a comprehensive system of Native education. The Department of Indian Affairs maintained three levels of schools: day schools, which were located on reserves, resi-

2.19. Court-house, Fort Macleod, Alberta, 1902–5. Plans prepared by the Chief Architect's Branch. The building, the best surviving example of a North-West Territories court-house, has been restored and now houses the town hall. (J. Wright, Parks Canada, 1991)

2.20. Second-floor courtroom, Fort Macleod Court-house. (J. Wright, Parks Canada, 1993)

dential or boarding schools, and industrial schools. Of these three types, the industrial schools were considered the most effective tools of assimilation. In 1879 a report prepared for the federal government stated that they were the most effective instruments in a recommended policy of 'aggressive civilization.'[52] Their purpose was to remove the child from the 'corrupting' influence of the family and the reserve, and then to provide basic instruction in reading, writing, and farming and domestic skills.

During the 1880s and 1890s the Department of Indian Affairs established a network of Native schools. Initially a number of existing church schools were expanded, but by the late 1880s the department had begun a substantial program of new construction throughout Manitoba, Saskatchewan, Alberta, and the interior of British Columbia. Although many of the smaller day and residential schools were built by the Department of Indian Affairs, the larger industrial schools required the services of the Chief Architect's Branch. While no standard plans were developed, St Paul's Industrial School in Manitoba, which was established in 1888 and administered by the Church of England, provides a fairly typical and early example of the branch's work in this field (Figures 2.21 and 2.22).[53] Also known as the Rupert's Land Industrial School, it was a large, rectangular, brick building with a hipped roof and a rear wing. As seen from the exterior, the building featured an eleven-bay, symmetrical façade with a central frontispiece accented by a pedimented gable. A small bell tower was centrally placed on the roof ridge. The floor plan was symmetrical, laid out with a central hall that had offices and two classrooms on either side. A dining-room and a kitchen were located in the rear wing. The second floor contained two large dormitories, one for girls and one for boys, as well as separate bedrooms for staff and sickrooms. Like other schools, it was also equipped with a number of outbuildings; these included usually a barn and a stable to support the agricultural training program. The main building was destroyed by fire in 1906, and the school closed at that time.

The Chief Architect's Branch proved to be efficient but very conventional in its approach to the design of schools. In terms of the work of the branch, these assignments in remote areas were probably considered of minor importance, and the projects were probably given to staff members who would then prepare a design in consultation with the Indian Department. Again, there is no indication in the quality or character of the architecture of the schools that Fuller had any input into their design. Nor does there appear to have been any consideration given to the specific problems or requirements of building educational facilities for Native students on the Prairies. Instead, the branch turned to established patterns for schools in eastern Canadian communities and transplanted them, with some necessary functional modifications, to new settings and conditions. Buildings like the St Paul's Industrial School, with its red-brick construction, symmetrical façade, and bell tower, could easily have been built in Brockville or Smiths Falls.[54] It was as if the staff of the Chief Architect's Branch, producing plans within the limited confines of their drafting room in Ottawa, viewed the whole country simply as an extension of their immediate central Canadian environment.

Industrial schools were not outstanding works of architecture, but neither were they temporary, makeshift buildings. In their scale and quality of construction, they formed permanent and imposing symbols of the dominance and supremacy of white society. The buildings demonstrated the government's commitment to and confidence in the industrial school system for absorbing and eradicating a distinct aboriginal society on the Prairies. In many respects, industrial schools reflected the same social and moral purposes as nineteenth-century penitentiaries; the architecture of the buildings was seen to play an active part in the reform of what was regarded as deviant behaviour. The design of these schools, which was firmly rooted in white society, was clearly intended to support and reinforce the values, skills, and codes of behaviour in which the students were so rigorously indoctrinated.

The Expansion of Facilities for Immigrants

Immigration was an essential component of western settlement, and during the 1880s and 1890s the Department of Agriculture upgraded and expanded its facilities to provide a more comprehensive and permanent

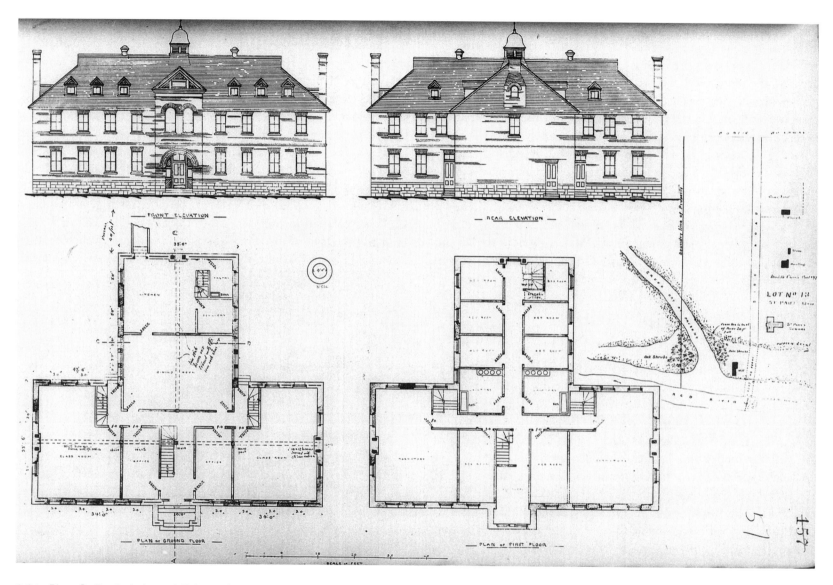

2.21. Plan, St Paul's Industrial School, St Paul's, Manitoba. Plans prepared by the Chief Architect's Branch in 1888. The building was destroyed by fire in 1906. (NA, RG11, Vol. 3911, C-138223)

2.22. St Paul's Industrial School, in 1898. (Manitoba Archives)

2.23. First-Class Detention Building, Grosse Île, Quebec, 1893. Plans prepared by the Chief Architect's Branch. Grosse Île was designated a national historic site in 1988. (J. Audet, Parks Canada, 1990, S-148-6)

network of buildings and services. The goal was the complete control of the immigration process, from the point of arrival to the final destination on the homestead lot.[55]

Much of the new building took place at the quarantine stations. Facilities were expanded at Grosse Île and at Lawlor's Island. On the West Coast a new station was established at William Head, near Victoria.[56] During this period, quarantine stations became increasingly sophisticated. The revolution in medical science brought about by men such as Louis Pasteur and Robert Koch had shed new light and understanding on the nature of diseases, how they were transmitted, and how they could be controlled. In the early 1890s buildings for disinfecting became a standard feature of all quarantine stations. These were large irregular-shaped buildings equipped with disinfecting chambers for baggage and personal effects, as well as showers for the arriving immigrants.

Quarantine stations also became more efficient at separating different classes of immigrants. First-class, second-class, and third-class detention buildings were provided at Grosse Île, Lawlor's Island, and William Head. Either new buildings were constructed or existing structures were altered, and each class of detention building had its own design standards and configuration. All were basic wood-frame buildings with simple gabled or hipped roofs, but the first-class buildings could usually be identified by a gallery that ran across the main façade. First-class buildings were typically divided into three parts, with a central section containing a large dining-room on the ground floor and a hall above. The two wings on either side contained washrooms and fourteen private rooms in each wing. The First-Class Detention Building at Grosse Île, which is still standing, was the largest example of this type (Figure 2.23).[57] Second-class and third-class detention buildings offered fewer amenities and less spacious accommodation. At William Head, two third-class detention buildings were constructed in 1893.[58] Both were long, one-storey, wood-frame buildings. A large dining-hall was located in the middle and two large open dormitories, which could accommodate 318 people, were situated on either side. Third-class accommodation appeared to be designed for non-British or non-white passengers; at William Head the third-class detention buildings were designated for use by Chinese and Japanese immigrants.

In major transportation centres, the federal government improved the quality of accommodation at the various immigration depots. The most notable example was the Immigration Depot at the Princess Louise Embankment in Quebec, which was designed in 1886 (Figure 2.24).[59] A long, L-shaped structure measuring 320 feet by 110 feet, this building was more sophisticated in its facilities and in its architecture than the 'sheds' of the 1870s. It also offered a more extensive range of services for the immigrant in transit. The ground floor consisted of a series of offices for government agents, a large waiting-room, a dining-room, and a kitchen. The upstairs contained two large dormitories, one for men and the other for women. Smaller bedrooms for men and women were also provided for first-class and second-class immigrants. The exterior design borrowed some features, such as the wide bracketed canopy, from those for railway stations and, like many stations of the period, reflected the influence of the Queen Anne or Shingle style. The decorative treatment of the woodwork, defined by a pattern of horizontal and diagonal planks, varied patterns of shingling on the second level and on dormers, and a heavy veranda and roof brackets, were characteristic of this style. It was indicative of the central Canadian focus of the Chief Architect's Branch that an immigration depot in Quebec would receive far greater attention to its design than a court-house in Calgary.

The arrival of immigrants on the Prairies created a demand for a new type of immigration building. Once new settlers had arrived, they required a certain amount of time to obtain a homestead lot and to equip themselves for farming. Given the undeveloped nature of the communities, there was often inadequate accommodation for new arrivals. This problem was the subject of an angry editorial in a Regina paper in 1886, which described the plight of a number of immigrants who were forced to seek shelter in tents provided by the town.[60] A few years later a new Immigration Hall was constructed in Regina. One of several immigration buildings built for Prairie communities, it provided up to a week of free but rudimentary accommodation (Figure 2.25). Two day-rooms were located on the ground floor. A rear wing contained a kitchen and the second storey was taken up by two dormitories. A two-and-a-half-storey building, it was constructed of wood and had a gabled roof and clapboard siding. Between 1881 and 1900 many similar buildings were built in communities across the Prairies.

The Dominion Experimental Farm Service

By the mid-1880s it was becoming apparent that the expected flood of immigrants to the Prairies would not take place. The government believed that it would not be able to build a strong national economy without a healthy and prosperous agricultural community in the Northwest and across the country, and so it decided it must play a more active role in encouraging agriculture. In 1886, it established the Experimental Farm Service to develop new techniques and crop varieties that would increase agricultural productivity and profitability.[61] The service initially consisted of a central farm in Ottawa, where most of the primary research was carried out, and smaller branch farms located at Nappan, Nova Scotia, Brandon, Manitoba, Indian Head, Saskatchewan, and Agassiz, British Columbia. The role of the branch farms was to test under local conditions the new crop varieties and techniques developed in Ottawa and to demonstrate the advances to farmers.

The Chief Architect's Branch was given charge of all the new construction for the Experimental Farm Service. The Central Experimental Farm in Ottawa, which was the most elaborate and extensive complex, consisted of several administrative and laboratory buildings, barns, five large residences for the director and the senior staff, and several small cottages for the foremen and other staff. All the buildings were designed according to a logical and coherent theme. The administration and laboratory buildings were visually linked together by their brick construction, but their designs tended to be the least inventive, based on plans that resembled those for very modest federal public buildings.

The Main Barn was the most imposing building at the Central Experimental Farm, and it was the first agricultural building designed by the Chief Architect's Branch (Figure 2.26).[62] A massive U-shaped structure, it featured a high, gabled roof, patterned shingling on the upper level, and, what would become a defining characteristic of the agricultural buildings on the farm, board and batten siding on the lower level. Al-

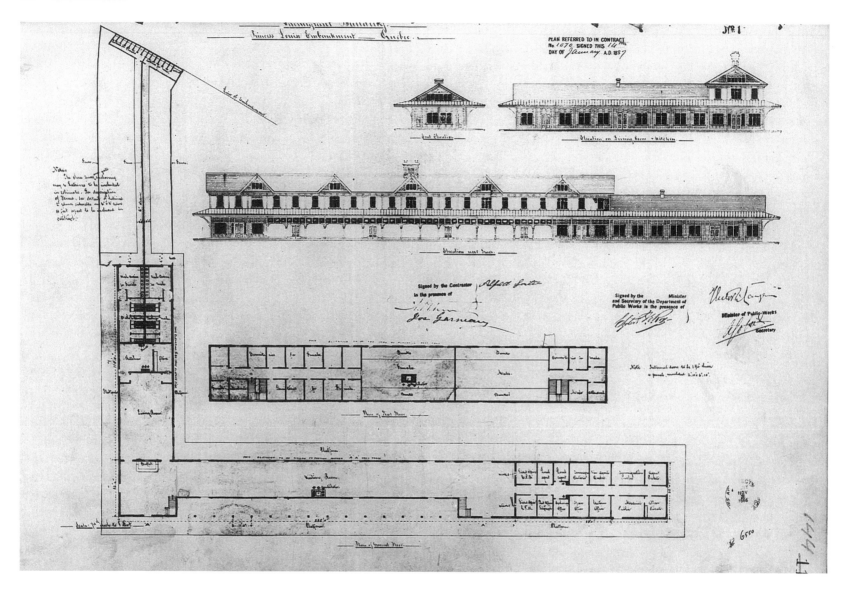

2.24. Plan and elevation, Immigration Depot, Princess Louise Embankment, Quebec, 1886–7. Plans prepared by the Chief Architect's Branch. Demolished in 1915. (NA, RG11, vol. 3917, C-138224)

though not a typical barn in its scale and detail, its design represented a fairly conventional and conservative solution. The central block could be described as a typical Ontario bank barn, featuring a hillside location that permitted ground-level access to two floors – one entrance to the threshing floor where heavy farm equipment was stored, and the other to the cattle stalls below. The structural framing also tended towards the conventional. By the 1880s plank-frame construction, which was a lighter, more versatile form of framing, had begun to appear and yet the Main Barn employed a heavy squared-timber frame that was more difficult to construct and resulted in a much less efficient interior space. The Main Barn was destroyed by fire in 1913. A new building was constructed in 1914; although some changes were made to the interior plan, the exterior replicated the original design.

Again the staff of the Chief Architect's Branch had proved to be very adaptable to new problems, but the scope of the work did not allow for the development of specialized skills or knowledge. Because of this limitation, there was a tendency for departments with specialized building needs to develop their own building services. By the early twentieth century the Experimental Farm Service had identified agricultural design as a relevant field of research and, with the exception of large administrative buildings, designed most of its own buildings. They may not have been as attractive to look at, but they incorporated the most recent developments in agricultural technology.

Residential Buildings

Federal government facilities, such as quarantine stations, penitentiaries, and experimental farms, also required buildings to house resident staff. In the 1870s the Chief Architect's Branch designed a few houses, but by the 1880s and 1890 the call for domestic buildings became greater. As a result, the branch developed a broader range of design types under Fuller's direction. The finest example of residential building by the branch was the now-demolished Director's Residence at the Central Experimental Farm (Figure 2.27). The rambling, two-and-a-half-storey building fea-

2.25. Immigration Hall, Regina, Saskatchewan, 1889. Plans prepared by the Chief Architect's Branch. Now demolished. (NA, PA-46555)

2.26. Main Barn, Central Experimental Farm, Ottawa, Ontario, 1913–14. This building replicates the exterior design of the 1886 barn that burned down in 1913. (M. Trépanier, Parks Canada, 1993)

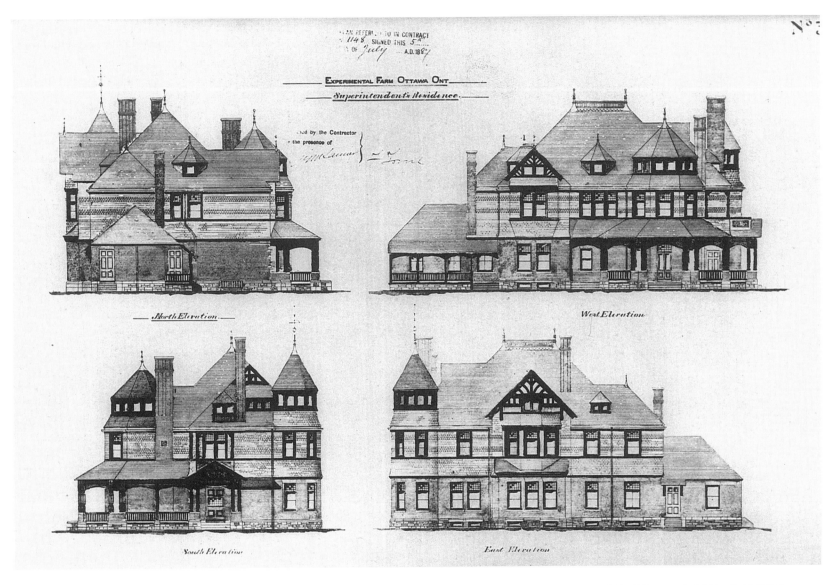

EXPERIMENTAL FARM OTTAWA ONT

Superintendent's Residence.

North Elevation

West Elevation

South Elevation

East Elevation

2.27. Plan, Director's Residence, Central Experimental Farm, Ottawa, Ontario, 1887–8. Demolished *ca.* 1935. (NA, RG11, vol. 3918, C-138228)

2.28. McNeely Residence, Central Experimental Farm, Ottawa, Ontario, 1889. Plans prepared by the Chief Architect's Branch. (M. Trépanier, Parks Canada, 1993)

tured a complex, irregular plan and a highly picturesque roofline composed of projecting half-timbered gables, dormers, bay windows, towers, and tall ribbed chimneys. The ground floor was sheathed on the exterior in brick, and the upper floor featured patterned shingles similar to those used on the immigration building in Quebec. The woodwork of the wide veranda and porches fully exploited the decorative potential of the lathe and the fretsaw, as is evident in the abundance of elaborately turned posts, railings and spool motifs. It was a very good example of the Queen Anne or Shingle style, which was popular for residential buildings of the period, and Fuller obviously enjoyed this opportunity to design a fine residence. In his enthusiasm for the project, however, he produced a building that really exceeded the basic requirements of a civil servant's residence.

Scaled-down versions of the Director's Residence were constructed for other staff members at the Central Experimental Farm and at the various branch farms.[63] At the federal penitentiaries, most construction was directed by the Penitentiaries Branch but the design of residential support buildings was generally given to the Chief Architect's Branch. Unfortunately most of these buildings have disappeared, but another surviving residence at the Central Experimental Farm in Ottawa illustrates the attention to detail sometimes given to small residential projects (Figure 2.28).[64] The McNeely Residence is a picturesque cottage in the Queen Anne or Shingle style; the design adopts the wood shingles, asymmetrical plan, and decorative gables characteristic of the style. This building represents a fairly elaborate example of the branch's work in small house design. The surviving Assistant Medical Officer's Residence at Grosse Île, built in 1893, provides an example of a larger but more functional design that often typified the branch's residential buildings in less accessible locations (Figure 2.29).[65]

Conclusion

The popular image of federal government building in Canada owes much to Thomas Fuller. By the turn of the twentieth century the eclecticism of the late Victorian era had fallen out of fashion, but Fuller had established patterns of design that, in many respects, transcended shifting architec-

2.29. Assistant Medical Officer's Residence, Grosse Île, Quebec, 1893. Plans prepared by the Chief Architect's Branch. (J. Audet, Parks Canada, 1990)

tural tastes. Although new architectural themes would enter into the vocabulary of government buildings by the early 1900s, Fuller's legacy, particularly in the area of small public buildings, remained strong. His buildings, distinguished by their effective siting, textured surfaces, simple yet well-crafted detail, and quality materials, defined an architectural tradition that would shape the work of the Chief Architect's Branch well into the next century.

As chief architect in the Department of Public Works, Thomas Fuller brought to the branch a professional credibility that it would never regain. In 1889 an architectural exhibition in Toronto prominently featured designs from the branch. The work was received with unqualified praise. One reviewer wrote: 'The series of colour drawings lent by Mr. Fuller of Ottawa, are specially fine, and from an artistic point of view, were the attraction of the exhibition.'[66] The architectural profession disliked, on principle, a self-sufficient Chief Architect's Branch that deprived private architects of lucrative government commissions, but in 1894 even one of its critics had to admit that 'If the present system is to be maintained it would be no easy matter to find, in the whole Dominion, a man better qualified for his position.'[67] No other chief architect could command the same degree of respect from his colleagues in private practice.

Many lamented the passing of this era, which came to an end in 1896 with Fuller's retirement, and wished for the arrival of an architect equal to his stature who would bring about a rebirth of a golden age in federal building. The Fuller years would, however, remain an anomaly in the history of the Department of Public Works. By the turn of the century, the role of the chief architect and that of the branch in general had undergone a transformation. Even Fuller must have come to realize by the late 1880s that the chief architect could no longer function as the master designer of federal buildings. The growing demand for public buildings to service a rapidly expanding nation would demand an increasing standardization and simplification of design. This trend was already evident in the public buildings constructed in the 1890s, and it had been noticed, even by Fuller's supporters. One critic commented that 'even the most versatile architect becomes in the course of time liable to repeat himself, he may even become stereotypical in his versatility. We cannot therefore look for much progress in our national buildings, when we continue . . . to engage services of only one man.'[68] In the twentieth century government architects would learn to operate within the rules of a more modern bureaucracy. Federal architecture of the early part of the century would be shaped by the basic premise that government buildings should reflect good design within the bounds of economy and efficiency.

Fuller's most significant contribution was to demonstrate to the government the advantages of maintaining a permanent architectural staff who were familiar with the basic requirements of the client department and who could deliver buildings quickly and within budget. The next generation of chief architects would come to the job equipped with very different skills and experience. Most would be recruited into the government architectural service at a young age and would work their way up through the ranks. These architects made no attempt to impose a personal architectural identity on the work produced by the branch, but they were well trained to work within a complex administrative and organizational structure that was designed to produce at a high volume, and to manage and maintain an ever-growing building inventory over an ever-widening geographical area.

CHAPTER THREE

The Architecture of Growth and Prosperity, 1896–1914

The years between 1896 and 1914 comprised one of the most productive eras in the history of the Chief Architect's Branch. It was a period of unprecedented growth and prosperity that was fuelled by a booming industrial and manufacturing sector, the development of new resource-based industries, and the successful agricultural settlement of the Prairies. Such growth created a demand for expanded federal institutions and for new public buildings. Rising federal revenues, generated by this prosperity, enabled the government to build at a rate that would not be equalled again until the 1950s. Between 1900 and 1914 the Chief Architect's Branch spent over $47 million on construction and improvements to public buildings.[1] That figure translated into over three hundred new public buildings, drill halls, and customs houses, as well as numerous minor structures for quarantine stations and immigration services, and some agricultural buildings. The federal building inventory of the Department of Public Works tripled in size and many more buildings were in the planning stages when the boom came to an abrupt end with the outbreak of World War I in 1914.[2]

The scope and character of the federal buildings designed by the Chief Architect's Branch were shaped and transformed by different and often contradictory forces. The High Victorian legacy of Thomas Fuller continued to influence federal architecture, but by the early 1900s a new architecture of classicism, inspired by the École des Beaux-Arts in Paris and the Edwardian Baroque style in Britain, introduced new patterns of design that would define government building until the 1950s. Although many outstanding monuments were produced, the majority of buildings reflected the aims and values that were associated with the emergence of a modern federal bureaucracy. In order to maintain a high volume of construction, the branch had to develop an efficient assembly line of architectural production through greater economy and standardization in design. This was the era of 'government-issue' architecture – good, solid buildings designed according to standard patterns that could be delivered on time and on budget to hundreds of towns and cities across the country.

One of the most important projects undertaken was the improvement of Ottawa and its transformation from a rough lumbering town into a more dignified national capital. The early 1900s were energized by a new sense of nationalism which, in Ottawa, manifested itself through a vision of the town as a symbol of the nation. Federal building and planning in Ottawa was guided by an attempt to define a distinct architectural and urban form that would give expression to Canada's unique cultural identity. From the beginning of the twentieth century, Ottawa emerged as a central but separate problem for the Chief Architect's Branch, and therefore this aspect of government building will be discussed separately in the next chapter.

Public Works and the Emergence of a Modern Bureaucracy

In June 1896 a Liberal government under the leadership of Wilfrid Laurier brought an end to almost thirty years of Conservative rule. Four months later Thomas Fuller retired as chief architect.[3] He was replaced by David Ewart, an architect who had been with the branch since 1871. Throughout his tenure, Ewart and his staff would be criticized by the architectural community for the general mediocrity of their buildings, and in many respects the criticisms were valid. Much of the work lacked the individual stamp that Fuller had brought to federal architecture. However, the decline in the quality of design of individual buildings should not be attributed solely to the chief architect and his staff. Rather, it was a reflection of fundamental changes in the nature of the job and of the working environment within the bureaucracy. The trend towards economy and standardization was already evident in the latter half of Fuller's term, but by the early twentieth century the rapid growth of the civil service and the increasing complexity of government programs demanded new approaches to government administration. During the early 1900s the government and the civil service were under constant attack from the Opposition in Parliament for inefficiency, blatant patronage, and corruption. In 1907 and 1911 royal commissions were established to investigate the civil service and to recommend reforms.

Although created by two different governments, the findings of the commissions had much in common.[4] Both concluded that the work of departments had become too big and too complex to be administered effectively by elected ministers who often held their portfolios for only short periods. Responsibility for managing the day-to-day activities of the department should devolve to permanent senior officials and their staffs. The aim was to create a permanent, self-sufficient bureaucracy that would serve the elected government but that would, to some extent, be independent of it. Both commissions saw the need for greater accountability and tighter control over expenditures. They also identified the need to eliminate patronage from the civil service by establishing a formal system of hiring, promotion, and classification based on merit. The government proved to be resistant to change. Patronage could not be eradicated, and although many of the recommendations of the commissions were implemented, others were ignored. The Public Service Commission was established in 1908 to administer personnel services and to remove this function from political hands. At the same time, a new breed of professional bureaucrat emerged. These individuals imposed on their departments the principles and priorities of bureaucracy – efficiency, consistency, and careful and conservative financial management.

In the Department of Public Works, the rise of the bureaucracy and the devolution of responsibility to the deputy minister and his senior staff was facilitated by the lack of strong political leadership. Between 1896 and 1914 the department was headed by six different ministers. Some, like Joseph-Israël Tarte (Liberal minister from 1896 to 1902) and Robert Rogers (Conservative minister from 1912 to 1917), were powerful and effective but most of the remaining four were not in office long enough to exert any discernible influence.[5] Instead, administrative power naturally fell to the deputy minister. During the early years this position was held by Antoine Gobeil, who had been in office since 1891; by 1907 he was nearing retirement and the government began looking for a suitable replacement.[6]

The importance of this appointment to the effective operation of the department was clearly appreciated by the government. In July 1907 Richard Cartwright, one of Laurier's senior ministers, wrote to the prime minister urging him to appoint a capable deputy minister, claiming that 'the choice of a good deputy head is almost more important than a minister.'[7] This same view was expressed more strongly a few years later by another member of Parliament: 'What does it matter who are the ministers and acting ministers of the department? They are only temporary, they are in and out; it is the permanent official who will carry on.'[8] In 1908 the government appointed James B. Hunter as deputy minister, and for the next forty-three years he would rule over the Department of Public Works.

Born in Woodstock, Ontario, Hunter had studied journalism at the University of Toronto but in 1900 he was persuaded by James Sutherland, a Liberal member of Parliament, to go to Ottawa as a clerk in the

Privy Council Office. In 1903, when Sutherland was appointed minister of public works, he brought Hunter with him as his private secretary.[9] Hunter epitomized the new breed of senior bureaucrat.[10] Although he had no professional background in public works, he was a smart, capable administrator with good political connections. His contribution to the department and his influence on government building is difficult to define precisely. As will be seen, there were few instances when he directly involved himself in the activities of the Chief Architect's Branch. Rather, his success seemed to lie in his ability to delegate responsibility to his senior professional staff while, at the same time, imposing on them a sense of order, efficiency, and responsible spending.

The selection of David Ewart as chief architect in 1896 had been an early indication of a new emphasis on careful, conservative administration. Ewart was a very different type of architect from Fuller, but it was Ewart, not Fuller, who would define the professional profile of the typical chief architect in the twentieth century. Whereas Fuller had come to the public service after many years in private practice, Ewart was a career civil servant who appears to have had little professional experience outside the confines of the Chief Architect's Branch. Born in Scotland in 1841, he was educated at the Edinburgh School of Art. Little is known of his early career in Scotland, but in 1871 he immigrated to Canada, where he found employment with the newly created Chief Architect's Branch.[11] When Scott retired in 1881 Ewart served briefly as the acting chief architect, but he was passed over for promotion in favour of Thomas Fuller. In 1896 he had a second chance at the job, and this time he was successful. Ewart promised consistency and predictability, and he also brought to the job a thorough understanding of the administration of the branch and of the workings of government. These qualifications were essential in the new bureaucracy.

During his tenure David Ewart oversaw the rapid expansion of the Chief Architect's Branch and its gradual transformation into an integrated component of the federal bureaucracy. In 1896 there were approximately fourteen employees engaged in designing public buildings; most were classified as temporary employees without any security or professional status within the government. By 1912 departmental records list approx-imately thirty-four staff members who were directly engaged in designing and supervising the construction of public buildings.[12] The new employees all tended to have been drawn from the same sector of the architectural community. Because the salary of an architect in the Department of Public Works was comparatively low and the position lacked prestige, it was difficult to hire architects with established reputations. Moreover, reforms in the hiring practices of the civil service encouraged recruitment at junior levels, with promotions to more senior levels being made from within the ranks.[13] For these reasons, the new recruits tended to be young and with little or no outside experience.[14]

But, despite youth and inexperience, the Chief Architect's Branch developed into a strong design team. The buildings demonstrated a confidence and maturity that results from the challenge of a large, amply funded building program. More importantly, it was a staff whose professional identity was inseparable from that of the department. Although a few members moved on to private practice, most remained with the branch throughout their professional lives. Some built highly successful careers in the government. By 1914 or 1915 four of the next five chief architects were working together in the branch.[15] It was a staff capable of producing public buildings of considerable sophistication and grandeur; at the same time, it was a staff that produced dozens of standardized 'government-issue' public buildings in response to bureaucratic strictures of economy and restraint. This balance of professional competence and a clear understanding of the priorities of government made the staff invaluable to the bureaucracy, and assured them an important role in the design and construction of new public buildings until the mid-1930s.

The volume of work carried out by the Chief Architect's Branch grew steadily throughout the early 1900s, but at the same time its clientele began to shrink. Although the Quarantine Branch of the Department of Agriculture and the Immigration Branch of the Department of the Interior remained loyal clients, by 1914 many departments, particularly those that managed large building inventories or had specialized needs, decided that they would be better served by hiring their own resident staff of specialists. This process of decentralization had begun in the 1880s, with the establishment of separate construction services in the Penitentiaries

Branch of the Department of Justice and, briefly, in the Department of Militia and Defence. It was not until the late nineteenth century that the government began to formally recognize these independent departmental services. By 1896 penitentiary design was taken over by the chief trades instructor at Kingston, and in 1906 he received the title of architect to the Penitentiaries Branch.[16] The Parks Branch of the Department of the Interior, which had originated with the establishment of the first park in the Rocky Mountains in 1886, had always constructed its own buildings, and in 1911 the arrangement was recognized by the creation of the Architectural and Engineering Service of the Parks Branch.[17] The Dominion Experimental Farm Service developed a compromise arrangement with the Department of Public Works: administrative and general-purpose buildings would often be constructed by the Chief Architect's Branch, while the design of agricultural buildings, which had evolved into a legitimate branch of agricultural science, was carried out by the Animal Husbandry Division. The construction of Native schools was also taken over by the Construction Branch in the Department of Indian Affairs. Militia and Defence struggled to take control of its own buildings from Public Works, but it had to accept an uneasy, cooperative arrangement, whereby large buildings were designed by the chief architect's staff and smaller projects were carried out by military engineers.

Federal Public Buildings and the Influence of the Grand Manner

The Post Office Department and the Department of Customs continued to provide the Chief Architect's Branch with the core of its work. Throughout its history the branch clearly considered the business of designing urban public buildings as its main function, and it is here that the evolution of design in government architecture can be traced most clearly. Ewart's appointment as chief architect had no immediately perceptible effect on designs produced by the branch. After ten years of service under Scott and sixteen years under Fuller, Ewart seems to have had no desire to remake federal architecture in his own image. It could be said that his personal style was indistinguishable from that of the

branch. The buildings produced in the late 1890s and early 1900s faithfully adhered to patterns of design that had been established by Fuller. Fuller's legacy would continue to influence government design, but by the early twentieth century new influences began to expand and transform the vocabulary of the Chief Architect's Branch.

The Vancouver Post Office (1905–10), although not the first of its type, clearly illustrates the shift in stylistic direction that took place around 1902 (Figure 3.1).[18] An imposing, four-storey, granite-faced building, it adopted the Edwardian Baroque style that dominated public architecture in Britain at the turn of the century.[19] Inspired by the work of such seventeenth-century and early eighteenth-century architects as Christopher Wren, James Gibbs, and John Vanbrugh, this style was influenced by French and Italian Baroque architecture, which it reinterpreted into a distinctive British design. The organization of the façade of the Vancouver Post Office, consisting of a rusticated stone base punctuated by round-arched openings and a row of monumental Ionic columns, was modelled after the Italian palazzo form. Features such as the broken segmental pediments and the high mansard roof were drawn from European, primarily French, Baroque architecture. The domed corner tower is a feature found on the buildings of Christopher Wren. This motif also represents a translation of the federal government's emblematic clock tower into a classical vocabulary.

In the design of this building, the Chief Architect's Branch was responding to a widespread shift toward a grander and simpler language of classicism. By the late nineteenth century, a reaction was setting in against the unrestrained eclecticism of the Victorian era. In the United States, architects turned increasingly to the French classical tradition, as promulgated by the teaching and principles of the École des Beaux-Arts. Characterized by a formal classical vocabulary, rational planning, and ordered composition, the École created a new architecture of grandeur and formalism that contrasted with the picturesque informality of Victorian design.

In Britain the reaction against the superficial excesses of Victorian design was first manifested in the aesthetics of the Arts and Crafts movement at the end of the nineteenth century.[20] It sought to return architecture to its vernacular, pre-industrial roots, but its influence was largely confined to the field of domestic architecture. Public architecture was dominated by the new classicism. The richness and grandeur of this style appealed to the new sense of imperial splendour that coloured popular opinion in the Edwardian era. By the second decade of the twentieth century the influence of the French École des Beaux-Arts would become more prevalent, but initially strong nationalistic sentiments encouraged the definition of a new language of classicism in terms of British sources. The architecture of the Baroque period provided Edwardian architecture its historical sources, but these forms were translated into a grandiose scale that earned work of this period of architecture the title of Grand Manner.[21]

In Canadian architecture the influence of the new classicism could be detected in the last years of the nineteenth century, but it was not until the early 1900s that the style began to dominate public, commercial, and institutional building.[22] The shift within the Chief Architect's Branch may have come about in response to developments within the larger architectural community in Canada; it may also have been prompted by David Ewart's tour of Europe in the summer of 1901.[23] The purpose of the trip was to examine public buildings that might serve as models for some new public buildings being designed in Ottawa. While in London Ewart would have seen some of the new public buildings in the Grand Manner then under construction in Whitehall.[24] Certainly the shift to a classical style coincided with Ewart's return. At this point, the branch became among the leaders in Canada in adapting Beaux-Arts and Edwardian Baroque styles to public architecture; in subsequent decades the Chief Architect's Branch would earn a reputation for its conservatism and resistance to new design influences.

The Vancouver Post Office also provides a good illustration of the impact that a new federal building could have on local development. Like many other Canadian cities, Vancouver experienced dramatic growth in the early 1900s. In the nineteenth century the commercial district had been centred along the waterfront of Burrard Inlet in the area now known as Gastown. The purchase by the federal government of a site for a post office at the corner of West Hastings and Granville streets played an important part in shifting the focus of development within the financial district away from the harbour. Within a few years a number of major

3.1. Vancouver Post Office, Granville Street, Vancouver, British Columbia, 1905–10. Designed by the Chief Architect's Branch. The building was incorporated into a government office complex, the Sinclair Centre, which in 1981–6 was converted to shops and offices. Richard Henriquez and Partners designed the renovations and redevelopment. (Public Works and Government Services Canada, Heritage Recording and Technical Data Services, 1992)

3.2. Public Building, Moose Jaw, Saskatchewan, 1911. Designed by the Chief Architect's Branch. The building now serves as the city hall. (J. Wright, Parks Canada, 1991)

bank buildings and prestigious office buildings had located near the new post office.[25]

The Vancouver building also played an important role in introducing new building technologies to the city. The interior structure employs steel posts and beams that support reinforced concrete floors. The exterior walls were constructed of traditional load-bearing granite walls backed with brick, to which the interior steel frame was tied. Within the context of Canadian building technology, this mix of construction techniques was relatively conservative. Independent steel-frame structures first appeared in Toronto around 1895 and soon afterwards they were being built in Montreal and Winnipeg.[26] In Vancouver, however, this building was the first to introduce steel beam construction.[27] Once again, federal buildings served, not as sources of innovation, but as disseminators of new ideas and new technologies to other parts of the country.

The Vancouver Post Office defined a prototypical design for a series of subsequent federal buildings. The public building of 1911 in Moose Jaw, Saskatchewan, provides a late example of the type. Its design, with a rusticated, round-arched base, a row of engaged columns, a mansard roof, and a domed, corner clock tower, represented a simplified and scaled-down version of the Vancouver building (Figure 3.2). Variations on this theme were repeated at Regina, Edmonton, Brantford, and Lethbridge.[28] These buildings were all well designed and solidly constructed, and yet they also demonstrated the tendency in the Chief Architect's Branch to define its work within established conventions. The trend toward standardization created recognizable symbols of the federal government but it also ensured a certain predictability and lack of individuality in design.

By the end of the first decade of the twentieth century new influences could be detected in the work of the Chief Architect's Branch. Paralleling a stylistic evolution evident in both British and Canadian architecture in general, federal buildings showed a marked shift towards the simpler but more monumental classical forms associated with the architecture of the École des Beaux-Arts in Paris. Two New Brunswick buildings, Postal Station A in Saint John and Postal Station A in Fredericton, both begun in 1913, provide good examples of this trend (Figures 3.3 and 3.4). The Saint John building is similar in many respects to the Vancouver Post

3.3. Postal Station A, Saint John, New Brunswick, 1913–16. Plans prepared by the Chief Architect's Branch; supervising architects: J.T.C. Mckean and G.E. Fairweather. The building is now an important element in the Prince William heritage streetscape, which consists of a homogeneous group of predominantly late nineteenth-century buildings. (NA, PA-46589)

3.4. Postal Station A, Fredericton, New Brunswick, 1913. Designed by the Chief Architect's Branch. (Canadian Inventory of Historic Building, 1985)

Office in its use of the palazzo form, with an arcaded base supporting a row of monumental Ionic columns, but the French and Baroque elements, such as the mansard roof, the domed tower, and the broken pediments, were eliminated.[29] The compact rectangular mass of the building is contained within the strong horizontal line of the flat roof, with its heavy cornice and attic. The detail retains the full sculptural quality of the Vancouver building but it takes on a less flamboyant character. Postal Station A in Fredericton represents an example of a mid-sized federal building in the Beaux-Arts style.[30] The classical vocabulary has a simplicity and restraint characteristic of the pure Beaux-Arts style. The use of inset columns next to simple piers would become a recurring motif in the work of the Chief Architect's Branch.[31]

Small Public Buildings and the Era of Government-Issue Design

In the early years of Ewart's term, before the volume of work became onerous, the staff had time to develop individual design variations for small public buildings. For example, the public building of 1901 in Nelson, British Columbia, featuring a rounded tower and a mixture of rusticated stone base with red brick above, was one of the more picturesque designs to come out of the branch. Like many federal buildings of this period, it now serves as the city hall (Figure 3.5). The public building of 1904 in Sydney Mines, Nova Scotia, offers quite a different variation in its use of stepped gables and an octagonal tower (Figure 3.6). It too now serves as the local town hall.

By 1905 and 1906, as the volume of construction rose, standardization in design was becoming increasingly evident. The public building in Humboldt, Saskatchewan, constructed in 1911, is typical of this period of construction; its design illustrates the conservative and sometimes anachronistic traditions within the Chief Architect's Branch (Figure 3.7).[32] The basic configuration of the design, with its corner clock tower, steeply pitched and truncated hipped roof, offset parapeted gables, and round-arched openings, referred back to Thomas Fuller's late Victorian public buildings. Unlike Fuller's buildings, however, this second genera-

tion of design reflected a growing trend toward simplification and economy. Brick replaced stone as the standard building material and decorative detail was reduced to a minimum. The building's visual effect depended on good massing and a rhythmic distribution of openings. Cut-stone dressing added a little colour and gave definition to the principal elements of the façade. Variations on this theme were developed for smaller buildings. The public building in Rock Island, Quebec, incorporated the same steep roofline, round-arched windows, and clock tower, but all compressed into a one-and-a-half-storey block (Figure 3.8).[33]

The public building in Campbellton, New Brunswick, represents another common design formula for small and medium-sized federal buildings that traced its architectural roots to the federal buildings of Thomas Fuller (Figure 3.9). Although built in 1910, fourteen years after Fuller's departure, it could easily have been constructed in the 1890s.[34] A two-and-a-half-storey brick block, the façade is dominated by the central parapeted gable that had become a Fuller trademark. The double flanking entrance, the heavy corbelling under the cornice, the central clock tower, and small details such as the stone balls on either side of the central gable were found on his buildings. Only the use of a slightly lower roof, the elimination of overtly medieval detail, the incongruous use of classical door mouldings, and the use of internal steel posts and beams indicate a later date for this building.

Occasionally a fresh design would emerge from the offices of the Chief Architect's Branch. For example, around 1914 a series of small public buildings were designed with a distinctive Italianate accent. The public building in Newmarket, Ontario, exemplifies the style. It adopted many of the same basic components as the Humboldt Public Building, but with a low pitch for the roof, semicircular windows, and wide overhanging eaves giving an Italianate character to the design (Figure 3.10).[35]

Postal Station C in Toronto introduced yet another type that would become closely associated with the Chief Architect's Branch (Figure 3.11). Designed in a stripped-down, economical classical style, it was a two-storey brick building with stone accents in the string-courses and door and window surrounds. The classical vocabulary was simplified and reduced to a minimum. Its symmetrical elevation, shallow pilasters mark-

3.5. Public Building, Nelson, British Columbia, 1901, in the early twentieth century. Designed by the Chief Architect's Branch. The building now serves as the city hall. (NA, PA53155)

ing the two slightly projecting end pavilions, and wide cornices would become clichés of government design. Sometimes a building of this type would also have a pediment or entablature over the principal doors. The interior organization conformed to the typical Department of Public Works pattern. The two flanking entrances provided separate accesses, one to the postal lobby on the ground floor and the other to government offices above. Often the window on the ground level would feature semi-circular heads allowing for extra ceiling height on the ground floor.

Over the next thirty years dozens of similar designs flowed from the drafting tables of the Chief Architect's Branch. Decorative details and the number of bays varied from building to building, but a red-brick block, marginally classical in style, provided a design that met the two basic requirements of government architecture: a building with a suitably dignified appearance and one that could be delivered at a reasonable cost. In 1907 the branch also developed its first true standard plans, although they were not widely used. 'Standard Plan B,' which was a typical two-storey, classicized block, is known to have been adapted to only two completed projects, the Maple Creek Public Building in Saskatchewan (Figure 3.12) and the Westville Public Building in Nova Scotia. The idea of using standard plans to mass-produce federal post offices appealed to both the Department of Public Works and the Post Office Department, but such a program would not be successfully implemented until the 1960s.[36]

These government-issue buildings were not outstanding works of architecture, but in some respects they represented the most important contribution of the Chief Architect's Branch to Canadian building. Because of their numbers, they formed a common urban imagery that was consistent and recognizable across the country. Although architecturally not as inventive as the buildings designed under Thomas Fuller, they had a greater impact on the character of the Canadian urban landscape. In the nineteenth century, few public buildings were constructed and they were generally located in communities that were already well established. In the boom years of the early twentieth century, public buildings were being constructed at a more rapid pace. Between 1900 and 1914 the population increased by 64 per cent, whereas the number of public buildings in-

3.6. Public Building, Sydney Mines, Nova Scotia, 1904. Designed by the Chief Architect's Branch. The building is now used as the town hall. (NA, PA-04621)

3.7. Public Building, Humboldt, Saskatchewan, 1911. Designed by the Chief Architect's Branch. Designated a national historic site in 1977, the building now houses the local museum. (Public Works and Government Services Canada, Heritage Recording and Technical Data Services, 1990)

creased by almost 200 per cent. This meant that many small towns were now receiving their own government buildings, and the visual and physical impact of these structures on these small and sometimes marginal communities was significant. The importance of a federal building was particularly evident on the Prairies, where hundreds of new towns and villages were being established.[37] In this competitive environment the construction of a new federal building was seen as proof of a community's stability and an assurance of future growth.

The visual impact of these buildings was owed partly to a conscious policy to improve the overall quality of construction and materials used. In the 1898–9 annual report, the deputy minister of public works stated:

> It is also the earnest wish of the department to dispense as often as will be practicable with the use of wood, and substitute iron, stone, concrete, brick, terracotta or other fireproof materials in the construction of public buildings, not only as a better protection against fire, but as an effective incentive to individuals and companies in small cities and large towns to follow the example of the government . . .[38]

Of course, some public buildings constructed in the nineteenth century had also adopted fire-resistant materials and methods, but they were relatively few in number and were generally built in well-established communities where the use of these measures was more common. In the early twentieth century, federal public buildings constructed of concrete, brick, iron or steel, and galvanized metal roofing and cornice moulding were introduced into smaller municipalities where the existing building stock was dominated by wood-frame structures.

The lasting significance of these buildings was augmented by the fact that they were the product of a boom. They were built on the assumption that the country would continue to expand, but this did not happen. In the 1920s and 1930s the rate of growth slowed. Many smaller urban centres experienced little or no increase in size and some lost population. The problem was accentuated after the 1920s by population increases that were concentrated more and more in the major urban centres. As a result, many of the early twentieth-century public buildings remain key landmarks within their communities. The image of main-street Canada owes much to these solid, red-brick buildings, many with their characteristic clock tower. Although the federal government has disposed of a large number of these buildings, many have been restored to house local institutions and have become town halls, libraries, and other public facilities.

Public Building Commissions to Private Architects

The Department of Public Works clearly preferred to work with its own staff, but by the early 1900s pressure was mounting from the architectural community at large to employ more private architects on government buildings. The debate over who should design public buildings intensified, creating a rift between the Chief Architect's Branch and outside professionals that was to resurface throughout the history of the branch. In the 1880s and 1890s Thomas Fuller had the respect of the architectural community and few questioned his ability to operate with an exclusive monopoly over government design. David Ewart, however, lacked Fuller's professional credentials and there was considerable resentment among independent architects that this unknown civil servant should command the nation's largest and most expensive construction program.[39]

The debate was further fuelled both by the example of the U.S. government and by a new sense of professional identity that was developing within Canadian architectural circles. In 1893 the United States had passed the Tarnsey Act, which allowed for and encouraged the employment of private architects on large federal buildings.[40] Although the act was revoked in 1912, Canadian architects continued to point to the legislation as a model for Canada.[41] At the same time, the architectural community's ability to influence the government had grown with the establishment of a number of provincial architectural associations at the end of the century, and finally with the creation of the Royal Architectural Institute of Canada in 1907.[42] With its headquarters in Ottawa, this organization functioned as a lobby for the profession. One of its priorities was to pressure the federal government to give more work to its members.

3.8. Public Building, Rock Island, Quebec, 1911. Designed by the Chief Architect's Branch. (C. Cameron, Parks Canada, 1982)

3.9. Public Building, Campbellton, New Brunswick, 1910–11, in 1972. Designed by the Chief Architect's Branch. (NA, PA-135567)

It argued that government buildings, as symbols of the nation, should reflect the highest standards of architectural excellence, which could only be achieved by private architects whose skills had been honed in the demanding and competitive world of private practice.

In response to pressure, the Laurier administration awarded a few contracts to outside firms, and the Borden administration, which assumed power in 1911, adopted an even more open policy. One of the earliest commissioned works was the post office in Winnipeg, which was built between 1904 and 1909 by Toronto architects Frank Darling and John A. Pearson (Figure 3.13).[43] Situated on Portage Avenue, the Winnipeg Post Office was designed in an Edwardian Baroque style. A four-storey building constructed of stone, it adopted a typical Renaissance façade composition defined by an arcaded base supporting a row of engaged Ionic columns above. Two slightly projecting pavilions, featuring large end-windows that were richly ornamented with broken segmental pediments and banded columns, marked the outer edges of the building. The mansard roof was punctuated by dormers with a semicircular pediment broken by decorative obelisks.

The Winnipeg Post Office demonstrated the strengths and weaknesses of engaging independent architects. The design was similar in many respects to the departmental design for the Vancouver Post Office, which would start construction the following year. The Winnipeg building, however, was distinguished by the quality and complexity of its finishing. Features such as the channelled stonework of the base and the intricately carved door and window surrounds, as well as elements such as the decorative obelisks, demonstrated a far greater range and sophistication in detailing. A comparison of the two buildings would tend to support the argument that private architects produced better buildings, but the high quality came at a price. Although there were always variables in expenses and in the way expenses were recorded, the department's accounts show that the construction costs for the post office in Winnipeg were as much as 60 per cent higher than those for the one in Vancouver, which was only slightly smaller and was built of similar materials.[44] In government and in bureaucracy, economy and cost control almost always had priority over excellence of design. It was for this reason that the government preferred to work with its own staff.

Postal Station G in Toronto, designed by E.J. Lennox, is an early example of the new federal building type known as a 'branch post office' (Figure 3.14). During the early 1900s, cities such as Toronto and Montreal expanded rapidly and it was no longer feasible or convenient for government postal services and offices to be located in one central location. Between 1902 and 1914 four branch offices were built in Toronto and eight were built in Montreal. Postal Station G represents a fairly typical example of this new building type. The temple form, with its portico across the façade, was characteristic of small banks. While it was not an exceptionally large building, a fundamental principle of government architecture was that its buildings should meet, if not exceed, the architectural standards of the immediate environment. For this reason, in cities such as Toronto and Montreal, where the prevailing architectural standards were higher or at least more costly than elsewhere, more elaborate standards were applied to government buildings.

The best of the commissioned work was generally located in the major cities, where the government could draw on the best architectural talent in the country. However, a number of fresh and original designs were also developed by private architects for buildings in small urban centres. One of the most remarkable is the public building in Collingwood of 1913–14 (Figures 3.15 and 3.16).[45] On the recommendation of a prominent local businessman, the commission was given to a local architect, Philip C. Palin, who was allowed to 'show what he can do.'[46] The building is a beautiful example of the Beaux-Arts style adapted to a small public building. A two-and-a-half-storey building, with a low, hipped roof, it is distinguished by the finely detailed and complex form of the projecting portico and colonnade. Its site, sandwiched between two ordinary, two-storey commercial blocks, was not particularly good, but the architect created a spatial presence by setting the building back from the street line and allowing the portico to project forward from the façade. The most remarkable aspect of the project was the unusually generous budget that was obviously lavished on a relatively minor public building.[47] The main

3.10. Public Building, Newmarket, Ontario, 1914–15. Designed by the Chief Architect's Branch. (J. Wright, Parks Canada, 1991)

3.11. Postal Station C, Toronto, Ontario, 1902. Designed by the Chief Architect's Branch. (J. Wright, Parks Canada, 1991)

3.12. Public Building, Maple Creek, Saskatchewan, 1908. Designed according to a standard plan by the Chief Architect's Branch. (J. Wright, Parks Canada, 1991)

3.13. Post Office, Winnipeg, Manitoba, 1904–9. Designed by F. Darling and J.A. Pearson. Now demolished. (NA, PA-46614)

3.14. Postal Station G, Toronto, Ontario, 1913. Architect: E.J. Lennox. The building now serves as a community centre. (J. Wright, Parks Canada, 1991)

3.15. Public Building, Collingwood, Ontario, 1913–14. Architect: Philip C. Palin. (M. Trépanier, Parks Canada, 1992)

façade was entirely sheathed in white marble, and the rich detailing, in the form of Corinthian columns, balustrades, and ornate frieze and cornice, fully exploited the sculptural potential of the material. In the interior, a spacious public lobby was finished with marble and bronze details and featured a coved skylight with leaded glass.

A less costly but more original design for a small urban post office in Stonewall, Manitoba, was built in 1914 by Ottawa architect Francis Sullivan (Figure 3.17). Sullivan had worked briefly in Chicago for Frank Lloyd Wright and had been employed by the Chief Architect's Branch between 1908 and 1911. He then set up a private practice in Ottawa but it was not very successful.[48] Perhaps to give the failing practice a boost, his former colleagues at the Department of Public Works commissioned him to design two small post offices: one at Stonewall and the other at Shawville, Quebec. The Stonewall Post Office is an early example of a one-room post office. Although it is a very modest building, the influence of Wright is evident in the sense of mass and strength created by the rusticated stonework, the strong horizontal lines, and the narrow slit windows. By the late 1930s hundreds of small semi-rural post offices would be built by the government, but none equalled this building for its fresh and novel interpretation.

The Customs Examining Warehouse

New buildings for the Customs and Excise Branch of the Department of Revenue were clearly a priority for the new Conservative government after 1911. Between 1900 and 1920 the gross revenue from import duties and excise tax increased from $28 million to $188 million.[49] To cope with the growing volume of goods entering the country, the government constructed eight large new customs buildings in the important transportation centres of the country in the first three years of its mandate.[50] Unlike the customs houses of the 1870s, they functioned primarily as storage warehouses and provided some support office space. The grand public space or long room, which had characterized the large customs house of the 1870s, was temporarily eliminated from this building type. The Montreal Customs House, begun in 1912, provides one of the most

3.16. Interior view, Public Building, Collingwood. (Public Works and Government Services Canada, Heritage Recording and Technical Data Services, 1992)

3.17. Post Office, Stonewall, Manitoba, 1914. Architect: F.C. Sullivan. (Canadian Inventory of Historic Building, 1974)

notable illustrations of this trend (Figure 3.18).[51] The building is situated on the corner of McGill and d'Youville streets with its main entrance located on the McGill Street façade. In the 1930s the building was doubled in size, and the new addition was designed to harmonize with the existing section. The exterior design, with its monumental row of Ionic columns, represents one of the most imposing examples of the Beaux-Arts style in government building, while the inside of the building is essentially a conventional warehouse. One of the first federal buildings to employ a skeletal steel frame, the layout featured a row of administrative offices across the front of the building on each level. The remainder of the floor area was taken up by roughly finished open warehouse space. Passenger elevators serviced the office areas and a larger freight elevator was located at the back of the building.

The location of this building in downtown Montreal seemed to demand a grand public face, whereas in other cities more modest plans were developed. The customs examining warehouse of 1912–16 in Calgary represented a fairly standard design solution to the type (Figure 3.19). The four-storey block, with applied pilasters, a heavy cornice, and a rusticated stone base, resembled a typical commercial warehouse. The same formula was adapted to other customs examining warehouses built at about the same time in Vancouver, Edmonton, Winnipeg, and Port Arthur. Following the example of the Montreal building, the customs offices for all of these were located on the ground floor and were finished in the manner of a typical post office. The areas above and behind these spaces were reserved for open warehouse storage.

Militia Reform and Drill Hall Construction

The Department of Militia and Defence remained one of the branch's most important clients. In the early 1900s the federal government initiated a program of reform in the Canadian militia. Issues such as the Alaska boundary dispute and the withdrawal of Imperial forces from bases at Halifax and Esquimalt pointed to the need for a Canadian military force. The Canadian experience in the Boer War had stirred a new nationalistic pride in the prowess of Canadian soldiers, but it had also highlighted inadequacies in their training, equipment, and leadership. The Militia Act of 1904 outlined a rigorous program of reform, including comprehensive training in the form of rifle practice, parade drill, physical fitness, and various educational plans. The aim was to transform a haphazard collection of weekend soldiers into a modern civilian army.[52]

The construction of an expanded network of drill halls and armouries was a key component of these reforms. Militia units were to be provided with permanent facilities that included a drill hall, rifle ranges, armouries for the storage of weapons and equipment, and lecture halls. The new facilities were also intended to strengthen the sense of identity and *esprit de corps* of the militia unit; many would be equipped with recreation rooms, mess rooms, and sometimes even basement bowling alleys. Drill halls or armouries of the immediate pre-World War I era would not differ substantially from those of the 1880s and 1890s; there were simply to be many more of them. In 1908 the Department of Militia and Defence estimated that approximately 360 new buildings would be required to serve adequately the needs of the militia.[53] Although this goal was never met, approximately one hundred new drill halls were built between 1900 and 1918. In addition, a number of militia stores buildings were erected in London, Winnipeg, Quebec, and Ottawa. These were large, plain brick or stone warehouses designed to store militia equipment.[54]

Responsibility for the design and construction of the buildings was shared by the departments of Public Works and of Militia and Defence, and the relationship between the two was not always easy. The military generally felt that the buildings designed by the department were too expensive and elaborate. Crenellations, towers, and decorative stonework were unnecessary and costly frills; the department argued for a simple, functional type of building to house militia regiments.[55] Over the next ten years, the role of the Chief Architect's Branch in designing and constructing militia buildings would gradually erode. In 1909 Militia and Defence won a significant victory when it gained the right to design and construct all military buildings that cost less than $15,000.[56]

In 1911 the new Borden government appointed Sam Hughes as

3.18. Customs House, Montreal, Quebec, 1912–14. Designed by the Chief Architect's Branch. Addition built in 1930. (J. Wright, Parks Canada, 1991)

3.19. Customs Examining Warehouse, Calgary, Alberta, 1912–16. Designed by the Chief Architect's Branch. (Canadian Inventory of Historic Building, 1974)

minister of militia and defence. Nicknamed 'Drill Hall Sam,' Hughes was determined to assume control of his extensive new program of drill hall construction. Between 1911 and 1915 fifty-nine new armouries were constructed: forty-three were designed and built by military engineers, and only sixteen were designed by the Department of Public Works, of which ten followed standard plans that had been developed by Militia and Defence.[57] Despite these constraints and restrictions, drill halls and armouries designed by the Chief Architect's Branch were among its most notable achievements. The drill hall at Trois-Rivières (1905–7) provides a good, representative example of the branch's work (Figure 3.20).[58] It was designed under the direction of T.W. Fuller, who in 1902 was appointed architect in charge of military buildings, a position he kept until 1918 when he was promoted to assistant chief architect under Richard C. Wright. The son of Thomas Fuller, he faithfully adhered to the architectural themes that had been established by his father. The twin octagonal towers flanking the troop door or portcullis of the Trois-Rivières drill hall, the corner pavilions accented by a circular tower, and the crenellated roofline maintained the appropriate architectural associations with medieval fortified castles. The red-brick walls that were accented by rusticated stone detail was characteristic of the work of both Fullers. Unlike his father's drill halls, those of T.W. Fuller often shifted the main entrance to the long elevation. At Trois-Rivières the drill hall itself was obscured behind two levels of offices and other rooms that were ranged across the front. As a result, the design lacked the clear articulation of internal space that had been characteristic of the earlier buildings.

T.W. Fuller was responsible for overseeing the design and construction of all drill halls produced by the Chief Architect's Branch after 1902.[59] They varied in size and design but all shared a common stylistic theme. The patterns of design that marked the early 1900s continued throughout the decade, but by the 1910s a subtle stylistic transition can be detected. The Mewata Armoury in Calgary (1917–18) was the last in a series of large western Canadian drill halls (Figure 3.21).[60] Although its design used the same plan as the earlier Trois-Rivières building and incorporated many of the same decorative elements, the detailing lost some of the picturesque quality. Rusticated stone was replaced by smooth-dressed stone, and the roofline was quieter and less picturesque, thereby accenting the simple, symmetrical massing of the building.

Immigration Buildings and Quarantine Stations

The Quarantine Branch of the Department of Agriculture and the Immigration Branch, which had been transferred to the Department of the Interior in 1892, generated much work for the branch prior to World War I. The Department of the Interior, under the direction of Clifford Sifton and his successor, Frank Oliver, initiated an aggressive campaign to attract new settlers to the West in the early 1900s. An integral component of the department's policies was an expanded and improved network of immigration facilities and services capable of efficiently processing the over 3.4 million immigrants who would arrive in Canada between 1900 and 1920.[61] The skeleton of this network had been established in the 1880s and 1890s, but as the volume of immigration grew many of the original buildings had to be replaced by larger, better-equipped ones. The new generation of buildings was also better and more substantially constructed. The wooden structures of the 1890s and the early 1900s gradually gave way to more permanent buildings of brick, steel, and concrete. The trend towards more permanent structures also reflected the government's assumption that immigration would continue to play an important part in Canada's long-term growth.

Immigration buildings of the early 1900s fell into three basic types. First, there were the large immigrant reception depots located in the major eastern ports. Like those built in the 1890s, they were located along railways and were designed to provide shelter (or, at most, overnight accommodation) while transportation was being arranged. Depots were constructed in Halifax (1896–7), Saint John (1900–1), and Quebec (1911–12). The early buildings at Halifax and Saint John were fairly simple wooden structures, while the later immigration building located on the Louise Embankment in Quebec was a solid two-storey building framed in steel and concrete. No new immigration buildings were built in the large Ontario cities; the thrust of immigration was to the West and the Prairies, thereby by-passing central Canada.

3.20. Armoury and Drill Hall, Trois-Rivières, Quebec, 1905–7. Designed by the Chief Architect's Branch. (Public Works and Government Services Canada, 1989)

3.21. Mewata Armoury, Calgary, Alberta, 1917–18. Designed by the Chief Architect's Branch. The Mewata Armoury is still in use. (NA, PA-53020)

The second type of facility, built in western Canada, was often referred to as an 'immigration hall.'[62] Here, immigrants received up to a week of free accommodation while they looked for work or made arrangements to settle on a homestead farm. Free room and board had been provided by the Immigration Branch since the 1880s but the early halls, like the eastern depots, were all simple wooden structures. By the early 1900s the Department of the Interior began to construct larger, permanent immigration halls in major urban centres. The first was built in Winnipeg in 1905 (Figure 3.22). The Winnipeg Immigration Hall was an imposing four-storey building, constructed of steel and reinforced concrete, and sheathed with brick. Although located alongside a railway track, it had the appearance of an important public building, with its classical elevation accented by an arcaded, stone base and detailed with pilasters and pediments.

Class distinctions were inherent in the immigration hall. Unlike the quarantine station, which housed all classes of immigrants, halls were used only by those who could not afford private accommodation. The facilities they provided were fairly basic: dormitories and sitting rooms segregated by sex and communal dining rooms. As immigration from Asia increased in the early twentieth century, the issue of racial segregation was also reflected in the design of the buildings. In 1914 a large new hall was constructed in Vancouver; in addition to separating men and women, it also identified segregated sleeping and sitting areas for Chinese and white immigrants. The plans also show a separate kitchen in the basement for Japanese immigrants.[63]

The third type of immigration building functioned as a secondary or satellite facility to the larger buildings located in major transportation centres. In Calgary, Lethbridge, Strathcona (Edmonton), and Regina smaller two-storey halls were built. Again, those dating from the first decade were generally wood-frame buildings, while the later buildings, such as the Calgary Immigration Hall of 1911, were constructed of brick with stone trim. The smallest but most numerous components in this system were small one- or two-room hostels that were built in more remote areas as they were opened to settlement. Some were built under the direction of the Chief Architect's Branch, but many were constructed by

local contractors, possibly with some supervision from the regional public works officer. The immigration building in Castor, Alberta, was a typical example of this type of facility (Figure 3.23).

The rapid increase in immigration also required a significant expansion of all five of the large quarantine stations at Partridge Island in New Brunswick, Lawlor's Island in Nova Scotia, Grosse Île in Quebec, and William Head and Prince Rupert in British Columbia. Between 1897 and 1905 new detention buildings were erected at Partridge Island and three new cottage hospitals were opened at Partridge Island, Lawlor's Island, and William Head. Grosse Île remained the most important station, receiving almost 50 per cent of the immigrants entering Canada. It developed into an increasingly complex and self-contained community. During this eight-year period, a bakery, several new staff residences, and even a school for the children of staff were constructed on the site.[64] Following the pattern of development noted in the buildings constructed for the Immigration Branch, they were usually constructed of wood with shingle or clapboard siding. The Third-Class Detention Hospital at Partridge Island, built around 1905, was typical of this period of construction (Figure 3.24).

Just before the outbreak of war, work that set new standards of construction began on a series of buildings at all the major quarantine stations. At Grosse Île and at William Head two large first-class detention buildings were constructed in 1912 and 1913 (Figure 3.25). Two third-class detention buildings were also built at Grosse Île and Prince Rupert. All were built of concrete that was reinforced by steel beams and columns, a material and construction technique just beginning to enter into the vocabulary of the Chief Architect's Branch.[65] The third-class detention buildings adopted the same standards of accommodation that were evident in the earlier periods. Each room was equipped with two or four berths and public halls were located at the end of each floor. The exterior design consisted of a long two-storey block with a low, pitched roof that was regularly punctuated by double-sash windows and a series of simple wall buttresses and decorative parapet gables. The first-class detention buildings also provided the usual facilities associated for this class of immigrant – large private rooms, a second-level hall with a fire-

3.22. Immigration Hall, Winnipeg, Manitoba, 1905. Designed by the Chief Architect's Branch. Now demolished. (NA, NMC 47137)

3.23. Immigration Building, Castor, Alberta, *ca.* 1911. (Glenbow Archives, Calgary, Alberta, NA-3635-7)

3.24. Third-Class Detention Hospital, Partridge Island, New Brunswick, *ca.* 1904, in 1914. Designed by the Chief Architect's Branch. This photograph shows a two-storey addition under construction. Demolished in 1941. (Bisson Family Collection, Partridge Island Research Project, Saint John, New Brunswick)

3.25. First-Class Detention Building, Grosse Île, Quebec, 1912–14. Designed by the Chief Architect's Branch. Identical buildings were constructed at William Head *ca.* 1914 and at Partridge Island in 1922. (J. Beardsell, Parks Canada, 1990, S-148-6)

place, and a large dining-room with a kitchen in the back. These buildings, with their Tudor half-timbered details under the gables and wide veranda extending across the front, could almost be mistaken for summer resorts.

Dawson: An Introduction to Building in the North

To the federal government, the North was a vast, largely unpopulated land; its potential worth to the nation was only dimly appreciated. In 1894 the North-West Mounted Police established Fort Constantine on the banks of the Yukon River in order to claim Crown sovereignty in an area that was attracting more and more miners and traders from the United States.[66] In 1896, however, a large gold deposit was discovered near the Klondike River; by 1897 the Yukon Gold Rush had begun. The townsite of Dawson was established near the gold-fields and it quickly became an important commercial centre. When the government created a separate Yukon Territory in 1898, Dawson was named the capital.

For the next few years federal and territorial government services were housed in rented quarters, but, as the staff increased and rents rose, it was decided to construct more permanent buildings. Initially the territorial government, which reported to the Department of the Interior, looked after its own accommodation, but in 1899 the minister, Clifford Sifton, recommended that the construction of the proposed new public buildings be turned over to the Department of Public Works. He also recommended that one of its best and most competent officers be sent to the Yukon to supervise the work.[67] In fact, two Public Works employees, J.B. Charleson and a young T.W. Fuller, were selected for the assignment. Charleson, who was appointed superintendent of public works, was primarily responsible for the construction of the Yukon telegraph; T.W. Fuller was named resident architect in Dawson.[68]

Between 1899 and 1901 Fuller designed and supervised the construction of an administration building, a post office, a court-house, the commissioner's residence, a school, and a telegraph office. Fuller, who had begun his career in public works under his father's tutelage in 1885, seemed to revel in the professional independence that he was allowed in this remote area. The freedom from the constraints and conventions of the Ottawa office was most evident in his final design for the administration building of 1901 (Figure 3.26).[69] In 1899 plans were prepared for two buildings, a recording office and an administration building. Both would be two-storey, hipped-roof buildings, resembling the solid but plain type of building that had been erected for government across the Prairies. Fuller, however, had become caught in the boosterism of the Yukon at the turn of the century and he persuaded the government to build something larger. Although the final proposal combined the two functions, the completed building provided twice as much floor space as originally intended. The cost was also double the initial estimates. The building was a long rectangular structure; its main façade featured three pedimented projections marking the centre and ends of the building. In contrast to the plain, serviceable quality of the 1899 plans, the new administration building was elaborately detailed. Its classical style included wood pilasters across the front, pedimented doorway and window surrounds, elaborate, moulded eaves and cornices, and highly ornate fretwork in the pediments.

The Dawson buildings introduced the Chief Architect's Branch to the problems of building in the Arctic. Permafrost did not permit the use of masonry foundations; instead, the administration building was constructed on wooden posts set every four feet and driven into the ground to a depth of ten feet. The main floor of the building was also raised five feet above ground level to insulate it from the cold ground. Sawdust in the wall cavities and a double thickness of building paper provided extra insulation. In 1900 Dawson was seen as the new commercial centre of the North, and the early government buildings reflected the sense of confidence in its future stability and prosperity. The city, however, failed to live up to its promise: by 1905 Dawson was in decline. The federal government undertook almost no new construction there until World War II. At that point, building in the North took on a more practical, functional appearance, but the problems that faced Fuller in 1900 resurfaced. Permafrost, the need for adequate insulation, and the difficulty in obtaining good quality materials – these problems were to challenge the branch into the 1960s.

Conclusion

The years between 1896 and 1914 were among the most productive in the history of the Chief Architect's Branch. As the economy prospered and the country expanded, the demand for new federal buildings and institutions grew. By 1914 over three hundred public buildings, drill halls, and customs houses, as well as numerous quarantine and immigration buildings, had been constructed across the country. The design of these buildings reflected the different architectural currents that shaped architecture in Canada during the Edwardian era. Important public buildings, such as the Vancouver Post Office and the now-demolished Winnipeg Post Office, were well-crafted examples of the ornate Edwardian Baroque style. Other buildings, including the Montreal Customs House and Postal Station A in Fredericton, reflected the influence of the more subdued but more monumental forms of the French-inspired Beaux-Arts style. At the same time, patterns of design that were rooted in the Victorian picturesque tradition persisted in the work of the Chief Architect's Branch. The public buildings at Nelson, British Columbia, and Humboldt, Saskatchewan, both referred back, in their general massing and detailing, to Thomas Fuller's late nineteenth-century public buildings.

The federal building program of the early twentieth century played, and indeed continues to play, an important part in defining the unique character of the Canadian urban environment. The red-brick public buildings with corner clock towers and the castellated drill halls continue to command their settings and to identify themselves as federal government institutions. During these years the Department of Public works constructed over two hundred urban public buildings or post offices, and today approximately 141 survive. Some are still owned by the federal government but many more have been transferred to municipalities or to private owners.[70] It is indicative of the importance of these buildings to their communities that many continue to function as important public institutions – city halls, libraries, museums, and community centres.

This period of construction, from 1896 to 1914, was also marked by a change in the nature of the working environment within the Chief

3.26. Territorial Administration Building, Dawson, Yukon Territory, 1901–2. Designed by T.W. Fuller. The building has been restored as part of the national historic site. (Public Works and Government Services Canada, Heritage Recording and Technical Data Services, 1987)

Architect's Branch. Designs from the branch reflected the new pressures imposed by the higher volume of construction and by the increasing emphasis on economy and efficiency within the bureaucracy. Although the branch produced a number of outstanding buildings, the majority became increasingly codified into a series of standard design types that were distributed to politically deserving communities. Under Ewart, the Chief Architect's Branch proved itself ideally suited to meet the demands.

By 1910 the branch had recruited a new generation of young architects; their individual contributions quickly became obscured within the corporate identity but as a group they formed a skilled and efficient design team that was capable of producing hundreds of public buildings. The team that emerged in the early 1900s formed the foundations of the branch that would remain in place throughout the 1920s and 1930s.

CHAPTER FOUR

Nationalism, Symbolism, and Architecture: Planning the Capital, 1899–1945

If Canada is to be a great nation the capital of Canada must in dignity and beauty be made worthy of a great people.

Harold Fisher, Mayor of Ottawa, 1918[1]

The idea that Ottawa should stand as a symbol of the nation dated from the turn of the century. Although Ottawa had been the centre of government since 1857, its status was seen largely as an accident of history. The Parliament Buildings, the main post office, the Langevin Building, and Rideau Hall represented the federal presence in Ottawa, but the identity of the city itself remained that of a remote and unpolished commercial centre of the square timber and lumber trade in the Ottawa Valley. The transformation of Ottawa from lumber town to national capital is traditionally seen to have begun with Wilfrid Laurier's promise in 1893 to turn Ottawa into the 'Washington of the North.'[2] The statement was made in reference to Laurier's intention to make Ottawa an important centre of intellectual life, but the phrase was quickly adopted by advocates of city beautification. It also provides historians with a convenient and emphatic beginning to the emergence of a grand design for a national capital.

The changed perception of the role of a national capital grew out of a number of factors and influences. The federal building boom experienced throughout the country in the pre-1914 period was magnified in Ottawa. An expanding civil service and the establishment of a number of national institutions created a demand for many new buildings. Rising revenues and a new sense of confidence that came with growth and prosperity encouraged the government to plan on a scale larger than anything previously envisioned.[3] A comprehensive approach to development was also fuelled by the emergence of the City Beautiful movement, which dominated urban planning in North America in the early twentieth century. City Beautiful planners sought to impose a new grandeur and beauty on the urban landscape by reshaping it on a monumental scale according to classical principles of order, harmony, and symmetry.

In Ottawa, the enthusiasm for civic beautification was fuelled by a new spirit of nationalism. The history, culture, and geography of Canada became a central theme to be explored and celebrated in literature, art, and academic study.[4] For the federal government, this sentiment was focused on the vision of Ottawa as the spiritual and symbolic core of the nation. For this reason, government building in Ottawa during this period did not follow the same patterns of design and stylistic trends that was evident in other parts of the country. Instead, the Department of Public Works sought to develop a distinct architectural and urban form that would define and express what was perceived as Canada's unique cultural identity.[5]

The Parliament Buildings as a National Symbol

To understand the evolution of federal building and planning in Ottawa and the vision of what the city might become, it is necessary to revisit the original Parliament Buildings (Figure 4.1). At the time of their construction, these buildings represented one of the finest examples of the High Victorian Gothic style in North America, but by the early twentieth century they had taken on a new significance that was specific to Ottawa and Canada. Once denounced as an extravagant folly, they were now seen as a symbol of the bold vision and confidence that had supposedly marked the founding of the country. The eclecticism of the design became an expression of Canada's fundamental cultural duality. In 1907 the poet Wilfred Campbell wrote: 'In the buildings we have as a people, both French and British . . . epics in stone, revealing to us not only universal beauty and inspiration but emblematic of our common ideal, our common artistic sense, our common ancestry, and our common Christianity.'[6] It is unlikely that the architects intended to express the bicultural foundations of the country in their design. Indeed, the choice of the Gothic mode is more generally interpreted as a statement of political and cultural allegiance to Britain. Meaning in architecture is in a constant state of flux, reflecting not only the values and aspirations of the people who built but also those imposed by future generations.

The acknowledged pre-eminence of the Parliament Buildings provided the common thread to the history of federal building and town planning in the national capital until the 1950s, but it also created a fundamental dilemma for architects and planners. By 1900 the popular image of public architecture and urban space in North America was dominated by the classical model associated with the École des Beaux-Arts and the City Beautiful movement. The Parliament Buildings, as examples of High Victorian Gothic, epitomized everything that architects of the early twentieth century rejected. Architects argued that the Gothic vocabulary could be reworked to reflect contemporary aesthetic standards. However, the basic incompatibility of this symbolically meaningful but architecturally outdated theme with the dominant trends in public architecture and urban design, would continue to hinder and undermine the planning process during the next half century.

Early Efforts: The Ottawa Improvement Commission, 1899–1903

Urban planning in Ottawa in the first two decades of the twentieth century reflected the gradual evolution and maturation of the City Beautiful movement. Although this movement represented only one manifestation of the emerging science of urban planning, it dominated the field in the United States and Canada during this period.[7] Rooted in the art of landscape design and the nineteenth-century Parks and Recreation movement, the City Beautiful was a concept articulated by architects and landscape designers and backed by business and commercial interests. Within this circle, the city was viewed as a work of art, in which development should be dictated by a single aesthetic vision.

The World Columbian Exposition, held in Chicago in 1893, profoundly influenced the emergence of City Beautiful planning in North America. Organized to celebrate the four hundredth anniversary of the discovery of America, the exhibition site was planned by Chicago architect Daniel Burnham and noted U.S. landscape designer Frederick Law Olmsted. The buildings were designed by Burnham and other leading American architects. Although a temporary installation, the exposition had a far-reaching impact on urban design by providing a life-size model of what the city of the future might look like. The imposition of classical and Beaux-Arts principles of order, harmony, and symmetry on the entire urban fabric would create beautiful and therefore more habitable and humane cities. Urban planning was a design problem rather than a political process.[8]

The earliest efforts in Ottawa at civic improvement date from 1899 and the establishment of the Ottawa Improvement Commission.[9] A federally appointed body, the commission was initially given an annual budget of $60,000. Under its direction, new parks were developed along the Rideau Canal and in Rockcliffe Park. A scenic drive was established along the banks of the canal, and King Edward Avenue was converted into a wide boulevard lined with trees. At this stage public building was not considered part of the commission's mandate. Its work can be interpreted in terms of the nineteenth-century Parks and Recreation movement, whereby cities were improved by introducing and enhancing nat-

4.1. Lithograph, Houses of Parliament, Ottawa, in 1868. From Charles P. DeVolpi, *Ottawa: A Pictorial Record, Historical Prints and Illustrations of the City of Ottawa, Province of Ontario, Canada, 1807–1882* (Montreal: Dev-Sco 1964), pl. 60. (NA, C-83946)

ural beauty within the urban fabric in the form of landscaped parks and picturesque drives.

In 1903 the first step was taken towards the development of an integrated plan for Ottawa. In that year Frederick Todd, a Montreal landscape architect, was hired to outline a planning strategy that would give direction to the efforts of the Ottawa Improvement Commission. The Todd report maintained a focus on natural landscape, but it adopted a broader and more comprehensive view of city improvement.[10] Todd identified the need to control the development and location of industrial areas so as not to interfere with beauty spots in the city. He sketched out a network of parks linked by scenic boulevards that would unite Ottawa with neighbouring Hull. He also recommended the establishment of a large natural reserve on the Quebec side of the river, an idea that would eventually come into being with the establishment of the Gatineau Park.

The Todd report also articulated a larger vision of Ottawa as a symbol of the nation. In his introduction, Todd wrote:

Not only is Ottawa sure to become the centre of a large and populous district, but the fact that it is the Capital of an immense country whose future greatness is only beginning to unfold, renders it necessary that it should also be the centre of all those things which are an index of man's highest intellectual attainments, and that it be a city which will reflect the character of the nation and the dignity, stability and good taste of its citizens.[11]

Public buildings would play a key part in creating this image of 'dignity, stability and good taste.' Todd was the first to identify formally the need for a unified architectural theme that would be compatible with the Parliament Buildings. He also suggested that Sussex Street, which linked the Parliament Buildings with Government House, should become the focus for government building.

The Development of Sussex Street, 1903–1911

The Todd report closely coincided with the government's decision to provide permanent buildings for some of Canada's recently founded national, cultural, and scientific institutions. Between 1899 and 1908 the Dominion Observatory (1899–1900), the Archives Building (1905–7), the Victoria Memorial Museum (1905–8), and the Royal Mint (1905–8) were erected in Ottawa (Figures 4.2 and 4.3). The Chief Architect's Branch had never undertaken projects like these, and David Ewart was sent in 1901 to study European examples.[12] Although there is no detailed account of his tour, the experience obviously had a profound impact on Ewart. As noted in the previous chapter, the Grand Manner of Edwardian Baroque and the more restrained classicism of the European Beaux-Arts style, which dominated public building in Great Britain, entered into the vocabulary of the Chief Architect's Branch after his return. The lessons were not, however, to be applied to the Ottawa buildings. While Ewart may have incorporated certain planning features of buildings that housed comparable European institutions, the stylistic program for Ottawa was clearly shaped by the recommendations of the Todd report.

With the exception of the Dominion Observatory, which was built prior to the Todd report, the Chief Architect's Branch opted for what it referred to as 'late Gothic.'[13] Preliminary sketch plans show a building similar in its vocabulary to the Parliament Buildings, but the design was quickly rejected in favour of a more austere Tudor Gothic style.[14] Ewart felt it was better suited to modern public buildings and, more importantly, it was a style that avoided the decorative excesses of the High Victorian Gothic.[15] In accordance with Todd's recommendations, the archives and the mint were located on Sussex Street, and thereby the first modest step was taken at creating a unified streetscape.[16]

The Victoria Memorial Museum, located about one mile south of Parliament Hill, was not part of the Sussex Street development, but it was the most important and accomplished building of the period. As originally designed, it consisted of a long narrow building with a projecting central tower and a semicircular wing to the rear containing a two-storey amphitheatre. Its outer corners were completed by projecting wings accented with octagonal turrets at the four corners. Here the staff of the Chief Architect's Branch defined the vocabulary that would be repeated on other Ottawa buildings: turrets, a crenellated roofline, buttresses,

4.2. Royal Mint, Sussex Street, Ottawa, 1905–8. Designed by the Chief Architect's Branch. (Public Works and Government Services Canada, Heritage Recording and Technical Data Services, 1987)

4.3. Victoria Memorial Museum, Ottawa, Ontario, 1905–8. Designed by the Chief Architect's Branch. (NA, C-9273)

ogee-arched openings for the main entrance, and strong horizontal lines created by raised string-courses punctuated by rows of flat-headed windows accented by dressed quoins. The randomly coursed, rusticated Nepean sandstone established a strong link with the Parliament Buildings, though the architecture was more severe and ordered.[17]

Unfortunately the building, as seen today, presents an even more sombre appearance than originally intended. The design called for a tall central tower, marked by corner turrets and surmounted by a highly ornate crown consisting of an open-ribbed frame decorated with croquets and topped by a delicate finial. Construction on the tower was well under way when it started to sink and pull away from the main wall. Apparently the subsoil, which had never been accurately surveyed, could not support the weight of structure. In 1916 eighty feet of the tower had to be removed, leaving the rather stubby entrance that remains today.

Built to house the botanical, zoological, and ethnological collection of the Geological Survey of Canada, the museum required well-lit exhibition spaces, an auditorium, a library, public facilities, and offices for staff. It would also serve as a major public institution with a high public profile. The focus of the design is the spacious central lobby, which extends through the four storeys of the building (Figure 4.4). A central stair at the opposite end of the hall provides access to the upper levels. Iron balconies encircle the hall at each level. It is not sumptuously detailed – the sense of frugality of the federal government still held strong – but it is an impressive space that gives the building a sense of grandeur not usually found in federal government building. The symbolic role of the Victoria Memorial Museum is also expressed in the decorative iconography. It was one of the first federal buildings to experiment with uniquely Canadian decorative motifs. Two moose heads appear in relief over the main entrance, and stained-glass windows over the doors depict indigenous flora and fauna. The search for Canadian decorative forms would become a recurring theme of the first half of the twentieth century.

Once these buildings were under way, the federal government turned its attention to providing more office space for the rapidly expanding civil service. In 1906 the Department of Public Works held a national competition for two new buildings, one for general departmental offices and the other to house the Supreme Court of Canada, the Exchequer's Court (now the Federal Court of Canada), and offices for the Department of Justice.[18] It was the first major architectural competition since the one for the Parliament Buildings in 1858. The buildings were to be located on the west side of Sussex Street, between Wellington and St Patrick streets. It was a long narrow site that faced onto Major's Hill Park and across the entrance valley of the Rideau Canal to Parliament Hill. The proposal was to include a bridge over the Rideau Canal that would link Parliament Hill with the buildings on Sussex Street (Figure 4.5). Any style of architecture was acceptable, but some form of Gothic was recommended.

In September 1907 the Montreal firm of W.S. and Edward Maxwell was awarded first prize. Its proposal for the two buildings, which was published in the *Canadian Architect and Builder* in December of that year, adopted a Gothic design slightly suggestive of the Elizabethan or Jacobean periods.[19] The introduction of some classical elements, evident in the decorative domed cupolas marking the central pavilions, suggests this mixed style of architecture. They were, however, to be constructed of rusticated Nepean sandstone, and design elements such as the shallow buttresses, the broken parapeted rooflines, and the Tudor-arched openings would have been very compatible with the Parliament Buildings and with the new Royal Mint and Archives buildings on the same street. Of the two designs submitted by the firm, the one for the Justice Building was more conventional in its layout but grander in its design (Figure 4.6). The architects dealt with the long narrow façade imposed by the shape of the site by creating a symmetrical but complex elevation defined by a series of distinct building volumes, each with its own roofline, wall definition and pattern of bays. These elements, in turn, corresponded with internal room functions. It was a rather rambling façade, and the composition was held together by the dominant central pavilion, with a stepped roofline, corner turrets, and massive arched window. It was a remarkably animated design that would have equalled the quality of design evident in the original Parliament Buildings.

When the competition results were announced, there was some surprise that the design of the Maxwells had placed first.[20] Regarded as leading proponents of the classical style in Canada, they were not well known as medievalists.[21] However, their training in the Beaux-Arts style and their ability to adapt its logical, rational approach to a Gothic shell gave them the advantage over their competitors. The Justice Building design was organized around four internal courts that were connected by a system of primary and secondary corridors. These served to create two largely separate circulation systems, one that linked the judges' chambers with the offices and the other for the general public. The exterior design of the Departmental Building was visually less dynamic than that of the Justice Building, but its interior plan reflected the most modern concepts of office layout. Organized around two large internal courtyards, each floor featured a wide hall running through the centre of the building. Narrow secondary corridors ran perpendicular to the main hall and around each of the courtyards. The interior office space had no fixed partition walls. These areas were left completely open, allowing for greater flexibility in the internal layout.

Although it was a good scheme, it turned out to be the first of many abortive efforts. No sooner had the winners been announced than the project began to unravel. The federal bureaucracy would always feel some discomfort with the competition process. Submissions were based on fairly general programs or guidelines, and for this reason plans tended to be sketchy in nature. It was intended that detailed drawings would later be worked out with the client departments once the architect had been selected, with the Chief Architect's Branch acting as liaison between the parties. In practice, however, there was often little direct contact between the commissioned architect and the client, as the latter was often quite happy to relinquish its involvement to the staff of the Department of Public Works. The staff in the Chief Architect's Branch, as professional architects, tended to usurp the designing role, and the commissioned architect would become increasingly redundant.

This was certainly the case for the Maxwell project. In 1909 the government announced that the staff of the Chief Architect's Branch had prepared a new set of plans for the buildings.[22] These did not resemble

4.4. Main lobby, Victoria Memorial Museum, in 1993. (M. Trépanier, Parks Canada, 1993)

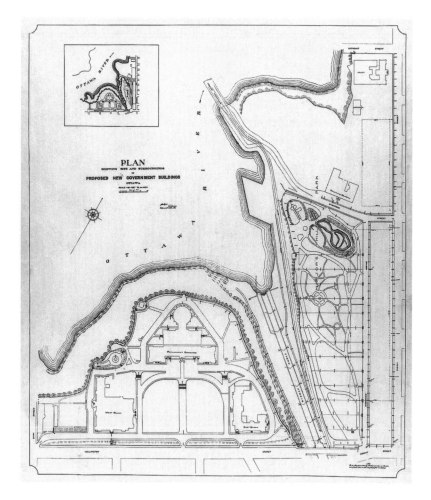

4.5. 'Plan shewing site and surroundings of the Proposed New Government Buildings, 1906.' The new buildings were to be located alongside Major's Hill Park, separated from Parliament Hill (lower right) by the Rideau Canal and the park. The Château Laurier, built at the bottom of Major's Hill Park, undermined the creation of a cohesive government centre. (NA, C-78961)

the Maxwell proposal at all. Instead, they represented a continuation of the architectural theme defined by the Victoria Memorial Museum but enlarged several times over (Figure 4.7). It is not clear why the Maxwell plans were abandoned – cost is the most likely reason – but in the end neither design was carried out. The government decided to erect a new customs house, the Connaught Building, on part of the site. It resembled a scaled-down version of the 1909 plans by the Chief Architect's Branch, and blended in with the other buildings along Sussex Street (Figure 4.8).[23]

David Ewart considered the Connaught Building one of his finest, but the architectural community attacked it with a vehemence unknown before this time: editorials in the architectural press described the buildings as being of 'puerile design and questionable construction.'[24] The air was heavy with petitions and letters to the minister, and editorials filed accusations of poor design that undermined the dignity of the national capital.[25] The intensity of the criticism was partly the result of a misunderstanding as to the purpose of the building that was finally erected on the site. The architectural community assumed that the Connaught Building was the government's meagre substitute for the grand architectural sweep displayed in the winning competitive design. The Connaught Building was, however, a completely separate project that had originally been intended for the central business district. When the plan for the Sussex Street development fell through, it was decided to make use of the vacant site for the customs house rather than purchase another.

The decision to abandon the proposal for a cohesive government precinct along Sussex Street was owing to a number of factors. The evolution and eventual demise of the project offers insight into the difficulties that were involved in carrying a large project through to completion within the federal government. Unsympathetic or conflicting decisions taken by other departments or agencies, changes in economic climate, and changes in government were all potential pitfalls. In this case, the first indication of a problem was the government's decision to allow the Grand Trunk Railway to construct the Château Laurier Hotel on Major's Hill Park in 1907. Although the completed building was viewed as an architectural asset to the city, its location – between the East Block and the site of the proposed government complex – undermined the integrity of

JUSTICE BUILDING, PARK ELEVATION

SCALE SIXTEEN FEET TO ONE INCH

⊛ DESIGN FOR PROPOSED NEW GOVERNMENT BUILDINGS, OTTAWA ⊛

4.6. Plans and elevations, proposed Justice Building, 1907. Architects: W.S. and Edward Maxwell. (*Canadian Architect and Builder* 20, no. 9 [September 1907]: 176)

4.7. Proposed government buildings, elevation, Major's Hill Park, Ottawa, Ontario. Plans prepared by the Chief Architect's Branch in 1909. (*Construction* 3, no. 6 [May 1910]: 70)

4.8. Connaught Building, Sussex Street, Ottawa, Ontario, 1913–16. Designed by the Chief Architect's Branch. (M. Trépanier, Parks Canada, 1993)

the site. It was planned and erected without any reference to the new buildings that were to stand across the street. Once completed, it was apparent that this châteauesque pile would overshadow the proposed government centre.[26]

More importantly, in 1911 the Laurier government was defeated by the Conservatives led by Robert L. Borden. At that point, no contracts had been signed for the Sussex Street complex and there had been no significant financial investment. A new government is always reluctant to implement a project initiated by its predecessor – particularly a project that has received negative publicity. As a result, the Borden government decided to begin the planning process all over again.

Ottawa as an Imperial Capital: The Competition of 1913

After 1911 the focus of federal building shifted to the north side of Wellington Street, west of Parliament Hill. The site had distinct advantages over Sussex Street. Situated on the edge of the limestone cliffs overlooking the Ottawa River, it was extremely dramatic and picturesque. It also offered easier, more direct access to Parliament Hill. Most important, it was much larger. Throughout the first decade of the century the civil service had grown steadily, and the two buildings that had been proposed in 1906 would not have met the government's current space requirements. In 1911 the new government started to develop a proposal for a much more ambitious project that would provide 1.2 million square feet of space spread out over approximately ten buildings.[27]

This project was directed by the Chief Architect's Branch. It represented a comprehensive integration of architecture and urban design, but it also marked a radical change in architectural direction. Initially, Frederick Todd was engaged to prepare a general plan for the Wellington Street property, but for some reason – perhaps a lack of confidence in the Canadian planner – the Department of Public Works decided to seek advice further afield.[28] In 1912 the minister of public works wrote to the Canadian high commissioner in London for information on two 'landscape artists' – Thomas Mawson and Edward White – as potential con-

sultants for the Wellington Street property.[29] Mawson was the logical choice, having established an international reputation as a leading landscape architect with strong City Beautiful movement sympathies. However, he was not selected. Mawson later wrote that he thought his appointment may have been blocked by the Canadian Pacific Railway, which, he claimed, felt threatened by his views on the need to control and limit the development of railways within an urban core.[30] The fact that the high commissioner was Lord Strathcona, a founder and principal shareholder of the Canadian Pacific Railway, would seem to confirm Mawson's suspicions. Instead, Strathcona recommended White, a well-known landscape architect from London who was primarily a garden designer. Unlike Mawson, White did not have strong credentials in architecture or town planning.[31]

White, however, compensated for his lack of experience in architecture and urban design by engaging the services of Aston Webb, one of the most successful British architects of the period.[32] Webb was responsible for such major projects as the extension to the Victoria and Albert Museum (1891) and the University of Birmingham (1901). He also redesigned the façade of Buckingham Palace, redeveloped the Mall and Admiralty Arch (1903–12), and designed the offices of the Grand Trunk Railway in London (1904). He had first established himself as a master of the English Baroque, but by the 1910s his work showed the sober influence of the École des Beaux-Arts.

The preliminary White-Webb proposal for Ottawa represented a direct transfer of the Edwardian Grand Manner to Canadian soil. Typical of Webb's work, it was a carefully ordered classical essay of domed pavilions, long colonnades, porticoes, and triumphal arches, all orchestrated on a grand scale. Two ranges of buildings were organized on both sides of a broad east–west mall (Figure 4.9). These buildings were linked together by a series of arches that brought the entire group into one grand design. The central focus of the composition was the Courts Building, which was set back on the cliff promontory. It faced onto a wide open plaza featuring a tall campanile, which was to provide an observation deck.[33]

4.9. Drawing and ground plan, proposed federal buildings, Wellington Street (north side), Ottawa, Ontario. Drawn by Edward White and Aston Webb in 1912. (*Builder* [May 1913], NA, L-14903)

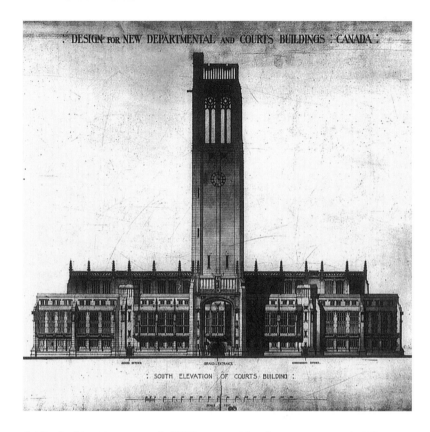

4.10. Architect's proposal, 1913 competition for government buildings, Ottawa, Ontario. Architect: Thomas Moodie. Moodie was among the six finalists. (NA, NMC, 142136)

The proposal had a distinctly British flavour in its complexity and in the stylistic reference to British architectural models, particularly to the work of Christopher Wren. The domed pavilions set on a columned drum and a square, pedimented base resembled the pavilions on Wren's eighteenth-century design for Greenwich Hospital. But the proposal also fell into the mainstream of City Beautiful planning. The symmetrical plan was dominated by the two principal crossing axes defined by the mall and the plaza. Individual buildings were subordinated into this tightly unified layout. The overall concept had a monumental quality created by the large open public spaces and broad sweeping façades that dominated the streetscape. The White-Webb plan offered a very seductive image. This vision of Ottawa represented the height of urban sophistication. If completed, the buildings would have vied with some of the grand new City Beautiful plans being developed in many North American capitals in the early twentieth century.

In 1913 the Department of Public Works set up an international competition open to any architect practising in Britain or its colonies. The Webb-White proposal was included with the terms of reference as a suggestion to architects of the type of design envisioned by the department. Sixty-one submissions were received – thirty-one from Canada, nineteen from England, two from Scotland, and one from South Africa.[34] In April 1914 an independent Board of Assessors selected six finalists: Thomas A. Moodie of London, Saxe and Archibald of Montreal, Hutchinson and Wood of Montreal, W.E. Noffke of Ottawa, David H. Macfarlane and Herbert Raine of Montreal, and Frederick G. Robb and G. Gordon Mitchell, also of Montreal.[35] Unfortunately most of the plans have disappeared, but the few that survive show a wide range of style and approach. Thomas Moodie's proposal adopted a perpendicular Gothic vocabulary that he adapted to a plan reflecting the École des Beaux-Arts influence in its use of a dominant central court building surrounded by a massive semicircular structure with radiating spokes housing government offices (Figure 4.10). W.S. and Edward Maxwell, who were not finalists, presented a reworked version of their original and winning proposal for the Sussex Street competition of 1906 (Figure 4.11). C.F.A. Voysey, a leading figure in the British Freestyle architecture who was best known for

4.11. Architect's proposal, 1913 competition for government buildings, Ottawa, Ontario. Architects: W.S. and Edward Maxwell. (National Gallery of Canada, Acc. no.1784)

his domestic work, submitted a proposal that was medieval in style but was executed with his characteristic restraint, evident in the clean, smooth wall planes and the simplicity of detail. Best at designing on a small scale, Voysey submitted an overall plan that lacked coherence. The submission by the Toronto architect John Lyle resembled Webb's preliminary proposal, though the ground plan reflected a much simpler approach to planning (Figure 4.12); the entire composition was centred around a vast plaza open to the street, which was encircled by the long, low sweep of a colonnade whose simple columned façade extended through to the Courts Building, creating one tightly unified but dramatic architectural statement.

The competition closed in April, but even before the finalists had been selected the basic concept was being questioned. From the beginning, the Board of Assessors had misgivings about the White-Webb plan. Although the board stated privately that there were definite weaknesses in the scheme, it recommended that architects be encouraged to take a free hand in their submissions in the international competition.[36] The White-Webb plan had been developed in isolation, with little attempt made to integrate the new construction into the existing urban fabric. The north–south axes did not line up with any existing streets, and, more importantly, the design made no attempt to acknowledge, either in terms of style or plan, the symbolic and visual pre-eminence of the Parliament Buildings. The new buildings were intended to function as subsidiary components within the larger federal precinct, and yet the architects had created a grouping that would have overwhelmed the buildings on Parliament Hill.[37]

The choice of a classical theme for the buildings in the White-Webb proposal ran counter to a strong sense of nationalism and the need to create an architecture that would express Canada's own cultural identity. Criticism of the proposal came from all sides. In April 1913 Thomas Mawson commented on the preliminary proposal:

> I shall be surprised if on mature thought Canadians will care to experiment in this style. If it had been the intention to rebuild the present parliament buildings and government offices, there might have been an excuse for this type of design which is foreign to Canadian sentiment. Surely the

picturesque qualities which the present parliament buildings undoubtedly possess should give the suggestion for the completion of the government group.[38]

Even the Board of Assessors for the competition lacked a commitment to this classical vision; it selected two proposals in Gothic style among the six finalists.

The 1913 competition was also criticized because it was too limited in scope and failed to conform to current approaches to urban design. By 1920 cities all over the United States and Canada had commissioned architects and urban planners to prepare master plans providing complete and comprehensive guidelines that would shape all future development. The project for Ottawa proposed by the Chief Architect's Branch focused only on one small part of the downtown area, and its development was seen as independent of the city and the region. While the branch was drafting the terms of reference for the Wellington Street competition, the cities of Ottawa and Hull and the Ottawa Improvement Commission were calling for the establishment of an independent planning commission. Just as the competition was made public, an order-in-council was approved by the Privy Council to set up the Federal Plan Commission.[39] The 1913 competition was never officially abandoned, but the Federal Plan Commission, which represented a competing player in the field, would put forward a very different vision of a national capital.

The Federal Plan Commission, 1913–1915

The Federal Plan Commission was given a mandate to draw up a comprehensive plan for the region, one that would provide particularly for the location, layout, and beautification of parks and connecting boulevards, and to propose adequate and convenient arrangements for traffic and transportation. It was also asked to make recommendations on the location and architectural character of public buildings. The commission itself, composed primarily of political appointees drawn from the business or political community, was not expected to prepare the plans.[40] Instead, it was the commission's job to ensure that plans addressed the needs and

4.12. Architect's proposal, 1913 competition for government buildings, Ottawa, Ontario. Architect: John Lyle. (Canadian Centre for Architecture)

aspirations of the community within an appropriate budget and time frame. Responsibility for the preparation of the detailed plan was given to Edward H. Bennett, a Chicago architect and one of the leading American practitioners of City Beautiful planning.[41]

The report of the Federal Plan Commission, issued in 1915, was typical of Bennett's work and represented a late or mature phase of the City Beautiful movement. No longer defining Ottawa purely in terms of grand public spaces and buildings, the plan addressed a wide range of civic issues, including transportation and zoning.[42] It expressed the view that the key to the civic improvement of Ottawa lay in the reorganization and rationalization of the railway transit system. The web of rail lines and stations, which criss-crossed the city and disrupted the flow of traffic, should be replaced by two main lines with overpasses and a tunnel in the city core. Bennett also recommended an end to the indiscriminate mixing of residential and industrial areas through the application of zoning by-laws.

In drawing up his recommendations for the architectural development for the downtown core, Bennett completely rejected the White-Webb proposal. He wrote: 'One cannot look without reluctance upon any project to change the general architectural character of the present group of buildings. Not that criticism may not be levelled at them, but because of the general harmony of the group, and the happy expression which has been given to them, seemingly in character with a northern country.'[43] Marking a return to Todd's recommendations, Bennett's report insisted instead on the adoption of an architecture that would harmonize with the Parliament Buildings. As expressed in his report:

> the architectural design of the proposed new building[s] should be in harmony and not in contrast. They should be planned to have an architectural character with vigorous silhouettes, steep roofs, pavilions and towers, never competing with, but always recalling the present group.[44]

At the same time, it did not recommend a re-creation of this style; it suggested instead that inspiration be found in the seventeenth-century architecture of France. The Château Laurier was cited as an appropriate model.

The identification of the Château style as the most appropriate form of architecture for government buildings in Ottawa and the specific reference to the Château Laurier were not dictated purely by formalistic, design values. The Château style had emerged out Victorian eclecticism and had manifested itself in its most familiar form in hotel and large residential architecture in Britain and the United States in the late nineteenth and early twentieth centuries. Its palatial and exotically picturesque appearance projected an image of luxury and romance that appealed to the travelling public. In Canada the Château style was influenced by both British (particularly Scottish) and American models, but it would also assume a symbolic meaning that was unique to the Canadian cultural context.[45]

The Château Frontenac in Quebec, which was designed in 1888 by American architect Bruce Price, was not the earliest example of the Château style, but it played a key role in defining its popular image in Canada.[46] Although the design reflected prevailing international trends in hotel architecture, the French associations of the style seemed ideally suited to its location in the heart of old Quebec. The architectural and commercial success of the Château Frontenac prompted its owner, the Canadian Pacific Railway, and later its major railway competitors to construct a chain of grand Château-style hotels across the country. These two factors – the strong association with the national railways, which in themselves were important icons of the Canadian identity, and the perception of this style as being rooted in French and Scottish baronial – imbued the style with iconographic and symbolic meaning when it was applied to public architecture in the national capital. It proved to be a potent national image that enabled it to endure in Canada long after its currency had been expended within the broader architectural community.

The Bennett proposal for the federal precinct was more extensive and more easily integrated into the urban fabric than the White-Webb plan (Figures 4.13 and 4.14). The main departmental group, situated on the north side of Wellington Street, again featured a wide east–west mall

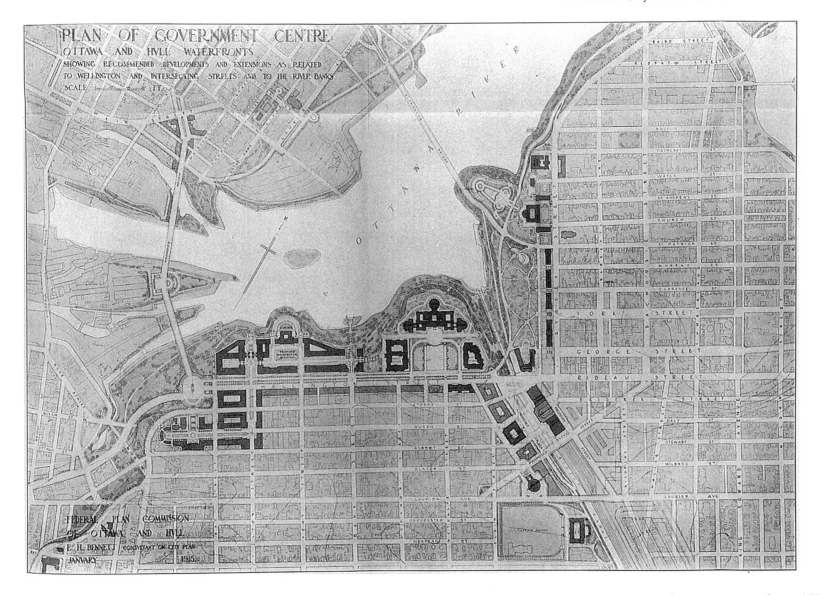

4.13. Federal Plan Commission proposal, Government Centre, Ottawa, Ontario, 1915. From *Report of the Federal Plan Commission on a General Plan for the Cities of Ottawa and Hull* (Ottawa 1916), pl. 14. (NA, NL 18068)

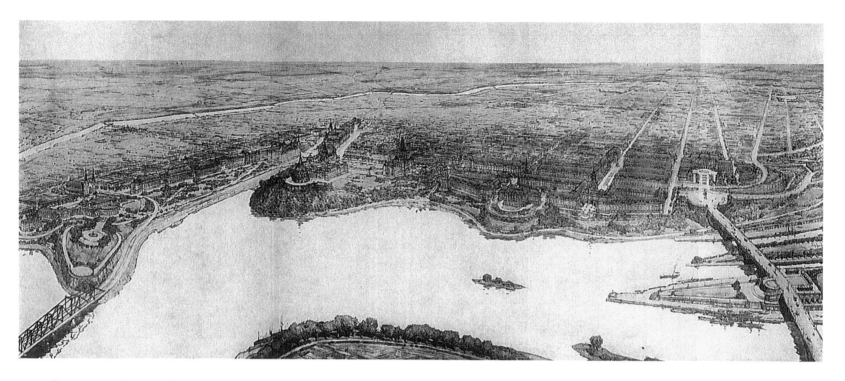

4.14. Perspective drawing, Government Centre. From *Report of the Federal Plan Commission on a General Plan for the Cities of Ottawa and Hull* (Ottawa 1916), pl. 15. (NA, NL 18069)

centred on the Mackenzie Tower of the West Block. The Courts Building was centrally placed and set back on the cliff edge. In the Bennett plan, however, the open plaza in front was surrounded by buildings on all sides. Clearly Bennett did not want to create a second major public space on Wellington Street that would compete with the Parliament Hill grounds. Bennett also identified Sussex Street as a secondary government avenue to be completed by a fine arts museum and other minor government buildings. A great civic centre, encompassing a new city hall, extended union station, post office, and auditorium, was to be located between Elgin Street and the train tracks. Future government development was also planned for Lyon Street and across the river in Hull. The overall view of the proposed development shows a central core dominated by consistently designed government offices with steep châteauesque roofs and ornate dormers. The quality and the definition of the individual buildings were secondary to the broader visual effects created by the dramatic sweep of uniformly designed streetscapes.

There was considerable merit to the report of the Federal Plan Commission. It attempted to address current conditions within the city and to provide practical and feasible solutions to problems such as rail transportation, industrial and residential zoning, and the need for an expanded network of public parks and playgrounds. But the report also displayed some of the limitations inherent in City Beautiful planning. Although general principles and parameters for development were identified, no attempt was made to define administrative, legal, or organizational mechanisms that would have to be instituted in order to implement the plan. It recommended the creation of a federal district commission that would replace elected municipal governments, but, given that the mayors of Hull and Ottawa both sat on the commission, this suggestion was never taken seriously. The report was also limited by the fact that it presented a fixed vision of Ottawa's future. The prescribed architectural theme was clearly rooted in the tastes of the Edwardian era, which quickly became outdated.

A modified version of some of the proposals in Bennett's plan would eventually be implemented, and had political and economic conditions remained stable more of it might have been. But in 1914 war was declared and all but essential government expenditures were redirected to the war

effort. By the time peace was restored in 1918 the federal government had incurred an enormous debt and, as a result, government building went into sharp decline. During the late 1910s and early 1920s government building in Ottawa was limited to two projects. The first was the reconstruction of the Centre Block, which had been destroyed by fire in 1916, and the second was the construction of the James B. Hunter Building in 1917, the first government building constructed to commercial office standards. Both projects were prompted by demands and events outside the existing planning and design guidelines. For this reason, they will be discussed separately in the next chapter.

Despite the delays and setbacks, the recommendations of the Federal Plan Commission were never abandoned. Throughout the 1920s the government intended to proceed with the work once funds were available. In preparation for this time, yet another committee – consisting of David Ewart, the retired chief architect, Richard C. Wright, the current chief architect, and Thomas Adams, a prominent British town planner – was established in 1919. The role of the committee, intended as informal and in-house, was to sift through the various proposals for new government buildings and to make recommendations on how to proceed.[47] It was not asked to prepare new plans, but the presence of Adams introduced a radically different perspective: he naturally sought to reshape the project according to his own ideas on urban design.

It is likely that Adams was included on the committee because he was already under contract to the federal government. He had been brought to Canada in 1914 as the town planning consultant to the Commission on Conservation set up in 1909 to investigate the nature of scientific farming and the management of Canada's natural resources, including the human and urban environment.[48] Adams was well known and well respected in his field, but his approach to town planning was very different from that of the other consultants who had worked on the Ottawa project. He had begun his career as a proponent of Ebenezer Howard's Garden City movement, and as a planner he gave priority to issues of social and municipal reform, housing, and public utilities rather than to the beautification of public spaces. Moreover, his aesthetic sensibilities were not rooted in the Beaux-Arts tradition. While in Canada Adams prepared several plans for townsites, and all were laid out in the informal, irregular manner of the picturesque landscape tradition.[49]

The committee agreed with the Federal Plan Commission that the Château style was most appropriate for new government buildings, but it did not accept Bennett's suggested ground plan. Nor could the members agree among themselves. David Ewart presented his own plan, consisting of two rows of long narrow buildings placed on either side of the east–west mall and centred on the Mackenzie Tower. Although supposedly adopting a châteauesque vocabulary, the general outline of the proposed buildings, each with projecting central and end pavilions, resembled the layout of the Victoria Memorial Museum and the Connaught Building repeated many times over. The buildings were set well back from Wellington Street, and Ewart intended landscaped grounds in front of each building. It was as if he wanted to transpose the original Sussex Street development, with its frontage on Major's Hill Park, to the new site. Unfortunately, Ewart did not live to promote his proposal further; he died in 1921 and his plan was put aside.[50]

A second plan, submitted jointly by Wright and Adams, clearly owed much to Adams (Figure 4.15).[51] In all previous proposals, whether in a Gothic or a classical style, the influence of Beaux-Arts – strict symmetry, monumental sense of space and scale, and formal design of the landscaped grounds – was very strong. The Wright-Adams plan, on the other hand, introduced a new informality and picturesqueness into the layout. Each building would be varied and irregular. The frontage along Wellington Street would have been made up of a sequence of broken, irregular planes that opened up into a variety of intimate and asymmetrical courtyards. The east–west mall was reduced in scale: no longer a grand, formal avenue, it took on the more intimate, human scale of a tree-lined street. Formal gardens were introduced where appropriate, but most of the grounds were laid out in the picturesque manner, with paths winding through a wooded park.

This last proposal was the product of an ad hoc committee working in relative obscurity within the federal bureaucracy, yet it was the one that would produce concrete results. It succeeded, not because it was better, but because it was the most recent and complete plan available when the

government summoned the will and the money to proceed with construction. Throughout the early 1920s the planning process had moved forward at a slow leisurely pace but nothing had been accomplished. By 1927, however, federal revenues were increasing, and estimates were finally submitted for the first of the new departmental buildings. Rather than enter into the perilous and apparently futile process of setting up a competition or of hiring an architect on contract, the project fell, almost by default, to the Chief Architect's Branch.[52]

The Confederation Building was the product of several decades of planning, revision, and compromise (Figure 4.16). The architectural style was defined by the Federal Plan Commission, the ground plan was determined by Wright and Adams, and the detailed working drawings were prepared by a departmental project team headed by T.D. Rankin, the senior staff architect.[53] Even the deputy minister of public works involved himself with the design, suggesting that the new Hotel MacDonald in Edmonton would provide a suitable model for the buildings.[54] Despite the complexity of the planning process, the Confederation Building is a remarkably well-designed building.[55] Nine storeyed and capped by a steep copper roof with ornate dormers, it was designed in a free interpretation of the Château style. Like the Hotel MacDonald, the focal point of the design was a tall central tower, located at the corner but recessed in from the first plane. The picturesque quality of the building was reinforced by the circular tower to the right of the main tower and by the asymmetrical treatment of the two main elevations running along Bank and Wellington streets. The profile and details are reminiscent of the Château Laurier at the other end of Wellington Street, but the warmly variegated Nepean sandstone walls with Wallace sandstone trim visually harmonize with those same materials in the Parliament Hill complex.

The architectural press and the professional organizations hated the building and decided to use it as a target for an attack on the quality of federal government architecture. In a petition to the federal government, the Royal Architectural Institute of Canada wrote: 'From the meagre illustrations which have come through the press, it does not appear that these buildings will measure up to the capabilities of the Canadian architects of today.'[56] The choice of the Château style was questioned

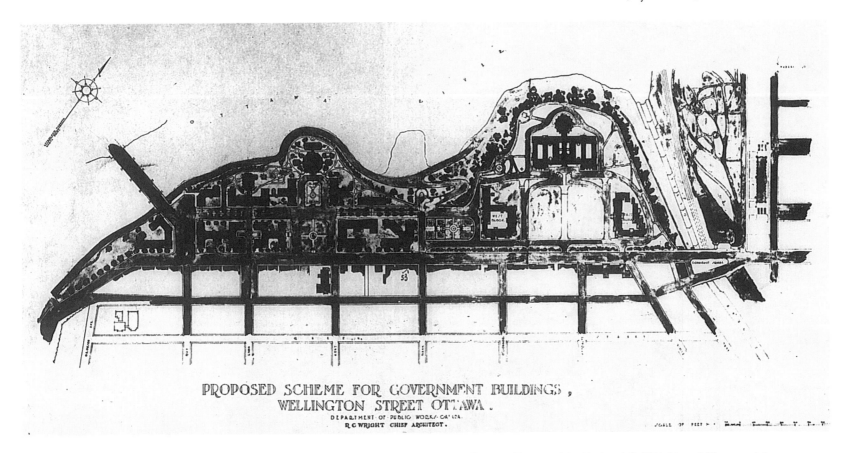

4.15. Proposed plan, government buildings, Wellington Street (north side), Ottawa, Ontario. Prepared by Richard C. Wright and Thomas Adams *ca.* 1920. (NA, NMC 121803)

4.16. Confederation Building, Ottawa, Ontario, 1928–31. Designed by the Chief Architect's Branch. (J. Wright, Parks Canada, 1992)

on its suitability for a modern office building, and the use of the 'arrow plan' was also severely criticized. One architect wrote that 'such a plan for any building, particularly a building of this importance, would not pass a student in the Department of Architecture in any reputable university.'[57] Such criticism was overly harsh, revealing a certain rigidity of thought within the architectural community at the time. Today the aesthetic qualities of the building can be better appreciated, but at the time of construction it was viewed as architectural anachronism. The designs retained an element of the Victorian picturesque that was incompatible with the new modern classicism dominating public architecture in Canada throughout the late 1920s and 1930s.

Seemingly oblivious to these criticisms, the Department of Public Works continued with its program of building along Wellington Street. In 1934 construction began on a second building, now known as the Justice Building, which was designed in the same manner as the Confederation Building. In 1937 the Chief Architect's Branch drew up plans for two more buildings to be located on Wellington Street on the far side of the proposed plaza, but they were never constructed (Figure 4.17).[58]

William Lyon Mackenzie King and Jacques Gréber: Rethinking the Capital

By 1937 the nature of development and design in the 'parliamentary precinct' had shifted focus. The change in direction owed much to the influence of William Lyon Mackenzie King, who, as prime minister, took a keen personal interest in the beautification of the national capital. In 1927 the Ottawa Improvement Commission had been renamed the Federal District Commission and given broader powers, more money, and an extension of its planning mandate into the province of Quebec.[59] While the Department of Public Works was excavating the foundations of the new Confederation Building, King turned his attention to the widening of Elgin Street and the development of an open public space and traffic circle that would become the present-day Confederation Square. A National War Memorial, being designed and sculpted in Britain, was to form the centre-piece of the square, which King likened to

Piccadilly Circus. To carry out the proposal the government expropriated a number of private properties in the area.[60]

The onset of the Depression and the election victory of the Conservatives in 1930 delayed work on the plan, but in 1935 King returned to power with his enthusiasm for the civic improvement of Ottawa undiminished. While in Paris in 1936, King had toured the site of the Paris Exhibition of 1937. His guide was Jacques Gréber, the chief architect to the exhibition and a noted town planner. King was very impressed by Gréber, and he immediately invited him to help guide the development of the new Confederation Square.[61]

Gréber's arrival in Ottawa in 1937 explains the demise of the proposal for two departmental buildings on Wellington Street (see Figure 4.17). The lingering Victorian picturesqueness in these designs, with their rusticated and random coursed stonework, would have been quite alien to Gréber's French architectural sensibilities. His initial report, prepared in 1937 and revised in 1938, supported many of the recommendations of the Federal Plan Commission in 1915, but it also gave more precise shape to the development of Confederation Square and Elgin Street. Although he advocated the retention of a Château-styled roofline with uniform cornice, he argued for greater architectural freedom in all other aspects of the design.[62] Gréber also recommended the use of a light-coloured stone, representing a marked departure from the darker, variegated colour of the Nepean sandstone that had, until then, been the standard material for government buildings in the central core.[63]

Gréber's work in Ottawa would be cut short by the outbreak of war in 1939, but two major government buildings – the Supreme Court of Canada, designed by Ernest Cormier (1938–46), and the Postal Station B, designed by W.E. Noffke (1938–9) – were begun during these years (Figures 4.18 and 4.19). Although both buildings retained the Château roof, it survived merely as an emblematic gesture to the stylistic program as defined by the Federal Plan Commission in 1915. In all other respects, the two buildings exemplify the architecture of modern classicism that dominated public building in Canada during the 1930s.[64] In fact, in both cases the architects had submitted plans without Château roofs and it was Gréber who insisted that the rooflines be modified.[65] Given Gréber's

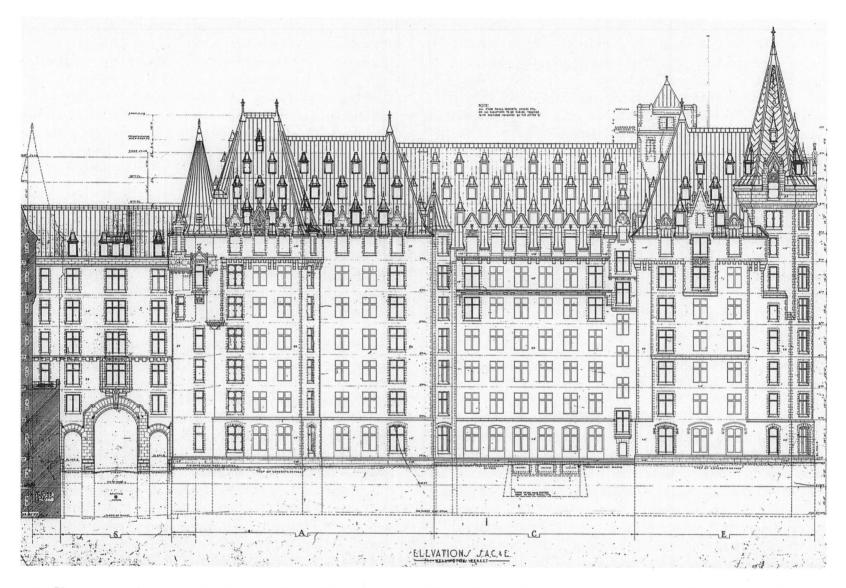

4.17. Plans, proposed government buildings, Wellington Street (north side), Ottawa, Ontario. Drawn by the Chief Architect's Branch in 1937. (Public Works Canada, Plan Room, file 149)

4.18. Supreme Court of Canada, Ottawa, Ontario, 1938–46. Designed by Ernest Cormier. (Paul Couvrette Photographs, 1993)

4.19. Grand entrance hall, Supreme Court of Canada. (Paul Couvrette Photographs, 1989)

strong classical background, one suspects he was merely voicing the preferences of his client, Prime Minister Mackenzie King, who remained committed to the idea that the steep copper roofs constituted an appropriate vision of the national capital.[66]

The Supreme Court of Canada was one of the most outstanding products of the federal government's building program of the 1930s. A massive granite building, it contained the Supreme Court chambers, two courtrooms for the Exchequer Court (now the Federal Court of Canada), and general office space. The main façade is defined by a seven-bay central core flanked by two projecting pavilions, a composition that echoes the principal public spaces of the interior. The design is clearly rooted in the classical tradition, but all precise historical references have been eliminated. The sense of rhythm and movement is created by the subtly shifting planes of the grey granite walls. In Cormier's work, classicism is expressed not in terms of a vocabulary of details but in terms of a set of underlying principles of order, symmetry, and balance.

The Supreme Court building also played an important part in defining a new architectural image that would briefly shape federal building in Ottawa in the postwar period. As will be discussed in Chapter 7, Gréber was invited back to Ottawa in 1945 to prepare a comprehensive plan for the entire region. Again, the development of a cohesive architectural plan for the federal precinct formed an important part of the report. Gréber's sketch plans and model for new government buildings bear a strong resemblance to Cormier's design of 1938, which was still under construction at the time. By 1950 three major government buildings, designed in minimalist classical style, were under construction.

Conclusion

A plan for Ottawa was a central preoccupation for the Department of Public Works during the early twentieth century. Between 1899 and 1939 the government established two planning commissions, produced two comprehensive planning reports, held two major architectural competitions (one national and one international), engaged four different town planners from four different countries, and set up an internal steering committee which, in turn, came up with its own set of recommendations. In the first decade of the century, four buildings were erected according to the Tudor Gothic mode preferred by the Chief Architect's Branch. This approach was then superseded by the recommendations of the Federal Plan Commission, which represented the culmination of the early planning efforts for Ottawa. A classic example of the City Beautiful movement, the commission integrated issues of architecture and landscape, and a range of more practical urban concerns, including transportation, zoning, and suburban development, into a comprehensive master plan. This plan shaped development in the capital through the 1920s and 1930s, but, ultimately, relatively little resulted from it. By 1935 only two buildings had been constructed, more or less according to the plan, and then it was abandoned. By this time the vision of Ottawa formulated in the pre-World War I era was no longer compatible with current architectural trends.

The failure of these efforts was partly due to the complexities and problems inherent in the bureaucratic process within the federal government. Responsibility for planning and building in Ottawa fell to the Chief Architect's Branch of the Department of Public Works and to the Ottawa Improvement Commission (the Federal District Commission from 1927). Both agencies worked to give architectural and urban shape to the city. Unfortunately, throughout this period the work of the two bodies was poorly coordinated. New initiatives were frequently derailed by the introduction of competing plans. Local municipal governments, particularly that of Ottawa itself, also had their own ideas as to how the city should develop.[67] The process was further complicated by changes in government and in spending priorities, which undermined any attempt to mount a sustained campaign for development and construction.

In addition, the implementation of a coherent and comprehensive plan was hindered by the fundamental dilemma of building within the national capital. All federal public buildings stood as symbols of the state, but in Ottawa the symbolic intent bore the burden of Canada's need for distinct cultural definition: building in the heart of the capital demanded the highest standards of design and an architecture that stood as a meaningful cultural symbol. The political and symbolic implications of building in the capital seemed to unnerve the various players involved in the business of planning the capital, and throughout the first half of the twentieth century there was a reluctance on the part of government to commit itself to a single vision of Ottawa. Hesitation and uncertainty constantly hampered the planning process. In 1945 the planning of the national capital would begin again under the direction of Jacques Gréber. Although Gréber's report in 1937 was the most successful planning document ever produced for the region, when measured in terms of concrete results it did not offer a convincing architectural solution to the problem of building in the shadow of Parliament Hill.

CHAPTER FIVE

Wartime Projects and the Dormant Years, 1914–1927

The outbreak of World War I in 1914 marked the end of an era in government building. Projects that were well under way were generally carried through to completion, but all other non-military construction was brought to an abrupt stop. Plans for the development of a federal precinct in Ottawa and many other large-scale projects, including a customs house in Toronto and federal buildings in Calgary and Vancouver, were relegated to the filing cabinets of the Chief Architect's Branch. Many other small public buildings, for which estimates had been prepared and urban lots purchased, were cancelled. The war ended in 1918, but the work did not resume. War had left the federal government with a large debt, a weak economy, and growing social and labour unrest throughout the country. Although the imposition of a federal income tax in 1917 provided the government with a new source of revenue, spending would be directed toward a reduction of the national debt and towards major expenditures, such as the acquisition of a number of private railways to form the Canadian National Railways. All other spending was curtailed, and the bureaucracy was gradually reduced in size.

Only three major projects, all of which grew out of wartime conditions or events, were carried out during the war years. These were the rebuilding of the Centre Block on Parliament Hill, which was destroyed by fire in 1916, the completion of a number of military hospitals begun by the Military Hospitals Commission and transferred to the Department of Public Works in 1918, and the construction of the James B. Hunter Building in Ottawa in 1917–18, a multi-storeyed office building to deal with the wartime shortage of government office space. These were the last projects before the program slipped into a quiet dormancy. Between 1918 and 1927 new projects were confined to minor public buildings and to a few secondary buildings at such federal institutions as the Experimental Farm Service and the Quarantine Branch. The yearly average of twenty new post office and urban public buildings in the pre-war decade fell to around two or three per year, and most were constructed between 1925 and 1927 when the pace of building started to gain momentum. The Chief Architect's Branch reacted to this lack of activity and lack of challenge by retreating into its past. With the exception of the three large projects, government architecture appeared to be immune to any new ideas and influences; until the early 1930s government design confined itself to set formulas that had been established in the early years of the century.

Wartime Projects: The Centre Block, Parliament Hill

On 3 February 1916 a fire broke out in the House of Commons reading room and within minutes of its discovery it was out of control. By the next morning all that was left of the original Centre Block were the exterior walls and the Library, which had been separated from the rest of the building by a fireproof door. Within a few days an all-party parliamentary committee was established to oversee the reconstruction of the building. James B. Hunter, the deputy minister, and E.L. Horwood, the new chief architect, participated in the meetings but not as voting members. Because of the national significance of the project, it was decided that the committee should be directed by elected representatives. It then engaged the services of John A. Pearson and J.-Omer Marchand to prepare a report on the condition of the building. These two architects had never worked together, but the fact that Pearson was an anglophone from Toronto and Marchand was a francophone from Montreal would suggest that the make-up of the team was determined by political factors as well as professional ones.[1]

At first the architects reported that the building could be restored. A few weeks later, however, it was decided that the surviving walls were structurally unsound, and they were demolished. This move angered the members of the committee, who claimed that they had not been consulted. Initially they blamed the architects, but it is unlikely that Pearson or Marchand would have taken such radical action without the knowledge of the minister and of senior officials within the Department of Public Works.[2] The decision to move quickly, without going through the committee, may well have been prompted by a desire for expediency. As noted in the previous chapter, the symbolic significance of the old building was deeply rooted in popular imagination, and there was a strong feeling within the committee and among the public that the building should be salvaged and rebuilt according to the original plan. For the architects and the department, however, this sentimental attachment to the building was moderated by aesthetic and practical concerns. By tearing down the old walls, Pearson, who was to become the principal designer, was free to develop a new design that respected many of the salient features of the original building but that also incorporated modern standards of construction and met the growing demands from Parliament for more office space.[3]

The parliamentary committee instructed the architects to build a larger version of the original building, 'without a change in the general character and the style of building.'[4] Pearson followed these instructions up to a point (Figures 5.1, 5.2, and 5.3). Many of the landscape features, including the walls and terrace that had been designed by Calvert Vaux in the 1870s, were retained. Nepean sandstone was again used as the principal building material and Ohio sandstone was used for the trim.[5] The general massing of the main façade – a central tower with two projecting wings accented at the corners by mansard pavilions – was almost identical to the original building. The distribution of windows across the main façade was also similar. But Pearson never intended his design to be a faithful reconstruction of the original, and he made many structural and stylistic changes.

By 1916 the architecture of the High Victorian period had fallen out of favour. Pearson wanted to redefine Fuller's decorative vocabulary and to tame its picturesque and polychromatic excesses so that it conformed more closely to Beaux-Arts principles of order and simplicity. The original roofline was considerably subdued. The ornate dormers were replaced by simple hipped dormers, and the extensive use of iron cresting along the roof was limited to a very simple metal railing on top of the corner pavilions. Pearson also decided to eliminate the red Potsdam sandstone trim that had figured so prominently in Fuller's design. Despite some protest from the public, he argued that its jarring colour detracted from the desired sense of solidity and massiveness.[6] The central tower was the last part of the building to be constructed and here Pearson departed quite substantially from the original. In contrast to Fuller's shorter and more ornate tower, the new tower soars above the main body of the building. Now known as the Peace Tower, it has become the strongest and most recognizable symbol of Ottawa and of the federal government.

The plan and internal structure of the building were completely changed. The original building was a three-a-half-storey structure laid out in a triangular configuration with the library forming the apex of the triangle. By adding a fourth storey and by extending the building back from the main elevation to form a rectangular plan, the architect was able to increase the amount of interior space by 50 per cent. The old stone, brick, and iron construction of the nineteenth-century building was replaced by an independent steel frame faced in stone and backed with hollow tile and brick.

5.1. Centre Block, Parliament Buildings, Ottawa, Ontario, 1916–27. Architect: John A. Pearson; associate: J.-Omer Marchand. (Public Works and Government Services Canada, Heritage Recording and Technical Data Services, 1991)

The interior design was also thoroughly reinterpreted. The plan is arranged around a central spine or axis. The main entrance under the Peace Tower opens into Confederation Hall, a large semi-octagonal space modelled after a medieval chapter house. Its central column, which is said to symbolize Great Britain, supports a complex fan vault that carries the weight to the other perimeters marked by ten Gothic columns (see Figure 5.3). The central axis is completed by the wide hall of honour, which leads to the Parliamentary Library. Unlike the original building, which was detailed in a typically Victorian mix of styles, the public areas of the new Centre Block represent a sophisticated expression of the Gothic vocabulary with particular reference to British sources. Features such as the pointed stone arches, the clerestory windows, and the five-part ribbed vaults with richly carved bosses at the junction of the ribs, were inspired by English Gothic architecture of the twelfth century. This period of Gothic building appealed to twentieth-century architects because it avoided the overly intricate ornamentation of the late Gothic and the undisciplined eclecticism of the Victorian Gothic.[7]

The central axis divides the ground floor into two halves, one allocated to the House of Commons and the other to the Senate (Figure 5.4). Each section has its own entrance and lobby, forming two secondary axes terminated by the House of Commons chamber on the west side and the Senate chamber on the east. Both chambers were conceived as medieval halls that extend through two storeys and that are lighted from above by arched windows situated high on the walls. The House of Commons is larger but the Senate, as the senior house, is more ornate in its decoration. Each chamber is equipped with its own reading-room, smoking-room, committee rooms, and a suite of rooms for the speaker. Two secondary corridors, which run perpendicular to the main halls, link the two sections. The upper floors contain offices for senators and members of Parliament. The parliamentary dining room is located on the top level above the Commons chamber. These secondary areas adopt a variety of styles suited to the different functions. For example, the suite of rooms occupied by the speaker of the Senate was designed in a Tudor Gothic style, while some of the reading-rooms, committee rooms, and the parliamentary dining room were designed in an elegant classical or Adamesque style.

Although Parliament sat in the new building for the first time in 1920,

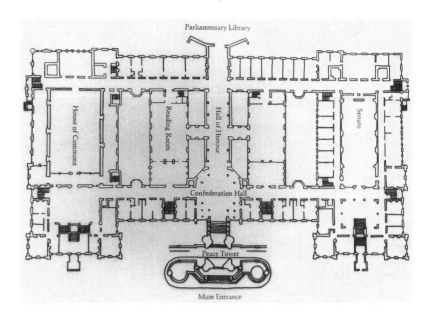

5.2. Floor plans, Centre Block. (National Film Board of Canada, *Stones of History: Canada's Houses of Parliament* [Ottawa 1967])

5.3. Hall of Honour, Centre Block. (Public Works and Government Services Canada, Heritage Recording and Technical Data Services, 1993)

work on the sculptural ornamentation still continues to this day. Since 1936 the work has been carried out under the direction of three principal artists – Cléophas Soucy (1936 to 1950), William Oosterhoff (1950 to 1962), and Eleanor Milne (1962 to the present). Although the artists developed their own distinctive styles, all three have sought to create forms that harmonized with the Gothic setting and at the same time introduced a distinctly Canadian iconography into the decorative program. In the past decade, several Native carvers have also been invited to prepare relief panels for the building. In the manner of a medieval cathedral, the construction of the Centre Block is an ongoing process, drawing upon the skills of many generations of artists and artisans.

Wartime Projects: Military Hospitals

Responsibility for the construction of military hospitals was first given to the Military Hospitals Commission, which was established under the direction of the Department of Militia and Defence in 1915.[8] In the early months of the war temporary hospitals and convalescent homes were set up in institutions and private homes that were loaned to the commission. By October 1916, 2,000 beds were available at over forty-seven institutions, but it quickly became apparent that this makeshift approach could not begin to cope with the growing number of casualties that were returning from the battlefields of Europe. Renovating existing buildings for hospital use was proving to be too costly and time-consuming. It was cheaper and faster to build from the ground up.

In 1917 Captain W.L. Symons was named chief architect to the Military Hospitals Commission, and for ten months he developed a series of standard plans for a number of temporary hospital buildings.[9] This work was well advanced when jurisdictional squabbling with the Canadian Army Medical Corps forced a major reorganization. In February 1918 the management of the military hospitals that provided short-term care for active soldiers was turned over to the medical corps. The Military Hospitals Commission, reconstituted as the Department of Soldiers' Civil Re-establishment, retained control of hospitals that provided care for

5.4. House of Commons, Parliament Buildings, Ottawa, Ontario. (Public Works and Government Services Canada, Heritage Recording and Technical Data Services, 1993)

veterans with permanent disabilities or requiring long-term hospitalization.[10] At the same time, responsibility for the design and construction of hospitals for both departments was transferred to the Department of Public Works. The chief architect was ultimately responsible for the program, but Captain Symons, who assumed the title of 'Architect for Military Hospitals,' seems to have remained in charge of the work.[11]

Canadian military hospitals were the product of two separate developments in the evolution of hospital planning, the pavilion plan and the concept of temporary buildings. The pavilion plan was first introduced in France in the late eighteenth century and reflected the growing awareness of the importance of light and fresh air in combating disease.[12] Rather than incorporating hospital functions into one building, each ward formed a distinct building linked to others by passages or walkways. Large windows on two or more façades provided good ventilation and natural lighting. The pavilion ward also permitted more effective isolation of patients into smaller groups.

Temporary and transportable field hospitals were first introduced during the Crimean War, and their practical and medical advantages were clearly demonstrated during the American Civil War.[13] In Europe, most military field hospitals constructed during World War I were rough wood or canvas structures that were one storey in height and were heated by wood- or coal-burning stoves.[14] In Canada, however, this type of flimsy structure was not practical. The harsh climate demanded sturdier, more weatherproofed buildings. Accordingly, the Military Hospitals Commission developed what were referred to as 'semi-permanent' structures. These were wood-frame buildings set on concrete or wood-post foundations, with gently pitched gable roofs. The studs were covered with tongue-and-groove boards, and a layer of heavy-duty building paper was applied both inside and outside the structure. The interior was finished with fibreboard. The exteriors of these predominantly wooden buildings were usually sheathed in stucco to provide some measure of fire resistance.[15]

The ward unit or pavilion formed the basic component of the military hospital. The commission experimented with various plans during the early months of the program, but by 1918 a standard layout had emerged (Figure 5.5).[16] It consisted of a long rectangular building with two wards at either end, each providing approximately thirty-eight beds. A solarium with windows on three sides was located on the outer end of each ward. A middle section contained the nurses' station and medical offices. In some of the early plans, facilities such as the washrooms and kitchens were located within the ward pavilion, but these were later removed to a separate unit linked to the ward by a narrow corridor. The ward pavilions were always two storeys in height, which was found to be the most economical yet efficient configuration. Any number of these basic units could be built to form complexes of a variety of sizes; moreover, the size of the complex could easily be adjusted by adding new units or tearing down old ones. The decision to adopt this type of plan was clearly made by the staff of the Military Hospitals Commission. In 1910–11 the Chief Architect's Branch had prepared plans for a five-pavilion hospital for the Grosse Île Quarantine Station, but the staff of the commission opted for a more complex radial plan with a central administration building.[17] It was characteristic of the military to adopt the simplest, most practical solution.

Most of the construction related to the military hospitals program was carried out within an eighteenth-month period. During that time over $15 million was spent on more than eighty facilities across the country.[18] The military hospital at Camp Hill in Halifax was the first project of this type, but the one at Ste-Anne-de-Bellevue near Montreal, providing one thousand beds, was one of the largest and typified the Canadian military hospitals during World War I (Figure 5.6).[19] The administration building, with its offices and operating rooms, and the service building, containing the kitchen and dining-room, formed the core of the complex. Seven separate pavilions, identified as active treatment, convalescent, neurological, or officers' wards, were linked by narrow corridors or sheltered walkways that formed the stem or spine of the complex. Small service units, equipped with washrooms and storage facilities, were located between pavilions. Subsidiary buildings, such as a vocational and recreation building, laboratories, and staff residences for medical officers, nurses, and orderlies, were placed around the central complex. These buildings were often a little more elaborate, featuring wooden galleries and verandas across the front, but they adopted the same type of structure, materials,

5.5. Standard pavilion ward, Rena Maclean Hospital, Charlottetown, Prince Edward Island, 1918. Plans prepared by the Military Hospitals Commission and the Chief Architect's Branch. (*Construction* 13, no. 3 [March 1920]:89)

5.6. View and ground plan, Ste-Anne-de-Bellevue Military Hospital, Ste-Anne-de-Bellevue, Quebec. (Department of Soldiers' Civil Re-establishment, *Canada's Work for Disabled Soldiers* [Ottawa (1919), 98)

and basic design elements (Figure 5.7). The powerhouse, which also included the laundry, was usually set apart from the rest of the buildings. Although many of these institutions are still in existence, few, if any, of the early temporary structures appear to have survived.

The Department of Soldiers' Civil Re-establishment adopted a similar approach to planning, but because its hospitals were designed to provide long-term care, they were generally constructed of brick. The two largest hospitals under this agency's jurisdiction were the Orthopaedic Hospital in Toronto, which became known as the Christie Street Hospital, and the London Psychopathic Hospital in Ontario.[20] Tuberculosis sanatoria, however, constituted the largest component of its network of hospitals. During World War I, more soldiers were disabled through disease and illness than by wounds suffered in battle. The leading cause of illness was tuberculosis.[21]

The sanatoria built by the Military Hospitals Commission and later by the Chief Architect's Branch for the Department of Soldiers' Civil Re-establishment conformed to standards of design and plan that had been developed during the 1880s and 1890s. Prior to the development of antibiotics, the accepted treatment for tuberculosis was rest, fresh air, sunshine, supervised diet, and controlled exercise. During the 1890s and early 1900s the National Sanatorium Association recommended that sanatoria should be located in rural settings and that the buildings should be aesthetically pleasing. It was believed that attractive surroundings would have a beneficial effect on a patient's rate of recovery.

Finding enough beds to accommodate the large number of soldiers who had contracted tuberculosis was a major problem for the commission. In order to avoid the high costs involved in building its own permanent facilities, the government put money into expanding existing sanatoria that were administered either privately or by provincial governments. When the Department of Soldiers' Civil Re-establishment had no further need of the buildings, they would be transferred back. At these sanatoria new pavilions designed under the direction of the Chief Architect's Branch differed considerably from the typical ward at a military hospital. The pavilion at the Mountain Sanatorium in Hamilton was characteristic of the type (Figure 5.8). The wards were situated across the front of a two-

storey building, with large windows providing ample sunlight and fresh air. The beds were located along the back wall and lounge chairs were placed in front of the windows so that the patients could sit and take in the healthful rays of the sun. Service areas and offices were located across the back of the building. In a typical western Canadian sanatorium the sitting area or 'cure veranda' was divided from the inside ward by a wall so that the sleeping area could be heated separately from the veranda, which was used only in the daytime (see Figure 5.7).

Although most of these buildings were designed to meet a temporary need, many experts who were involved with the program believed they had developed a model that could be applied to permanent hospital facilities. The cost of building a modern hospital had become too high for many communities, and those that were built often became outdated within a short period of time. Some people argued that the military hospitals met the basic needs of medical services at a fraction of the cost of conventional city hospitals. By adopting a more economical, semi-permanent type of construction, hospitals could easily be enlarged or altered to meet new requirements at a relatively low cost.[22] The military hospitals, however, would have little impact on subsequent hospital design. Within two decades another war would break out and once again the federal government would be in the business of building hospitals, but by this time modern technology and sophisticated systems of sanitation and climate control offered very different solutions.

Wartime Projects: The Hunter Building

The Centre Block and military hospitals fell under the administrative control of the Department of Public Works, but in both cases the role of the Chief Architect's Branch was primarily to provide technical and administrative support, with limited input in the design process. The only wartime project that was generated from within the branch was the James B. Hunter Building in downtown Ottawa (Figure 5.9). While not as prestigious as the Centre Block or as extensive as the military hospitals program, it represented a significant development in the government's concept of a public building. The project was conceived by the deputy

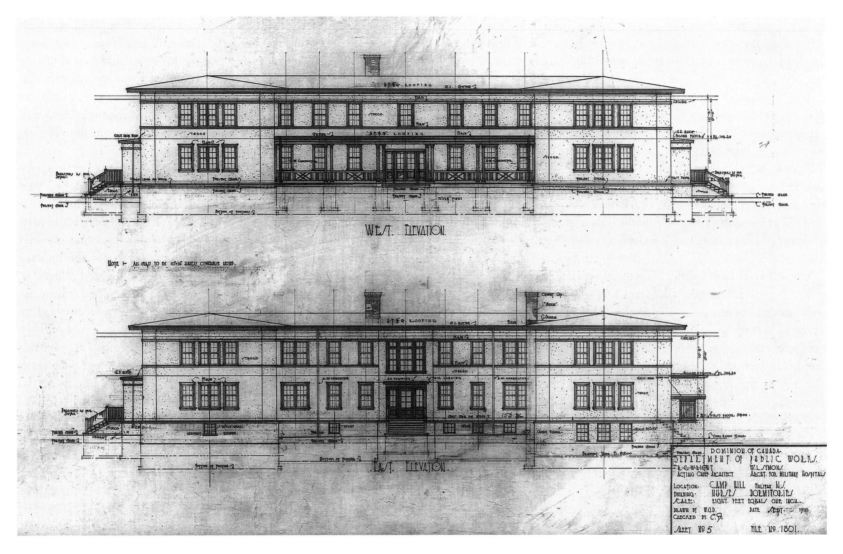

5.7. Plan, Nurses' Dormitory, Camp Hill Military Hospital, Halifax, Nova Scotia, 1918. Designed by the Chief Architect's Branch (W.L. Symons, architect for military hospitals). (NA, NMC 0059439)

5.8. Mountain Sanatorium, Hamilton, Ontario. (Department of Soldiers' Civil Re-establishment, *Canada's Work for Disabled Soldiers* [Ottawa (1919], 122)

5.9. James B. Hunter Building, Ottawa, Ontario, 1917–20. Plans prepared by the Chief Architect's Branch. Demolished in 1982. (NA, PA-151668)

minister after whom the building was named, and it was developed in response to the government's need for more office space. During World War I the number of civil servants and military staff had increased rapidly, and by 1917 the federal government was forced to lease almost 900,000 square feet of office space from the private sector.[23] Hunter saw this as a wasteful and unnecessary expenditure, and he successfully argued that the government could save money by constructing its own office buildings.

The Hunter Building introduced the concept of the government 'office' building as a type that was distinct from the 'public' building. As explained by Hunter, the building was not intended as a monument to the government; instead, it was designed to conform to the basic requirements of standard commercial office space.[24] After the initial proposal was rejected as too costly, the staff in the Chief Architect's Branch accepted 'wartime imperatives' and 'overcame that distaste which nearly all architects have to changing their original conception and trimmed from the building everything that was not absolutely necessary.'[25] The result was a nine-storey, steel-frame building with concrete-slab floors. The limestone facing, which was originally intended to sheath all three street elevations, was limited to the first two floors. The three main entrances were accented by a modest range of classical detail in the form of free-standing columns and a row of shallow pilasters. The remaining storeys were finished in a red tapestry brick, a lightly textured material that was used frequently on public buildings during this period.[26] The Hunter Building was a solid, serviceable, yet architecturally undistinguished building. The fact that it was one of the few government buildings to receive the whole-hearted approval and praise of the House of Commons reveals something of government priorities.[27] One of the first tenants to move into the building was the Department of Public Works.

The exterior design and interior plan of the Hunter Building followed standard conventions for a modern office building. The tripartite division of the façade, with its two-storey stone base, five-storey shaft, and two-storey attic or capital topped by a heavy projecting cornice, represented the most common design solution for a multi-storeyed office building in the early twentieth century. The interior plan was also typical of the period. The rectangular block plan, which filled its site, obeyed the economical imperative to maximize interior floor space. The office space was organized around a central court, which was a necessary feature in the days before fluorescent lighting and modern climate controls. A narrow corridor ran through the middle of the surrounding office space. Three elevator banks, each consisting of two elevators, serviced the various floors. The interior structural columns were placed on either side of the encircling corridor, thereby maximizing the amount of unobstructed office space.

During the early twentieth century, the design of office space had become a central preoccupation not only of architects but also of business management specialists and commercial real estate brokers. These groups were interested in developing ideal spatial configurations for offices that would provide efficient working environments and command high rents. Offices of between twenty and twenty-five feet in depth and no less than nine feet in width were identified as the smallest acceptable units. The maximum recommended depth was determined by how effectively natural light could penetrate into a building; the width was determined by taking half of the typical structural span of between eighteen and twenty-five feet.[28] The structural grid of the Hunter Building, which was based on a twenty-foot span, conformed to the guidelines. All offices were twenty feet in depth, but they ranged considerably in width from approximately 10 ten for small private offices to large, open working areas for clerical staff and for records storage. The exterior appearance of the building was also determined to a large extent by the internal layout of the offices. The paired-sash windows, a feature characteristic of many commercial office buildings of the period, corresponded to a basic ten-foot office unit rather than to the underlying steel grid. From a structural standpoint, it would have been possible to open up the wall area completely between each span, but this would have limited the number of possible office divisions.

The modern office building was a product of advances in construction technology, rising land values, and the increasing density of urban cores. But the success of this type of building was also connected to the rise of the large corporation which needed a compact and centralized administrative centre.[29] The suitability of this form of building to the federal government reflected similar changes in the nature and structure of government and bureaucracy. In the nineteenth century the civil service in Ottawa had been contained within a compact, close-knit community centred around Parliament Hill. Between 1900 and 1914 the expansion of government programs brought a significant increase in the civil service, and this growth continued through the war years. By 1920 it numbered approximately 50,000 full-time employees; the Department of Public Works alone employed 350. A building like the Hunter Building was well suited to the increasingly complex corporate reality of the federal bureaucracy of the twentieth century.[30] Its compact tiers of offices and flexible interior plan allowed for the efficient management and coordination of a large number of employees within a hierarchical structure.

The Hunter Building was originally intended as a temporary solution to a short-term problem. Once the war ended and the proposals of the Federal Plan Commission were carried out, it would be declared surplus and sold. In the end, however, the idea of housing civil servants cheaply and efficiently proved to be too appealing to the government and the bureaucracy. The Hunter Building introduced a two-tiered approach to building, which in Ottawa led to an erratic pattern of government development. Within the parliamentary precinct the government accepted that only the most imposing public buildings should be erected. But these were expensive; it was often easier and more expedient to build lower-grade office space outside that symbolically sensitive core. The full impact of this double architectural standard would become most apparent in the 1950s and 1960s when a federal building boom in the suburbs contrasted with the painfully slow development of the central core. Even today prime undeveloped lots in the shadow of Parliament Hill bear witness to the aesthetic, symbolic, and financial dilemma of building meaningful icons to the nation in the heart of the capital.

Postwar Restraint and the Dormant Years

The three large projects described above were the products of wartime conditions or events. When the war ended, the work of the department did not pick up where it had left off in 1914. The federal election of 1921 brought about the defeat of Arthur Meighen's Conservatives in favour of the Liberal Party under the new leadership of William Lyon Mackenzie King. Despite an economic recession and high unemployment, the new government did not believe it should play an interventionist role in stimulating an economic recovery. Instead, it adopted a strict policy of debt reduction and a return to a balanced budget. The Liberals' first budget reduced government spending by one-quarter.[31]

Government construction was a convenient target for some of these cuts. Under the direction of J.H. King, the new minister of public works, government spending on public buildings fell in 1921, 1922, and again in 1923.[32] Much of the money allocated to new construction went to military hospitals and to the completion of the Centre Block. During the early 1920s only those buildings that were considered essential were approved, and they tended to be subsidiary buildings in large government complexes such as quarantine stations and experimental farms. Restrictions on spending began to lessen slightly by 1925, but it was not until the following year that approval was given to begin work on many of the major projects that had been postponed in 1914.

The cuts in new construction were made easier by a decrease in demand. In the 1920s the rate of population growth declined and, more significantly, demographic distributions in Canada were changing. The early 1900s had seen the establishment and expansion of many small and mid-sized urban centres that required new or larger public buildings. The process of urbanization observed in the pre-war era would continue, but growth became increasing concentrated in such major cities as Toronto, Montreal, Hamilton, and Vancouver. Many smaller towns and cities experienced little or no population growth. Some communities, particularly in the Maritimes, which was hardest hit by the recession, even declined in size during these years. In the circumstances the need for new public buildings lessened.[33] While more government office space was required in the big cities, the demand could be met by an ample supply of rental accommodation.[34] When construction revived in the late 1920s and 1930s, much of the new building would take place in the large cities.

Within this climate of restraint, the Chief Architect's Branch slipped into a quiet dormancy. The two chief architects who directed the branch in the period after the war and until the late 1920s had little opportunity to make a noticeable impact. In 1914 David Ewart had retired as chief architect, but he remained active as a consultant to the department until his death in 1921.[35] He was replaced by E.L. Horwood, who was recruited from private practice in Ottawa. Horwood was an unusual choice, as he had neither experience in a government department nor a strong professional reputation. The appointment was also made over the vigorous protests of the Public Service Commission, which regarded it as one of the more blatant examples of government patronage.[36] Horwood's stay was brief; in 1918 he was replaced by Richard C. Wright, who had served as assistant chief architect since 1906.[37]

Wright's appointment promised consistency and continuity in the work of the branch, and these conservative qualities were reinforced by the branch staff. Between 1914 and 1934 the personnel of the Chief Architect's Branch remained remarkably stable. Only a few left or retired, and almost no new staff was hired. It was a difficult time to be an architect in government service. Salaries fell well below the standards set in the private sector.[38] At the same time, the self-esteem of Chief Architect's Branch continued to be undermined by members of the architectural profession who were constantly questioning the professional competence of the branch.[39] These factors, combined with the lack of challenging work, created a stagnant and lethargic atmosphere within the branch, which was then reflected in the buildings designed.

In the 1920s the work of the Chief Architect's Branch conformed to a few basic patterns. The public building of 1923–4 in Sackville, New Brunswick, represented one standard formula (Figure 5.10). A two-storey brick block, it was modestly detailed with a stone portico over the main entrance. A simple metal cornice accented the roofline, but the stone dressings that had often enriched this type of building in the pre-war era were almost completely eliminated. In general, architectural details, such as string-courses and lintels, were translated into cheaper brickwork, either in the form of decorative panels, sometimes in a basket-weave, pattern (as in the Sackville building), or by rows of vertically laid brick. Buildings with government offices on the second floor would either have two principal entrances on the main façade or a side entrance if the building was situated on a corner lot.

The public building with the corner clock tower, which had been the most characteristic design type in the early 1900s, almost completely disappeared from the repertoire of government building. The one constructed in Edmunston, New Brunswick, in 1925 was a rare exception, but its main block conformed to the basic classicized brick box, typical of this period (Figure 5.11). Features such as the steeply pitched roof, the asymmetrical tower, parapeted gables, and the variety of round- and flat-arched opens, characteristic of Ewart public buildings, were gone. The sense that a government building should form a central landmark on the main street of a small urban community was clearly in decline.

The post office in Stouffville, Ontario, represented a new type of government building (Figure 5.12).[40] A one-and-a-half-storey brick structure, with a low, truncated hipped roof and a central door accented by a small parapet dormer, it was one of several one-room post offices built in the mid-1920s. Typically, they provided a small entrance vestibule that led into the postal lobby and mail-sorting area located behind a counter. A caretaker's apartment, at that time a basic feature of all federal government buildings, was located in the attic storey. Although the prototypical design appeared in the first decade of the century, it was not until the mid-1920s that it would become a standard item in the federal building inventory.[41] Its small size was not necessarily a reflection of government restraint; instead, it marked the beginning of a new program of building that would deliver purpose-built federal buildings to smaller semi-rural communities. Starting in the mid-1920s, one-storey, one-room post offices would account for the majority of new buildings constructed by the department.

Other departments suffered from the same budgetary restraints. The program of armoury and drill hall construction continued into the early years of the war, with the construction of new armouries at Edmonton (1914–15), Lévis in Quebec (1915), Winnipeg (1914–15), and Calgary

5.10. Public Building, Sackville, New Brunswick, 1923–4. Plans prepared by the Chief Architect's Branch. (NA, PA-46378)

5.11. Public Building, Edmunston, New Brunswick, 1925. Plans prepared by the Chief Architect's Branch. (NA, C-70479)

(1916–17), but these were the last. A few military structures did go up but they were initiated and paid for by the individual regiments, with the Department of Militia and Defence assuming responsibility for their maintenance;[42] no new buildings would be constructed by either the Department of Militia and Defence or the Department of Public Works until the mid-1930s. Although the Royal Canadian Mounted Police usually looked after their own building needs,[43] they did request the services of the Chief Architect's Branch on a few isolated projects. The Royal Military College also generated some work for the branch. Other agencies, including the Immigration Branch of the newly formed Department of Immigration and Colonization, initiated no new construction.[44] Immigration dropped sharply during the postwar era, and the extensive network of immigration facilities erected in the early 1900s met all current needs.[45]

The Quarantine Branch, which had been transferred to the new Department of Health in 1919, was able to maintain a modest construction program from the late 1910s to the mid-1920s. Most of the work was concentrated at Partridge Island in New Brunswick in an effort to bring its facilities closer to the standards that had been developed at Grosse Île and William Head prior to World War I. In the 1920s a disinfecting plant, first- and second-class detention buildings, a large two-storey, forty-bed hospital, a smaller sixteen-bed smallpox hospital, and a number of residences and service buildings were constructed. The First-Class Detention Building was identical to those built at Grosse Île and William Head around 1914. Other structures, such as the Second-Class Detention Building, were less durably constructed of wood-frame sheathed in clapboard (Figure 5.13). The only other building of note for the Quarantine Branch was a nurses' residence at William Head, dating from 1915 (Figure 5.14). Although not a major project, its vaguely Tudor Gothic style defined a new design that would be used on several other buildings in the 1920s. It was a type most commonly associated with small buildings situated in government complexes in a non-urban setting.[46]

These were the last projects for the Quarantine Branch. During the 1920s immigration and public health policy would undergo radical changes. Immigration to Canada was falling off. More importantly, factors such as advances in epidemiology, greater international cooperation in monitoring contagious diseases, and the development of a comprehensive vaccination program gradually eliminated the need for large quarantine stations.[47] In 1923 it was decided that all ships entering Quebec would now stop at Pointe-au-Père, near Rimouski, for clearance by a medical officer; only those ships suspected of carrying serious illnesses, such as cholera or typhus, would be sent to Grosse Île. Passengers with less serious diseases would be detained at the immigrant hospital in Quebec.[48] Grosse Île was closed in 1938 and the other quarantine stations soon followed.[49]

Agriculture was one of the few departments that did not appear to be paralysed by the budget cutbacks. Both the Dominion Experimental Farm Service and the Health of Animals Branch experienced steady growth. In the early twentieth century agricultural science had become increasingly sophisticated and complex, and these changes were reflected in the expanded structure of the Experimental Farm Service. During the 1910s several new research branches were established and they required new facilities. Although the Chief Architect's Branch was asked to design and construct a few buildings at some of the branch farms, most of its work was focused on the Central Experimental Farm in Ottawa.

One of the earliest projects was the new Cereal and Agrostology Building, built in 1915–16 to replace one from 1911 that had been destroyed by fire in 1915 (Figure 5.15).[50] Half of the building was designed as a granary, complete with a threshing floor and a wide central drive where cereals could be directly transferred vehicles to the storage bins inside. The other half of the building was occupied by offices and the various workshops and laboratories that were required for the processing and analysis of cereals and grasses. Despite the building's dual function, the Chief Architect's Branch decided to interpret its exterior design as a barn rather than as an administrative and laboratory building. The treatment of the exterior wall surface with board and batten siding at ground level and with wood shingles above had been established by the Chief Architect's Branch under Thomas Fuller in the 1880s as an appropriate decorative theme for its barns and agricultural buildings. The staff of the

5.12. Post Office, Stouffville, Ontario, 1926. Plans prepared by the Chief Architect's Branch. (NA, PA-46262)

5.13. Second-Class Detention Building and Chief Quarantine Officer's Residence, Partridge Island, New Brunswick, *ca.* 1923. The solid, square-brick residence was typical of the branch's residential designs of the period. The two-storey veranda was added later. Both buildings were demolished in 1941. (Bisson Family Collection, Partridge Island Research Project, Saint John, New Brunswick)

FRONT ELEVATION

SECTION 'A.A'

5.14. Nurses' Residence, William Head Quarantine Station, British Columbia, 1915. Designed by the Chief Architect's Branch. The building is now managed by the William Head Institute, a federal correctional institution under the control of the Department of the Solicitor General. (NA, NMC 106187)

5.15. Cereal and Agrostology Building, Central Experimental Farm, Ottawa, Ontario, 1915–16. Plans prepared by the Chief Architect's Branch. (M. Trépanier, Parks Canada, 1993)

Animal Husbandry Division had long since abandoned these picturesque affectations in their own work in favour of a simple and straightforward type of construction that could be taken as a model of design for the average farmer.

Other projects at the Central Experimental Farm ranged from small storage and implement sheds to more substantial one- and two-storey brick and stucco buildings housing laboratories and offices. These buildings were usually small in scale, but the designs were clearly meant to reinforce the image of the farm as a prosperous agricultural estate rather than as a government research institution. The administrative buildings generally evoked an informal domestic quality. There was still considerable variety in design, but the Tudor Gothic theme, with its characteristic simulated half-timbering, which was applied to the new Botanical Laboratory Building of 1926, would emerge as a recurring architectural theme for administrative offices on the farm.[51]

The Health of Animals Branch of the Department of Agriculture was a separate research program that had occupied laboratory space at the Central Experimental Farm since 1902.[52] In 1918, however, the branch acquired its own farm situated just north of Hull. The approval to buy property during a time of restraint indicates the high priority given to the project and particularly to its principal mandate – to control or eradicate bovine tuberculosis, which had become a serious and expensive problem in Canada. Initially the program was housed in the old farmhouse that had been purchased with the property and in the few barns and sheds that were constructed soon after.

By the early 1920s the staff of the Health of Animals Branch began lobbying for a modern laboratory; in 1925 construction began on a new building that would be opened in 1928 as the Animal Diseases Research Institute (Figure 5.16). According to departmental correspondence, members of the staff had visited similar institutions in the United States, and then drawn up general design and construction guidelines that included fireproof construction and a separate incinerator for contaminated waste, as well as a detailed outline of the space requirements. In contrast to the designs it produced for the research offices and laboratories at the Central Experimental Farm, the Chief Architect's Branch made no at-

5.16. Animal Diseases Research Institute, Hull, Quebec, 1925–8. Plans prepared by the Chief Architect's Branch. (M. Trépanier, Parks Canada, 1993)

tempt to clothe this one in picturesque Tudor vocabulary. The narrow main façade, with its classical architrave around the main entrance and its stylized domed tower featuring narrow-slit windows, resembled a typical urban public building, such as the near-contemporary Edmunston Public Building. As seen from the side elevation, the building was much more industrial in character than agricultural. It had a steel-frame construction with reinforced concrete floors, and the wall space between the structural beams opened up to large windows that provided ample natural light to the various laboratories inside and gave the design a light skeletal appearance not generally evident in government buildings of the period. The resulting design – an awkward blend of building styles and types – suggests that the bold treatment of the windows reflected the preferences of the research staff rather than a decision taken by the Chief Architect's Branch.

Conclusion

By 1925 and 1926 the federal budget was less restricted, and in 1927 the strength of the economy encouraged the government to begin work on some of the large projects that had been deferred in 1914. The preceding decade and a half had been marked by only a few major challenges and achievements. The rebuilding of the Centre Block represented the most significant project of the period, but it was a design that was developed outside the Chief Architect's Branch. By 1927 many of the military hospitals that had dominated the construction program at the end of the war had already been dismantled. The Hunter Building stands out as the most important development during the period in the evolution of Canadian federal architecture. It defined a new level of government building whose primary function was to provide modern, efficient, and economical office accommodation for the growing number of civil servants working in Ottawa. Architecture is always imbued with meaning, but here the symbolic message was not the dignity of the state but rather an expression of the modern corporate identity of the bureaucracy.

Once these major projects were completed, the work of the Chief Architect's Branch went into decline. Cloistered in their new offices in the Hunter Building, the branch occupied itself with the mundane, day-to-day business of maintaining existing federal buildings and of designing a few low-profile projects. Public buildings continued to follow a few basic patterns of design that had been established in the early 1900s, but in the face of tight budgets they were scaled down both in size and in quality of the finishing. When work did resume in 1927, the aging staff of the Chief Architect's Branch found itself ill-equipped to respond creatively to the challenge of an ambitious new program of public works.

CHAPTER SIX

Building in the Depression, 1927–1939

In May 1927 the Canadian journal *Construction* announced that the federal building program would resume after more than a decade of restraint.[1] The decision reflected a new mood of confidence and well-being that prevailed in the latter half of the 1920s. By mid-decade the country was entering into a brief but intense period of economic growth, based largely on expanding resource industries in pulp and paper, mining, and hydroelectricity. At the same time, the election in 1926 of a solid majority government under the Liberal leadership of Mackenzie King brought to an end years of political instability and turmoil, which had been marked by a series of rancorous and short-lived governments.[2] The next twelve years were marked by major economic and political upheavals, but for the Department of Public Works and the Chief Architect's Branch it was a period of sustained activity and growth. The stock market crash of 1929 and the onset of the Depression brought about a temporary halt to federal building in 1932, but the implementation of the 1934 Public Works Construction Act, designed to stimulate the flagging national economy through government expenditure on public works, restored the fortunes of the branch. This period of expansion did not quite equal the building boom of 1896 to 1914, but by 1939 almost three hundred new federal buildings, mainly post offices and urban public buildings, had been constructed across the country.[3]

Federal architecture during these years falls into two distinct periods.

Between 1927 and 1933 most buildings were designed by the staff of the Chief Architect's Branch. The work maintained consistently good, competent standards of design and construction, but the buildings tended to adhere to stylistic patterns that had been established in the early 1900s. The familiar vocabulary of Beaux-Arts classicism, with the Château and Gothic styles as acceptable alternatives, had become indelibly linked with the branch's perception of what a federal building should look like. This conservatism was not unique to the Chief Architect's Branch, but the latter's resistance to new ideas had been accentuated by the long years of inactivity during which the staff had little opportunity to develop or explore new ideas. When work started up again in 1927, the branch simply picked up where it had left off in 1914.

In 1934 the architectural image of the federal government underwent a significant transformation. The late 1920s had been a dynamic period in Canadian architecture as new ideas of simplicity, restraint, and functionalism associated with the Art Deco and modern classical styles began to infiltrate and subtly transform, without overthrowing, established architectural traditions. In 1934 the branch's isolation from outside architectural influences was brought to an end by the government's decision to abandon its policy of 'in-house' design and to employ private architects on many projects as part of a policy to provide employment to all sectors of the construction industry. This decision had a revitalizing effect on federal architecture. Many of the architects introduced new design models into the repertoire of federal building; in turn, these models influenced the work of the Chief Architect's Branch. Over the next six years the federal government erected some of Canada's most notable examples of public building in the Art Deco and modern classical styles.

Federal Building, 1927–1933: Reviving the Chief Architect's Branch

In 1927 the federal construction program, which had been showing signs of renewed activity in 1925 and 1926, quickly moved into high gear. Projects that had been 'on the shelf' since 1914 were revived and many new ones were proposed. By 1929 over one hundred buildings were either under construction or in planning stages across the country. The sense of optimism was also reflected in the government's willingness to commit itself to a number of large-scale projects. The most costly item was the development of the parliamentary precinct in Ottawa in accordance with the recommendations of the Federal Plan Commission of 1915. As discussed in Chapter 4, work on this project began with the construction of the Confederation Building (1928–31), and it was followed by the Justice Building (1934–8), the Supreme Court building (1938–46), and Postal Station B (1938–9). At the same time, a number of other equally large and expensive buildings were constructed outside the capital, including a customs house in Toronto, a postal terminal in Montreal, a new headquarters for the National Research Council in Ottawa, and large federal office buildings in Calgary, Windsor, and Saskatoon, as well as dozens of smaller post offices and federal public buildings.

Responsibility for the implementation of this construction program fell to the staff of the Chief Architect's Branch; the buildings that it designed revealed both its strengths and its weaknesses. During the lean times the branch had been protected from major cuts by the deputy minister, James B. Hunter. Although a few architects had left voluntarily, most had stayed on in the face of limited opportunities elsewhere.[4] The only major change to take place within the branch was the appointment

of T.W. Fuller as the new chief architect in 1927.[5] Fuller would fulfil his duties with competence and assurance, but his appointment had no perceptible impact on the organization or character of the branch. Like many of his predecessors, Fuller was a career civil servant with no professional life outside the confines of the Department of Public Works. He had been hired as a draughtsman by his father and had slowly worked up through the system. In 1918 he became the assistant chief architect to Richard C. Wright; when Wright died in 1927, Fuller was the obvious successor.[6]

The pattern would repeat itself in 1936 with the appointment of Charles D. Sutherland as Fuller's successor. Sutherland had followed almost the same path in his career as Fuller. He had been hired in 1901 and had been promoted up through the ranks. In 1928 he became Fuller's assistant chief architect and his heir apparent. Both appointments assured a smooth, seamless transition in senior administration and an adherence to the status quo.

The members of the professional staff within the Chief Architect's Branch were moulded by the same bureaucratic environment. By 1927 there were thirty-one architects and engineers working within the branch; all but two had been hired prior to World War I, and their average age was approaching fifty. Although most had little or no professional experience outside the civil service, they were all very familiar with the business of designing buildings for government. Despite years of low productivity, the staff of the Chief Architect's Branch clearly demonstrated maturity and experience by successfully planning, designing, and supervising the construction of dozens of federal building projects with no major charges of poor planning or overspending. At the same time, the lack of challenging work over the previous decade had transformed the branch into a cloistered, insular world cut off from new architectural influences. The staff had formed their aesthetic sensibilities in the Edwardian era; these had also become fixed, and it showed in the work they produced.[7]

The conservative character of federal building during the late 1920s and early 1930s can only partly be explained as a case of arrested architectural development on the part of the Chief Architect's Branch. In some cases, it was the inevitable result of reviving projects that had been planned in the 1910s. For example, the Confederation Building in Ottawa, construction of which began in 1928, had grown out of the recommendations and drawings presented in the report of the Federal Plan Commission. In Calgary, plans for a new federal building had been prepared in 1918; when money once again became available in 1927, the staff simply dusted off the old files and set to work.[8]

One of the largest projects of this period was a new customs house in Toronto; it too could trace the origins of its design to the pre-war era.[9] The issue of a new customs house was first raised in the early 1900s, and in 1911 a public building on the same site and of the same general scale was included in a proposed redevelopment of the downtown area by John Lyle, a project that had been commissioned by the Civic Improvement Committee of Toronto.[10] In Lyle's plan the building was depicted with a straight façade, but by 1913 a recommendation had been put forward for a large curved front that would follow the existing line of Front Street. Although it is not known whether detailed drawings were prepared, the building was obviously intended to conform visually to Lyle's grand Beaux-Arts design for the new Union Station (1915–20) further down the street.

The Toronto Customs House epitomizes the competent but conservative designs produced by the Chief Architect's Branch during these years (Figure 6.1). It is a well-balanced, well-proportioned composition; combined with the neighbouring Union Station, it creates a grand and visually coherent streetscape reflecting the sense of urban drama and grandeur that defined City Beautiful aesthetics. Its design is similar in many respects to the Montreal Customs House that was begun almost twenty years earlier. Following typical classical conventions, the design is built on a heavy stone base articulated by deeply channelled stonework and is punctuated by semicircular bays. The main façade is divided horizontally into three main components: a central projecting pavilion featuring six free-standing Ionic columns is balanced by two slightly projecting end pavilions. The intervening walls are accented by a row of Ionic pilasters that support the strong vertical lines of the cornice and attic. Queenston limestone exterior masks a reinforced concrete frame that was constructed in two phases. The east wing and the central pavilion were built in 1929–31, and the west wing was built in 1934–5. Although the two sections are expressed as one unified design, originally there was no internal connection between the two sections and the floor levels of the two sections did not match up.

In 1936 Percy Nobbs, a well-known Montreal architect, teacher, and critic, wrote of the work of the Chief Architect's Branch: 'The architects of the Department of Public Works may be occasionally somewhat wanting in their detailing, but they are wonderfully competent in their planning and most of their buildings mass and group well.'[11] This perceptive comment might well have been made in reference to the Toronto Customs House. The overall design projects an air of grandeur and dignity appropriate to a major federal building, but a closer look at the building reveals an economical, 'no frills' approach to the finishing. On the exterior the shafts of the pilasters and columns have been left plain, the cornice features a very simple moulding, and the keystones and spandrels, which were typically enriched with carved ornamentation, have been left unadorned. The main entrance under the central portico opens into a fairly modest hall and elevator lobby that is finished with marble floors and dado. Only the customs long room, which is the focus of the interior, escaped this frugal treatment. Continuing a tradition that dated back to the original Toronto Customs House of 1873–6, the long room is an impressive public space that extends through two storeys. It features a coffered ceiling supported by two rows of piers with gold-painted Corinthian capitals (Figure 6.2). The remainder of the building contained standard government office space and an examining warehouse.[12]

Small Federal Buildings: Design by Precedent

Large projects represented only a small percentage of the buildings constructed during the late 1920s and early 1930s. As always, most of the branch's work was concerned with the construction of smaller, less expensive public buildings. The talents of the staff of the Chief Architect's Branch and their facility with classical composition were most obvious on mid-sized public buildings constructed in small cities and regional centres. Two of the best surviving examples of this type are the public buildings in Moncton, New Brunswick, and in Fort William (now Thunder Bay),

6.1. Customs House, Front Street, Toronto, Ontario, 1929–31 and 1934–5. Designed by the Chief Architect's Branch. (J. Wright, Parks Canada, 1991)

Ontario (Figures 6.3 and 6.4).[13] They belong to a group of buildings that were designed in 1931 but whose construction was temporarily delayed by cutbacks in spending imposed between 1931 and 1933. Both feature a deeply channelled and rusticated base that supports the top two floors and is articulated by pilasters interspaced by deeply set windows and separated vertically by metal spandrels. On this slightly reduced scale, the branch's characteristic economy in detail is not as evident and the façades, with their projecting pavilions and free-standing columns recessed between two heavy piers, impart a sense of monumentality and sculptural variety.

The largest single group of buildings constructed by the Chief Architect's Branch was made up of small public buildings and post offices that were erected in small towns and rural municipalities. They were designed to meet fairly standard functional and spatial requirements, and so a few basic patterns were developed which could then be modified to individual sites. Some of these patterns were already very familiar in the repertoire of federal architecture. For example, the public building in Lloydminster, Saskatchewan, constructed in 1931–2, with its corner tower and round-arched windows, is a direct descendent of the typical Ewart post office of the pre-war era (Figure 6.5). Only the use of flat roof and a domed tower sets this building apart from the earlier generation of design, which usually featured a hipped roof with a pyramidal clock tower.

Other common formulas show no discernible evolution in design from the early 1900s. The public building in Parry Sound, Ontario (Figure 6.6), was atypical in its use of a third storey, but the basic brick block, with two flanking entrances, round-arched windows on the ground floor, and the branch's 'stock' classical detail, could easily be mistaken for the architectural contemporary of Postal Station C in Toronto built in 1902.[14]

The post office at Hantsport, Nova Scotia, illustrates a very common pattern of design, which first appeared in the late 1920s (Figure 6.7). A one-and-a-half-storey block surmounted by a truncated hipped roof, it was built of brick and featured a three-bay façade with a central projecting frontispiece capped by a small parapeted gable. The main floor was occupied by the post office, which was divided in half by a counter and

6.2. Customs Long Room, Customs House, Toronto, Ontario. (Public Works and Government Services Canada, Heritage Recording and Technical Data Services, 1993)

6.3. Dominion Building, Moncton, New Brunswick, 1934–6. Plans prepared by the Chief Architect's Branch in 1931. (NA, PA-135584)

Dominion Observatory, Central Experimental Farm, Ottawa, Ontario, 1899–1900. Designed by the Chief Architect's Branch. (Wayne Duford, Canadian Inventory of Historic Buildings, 1986)

Centre Block, Parliament Buildings, Ottawa, Ontario, 1916–27. Architect: John A. Pearson; associate: J.-Omer Marchand. (A. Guindon, Parks Canada, 1993)

Federal Building, Regina, Saskatchewan, 1935–7. Architects: Reilly and Portnall. (Public Works and Government Services Canada, Heritage Recording and Technical Data Services, 1981)

First-Class Detention Building (top), lavatories (bottom), Grosse Île, Quebec, 1912. Designed by the Chief Architect's Branch. (J.P. Jérôme, Parks Canada, 1996)

Detail of relief panel, City Delivery Building, Toronto, Ontario, 1939–40. Designed by Charles B. Dolphin (C. Cameron, Parks Canada, 1989)

Connaught Building, Sussex Street, Ottawa, Ontario, 1913–16. Designed by the Chief Architect's Branch. (M. Trépanier, Parks Canada, 1993)

Drill Hall, Halifax, Nova Scotia, 1893. Plans prepared by the Chief Architect's Branch. (Public Works and Government Services Canada, Heritage Recording and Technical Data Services, 1988)

Dominion Building, Winnipeg, Manitoba, 1934–7. Designed by George W. Northwood. (Public Works and Government Services Canada, Heritage Recording and Technical Data Services, 1982)

Lobby, Dominion Building, Hamilton, Ontario, 1935–7. Architects: Hutton and Souter. (Public Works and Government Services Canada, Heritage Recording and Technical Data Services, 1993)

Post Office, Dawson City, Yukon, 1900–2. Designed by T.W. Fuller
(J. Butterill, Parks Canada, 1996)

Victoria Memorial Museum, Ottawa, Ontario, 1905–8. Designed by the
Chief Architect's Branch. (M. Trépanier, Parks Canada, 1993)

supported down the middle by two steel columns. A one-storey customs examining warehouse was often located in a rear wing in this design, and a caretaker's apartment was provided in the attic. Although there were some exceptions, most were built for communities with populations of less than 1,500, at an average cost of around $16,000.[15] Between 1927 and 1935 approximately thirty post offices of this type were constructed in all provinces of the country.

The 'bungalow style' post office was another recurring design. Most were one-storey, hipped-roof buildings with a centre door flanked by tripartite sash windows; a few employed a more steeply pitched mansard roof (Figure 6.8). Built at a cost of between $7,000 and $10,000, this type represented the bottom end of the public building chain and was usually found in small rural communities with populations of less than 1,000.[16] About twenty were constructed between 1927 and 1939. The number would probably have been higher had the deputy minister, James B. Hunter, not intervened. He rarely interfered with the design work of the Chief Architect's Branch, but on seeing plans for one more of these post offices cross his desk, he was compelled to write: 'I do not think I would have any more public buildings designed along that line because, in my opinion, it does not look like a public building at all, but rather like a bungalow. I think the staff can do a great deal better than that.'[17] After that comment, the 'bungalow style' post office was dropped from the repertoire of the branch.

The Postal Terminal: Industrialization of the Mail

The late 1920s saw the development of a new building type known as the postal terminal. During the 1920s the volume of mail in Canada had increased rapidly in response to a general growth in population and, more importantly, to the rapid expansion in mail-order businesses and their catalogues. The postal terminal did not replace the standard urban post office; instead, it functioned as a central mail distribution and forwarding centre for an entire region.

The Montreal Postal Terminal, designed in 1931 and constructed in

6.4. Dominion Public Building, Fort William (now Thunder Bay), Ontario, 1934–5. Plans prepared by the Chief Architect's Branch in 1931. (Public Works and Government Services Canada, Real Property Branch, Ontario, 1994)

6.5. Public Building, Lloydminster, Saskatchewan, 1931–2. Designed by the Chief Architect's Branch. The building was sold by the federal government and it now houses the municipal offices. (Frank Korvemaker, Heritage Branch, Government of Saskatchewan, 1990)

1934–7, was the first purpose-built example of this type in Canada (Figure 6.9).[18] During the 1920s the post office began to apply 'straight line' production systems to the business of mail handling and sorting, and these systems, first developed for the mass-production of manufactured goods, called for a very different type of building. Like the customs examining warehouse, which fulfilled a similar function, the Montreal Postal Terminal featured a steel-frame, fireproof construction, an open plan, and large windows to let in ample natural light. Although a public post office was located on the ground floor, most of the interior of this massive seven-storey structure was taken up by the industrial style work space that was required to accommodate the new mail processing equipment. The very simple exterior design, with its tall slender brick piers linked by flattened Gothic arches, was developed to accommodate this interior configuration.

Border Crossing Stations: Monitoring the Frontier

During the 1920s the volume of private and commercial traffic on the road and crossing the Canada–United States border rose steadily as automobile transportation became more efficient and more reliable and as the cost of the new mass-produced cars fell to within the means of the middle class. A few border crossing stations had been built after the World War I, but the system of monitoring goods and people moving in and out of the country remained very lax.[19] The need for tighter controls became a political issue when it was revealed in the House of Commons that some customs officials in Quebec were accepting bribes to 'look the other way' when large quantities of liquor were illegally shipped across the border into the United States.[20] The resulting scandal brought down the Liberal government in 1926. When the party was returned to power later in the year, one of its first building priorities was to establish a network of permanent customs and immigration stations at the major points of entry along the border.[21]

The stations built in the late 1920s tended to be simple brick or wood-frame buildings with wide canopies extending out on both sides to shelter cars as they stopped at the checkpoint.[22] In 1932 a new design emerged that reflected the growing appreciation of these roadside buildings as the gateways to the nation. In the early 1930s this interest was partly spurred on by the building campaign in the United States to erect substantial brick customs offices at important border crossings. On several occasions the Department of Public Works justified the construction of a new customs and immigration building on the grounds that there was a fine new building under construction a few hundred yards down the highway.[23] The new design type, which was used at Beebe (1932), Trout River (1932), and Lacolle (1934–5) in Quebec, and at Pacific Highway, in Surrey, British Columbia (1935–6), was a one-and-a-half-storey building with white stuccoed walls that were accented with half-timbering under the gables (Figure 6.10). Although modest in comparison with its American counterparts, the picturesque Tudor style of these buildings contrasted with the predominantly colonial Georgian style of buildings on the other side of the line. The Canadian government obviously chose an architectural theme that would set their buildings apart, thus symbolizing the cultural and political differences between the two nations.

Building for Research

The federal government's research programs were becoming an increasingly important client group for the Department of Public Works. The Department of Agriculture continued to maintain its own engineering branch, but it called upon the services of the Chief Architect's Branch for many of its general-purpose office and research buildings. The design of the Horticultural Building at the Central Experimental Farm in Ottawa, built in 1928–9, represented a recurring theme in the work of the Chief Architect's Branch. Since about 1910 the Tudor Manor style, with its pitched roof, gables, and decorative half-timbering, had been the preferred style for small government structures, such as quarantine stations and experimental farms, that were situated in rural, park-like settings characteristic of non-urban federal complexes.

The Department of Mines (reorganized as the Department of Mines and Resources in 1936) was in the 1930s in the process of expanding its

6.6. Public Building, Parry Sound, Ontario, 1931–2. Designed by the Chief Architect's Branch. (Public Works and Government Services Canada, Real Property Branch, Ontario, 1994)

6.7. Post Office, Hantsport, Nova Scotia, 1929–30. Designed by the Chief Architect's Branch. (J. Wright, Parks Canada, 1985)

research facilities on Booth Street in Ottawa with the construction of three new buildings.[24] The site, located in an industrial area, did not invite the use of the Tudor Manor style. Instead, the three buildings, which were commissioned to Ottawa architect W.E. Noffke, resemble a common post office plan, and are defined by a two-storey brick block modestly detailed in a classical style. The rear wings adopted quite a different plan. Designed to accommodate the heavy equipment and machinery required to carry out research studies in fuels and metallurgy, these spaces were open work-areas with high ceilings, fireproof construction, and steel-sash windows. One of the wings had a monitor roof to provide natural overhead light and ventilation. Although some modifications have been carried out to meet current construction standards as well as changing program research needs, all three buildings still function as research laboratories.

The most important project in this area was the new headquarters of the National Research Council of Canada. Established in 1916 as the Honorary Advisory Council for Scientific and Industrial Research, the council's original function was to advise the government on the state of industrial research in Canada, provide leadership and guidance to the broader scientific community, and promote research through a system of grants and fellowships. In 1925 its mandate was expanded. Renamed the National Research Council (NRC), it began to hire staff and to maintain an active research program. At first NRC staff occupied rented and borrowed quarters, but in 1928 a proposal for a new building and powerhouse was given government approval. The government suggested a national design competition but the council argued against this time-consuming process. In 1929 the prominent Toronto firm of C.B. Sproatt and E.R. Rolph was appointed architect to the new National Research Council Building (Figure 6.11).[25]

The NRC building was the first major project commissioned to a private architect since the reconstruction of the Centre Block on Parliament Hill. A finely crafted building, noted for the high quality of its materials and for the richness and sophistication of its detail, it contrasted with the more frugal standards applied to departmental designs, such as the Toronto Customs House. The challenge of the project was to develop an interior plan that could accommodate the building's dual function as the administrative headquarters of an important national institution and as a practical laboratory facility devoted to industrial research.

To address the problem the architects created a plan that ingeniously integrated the two functions into a hierarchy of spaces. The central axis of the building contains the formal public spaces. The main entrance opens into an elegant stair hall with a double elliptical staircase executed in cream-coloured travertine marble. The main floor rotunda, which features a fresco on the ceiling depicting the night sky, leads into a 300-seat auditorium. Above this level is a two-storey library and reading-room, with a monumental arcade broken by a mezzanine level lit by clerestory windows. The rest of the building is organized around two courtyards on either side of the main axis. The front half of the building is allocated to administrative offices and conference rooms, while the outer wings and the rear of the building are taken up by research laboratories. As requested by the council, the latter areas were equipped with moveable wall partitions to allow for easy rearrangement of work spaces and were finished with fireproof materials, including industrial style steel-sash doors.

The exterior design expresses little of the building's function as a centre of applied industrial research. Instead, the architects chose to encase this dual-function structure in a grand Beaux-Arts shell that could easily be mistaken for a court-house, a town hall, or any other important public building. The principal elevation adopts a symmetrical pattern that is divided into four sections arranged on either side of the central frontispiece and separated by two secondary pavilions. The main entrance, which is marked by a pediment supported by two heavy piers and two free-standing Doric columns, provides an impressive introduction to the principal public spaces – the hall, an auditorium, and a library. The two flanking sections, which are marked by the rich Doric colonnade, correspond to the main administrative offices. The two outer wings and the rear and side elevations, which are more plainly articulated and feature a wider window, correspond to the laboratory space.

The choice of a classical style for this building, and the apparent dichotomy between its Beaux-Arts form and its industrial research function, brought criticism from Toronto architect Eric Arthur:

6.8. Post Office, Broadview, Saskatchewan, 1936–7. Designed by the Chief Architect's Branch. (Public Works and Government Services Canada, Western Region, 1987)

6.9. Postal Terminal, Montreal, Quebec, 1934–7. Designed by the Chief Architect's Branch in 1931. (NA, PA-61866)

If you sent an architectural student such a problem, he would think immediately of those mighty factories of Erick Mendelsohn in Berlin. He would think of light and power and the majesty of science. Sproatt and Rolph have been concerned only with the majesty of state . . . Its great façade suggests nothing but the civil service; of myriads of clerks in myriads of offices.[26]

Arthur's suggestion that the architects should have sought inspiration from the German modernists indicates a new interest, in some circles, in the new functionalist architecture of Europe. He did not, however, reflect the architectural values dominant in Canada in the 1930s.

The decision to adopt a monumental classical style for this building was dictated, to some extent, by its site on Sussex Drive, which continued to be regarded as an important scenic and ceremonial route linking Government House with Parliament Hill. More significantly, the choice of style is indicative of the enduring strength of the Beaux-Arts tradition in Canadian architecture. To Eric Arthur the design represented a clichéd response to public building, but for most Canadian architects the language of classicism was deeply ingrained in their perception of what a public building should look like and what sort of image it should project. Sproatt and Rolph belonged to an older generation of Canadian architects who were nearing the end of their professional careers, and, like many of the staff of the Chief Architect's Branch, they represented the most conservative trends in Canadian architecture. As will be seen, architects of a slightly younger generation were reacting against the academic historicism of the Beaux-Arts style but their concept of public architecture would still be defined within the framework of the classical tradition.

The Public Works Construction Act, 1934

The stock market crash of October 1929 did not bring about the immediate collapse of all sectors of the economy. The momentum of growth of the late 1920s sustained the economy through the early years of the Depression, thereby masking the long-term implications of the decline.[27]

6.10. Pacific Highway, Customs and Immigration Building, Surrey, British Columbia, 1935–6. Plans prepared by the Chief Architect's Branch. Demolished in the 1980s. (E. Mills, Parks Canada, 1984)

6.11. National Research Council Building, Ottawa, Ontario, 1929–32. Designed by C.B. Sproatt and E.R. Rolph. (Public Works and Government Services Canada, Heritage Recording and Technical Data Services, 1982)

In 1930 the Conservative Party under R.B. Bennett defeated the Liberal government with a promise to revitalize the economy and to bring a quick end to unemployment. Its strategy was based upon conventional remedies of increased tariffs to protect and stimulate growth in Canadian industry and manufacturing. Unemployment was seen as a short-term problem to be dealt with through direct relief and through the creation of labour-intensive make-work projects, such as highway construction.

By 1932 the situation had worsened. In February, 25 per cent of the labour force was unemployed and the cost of relief, coupled with declining government revenues, produced growing deficits at all levels of government. The unstable economy was further undermined by the British decision to drop the gold standard in favour of sterling. Because the Canadian dollar was closely tied to the British pound, its value against the U.S. dollar plummeted. To reinforce Canada's currency and achieve a balanced budget, the government quickly imposed a policy of strict fiscal restraint. Relief programs were cut back, taxes were raised, and all federal expenditures were slashed.[28]

The momentum created by the building boom begun in 1927 kept the budget of the Department of Public Works at high levels through the early years of the Depression. In fact, the largest annual budget for new construction was recorded in the fiscal year 1930–1, when many of the big projects begun in the late 1920s were brought to completion. In 1932, however, the government's policy of restraint had an immediate impact on the activities of the Chief Architect's Branch. Many projects for which plans and estimates had been prepared were cancelled, and no new projects were initiated. In less than two years the budget for new construction fell from a high of $8,760,000 to $833,730 in 1933–4.

During the first quarter of 1933 the Canadian economy was at its lowest point. Unemployment had risen to 30 per cent and the cost of maintaining basic relief programs was threatening to bankrupt many provincial and municipal governments. If the federal government was to survive the next election, it would have to demonstrate an ability to turn things around. In 1932 Franklin D. Roosevelt had won an impressive presidential victory on a platform of economic recovery. Roosevelt's New Deal was influenced by the writings of John Maynard Keynes, a British economist who argued in favour of deficit government spending on useful capital projects. They would provide employment and stimulate the economy of the private sector while improving the country's infrastructure of public works. An important component of Roosevelt's platform was the creation of the Public Works Administration (PWA), which allocated $3.3 billion in supplementary funds for public works projects.[29]

The PWA was introduced to Congress in May 1933 and throughout that year pressure mounted on the Canadian government to implement a similar program.[30] In January 1934 Prime Minister Bennett instructed Major-General Andrew McNaughton, a co-director of the government's relief camps, to draw up plans and estimates for a Canadian version of the PWA. McNaughton's proposal outlined an ambitious program of works, which included the extension of the Trans-Canada Highway, airport construction, dams and irrigation projects, housing, reforestation, aid to municipal and provincial public works, and many new government buildings. The cost of this proposal was estimated at $70 million annually.[31] The prime minister was politically committed to some sort of spending program, but he was also a fiscal conservative who was reluctant to run up such a huge deficit.

The Public Works Construction Act was finally presented to Parliament in June 1934. It outlined a comparatively modest program that allocated only $40 million to be spent on 185 projects over the course of several years.[32] Of this budget, $19.5 million was to be spent on new government buildings. At the same time, the normal operating budget of the Department of Public Works for new construction and for maintenance and repair was also restored to pre-Depression levels. Priority was given to projects that would provide long-term employment or where government rental costs were high.[33] These criteria tended to favour large-scale projects in major urban centres. To maximize their stimulative effect, wage tables were established, the use of manual labour was encouraged, and the use of Canadian materials was made mandatory wherever possible. The type of construction – either steel or reinforced concrete – was also dictated by the department in order to ensure an equitable distribution of work between the two most powerful sectors of the construction industry. The program was also strategically designed so that most of the money went to Conservative-held ridings. Not surprisingly, the seat of Calgary West, held by R.B. Bennett, was the largest single beneficiary, receiving projects amounting to $1.5 million.[34]

The program, however, was not a political success, and from the beginning it was criticized as 'too little, too late.'[35] Although the economy in general was showing signs of improving by 1935, the program failed to revive the credibility of the Conservative government; in the election of October 1935 it suffered one of the biggest electoral defeats in history.

The Public Works Construction Act did, however, have a profound effect on the character of federal architecture and it signalled a change in the role of the Chief Architect's Branch in government construction. Initially the branch had assumed that it would be responsible for most of the new design work. Over the summer and fall of 1934 the branch prepared for the increased workload by hiring two assistant architects, six junior architects, five draughtsmen, and four structural and mechanical engineers.[36] Meanwhile, architectural organizations, such as the Royal Architectural Institute of Canada and the various provincial associations, pressured the government to turn more of the work over to independent architects. This professional lobby, which had first emerged in the early 1900s, had been relatively quiet after the war, primarily because there was so little government work. When construction started up again in 1927, so did the lobbying campaign, and it intensified in the 1930s when work in the private sector dried up.

The tone and content of the debate had not changed since the early 1900s. Government buildings should reflect the highest standards of architecture in the country, and government architects had fallen well short in their pursuit of this ideal. As expressed in a petition of 1928 from the Royal Architectural Institute of Canada: 'Public buildings, especially when of any magnitude, are expected to exemplify the culture of the community, but as yet this is hardly true of Canada.'[37] Government architects were not incompetent but, as was pointed out in many letters, they were salaried civil servants who did not depend upon their good reputation to maintain a healthy practice. For this reason, there was little incentive to keep pace with new developments. Moreover, government architects lacked the freedom of action and the sense of competition with confrères that produced good architecture. The working environment within a big federal bureaucracy – the division of responsibilities and the limitations imposed on individual creativity – gave them 'little or no opportunity to give the problem their best individual effort.'[38]

At first the department defended the use of its staff. In a letter to the president of the Royal Architectural Institute of Canada, the minister of public works pointed out that it was cheaper to pay civil service salaries than to pay the 5 per cent commission due a private architect. Government architects were more familiar with the needs of the clients and could prepare designs faster, more efficiently, and with minimal cost overruns. Private architects, on the other hand, tended to exceed appropriations and their designs did not always meet acceptable standards. By relying on permanent staff, the department was also able to avoid the sensitive issue of patronage appointments, which resulted in little real political benefit to the party. In the previous seven years the Chief Architect's Branch had demonstrated its ability to carry out successfully a large building program, and the bureaucracy clearly intended that it should take charge of the work generated by the Public Works Construction Act.

Political pressure and the desire to provide employment to a profession hard hit by the Depression forced a change in policy. By November 1934 twenty-seven architects had received government commissions; almost all of the big, 'high-profile' projects had been commissioned.[39] As always, the selection process was tinged by patronage. Responsibility for appointments lay with the minister of public works, who in turn acted on the recommendations of the party caucus. As soon as the program was announced, letters from architects soliciting work began flooding in to the minister and to members of Parliament. The unabashedly political nature of the process is well illustrated by a letter in 1934 from a Montreal member of Parliament to the minister regarding the possible appointment of an architect to supervise an extension to the Montreal Customs House: 'His name would certainly not be well received by our Conservative friends and for obvious reasons. Although he comes from a Conservative family, he has never taken any part in our organizations and has always been with our opponents.'[40] The member recommended another, 'more acceptable,' architect, who was subsequently given the contract.

Redefining the Federal Image: The Influence of Modern Classicism

Although the program produced its share of mediocre buildings during the Depression, the decision to employ outside architects clearly had a revitalizing effect on federal architecture. The late 1920s and early 1930s had represented an exciting and dynamic phase in the history of Canadian architecture. It was a period of change and transformation created by a tension between divergent and often conflicting architectural and aesthetic values. By the mid-1920s the new modernism of the European avant-garde – exemplified by the work of De Stijl in the Netherlands, the Bauhaus in Germany, and Le Corbusier in France – was becoming familiar to a broader audience and attracting followers in Britain, Europe, and, to a lesser extent, the United States. Canadian architects were aware of these developments and they found much to admire, but they could not deny the architectural traditions in which they had been trained. As expressed by one architect: 'The difficulty of putting scholarship and tradition into the waste paper basket is that we deprive ourselves of the very phrases out of which we make our sentences, the paragraphs and the whole compositions in architecture.'[41] Instead, Canadian architects, like most North American and European architects, advocated a middle road between past and present.

Mainstream architecture of the late 1920s and the 1930s sought a fusion or reconciliation of academic traditions and modernity that would avoid the restricting historicism of the former and the decorative and cultural poverty of the latter.[42] It was a period and an approach to design that is identified by a variety of stylistic labels. The most widely used term, Art Deco, was derived from the Exposition des Arts Décoratifs et Industriels, an industrial exhibition held in Paris in 1925 that had brought to popular attention the new modernistic trends in decorative design. Art Deco is a general term that can be applied to a wide variety of architectural styles for which more specific and descriptive labels have been developed. The 'moderne' style, with its curved lines and streamlined form, is most readily identified with movie theatres, gas stations, and commercial buildings. 'Modern' or 'stripped' classicism is a term used to describe an architecture rooted in the classical tradition but reinterpreted by new modernist concepts of simplicity, purity of form, and restraint in detail. Modern classicism is most commonly associated with public architecture.

The Chief Architect's Branch had continued during the late 1920s and early 1930s to build according to conventions that had been established twenty years earlier. In 1934 outside architects began introducing new ideas that would redefine the architectural image of the federal government.[43] The nature of this stylistic change is illustrated by a comparison between the Customs House in Toronto (which was still under construction in 1934) and the new Dominion Building in Hamilton, which was one of the first projects initiated under the Public Works Construction Act (Figure 6.12). Both are steel-frame buildings sheathed in limestone; their façades adopt the familiar classical syntax composed of a clearly defined base, column, and cornice. The difference between the two buildings lies in the quality of the detail and its relation to the underlying volumes. On the Toronto building the free-standing Ionic columns, string-courses, cornice, and entrance architrave project out from the structural wall, giving the façade a three-dimensional and sculptural quality. The Hamilton Dominion Building, on the other hand, adopts a reductive, rather than additive, approach to detail. The pilasters have been reduced to simple fluted strips and the classical 'orders' have been replaced by narrow bands decorated in a simple geometric pattern of circles and squares. The cornice is defined as a simple band, shallowly carved with stylized leaf and floral motifs. The detail has a flat, two-dimensional quality that looks as if it has been carved out of, or incised into, the taut skin of the limestone walls. This approach, which tends to accentuate the bold, simple volumes of the design, is a defining characteristic of modern classicism.

Breaking free of the rules and conventions of academic historicism also gave architects licence to develop a new decorative vocabulary drawn from

6.12. Dominion Building, Hamilton, Ontario, 1935–7. Designed by Hutton and Souter. (Public Works and Government Services Canada, Heritage Recording and Technical Data Services, 1984)

contemporary experience. The relief panel over the main entrance of the Hamilton Dominion Building is typical of the style and nationalistic imagery associated with the public architecture of the period (Figure 6.13). It depicts a series of allegorical figures representing industries and natural resources of Canada – agriculture, lumbering, fishing, and transportation. The images refer to Canadian themes but the style of rendering maintains a link with artistic conventions of the past. The heroic figures, with their muscular, twisting torsos, adopt poses that immediately recall Greek and Roman sculpture. This meshing of the contemporary with the historical, of modern with traditional, defines the unifying theme of Canadian architecture in the 1930s.

As was often characteristic of buildings designed on commission, the Hamilton Dominion Building was, by the standards of the Department of Public Works, unusually lavish in its finish and detail. This high quality of design and craftsmanship is most evident in the treatment of the principal public spaces inside. The main postal lobby, located on the ground floor to the left of the main entrance foyer, is classical in inspiration, but the space and the detail exudes a light, airy quality and imparts a sense of cool calmness that is characteristic of the modern classical style (Figure 6.14). Natural light floods in through the tall windows that punctuate the outside wall. The floor features four shades of marble, which is laid in a geometric pattern. This pattern is then echoed in the coffered ceiling above. The ceiling and the encircling frieze are executed in a soft, subtle mix of colours – mottled green, bronze, grey, silver, and touches of red. The interior detail is similar to the stylized geometric patterns found on the exterior. Canadian images also appear in the inlaid map of Canada situated over the counter area and in a series of medallions depicting a ship, a plane, a dogsled, and a train – all common themes in the realm of post office iconography. The interior has been beautifully maintained and still possesses many of its original furnishings, including beautifully wrought metal light fixtures and tall public writing tables in a light slender Greek style.

The Hamilton Dominion Building was just one of several major projects initiated under the provisions of the Public Works Construction Act. In Halifax, London, Winnipeg, Regina, and Vancouver large new

6.13. Detail of relief panel, Hamilton Dominion Building. From left to right are allegorical figures representing fishing, agriculture (harvesting and sowing), and the fur trade. (J. Wright, Parks Canada, 1985)

6.14. Postal Lobby, Hamilton Dominion Building. (Public Works and Government Services Canada, Heritage Recording and Technical Data Services, 1984)

buildings were begun in 1934 and 1935 and they all reflected the influence of the Art Deco or modern classical style. The Winnipeg Dominion Building, designed by George W. Northwood, represents a design solution that is not as obviously tied to the classical form (Figure 6.15).[44] Although its overall dimensions are not substantially different from those of the Hamilton building, the triangular plan, with its main façade focused on the apex of the triangle, gives the building a strong vertical emphasis. This effect is further accentuated by the tall thin piers that extend through the cornice line to create a visually open-ended form. The ornamentation along the top of the building resembles shafts of wheat. The motif seems particularly appropriate to Winnipeg but it is also a recurring element in the vocabulary of the Art Deco style.

The Halifax Dominion Building was the only major federal building assigned to the Chief Architect's Branch, and it demonstrates the adeptness of the branch staff in absorbing and mastering new approaches to design (Figure 6.16). Originally the project had been contracted to a private architect but he was dismissed when his proposal failed to meet departmental approval.[45] The branch's own proposal was clearly inspired by the new designs that would have been coming into the office at the time, in particular public buildings in London and Winnipeg.

The Halifax Dominion Building is a massive, seven-storey building occupying most of a city block. The ochre-coloured, Wallace sandstone walls sheath an unusual and experimental structural frame that combines steel and reinforced-concrete technologies.[46] The design avoids the simple rectangularity of the typical office block by breaking up the building's mass into a series of smaller volumes that build up towards the tall, central domed tower, which is set back from the street. Like the Winnipeg building, the sense of height is accentuated by the tall thin piers that separate the windows. The overall design compares well with those by private architects but, once again, the branch's more frugal standards in construction prevailed. Some maritime motifs – anchors, dolphins, sea horses, waves, and ships – have been worked into the decorative vocabulary but these enrichments are generally limited to the main entrance, some of the metal grill work over the ground floor windows, and the entrance lobby. Generally the quality of finish – both exterior and interior – lacks the richness and variety of the commissioned buildings that have been discussed.

The influence of modern classicism was equally evident on smaller projects designed either on commission or by the branch. The federal buildings in Prince Rupert, British Columbia, and in Kitchener, Ontario, provide two good examples of this level of facility (Figures 6.17 and 6.18). In both, the symmetrical massing, with a central entrance and two flanking wings, conforms to a standard classical formula, but the walls adopt the flat planar quality and shallow, stylized detail characteristic of the period. The Kitchener building is sheathed in the local Queenston limestone, but the Prince Rupert building provides an unusual example of monolithic concrete construction. The original specifications had called for brick but the architect recommended concrete as a versatile and inexpensive alternative.[47] Most commonly employed on the West Coast, particularly in California, concrete could be painted any colour and its smooth, highly finished surface could be scored to resemble stone. It was ideally suited to the tastes of the period for light colours and clean, crisp lines. The exterior of the building, which now serves as the Prince Rupert City Hall, has been embellished with decorative motifs drawn from Native art of the West Coast; although the work on the exterior is a recent addition, it has a natural aesthetic affinity with the original style.

By the late 1930s some architects employed by the branch were moving further away from their classical roots to a more progressively modern vocabulary. Two of the best examples of this trend can be seen in Postal Station K and the City Delivery Building, both in Toronto (Figures 6.19 and 6.20).[48] Postal Station K retains a sense of classical symmetry and order but recognizable classical forms have been eliminated. Two obelisks, surmounted by a lion and a unicorn, provide decorative accents to the main entrance. They are detached from the building to appear as free-standing sculptures that do not detract from the simplicity of the basic building volume.

The slightly later City Delivery Building, which, like the Montreal Postal Terminal, served as a mail sorting and distribution centre, is an

6.15. Dominion Building, Winnipeg, Manitoba, 1934–7. Designed by George W. Northwood. (Public Works and Government Services Canada, Heritage Recording and Technical Data Services, 1982)

6.16. Dominion Building, Halifax, Nova Scotia, 1935–7. Designed by the Chief Architect's Branch. (NA, PA-124522)

idiosyncratic mix of styles.[49] The main façade prominently features a row of simple pilasters – a common motif of modern classicism – but the wraparound windows on the outer corners of the building are associated with the more radical European modernism of the International style. By the mid-1930s the influence of modernism was becoming increasingly evident in the work of some Canadian architects, particularly in the area of residential and commercial design. In the City Delivery Building the architect simply borrowed a motif associated with the movement and applied it to a modern classical design. The City Delivery Building is also notable for its series of relief panels that are embedded into the stonework. Typical of the period, they depict Canadian themes to represent the many ways in which mail was transported in Canada but interpreted very differently than those on the relief panel on the Hamilton Dominion Building. Set at eye level, the panels more closely resemble landscape paintings that are applied to the walls than architectural ornamentation that is integrated into the design of the building.

Not all federal buildings constructed during the Depression conformed to this architectural image. Canadian architects of the 1930s and even the 1940s maintained an eclectic approach and felt free to draw upon a variety of vocabularies and styles, often moving back and forth with considerable ease between a very traditional historicism and designs inspired by the new modernism. For example, the Dominion Public Building of 1935–6 in Amherst, Nova Scotia, is a beautifully executed building designed in a very academic interpretation of the Greek Doric style (Figure 6.21).[50] The architect, Leslie Fairn of Halifax, was a leading exponent of the modern classical idiom in the Maritimes, but for this commission he decided that a more traditional vocabulary would be appropriate.

The Château style, although certainly declining in fashion, was considered symbolically appropriate in certain situations. In Ottawa it was still regarded as the official style for government buildings within the parliamentary precinct, but by the late 1930s it had been substantially redefined in terms of modern classical values. Ernest Cormier's design for the Supreme Court in Ottawa represents modern classical reduced to the most simple and pristine forms. In accordance with government policy Cormier added a steeply pitched Château roof, but it is treated as an

6.17. Federal Building, Prince Rupert, British Columbia, 1937–8. Designed by Max Downing. (J. Wright, Parks Canada, 1993)

6.18. Public Building, Kitchener, Ontario, 1937–8. Designed by the Chief Architect's Branch. (J. Wright, Parks Canada, 1985)

emblematic gesture rather than an integral part of the design.

More orthodox examples of the Château style are found in Quebec, where the cultural associations of the style retained their symbolic relevance. The postal terminal in Quebec City (Figure 6.22), begun in 1939, was an unusually picturesque interpretation of the Château style, with its asymmetrical plan, irregular roofline with towers and ornate Gothic dormers, and rich polychromatic surfaces composed of red brick with cut-stone quoins and trim. Designed to harmonize with the nearby CPR railway station of 1915, it reflects a long tradition of important public buildings that promoted a romantic French image for the City of Quebec. The Chief Architect's Branch also developed a 'French' style building for several smaller communities. The earliest examples date from the late 1920s but most were built between 1934 and 1939.[51] The post office of 1938–9 at Pointe-au-Pic, with its steeply pitched, *pavillon* roof and cut-stone frontispiece, provides a good example of this type (Figure 6.23).

Small Federal Buildings: Developing New Policies

The Chief Architect's Branch maintained exclusive design control over small federal buildings and post offices, and here the institutional stamp of the branch, with its tendency to work within two or three basic formulas, is evident. The first buildings erected under the Depression works program conformed to patterns that had been established in the 1920s. The typical red-brick, two-storey post office, with government offices and a caretaker's apartment on the second floor, remained the standard for small towns. The only visible change was in the definition of the detail, which by 1935 began to show the influence of modern classicism. The Federal Public Building of 1935–6 in Kingsville, Ontario, illustrates the nature of these transformations (Figure 6.24). The basic plan and elevation of the early twentieth century remain unchanged but the detail has been reduced to the simplest forms. The projecting moulded cornice and the pedimented entrance has been replaced by a flat, stylized stone trim along the roofline and around the two principal entrances.

Around 1936 the federal government began to implement new policies that would have significant impact on the character of these small

6.19. Postal Station K, Toronto, Ontario, 1936–7. Designed by Murray Brown. (J. Wright, Parks Canada, 1985)

6.20. City Delivery Building, Toronto, Ontario, 1939–40. Designed by Charles B. Dolphin. (University of Calgary, Canadian Architectural Archives, Panda Collection, 541132-2)

6.21. Dominion Building, Amherst, Nova Scotia, 1935–6. Designed by Leslie Fairn. (Public Works and Government Services Canada, Heritage Recording and Technical Data Services, 1982)

6.22. Postal Terminal, Quebec City, 1939–40. Designed by Raoul Chênevert. No longer occupied by the Post Office, the building now houses Health Canada offices. (M. Trépanier, Parks Canada, 1989)

buildings and their role in their communities. By the 1930s all communities, no matter how small, had come to expect their own post office, and they enlisted their member of Parliament to ensure its delivery. Rather than refuse and take the political consequences, the Liberal government developed new standards of accommodation that would allow it to build more post offices at a lower cost per unit. In March 1936 Minister of Public Works P.-J.-A. Cardin handed down new guidelines to Fuller, who was then nearing retirement. Fuller responded: 'My understanding of the instructions given yesterday by the Honourable minister, is to the effect that we are to design small inexpensive, one-storey buildings, without caretaker's quarters.'[52] The instructions also specified that construction was to be in brick veneer, wood shingle, or stucco instead of stone. The buildings would provide only a slight increase in the amount of space previously occupied by the departments. The branch would also discourage ongoing consultations with the client departments in order to curb their tendency to demand larger, more expensive buildings than deemed necessary.

The implementation of these new policies had an immediate impact on the design of post offices. In 1936 several standard one-and-a-half-storey post offices, which had been planned and for which estimates had been submitted, were withdrawn and new plans for smaller, one-storey buildings were substituted. The change resulted in a 50 per cent reduction in construction costs – a decrease from an average of $16,000 to $8,000 per building. After 1936 the typical federal post office was a one-storey brick block with a three-bay façade and either a central or an off-centre entrance. At first, the designs favoured a more conventional classical detail, as illustrated by the post office in Salmon Arm, British Columbia (Figure 6.25).[53] As the decade progressed, the plan and elevation changed little but the detail and finish showed the influence of modern classicism. The 1939 post office in Woodville, Ontario, with its simple stone frontispiece with inset quarter-round columns, represents a variation of the most common design theme (Figure 6.26). Between 1935 and 1939 more than fifty of these one-storey post offices were constructed by the Chief Architect's Branch.

6.23. Post Office, Pointe-au-Pic, Quebec, 1938–9. Designed by the Chief Architect's Branch. (NA, PA-124534)

6.24. Federal Public Building, Kingsville, Ontario, 1935–6, as seen in the 1930s. Designed by the Chief Architect's Branch. Now demolished. (NA, C-70536)

Communities were not entirely pleased with the new policy. The larger the building, the larger the capital investment and the greater the prestige to the community. The department had been trying to cut costs in this area for some time but it had always met with resistance at the local level. As the chief architect reported in 1931: 'As you are aware, strenuous protest has been received in nearly every instance where we have attempted to erect a one-storey building.'[54] The job of caretaker, with its accompanying apartment, was regarded as a local perk that was usually given to a deserving supporter of the party in power, and local politicians hated to see it go. Communities were particularly annoyed when a neighbouring town had received a larger building only a few years earlier. Yet despite the protests, the government continued to press its policy. It was a compromise between the government's desire to control construction budgets and its attempt to satisfy the ambition of every small town to have its own federal building.

Armouries and the Royal Canadian Mounted Police

The latter half of the 1930s also brought the return of two clients that had bypassed the department's construction services for a few decades. Since the end of the nineteenth century the Royal Canadian Mounted Police (RCMP, previously the Royal North-West Mounted Police) had managed its own building inventory, contracting private architects to design and construct all new buildings. The working relationship between the RCMP and the Chief Architect's Branch would remain ambiguous throughout the 1930s, but in 1934 the branch was asked to manage several new building projects for several divisions in Ontario and the West. This work included a large addition to the barracks at Edmonton, a workshop, gymnasium, and small lecture hall at the Depot in Regina, and five new buildings for the RCMP headquarters at N Division near Rockcliffe Park in Ottawa. The main barracks in Ottawa is a red-brick structure with a very simple castellated roofline. Although designed by Ottawa architect A.J. Hazelgrove, the building respected the architectural traditions of the RCMP, which favoured a Gothic castellated style.[55]

Later buildings, such as the stables (1939–40), would adopt a more streamlined, modern classical style typical of the period.

The Department of Public Works also renewed a working relationship with the Department of National Defence (formerly Militia and Defence) with the construction of four new armouries under the provisions of the Public Works Construction Act and with supplementary funds.[56] The last armoury constructed by the Chief Architect's Branch had been the Mewata Armoury in Calgary of 1917–18, but judging from the buildings produced under its direction in the late 1930s the old design formulas were still acceptable. The 1939 armoury in Cornwall, Ontario, which was designed on contract by W.C. Beattie, features a two-storey administrative block that masks the large drill hall behind it (Figure 6.27). Constructed of stone with a steel-truss roof, it was the last federal armoury to adopt the medieval castellated theme that had defined the armoury in Canada since the late nineteenth century. Around 1935 the 14th Infantry Brigade would commission the Toronto firm of Marani, Lawson and Morris to design the Fort York Armoury in Toronto. Their innovative design, with parabolic reinforced-concrete roof and restrained classical exterior, would define new standards of design and engineering that would provide the model for later armouries in Canada.

Conclusion

The Depression decade had been creative and productive in federal architecture. In 1927 the Chief Architect's Branch was transformed from a sleepy backwater of bureaucracy into a busy architectural office. By 1930 over one hundred projects were under construction or in the planning stages. For the first six years of this program, the staff of the Chief Architect's Branch was responsible for almost all new designs and, once again, it clearly demonstrated its ability to manage a national construction program with efficiency and assurance. The buildings it produced were solidly constructed and competently designed, but they also reflected the most conservative trends in Canadian architecture. Beaux-Arts classicism and the Château style – dominant stylistic themes of the pre-war era –

6.25. Plan of the Post Office, Salmon Arm, British Columbia, 1935. Designed by the Chief Architect's Branch. (NA, PA-139630)

6.26. Post Office, Woodville, Ontario, 1939. Designed by the Chief Architect's Branch. (J. Wright, Parks Canada, 1992)

continued to shape the character of government buildings into the mid-1930s.

In 1934 the Department of Public Works abandoned its policy of in-house design. It was a political decision but it had a revitalizing effect on federal architecture. Outside architects introduced new models of design into the repertoire of federal building, and between 1934 and 1939 some of Canada's best examples of the Art Deco and modern classical style were constructed under the patronage of the federal government. The use of private architects also marked a turning point for the Chief Architect's Branch. Never again would it play a dominant role in the design of new buildings. As a result, federal architecture, although cautious and conservative by nature, would lose the distinct 'departmental character' that had defined government buildings since the era of Thomas Fuller in the late nineteenth century. The outbreak of war in 1939 would create a lull in business, but in the two decades following World War II the department would undertake the most extensive and expensive building program in its history. In these years the Chief Architect's Branch would have to adjust slowly to its loss of pre-eminence as the central design office and develop new roles for its staff as policy advisers, contract administrators, and real property managers.

6.27. Armoury, Cornwall, Ontario, 1939. Designed by W.C. Beattie. (Public Works and Government Services Canada, Heritage Recording and Technical Data Services, 1990)

CHAPTER SEVEN

Federal Architecture in Transition, 1939–1953

The period between 1939 and 1953 saw fundamental changes in both government and architecture that would challenge the old bureaucratic structures and the established approaches to federal building design. The rapid expansion of government – brought about by the introduction of new social programs, the growth of federal responsibilities in the areas of taxation, scientific research, and health, and, finally, the entry of Newfoundland into Confederation in 1949 – created a growing demand for many new public buildings. At the same time, architecture in Canada was entering a period of transformation. During the 1930s modernism had represented an aesthetic undercurrent in an architecture that remained tied to established traditions. By the 1940s federal design, like Canadian architecture in general, had entered a transitional phase as architects began to explore – tentatively and cautiously but with an increasing fluency – the language of modernism.

The 1940s and early 1950s also marked the end of an era for the Department of Public Works and the Chief Architect's Branch. The generation of administrators and professional staff that had dominated the branch since the early twentieth century all reached retirement during these years, leaving room for a new generation to take over. At the same time, the need for a reorganization within the branch was becoming increasingly apparent because the administrative burden of maintaining an expanding construction program and managing an ever-increasing federal building inventory threatened to overwhelm and immobilize the branch. During the 1940s the branch was able to continue its successful and active building program by delegating more and more work to the private sector, but it was also becoming apparent that the system could not sustain itself. By the early 1950s the bureaucracy's voracious appetite for new buildings was no longer being satisfied, and by 1953 the need for major reform within the Department of Public Works and the Chief Architect's Branch was widely acknowledged.

Wartime Building: Architectural Experimentation at the National Research Council

Following the outbreak of war in September 1939 all federal construction that was not directly tied to the war effort came to a halt. Once again, the Department of Public Works was primarily occupied with the construction of military hospitals and the provision of more office space in Ottawa for the temporarily swelling ranks of the civil service. In contrast to the last war, the infrastructure required to support the war effort in Canada was considerably more complex and sophisticated. The presence of a resident army assigned to home defence, the growth of the Canadian Navy to provide convoy protection on the East and West coasts, and new initiatives such as the British Commonwealth Air Training Plan created the need for new and expanded military bases across the country. The war effort also included an expanded program of scientific research for the National Research Council of Canada in areas that had a direct military application.

One of the first war projects was the construction of new NRC laboratories located on the eastern outskirts of Ottawa. The original NRC building, which had been completed in 1932, was an impressive work of architecture, but its laboratories were too small and inflexible for the large-scale engineering research carried out by the Division of Mechanical Engineering in fields such as aeronautics, hydrodynamics, structures, high-voltage electrical transmission systems, and radio direction finders.[1] The need for a new type of facility had been identified prior to the war by Major-General A.G.L. McNaughton, who had taken over as director of the council in 1935. Initially his requests for new buildings were ignored, but the threat of war in Europe pushed defence research to the forefront of government spending priorities.[2]

In May 1939 the government acquired 130 acres of farmland on the Ottawa River and in December of that year work began on the first of nine new buildings for the Division of Mechanical Engineering (Figures 7.1, 7.2 and 7.3).[3] Most were designed by Ottawa architect H. Gordon Hughes in close cooperation with the staff of the NRC. According to Montreal architect John Bland, who worked on some of the buildings as a student during the summer of 1941, the clients – the research scientists – had a good idea of the type of buildings that were required and they were also open to innovative ideas in design.[4] As requested by NRC staff, the new facilities were to be modelled after industrial buildings that could be quickly and inexpensively constructed, and easily adapted, altered, or even torn down and replaced as required.[5] A suburban site was chosen to provide better security and to isolate the research, which could be noisy and involve hazardous materials, from close contact with developed areas. The general appearance of the complex, with its uniformly designed buildings widely spaced along a central avenue, a gatehouse at the entrance and broad expanses of lawn, suggests something between a university campus and an industrial complex. Today, the Montreal Road campus in Ottawa has expanded to over thirty buildings.

The Aerodynamics Building was the first building to be erected on the site and its design and construction set the pattern for subsequent development (see Figure 7.1). The J.H. Parkin Building, as it would later be called, is a two-storey building constructed of steel frame with cinder-block infill and sheathed in stucco with a final coating of cement paint. It adopts a widely splayed V-shaped plan; the rounded front accents the cylindrical form of the vertical (or spinning) wind-tunnel behind it. The main block of the building contained laboratories, a library, seminar rooms, and executive offices on one side, and a horizontal wind-tunnel on the other. The unique function of this building demanded innovative solutions. For example, the eighty-foot vertical wind-tunnel, which was formed by an outer shell of quarter-inch steel plates held together by a system of welded braces, was considered an engineering triumph because it permitted the testing of much larger models than had been possible previously. Electrical raceways were located behind removable baseboards so that new wiring could be installed with minimal structural intervention.[6]

The Parkin Building and other wartime buildings at the NRC were clearly influenced by the example of early modernism as it had emerged in Europe and, to a lesser extent, in the United States in the 1920s. These structures, with their broad, smooth planes of stucco wall surfaces, low-slung profiles, rounded corners, and ribbon windows that sometimes wrapped around the corners, most closely resemble the work of some of the early Dutch modernists, including architect J.J.P. Oud. Materials such as glass brick, enamelled-steel panels, and aluminum detail were also typical of early modernist design. The architecture of the German Bauhaus, characterized by its transparent rectangular volumes formed by a thin post-and-slab structure sheathed in a light curtain wall, would not enter into the vocabulary of mainstream Canadian architecture until the 1950s.

The NRC buildings were much admired in succeeding years as pioneers in the emerging 'Modern movement' but they also belong to a period when modern architecture was accepted as an alternative style rather than a new way of building that was freed from the historicism of the past.[7] During the late 1930s and the 1940s Canadian architecture

7.1. J.H. Parkin Building (Aerodynamics Building), National Research Council, Montreal Road, Ottawa, Ontario, 1939–40. Designed by H. Gordon Hughes. The exterior walls of the building have recently been reclad to bring the building up to current insulation standards. The original colours and materials were respected but changes in the windows and the pattern of mullions have altered the character of the design. (J. Wright, Parks Canada, 1992)

7.2. Instrument and Model Shop, National Research Council, Montreal Road, Ottawa, Ontario, 1940–1. Designed by H. Gordon Hughes. (Royal Architectural Institute of Canada, *Journal* 23, no. 5 [May 1946]:114)

7.3. Bird's-eye view of the Montreal Road campus of the National Research Centre. (NRC, 1993)

was dominated by a generation of designers who, for the most part, had been trained in the academic traditions of the early part of the century. By the mid-1930s the vocabulary of modernism was familiar to them and they had become relatively comfortable in its use, but they could not accept its antitraditional and, to some extent, anti-aesthetic ideology as defined by the left-wing avant-garde European modernists in the interwar period. For most Canadian architects, modernity was expressed in two ways, as an aesthetic quality based on principles of simplicity and restraint in form and detail, and as a rationalization of structure and planning that acted as a modifying influence on established architectural traditions. By the mid-1930s in Canada modernism was also seen as a style of architecture most appropriate to certain types of projects, including scientific research centres.[8] Architects of this period, among them Gordon Hughes, were equally comfortable working in a variety of historical styles.

Veterans' and Military Hospitals

A jurisdictional squabble between the Department of National Defence and the Department of Pensions resulted in a slow and rocky start to the construction of new military and veterans' hospitals. In 1928 the Department of Health had absorbed the old Department of Soldiers' Civil Re-establishment, including its network of military and veterans' hospitals. The new department, now known as Pensions and National Health, regarded hospital construction as falling within its mandate.[9] Of course, the Department of National Defence, which was always reluctant to surrender any of its autonomy to a civilian department, argued that it should maintain its own system of hospitals for all military personnel. Although the dispute was never entirely resolved, in 1942 the interdepartmental Wartime Committee on Hospitalization worked out a compromise agreement whereby the military would construct its own hospitals at military bases and training centres, while the Department of Pensions and National Health would manage hospitals in the cities.[10] The military would design and construct all its own buildings. The Department of Pensions and National Health maintained a small design office, which developed the preliminary building program, but the preparation of working drawings and project management was the responsibility of the Chief Architect's Branch.

The hospitals constructed during and after World War II were quite different from those built during the first war. The semi-permanent wood-frame pavilions gave way to more permanent buildings constructed of steel, concrete, and brick. Moreover, the design of the sprawling World War I hospital complexes, consisting of separate pavilions and services buildings linked by enclosed corridors or passageways, was abandoned in favour of more unified and compact plans. Although most construction during World War II consisted of expanding and upgrading older military hospitals, three large new facilities were developed. They were the Shaughnessy Hospital in Vancouver (1940–1), the Colonel Belcher Hospital in Calgary (1942–3), and the veterans' hospital in Victoria (1945–6), now known as the Memorial Building at the Royal Jubilee Hospital (Figure 7.4).

The two hospitals on the West Coast were designed by the Vancouver firm of Mercer and Mercer, but all three were similar in plan and layout. Built to accommodate between 200 and 240 patients, they adopted an H-plan. The ground floors were taken up with administrative and specialized medical services and the upper floors contained wards that were broken down into twenty-four–bed wards and a number of private and semi-private rooms (see Figure 7.4).[11] The Colonel Belcher Hospital was a steel-frame building sheathed in brick and stone trim, while the hospitals in British Columbia were both built of monolithic concrete, a structural type most common to the architecture of the West Coast. The designs by Mercer and Mercer were also more modern in conception. The smooth white surfaces of the cement coating and the strong horizontal lines of the windows gave the designs the low, sleek profile characteristic of modern architecture. The windows, which wrapped around corners, featured steel mullions that formed a distinctive grid pattern consisting of two vertical rows of eight panes laid on the long end. This window treatment would become a decorative cliché of early modern design in Canada, and it was a recurring motif in federal architecture of the late 1940s and early 1950s.

During the war the Chief Architect's Branch also constructed five

7.4. Memorial Building, Royal Jubilee Hospital, Victoria, British Columbia, 1945–6. Architects: Mercer and Mercer. (E. Mills, Parks Canada, 1993)

health and occupational centres. The Rideau Centre in Ottawa (1943–4) was the first and served as the prototype for the centres that followed at Ste-Anne-de-Bellevue in Quebec, Toronto, London, and Vancouver (Figure 7.5). These centres, which functioned as convalescent homes, consisted of a series of one-storey bungalows, each equipped with wards, a common room, and a veranda. The bungalows were arranged in a curved line on either side of a main adminstration building that housed offices, the dining-room, and kitchens. They were built to provide an informal, non-institutional environment that would be conducive to rest and recuperation. Like tuberculosis sanatoria of the late nineteenth and early twentieth centuries, the buildings affected a domestic style, with clapboard siding, gabled and hipped roofs accented with dormer windows, chimneys, and a small lantern over the administration building. More importantly, the centres were always set in spacious, informally landscaped grounds to give the complexes a resort-like atmosphere.[12]

In 1944 responsibility for veterans' hospitals was transferred to the newly created Department of Veterans Affairs, and with this change hospital construction entered into its most active period. Although the number of beds would gradually decrease, the new department initiated a program to eliminate all the old substandard buildings and to consolidate hospital services in large modern treatment centres.[13] Once again the buildings were the product of a cooperative effort between the Department of Veterans Affairs, which did much of the preliminary planning, and the Chief Architect's Branch, which managed the contracts and the contract architects.[14]

The first and the most important product of this new program was Sunnybrook Hospital in Toronto, which was begun in 1944 and opened in 1948 (Figures 7.6 and 7.7).[15] At the time of its completion it was the largest, most modern hospital in Canada, and was considered a major achievement in terms of design and planning. The size of the project, which involved dozens of subcontracts, was also considered a model in effective management for a large-scale project. Designed by the Toronto firm of Allward and Gouinlock, the complex consists of a main active treatment building, an up-patient (for ambulatory patients) building, a psychiatric unit, a nurses' residence, an administration building, a staff residence, a gymnasium, a chapel, a gate lodge, and a bus terminal. These different functions are expressed as distinct but interconnected building volumes, which are uniformly faced in a soft sand-coloured brick punctuated by a simple grid of windows. The budget did not allow for a high quality of exterior finish, and so the strength of the design is in the overall massing of the distinct building units. The active treatment building, with a central clock tower and elevator shaft, is the dominant structure in the complex; the other buildings pivot around this building in an asymmetrical composition that reaches out and down into the landscape. The surrounding grounds, situated on the edge of one of Toronto's spectacular ravines, also serve to soften the institutional character of the complex.

Built to accommodate 1,450 patients, Sunnybrook Hospital reflected the advances in medical science and hospital planning that had taken place during the 1920s and 1930s.[16] The introduction of sulpha drugs and antibiotics had reduced the risk of infection and the need for isolated wards. Hospital stays were also shorter in duration, but the development and expansion of medical support services, such as radiology and pathology, required increasing amounts of floor space.[17] The sprawling plan of the old pavilion hospital, which isolated groups of patients in separate buildings but which also placed medical support services far from the patients in the wards, was neither practical nor necessary. As early as 1900 doctors in the United States had begun to discuss the possibility of adapting multi-storeyed structures, but it was not until the 1920s and 1930s that this solution gained widespread acceptance.[18]

Sunnybrook Hospital, with its eight-storey active treatment building, was one of the first modern high-rise hospitals in Canada. The ground plan consisted of a long narrow spine, which housed the medical and administrative services and some of the smaller wards. A series of five projecting wings, containing the various wards and a solarium, stretched south towards the sun. This type of plan was promoted by hospital designers through the 1920s and 1930s and was employed by a number of major hospitals and medical institutions in Europe and the United States. The earliest Canadian example was developed in 1927 by Ernest Cormier for the proposed hospital at the Université de Montréal.[19] New standards of accommodation were also introduced at Sunnybrook. The

7.5. Rideau Health and Occupational Centre, Ottawa, Ontario, 1943–4. Designed by the Chief Architect's Branch with the Medical Services Branch, Department of Pensions and National Health. (J. Wright, Parks Canada, 1992)

7.6. Aerial view, Sunnybrook Hospital, Toronto, Ontario, 1944–8, in the 1940s. Architects: Allward and Gouinlock. (University of Calgary, Canadian Architectural Archives, Panda Collection, 451132-4)

7.7. Sunnybrook Hospital (Active Treatment Centre) as seen in 1993. (J. Wright, Parks Canada, 1993)

large open wards that had characterized older hospitals were replaced by smaller units. The standard ward accommodated twenty-four beds and was subdivided by permanent partitions into semi-enclosed units of four beds. A number of rooms for one to four patients were also built. The interiors were fairly inexpensively finished and furnished but had a unity of style and colour that gave the complex a visual coherence and design integrity. During the 1950s hospital facilities were expanded and modernized and new hospitals were built across the country, including an enlarged Shaughnessy Hospital in Vancouver, a new hospital, Deer Lodge, in Winnipeg, and a new veterans' hospital in Ste-Foy, Quebec.[20]

Building for the Department of National Defence

Building for the military accounted for the lion's share of federal construction expenditure during the war, but most of this work was allocated to the Works and Buildings Directorate within the Department of National Defence. The Chief Architect's Branch played only a minor, support role. Between 1939 and 1942 it was asked to build a number of structures at the two main naval bases at Halifax and at Esquimalt, British Columbia, ranging from temporary wood-frame buildings to more permanent administrative buildings, hospitals, barracks, warehouses, and training facilities.[21]

The Ordnance Depot at the Esquimalt Dockyard was typical of the serviceable but conservative design carried out at bases during the war years by the Chief Architect's Branch (Figure 7.8). Like the NRC buildings, its design met industrial standards with open floor areas, fire-resistant steel construction, and steel-sash windows, but there the comparison ended. In contrast to the modernism of the NRC buildings, the Chief Architect's Branch encased the Ordnance Depot in an architectural shell in which the vocabulary had not changed significantly since the 1910s. The brick sheathing, with its stone trim, applied pilasters, and small windows, represented a continuation of a line of warehouse, semi-industrial federal buildings that can be traced from pre-World War I military stores buildings, to such research laboratories as the Animal Diseases Research Institute in Hull in the 1920s and the the Montreal Postal Terminal in the 1930s.

Temporary Buildings in Ottawa: Accommodating Civil Servants

Wartime conditions also created an immediate demand for more office space for a rapidly expanding civil service in Ottawa. Between 1939 and 1945 the number of government employees increased by 300 per cent.[22] In 1917 the Department of Public Works had dealt with the same problem by building its own 'office block,' which was to be sold as soon as more suitable government buildings were constructed. In 1939 the government decided upon a much cheaper remedy. Within three years the Chief Architect's Branch created approximately 1.2 million square feet of office space in twelve wood-frame temporary buildings that were located in prime but still underdeveloped government land along Elgin, Wellington, and Sussex streets (Figure 7.9).[23] Like the earlier generation of military hospitals, the temporary buildings were two or three storeys in height and were set on concrete foundations. Most had gently pitched roofs and walls sheathed in clapboard or asbestos shingles. Although a thin appliqué of a portico sometimes dignified the entrances, these buildings were intended to meet short-term needs and were not meant to impress the public. Ironically, many were standing in the 1980s and in the mid-1990s one still survives. At over forty years of age, the Justice Annex, which sits in the shadow of Parliament Hill, now qualifies as a potential heritage building under federal policy.

Reconstruction and Public Building in the Postwar Period

In the spring of 1945 the Liberal government tabled a white paper on employment and income that outlined an ambitious program of postwar reconstruction and promised a high and stable level of employment and income for the entire country. The last war had been followed by a

7.8. Ordnance Depot (Buildings D192 and D192B), Esquimalt, British Columbia, 1940–1. Designed by the Chief Architect's Branch. Additions built in 1943 and 1944. (Ian Doull, Parks Canada, 1989)

7.9. Temporary Office Building No. 4, Elgin Street, Ottawa, Ontario, 1941–2. Designed by the Chief Architect's Branch. The building in the foreground was used by the Royal Canadian Navy. (NA, PA-166791)

recession and a long period of political and social upheaval, and the federal government was determined to avoid a similar crisis. Senior bureaucrats within the Department of Finance led the argument for a strong central government equipped with the financial and legislative tools that would allow it to regulate and balance the national economy and, at the same time, provide basic social security to the general population. Some of these mechanisms had been put in place during the war. In 1940 the provinces had agreed to allow the federal government to collect personal income, corporation, and inheritance taxes on their behalf in exchange for a system of transfer payments. Ottawa also assumed responsibility for a national program of unemployment insurance. The reconstruction program, which was given public approval in the federal election of 1945, was designed to stimulate the economy and trade through a variety of measures, including tariff reductions, export incentives, and support to industry. Other initiatives, such as the National Housing Act and the Family Allowance Bill, would stimulate spending and provide greater financial security to individual Canadians.[24]

The program had a direct impact on the activities of the Chief Architect's Branch. Although the percentage of the federal budget spent on construction declined after the war as the new and expensive social programs came into effect, the public works budget, in real dollars, rose steadily.[25] In the four years following the end of the war the federal government was a major force in the Canadian construction industry, accounting for 25 per cent of the total spent in Canada.[26] Much of this money was directed to the departments of Transport and National Defence and to large projects such as the many veterans' housing developments, but the Department of Public Works also had an important role to play. New and expanded programs involving taxation, unemployment insurance, and family allowance required an extensive network of regional and local offices. This burgeoning bureaucracy had a voracious appetite for office space in almost every urban centre across the country. The first signs of growth were evident in the large number of additions that were built to existing federal buildings just after the war.[27] By 1947 and 1948,

when the Liberal government was preparing itself for an election in 1949, the pace of new construction increased substantially. In the four years between 1949 and 1953 the branch oversaw the construction of almost two hundred new federal buildings, and they ranged from small public buildings and RCMP detachment buildings to large, multi-storeyed office blocks.

Most large federal buildings of the postwar era were designed by private architects who worked under the general supervision of the Chief Architect's Branch. Their buildings continued to reflect the modern-traditional dichotomy that defined Canadian architecture during this period. Two of the largest projects begun in the late 1940s were Postal Station B in Montreal, designed by I.P. Isley of the Montreal firm of Archibald, Isley and Templeton, and Postal Station Q in Toronto, which was designed by Toronto architect Charles B. Dolphin (Figures 7.10 and 7.11).[28] Both projects were originally planned on a much smaller scale. The initial estimates for Postal Station Q, which were submitted in 1948–9, described a one-storey building with the Post Office as the primary tenant.[29] In Montreal the original estimates called for a small addition to an existing federal building on Rue Ste-Catherine.[30] By the end of that year, however, both projects had grown from two to ten storeys. Clearly the impact of the new government programs and their need for office space was sudden and intense, resulting in major expansions to projects already under way. At Postal Station Q, the Post Office and the Department of National Health and Welfare both claimed space but the single largest tenant was the Unemployment Insurance Commission.

Both buildings provide a good illustration of the type of tentative modernism characteristic of the period. Neither design seriously reconsidered the standard office block formula represented, for example, by the Hunter Building in Ottawa. The urban grid defined the basic architectural volume. The height was determined by the amount of space required by the federal government. The job of the architect was to dress the outer skin of the building, and here the emergence of a new vocabulary can be seen that was not evident in pre-war federal buildings. In the design of the Montreal building the ribbon windows, the rounded edges, and the smooth surfaces bring to mind the streamlined forms of early Dutch and European modernism. The building is notable for its extensive use of large plate-glass windows at the ground level, which imparts a sense of weightlessness and structural transparency to the overall design. Postal Station Q is more conventional in its treatment. The first two floors are visually defined as a solid masonry base, which contrasts with the light, airy quality of the upper storeys. The main entrance, with its two granite columns, can also be read as a much simplified and stylized interpretation of a classical portico. Typically for this period of architecture, both buildings use natural materials on the exterior but these are handled in new ways. Postal Station B is sheathed in limestone, but the stones are laid in a grid (one on top of the other) rather than staggered as in a load-bearing masonry wall. The stone panels are clearly attached to the wall; they do not support it. The highly polished finish of the red and black granite detail used on Postal Station Q is also characteristic of this period. The glassy, reflective surfaces are well suited to an architecture that strives for a clean simplicity of line and form.

Other federal buildings of the period adopted more traditional solutions. Postal Station P in Port Arthur (now Thunder Bay) in Ontario and the Government of Canada building in Victoria were both constructed between 1950 and 1953 (Figures 7.12 and 7.13). Their designs descended directly from modern classical architecture prevalent in the 1930s but the detail has been reduced and simplified even further. In F.W. Watt's Port Arthur Federal Building, historical references in the detail have been completely eliminated. Instead, the polished granite base and crisply cut limestone create a design dependent on bold simple volumes and smooth, pristine surfaces. The rounded corners at the two principal entrances serve to soften the strict rectangularity of the structure. The composition of the entrances, consisting of large open bays that extend through two storeys and are infilled with walls of glass divided by aluminum mullions, was a recurring motif in federal architecture of the 1950s. A tenuous link with the architecture of the past is expressed in the symmetry of the façades and in the visual definition of the buildings as solid masonry structures. The Victoria building, which was designed in 1947

7.10. Postal Station B, Montreal, Quebec, 1949–51. Designed by I.P. Isley of Archibald, Isley and Templeton. (J. Wright, Parks Canada, 1991)

7.11. Postal Station Q (now known as the Arthur Meighen Building), Toronto, Ontario, 1951–4. Architect: Charles B. Dolphin. Designed in 1950. (J. Wright, Parks Canada, 1991)

by local architect P. Leonard James, is more overtly classical in style.[31] Although concessions to modernism can be seen in a simplification of the cornice lines and window surrounds and in the use of aluminum spandrels and door-frames, features such as the fluted pilasters along the main façade and the tripartite articulation of the façade are rooted in traditional forms.

Private architects took on most of the large and mid-sized projects, leaving the staff of the Chief Architect's Branch with small urban post offices and public buildings. During the late 1940s and early 1950s the Chief Architect's Branch produced about sixty of these buildings which it designed according to two or three basic patterns. The public buildings in Leduc, Alberta, and in Geraldton, Ontario, illustrate two of the most common design formulas (Figures 7.14 and 7.15).[32] Both were built to accommodate a post office on the ground floor and general offices and a caretaker's apartment on the second level. (Residential apartments continued to be provided in many government buildings, despite the department's attempts to eliminate this local perquisite from federal buildings.) Brick with limestone trim remained the preferred exterior material but the basic post office 'box' of the past was redefined as a more complex and irregular composition of simple volumes. The Leduc Public Building features a T-shaped plan with low one-storey porches on either side of the projecting front section. The Geraldton Public Building adopts an asymmetrical massing composed of a low-lying block, which relates functionally to the ground floor post office, a second storey that is set back and contains the caretaker's apartment, and a two-storey, horizontal volume that defines the entrance and the stairwell. The distinctive grouping of windows within a rectangular grid delineated on the outer perimeter by a stone trim was another recurring motif in the work of the Chief Architect's Branch.

Border Crossing Stations: Gateways to the Nation

Some of the most innovative designs produced by the staff of the Chief Architect's Branch were built as border crossing stations for the departments of Customs and Immigration. After the war the number of vehicles

7.12. Postal Station P, Port Arthur (now Thunder Bay), Ontario, 1950–3, as seen *ca.* 1953. Architect: F.W. Watt. (NA, PA-185817)

7.13. Federal Building, Fort Street, Victoria, British Columbia, 1950–3 (designed 1947–8). Architect: P.L. James. (E. Mills, Parks Canada, 1992)

7.14. Public Building, Leduc, Alberta, 1950–1. Designed by the Chief Architect's Branch. (J. Wright, Parks Canada, 1994)

7.15. Public Building, Geraldton, Ontario, 1949–50. Designed by the Chief Architect's Branch. (Public Works and Government Services Canada, Real Property Branch, 1994)

on the road, both private and commercial, increased sharply. Gas rationing was lifted, roads were being improved, and, because of the savings that they had been forced to make during the war, many Canadian families had money to spend on new cars. Border crossing stations had been built in the 1930s but they were no longer able to cope with the volume of cross-border traffic; moreover, the quaint rustic buildings that had been built in the previous decade were no longer considered appropriate for a leading industrial nation like Canada. As was pointed out by one member of Parliament, many of the existing stations would indicate to the visitor that 'we [Canada] are not so up and coming.'[33] Around 1947 the Department of Public Works began a nation-wide program to upgrade these stations. By 1953 new and expanded facilities had been provided for at thirteen border crossings.[34]

The automobile was an evocative symbol of the new machine age. Border crossing stations, which monitored and processed car traffic into and out of the country, were well suited, both functionally and symbolically, to the architecture of modernism. A good example of this period of design was the Bus Terminal and Examining Warehouse at St-Bernard-de-Lacolle in Quebec (1950–1) (Figure 7.16). It was one of the largest and most accomplished of several standard designs developed by the branch during the late 1940s and, unlike some of the branch's urban public buildings, it demonstrated a considerable confidence and assurance in the forms of modernism. The design consists of an asymmetrical massing of distinct volumes. The exterior walls are sheathed in limestone veneer which, like Postal Station B in Montreal, is laid out in a regular grid pattern. Together, the curved front wall with floor-to-ceiling glass and the flat slab roof extending out beyond the wall impart the sense of structural clarity and transparent volumes that characterized modernism of the International style.

The National Capital Plan, 1950

The end of the war also rekindled the government's enthusiasm for building the national capital. Throughout the 1920s and 1930s the report of

7.16. Bus Terminal and Examining Warehouse (border crossing station), St-Bernard-de-Lacolle, Quebec, 1950–1. Designed by the Chief Architect's Branch. The wing to the right of the curved front office is a later addition. (Revenue Canada, 1989)

the Federal Plan Commission was still regarded as the official plan for federal development in Ottawa. By 1945, however, its recommendations were outdated. The growth of services and programs across the country and the pressure for more office buildings was magnified in Ottawa, and the 1.2 million square feet of office space that had been proposed in 1915 would no longer satisfy needs. The development of a new plan for the national capital was given top priority by Prime Minister Mackenzie King. In 1945 he redefined the Federal District Commission as a national body with representation from across the country, and he also enlarged the boundaries of the federal district area to encompass over nine hundred square miles on both sides of the Ottawa River.[35] A few months later French town planner Jacques Gréber was invited to return to Ottawa with a new and broader mandate to develop a comprehensive plan for the expanded national capital region under the direction of the commission.[36] The whole project was put forward as Canada's memorial to those killed in the war, but the speed and enthusiasm with which it was set up owed much to the personal influence of Mackenzie King. Now nearing the end of his political career, King regarded the creation of a dignified and beautiful national capital as his final legacy to the nation.[37]

The National Capital Plan, which was tabled in 1950, represented a continuation and a revision of the 1915 report of the Federal Plan Commission.[38] Gréber, whose early urban design work dated from the early part of this century, clearly belonged to the generation of City Beautiful planners, and he approached urban planning primarily as a problem of design and beautification. Many of the recommendations found in the 1915 plan reappear in only slightly altered form in the Gréber report. Again, the most pressing issue for civic improvement was considered to be the removal of the railway tracks and yards from the city's core. The report also called for more effective zoning by-laws to separate residential and industrial areas, and it recommended improving the visual appearance of the city streets by removing the visual clutter of overhead wires, utility poles, and fire escapes.

The beautification of the central parliamentary precinct and the definition of a suitable architectural theme were the central preoccupations of the report. The picturesque Château style, which had dominated federal building in the capital since the 1910s, was not compatible with Gréber's vision. Although he felt that the Château roof theme should be retained for any new construction on the north side of Wellington Street for the sake of continuity, he criticized the design of the Confederation and Justice buildings for their awkward alignment to the street and for their 'incorporation of outmoded forms' of architecture.[39] Of the East and West blocks – those icons of Canadian nationalism – he wrote: 'Due to an excessive adaptation of the picturesque and of forms having medieval inspiration, the function of the structure has been rendered subservient, resulting in difficult working conditions, inadequate lighting and environments adverse to operational efficiency.'[40] He also dismissed the 1932 National Research Council building for its rigidly classical design.

Gréber did write favourably of the new NRC buildings at the Montreal Road campus, which he described as 'functional and satisfactory in aspect,' but he clearly did not think that this industrial type of design provided a suitable model for important government institutions in the central core. Instead, he envisioned a capital designed in a style that retained the proportions, massing, and symmetry of classicism, but which avoided any precise historical references.[41] This 'stripped' classical style could be described as a further modernization and simplification of modern classical or Art Deco style of the 1930s. It is a style of architecture most strongly identified with the official architecture of Nazi Germany and Fascist Italy of the 1930s and early 1940s, and it represented a conservative stream in public architecture that persisted in Europe and North America into the 1950s.

Like Edward H. Bennett in 1915, Gréber envisioned a grand and dignified capital in the tradition of Paris and Washington. He saw broad boulevards lined with buildings designed according to a unified stylistic theme. Major public buildings would be artfully placed at the end of long vistas or on the edge of spacious plazas, providing dramatic focus to Gréber's urban compositions orchestrated on a grand scale (Figure 7.17). His proposal for a civic plaza, consisting of a city hall at one end counterbalanced by a new national art gallery at the other and linked by a broad bridge and boulevard over the Rideau Canal, illustrates the nature of Gréber's vision for Ottawa.

7.17. Illustration from the National Capital Plan showing the 'Proposal with the City Hall Dominating Confederation Park from the Easterly Approach to the New Bridge,' *Plan for the National Capital: General Report* (Ottawa: 1950), fig. 158. (Malak Photographs, 1950)

Only a few federal public buildings were constructed according to the architectural models presented in the National Capital Plan. The East and West Memorial Buildings, designed by the Toronto firm of Allward and Gouinlock, was the largest project of the period (Figure 7.18).[42] (Allward and Gouinlock appear to have been much favoured by the Liberal government: they were currently working on Sunnybrook Hospital in Toronto, and in 1956 they were commissioned to design and construct the massive multi-building complex for the Department of Mines and Technical Surveys in Ottawa.) The East Memorial Building, to house the Department of Veterans Affairs, was begun in 1949; the West Memorial Building was constructed a few years later for the Department of Trade and Commerce. Both were designed in the stripped classical style that was so prominently featured in Gréber's plan. He felt that the buildings on the south side of Wellington Street should adopt a flat roof, but Prime Minister Mackenzie King was reluctant to abandon Ottawa's distinctive architectural emblem and a rather squat version of the Château roof was added.

According to Gréber's model, the two buildings were designed to mark the entrance to a grand plaza leading up to a convention centre and an auditorium. A memorial colonnade was built to link the two structures but the boulevard, which was to lead up to the plaza, was never completed. It now extends only half a block on the other side of the colonnade, then recedes into an ordinary mixed-use streetscape. The East and West Memorial Buildings were the last buildings in the parliamentary precinct to acknowledge the tradition of the Château style in Ottawa – that is, until the 1980s when Château roofs, or rather, steeply pitched green metal roofs, made a reappearance on Wellington Street in response to the fashionable eclecticism and historicism of post-modern architecture.

The National Printing Bureau, which was designed in 1949 by Montreal architect Ernest Cormier, was part of a scheme to beautify the City of Hull with boulevards, plazas, traffic circles, and several important public buildings, including a new train station and a hospital. Originally a public square was to be opened up in front of the printing bureau but this, like other proposals for Hull, was never realized. The National Printing Bureau

was far removed from the central parliamentary district but its design comes closest to realizing Gréber's architectural image for the national capital area (Figures 7.19 and 7.20).[43] Cormier, who had been trained in Montreal at the École Polytechnique and at the École des Beaux-Arts in Paris, had developed a distinctive personal style that was ideally suited to express the sense of civic grandeur and modernity that Gréber had envisioned for the national capital.[44] Cormier's earlier design for the Supreme Court Building harmonized perfectly with Gréber's plan and, in fact, might well have influenced Gréber in defining the architectural character of the proposed capital.

The National Printing Bureau, which was begun in 1949, functioned both as an industrial printing plant and as the headquarters of an important federal institution. This dual role was clearly articulated in Cormier's design. As seen from the front, the building bears much in common with the architecture of modern classicism, but Cormier's interpretation of this style was uncompromisingly severe. It is a three-storey structure with two two-storey wings that project forward from the main building mass. The central entrance portico is formed by six massive piers, which cut deeply into the wall and create a sharp contrast of light and shadow. Like those at Postal Station B in Montreal, the walls are faced with stone that has been laid in a grid pattern, but here this treatment conveys a sense of weight and mass. The exterior design is dominated by the cold, grey granite of the walls, and the windows – their size and pattern dictated by the uncompromising grid of the masonry – appear to be formed by the removal of a few blocks of stone from this massive pile. The central block corresponds with the public and administrative functions of the building.

The industrial plant, which surrounds the central section on three sides, is expressed in radically different terms. A granite base continues around the building, but the upper two levels contrast with the weighty monumentality of the main elevation. The glass and steel-panelled curtain wall has the light, transparent quality reminiscent of the architecture of the German Bauhaus. Cormier is an architect who eludes conventional categorization. The design of the National Printing Bureau cannot be

7.18. East (1949–56) and West (1954–8) Memorial Buildings, Ottawa, Ontario. Designed by Allward and Gouinlock. (B. Dewalt, Parks Canada, 1987)

7.19. National Printing Bureau, Hull, Quebec, 1949–57. Architect: Ernest Cormier. (M. Trépanier, Parks Canada, 1993).

7.20. Rear elevation, National Printing Bureau. (J. Wright, Parks Canada, 1992)

7.21. Tunney's Pasture with a view of the Dominion Bureau of Statistics (1950–3) at the end of the road. Designed by Ross, Patterson, Townshend and Heughan. (J. Wrights, Parks Canada, 1992)

described as a modernized or streamlined classicism. Instead, Cormier created two distinct buildings, drawn from two separate and antithetical approaches to design, and fused them into one composition.

Gréber's proposals for the central core of Ottawa represented a re-working of the ideas and principles inherent in the 1915 plan. The most innovative recommendations in his report addressed problems of subur-ban sprawl and urban congestion. He recommended the establishment of a 'green belt,' a rural or agricultural buffer zone around the city that would contain urban sprawl and the linear, fringe development that were scarring the appearance of the suburban outskirts. The concept of the green belt had originated in the late nineteenth-century writings of British urban planner Ebenezer Howard as a component of the self-contained Garden City, but in the interwar period green belts were seen as useful tools to control development around established cities.[45]

The Gréber report also introduced the idea of decentralized develop-ment. The traditional urban plan, with a central downtown core ringed by residential and industrial areas, was becoming obsolete as city streets became increasingly congested by private automobile traffic and as pop-ulation density within the city centre rose. During the 1920s the idea of a decentralized city had attracted a number of advocates, particularly in the United States. The Gréber report redefined Ottawa as a hierarchy of communities and functions. The central core could no longer support all government development and it was recommended that a series of satellite centres be established in the suburbs. New residential communities, each with their own commercial districts, schools, churches, and community centres, would be established around these government centres so that employees could live close to their work.[46]

Tunney's Pasture in the west end of the city was the first satellite government centre.[47] As originally conceived in the late 1940s, the build-ings formed a visually cohesive grouping arranged around a network of avenues and boulevards. The new Dominion Bureau of Statistics (1950–3), designed under contract by the firm of Ross, Patterson, Townshend and Heughan, was the first building on the site (Figure 7.21). It is a long, narrow, four-storey building, with eight wings projecting front and back in a double-H plan. The main entrance, which is set back between two projecting wings and is marked by an entrance gate with two wrought-iron lamp standards, provides the central focus to the design. Like many of the public buildings of the period, the main entrance is set in a large glass and aluminum opening that extends through three storeys. The exterior buff brick walls are uniformly articulated by horizontal bands of windows accented by an outer band of stone. Although subsequent buildings at Tunney's Pasture tended to be more 'modern,' the general massing, materials, and profile of this building defined an architectural theme that would survive until the early 1970s, when multi-storeyed office blocks were set down in the middle of this low-rise, campus-like setting.[48]

The concept of the satellite government centre would have a far-reaching impact on the nature of federal development in Ottawa. It had been introduced as a means to avoid congestion and over-development in the urban core but, in practice, it proved to be too successful. It introduced a double standard in government building, which tended to undermine efforts to implement Gréber's grand vision for the parliamentary precinct. The central core defined the symbolic heart of the city and the nation, and the buildings constructed there were expected to meet the highest standards of design and construction. In the satellite developments, however, it was always understood that design standards could be relaxed somewhat and that a more practical and functional type of building was appropriate. The government quickly realized that it was easier and cheaper to erect office buildings in the satellite centres. As a result, these areas were built up quickly in the 1940s and 1950s, while development in the downtown area was painfully slow. Even today, land identified for development in 1913, 1915, 1937, and 1950 is still vacant.

Of all the urban plans developed for Ottawa in the twentieth century, Gréber's was the most successful. It owed its success to opportune timing. The Holt report of 1915 was presented at the beginning of a long period of restraint; by the time the government was ready to build, its vision of Ottawa had become dated. In contrast, Gréber's National Capital Plan was prepared just as the nation was entering into a period of sustained growth. As a result, the government was able to move quickly on many of its more ambitious recommendations, such as the creation of a green belt, the removal of railway tracks from the city core, and the establishment of satellite government centres. The development of an architecturally cohesive parliamentary precinct remains to be resolved.

Building for the Scientific Community

The postwar period was a time of plenty for scientific research in Canada.[49] C.D. Howe, one of the most powerful Liberal cabinet ministers, believed that a generously funded research program was an essential tool in maintaining a progressive and competitive industrial and manufacturing sector in Canada. Howe had reluctantly agreed in 1944 to take over the newly created Department of Reconstruction on the condition that he also be given authority over the National Research Council. Under his direction the NRC budget increased from $5.2 billion in 1945 to $12.9 billion in 1951–2. Some of this money was directed toward the creation of a national network of government laboratories.[50] It was felt that a decentralized research program could better address the specific needs and concerns of each region. The government also hoped to encourage greater cooperation and sharing of resources with the broader academic and industrial community. In 1948 the Prairie Regional Laboratory was opened at the University of Saskatchewan campus in Saskatoon and in 1952 the Atlantic Regional Laboratory was opened at Dalhousie University in Halifax.

The research program of the Department of Agriculture also did very well during these years. In 1937 the department had integrated many of its diverse research branches into an organization known as the Science Service Branch.[51] Beginning in the nineteenth century a network of experimental farms had been established across the country, but in the postwar era new emphasis was placed on providing modern laboratory facilities in each of the regions. By 1953 seven Science Service branch laboratories, as well as several smaller specialized laboratories, had been constructed.[52] Other departments, such as Fisheries and Oceans,

Northern Affairs and Natural Resources, and Mines and Technical Surveys, maintained research divisions and built laboratories.[53]

Research laboratories tended to adopt fairly modest, economical standards of design. The NRC's Atlantic Regional Laboratory at Dalhousie University was typical of the work of the Chief Architect's Branch in this area (Figure 7.22). The design type – a rectangular block with a symmetrical elevation, a central entrance, and regularly spaced windows linked horizontally by an outer band of stone – resembles several other federal research buildings of the period. Stone, instead of the cheaper brick, was used in deference to the many stone and classical buildings at Dalhousie University. The need to conform with the dominant architectural character on other university campuses resulted in the development of alternative designs. The Prairie Research Station at the University of Saskatchewan and the Science Service Branch laboratory for the Department of Agriculture at the University of Western Ontario were both designed in a vaguely collegiate Gothic style similar to other buildings on the campuses. A few years later at Mount Allison University at Sackville in New Brunswick the Department of Agriculture's Science Service Branch laboratory (begun in 1955) was designed in a British Georgian style; it is a two-and-a-half-storey building with a steeply pitched roof and an imitation stone facing over a reinforced concrete frame.[54]

Several new buildings were built on the Montreal Road campus of the National Research Council in Ottawa to accommodate its new and expanded research programs. The Institute for Research in Construction (1951–3) was one of the most innovative designs of the period (Figure 7.23).[55] Designed by J.C. Meadowcroft of Montreal, its white stucco and cement walls and its low-lying profile respects the established architectural character of the existing complex, but the design also more convincingly embraces the International style. As seen from the front, the building is a long low structure with an off-centre entrance that is marked by slabs of polished black marble. The continuous bands of windows with glass blocks and an aluminum *brise-soleil* were motifs associated with early modernism. Built prior to the widespread use of central air conditioning, this window treatment protected the interior from the radiant heat of the sun while still providing ample natural light. The side elevation is an irregular composition, made up of distinct masses or volumes that reflect internal functional requirements. The main entrance opens onto a fairly impressive foyer with green marble flooring and a gracefully curved staircase with light aluminum railings. This formal public space directly overlooks the main project area rising up through three storeys (Figure 7.24). Only a wall of glass separates the two spaces, thereby clearly expressing and visually integrating the building's dual function as a public institution and a working research laboratory.

The RCMP and Indian Health Services

Urban public buildings, border crossing stations, and buildings for research accounted for most of the work of the Chief Architect's Branch in the 1940s, but by the end of the decade other departments were encouraged to use its services. The Royal Canadian Mounted Police had looked after most of its own building needs since the early part of the century, but by the late 1940s it had re-established an active working relationship with the branch. Much of the work was of a fairly routine nature and most of it was handled by the branch staff. In addition to some new garages and a few residences erected at the divisional headquarters in Ottawa (Rockcliffe Park) and at the Depot in Regina, the latter also received a stable and riding school and a new barracks (Barracks C).

The most commonly requested type of building was the small detachment building. Prior to 1945 many RCMP detachments were located in rented or purchased buildings, but after the war the force's new chief commissioner felt that accommodation of a better standard should be provided for officers.[56] Between 1945 and 1953 approximately thirty new detachment buildings were erected – ten of them between 1951 and 1953 in the new province of Newfoundland.[57] These structures tended to follow standard patterns. Resembling residential buildings, they were two storeys high, had low, hipped roofs and double garages, and were sheathed in asbestos shingle. They combined residential quarters and office accommodation.

7.22. Atlantic Regional Laboratory (NRC), Dalhousie University, Halifax, 1949–50. Designed by the Chief Architect's Branch. (I. Doull, Parks Canada, 1994)

INSTITUTE FOR RESEARCH IN CONSTRUCTION·INSTITUT DE RECHERCHE EN CONSTRUCTION

M·20

7.23. Institute for Research in Construction (NRC), Ottawa, Ontario, 1951–3. Architect: J.C. Meadowcroft. (J. Wright, Parks Canada, 1992)

The Medical Services Branch of the Department of National Health and Welfare also provided a new source of work for the branch. The government had maintained an Indian Health Services Division within the Indian Affairs Branch of the Department of Mines and Resources since 1928. In the 1920s and 1930s a number of hospitals for Native people had been established either by the federal government or by religious institutions, but the program had been a failure. By the mid-1930s tuberculosis claimed the lives of over six hundred people a year – a mortality rate that was as much as thirty times that of non-Natives. In 1935 the Canadian Tuberculosis Association devoted its annual meeting to a discussion of the problem, but its efforts were undermined by the Department of Mines and Resources, which was in the process of cutting back on its health services to Indians.[58]

The situation improved in 1945 when the Indian Health Services Division was transferred to the Department of National Health and Welfare. The effect of the reorganization was to move health care out of a department where Indian affairs was peripheral to its central mandate of resource development and into a department where it could be integrated into a broader national health care policy. Although health standards for Native communities continued to fall below those of the population as a whole, the reorganization did lessen the gap. By 1955 eighteen hospitals and forty nursing stations had been built and the death rate from tuberculosis had dropped to about sixty deaths per year.[59]

Construction for the Medical Services Branch consisted of a series of small nursing stations, which generally provided accommodation for nursing staff and about four patients.[60] Situated on or near reserves, these stations were usually small, one-and-a-half-storey buildings with gabled or hipped roofs. Like the small RCMP detachment buildings, the walls were sheathed in asbestos shingle.

The branch also constructed a series of larger hospitals throughout the North. One of the earliest was the combined hospital and sanatorium at Moose Factory, Ontario, which was constructed in 1948–9 (Figure 7.25).[61] Built to provide 150 beds, the hospital is a two-storey building that has a central section with four wings projecting at right angles. The

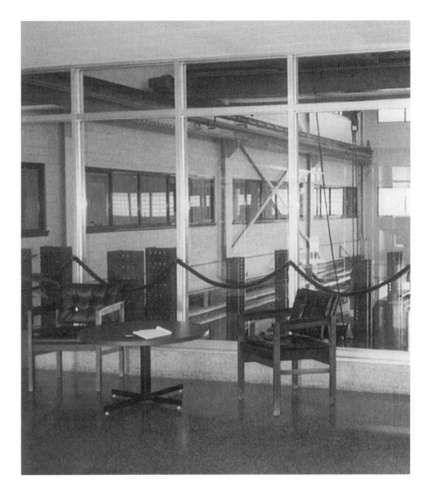

7.24. Institute for Research in Construction. View of the entrance foyer overlooking the main workshop. (J. Hucker, Parks Canada, 1991)

7.25. Moose Factory Indian Hospital, Moose Factory, Ontario, 1948–9. Designed by the Chief Architect's Branch with the Hospital Design Division. Department of National Health and Welfare. (NA, C-37472)

wings define the wards with solaria at each end. The exterior design was kept as simple and functional as possible. It is a wood-frame building with concrete foundations and asbestos siding. The windows are visually grouped in horizontal bands and separated from each other by tinted plywood panels. The Department of Public Works was responsible for the construction of the building, but much of the planning and design work was probably done by the Hospital Design Division in the Department of National Health and Welfare, which was headed by H. Gordon Hughes. Hughes, who had been the architect for wartime buildings at the National Research Council in Ottawa, became a leading expert in hospital design in Canada.[62]

A Crisis of Organization: The Chief Architect's Branch

Between 1945 and 1953 the Chief Architect's Branch oversaw the design and construction of approximately two hundred new buildings, a level of production that equalled the peak construction years of the 1930s. Despite this achievement, there was a growing perception within the government that the Department of Public Works and the Chief Architect's Branch had become obsolete and inefficient organizations, riddled with patronage and corruption.[63] This perception was owed, in part, to problems of personnel and staffing. James B. Hunter, who had served as the deputy minister since 1907, died in 1941, leaving behind a leadership vacuum. Emmett Patrick Murphy was appointed to the position in 1942, but his effectiveness was hampered by the fact that he was also expected to continue in his old job as director of construction for the Department of Munitions and Supply.[64]

Within the Chief Architect's Branch, Charles Sutherland carried on as chief architect during the war, but in 1946 he retired. His departure rekindled the recurring debate as to what sort of architect should serve as chief architect. The logical successor was J.-C.-G. Brault, who had been on staff since 1915 and who had served as the assistant chief architect since 1937.[65] Brault was appointed acting chief architect when Sutherland left but the Civil Service Commission was reluctant to approve the ap-

pointment. In 1947 an internal memo recommended that 'the position of Chief architect . . . be filled by an architect of recognized ability who . . . has an international reputation as a designer and executive.'[66] The department, however, was reluctant to hire an outsider and countered with the old argument that it would be difficult to get such an architect at the salary offered; moveover, it asked: 'Why should this long service employee [Brault] be denied promotion near the end of his official career?'[67] The careful and conservative choice won out and Brault was appointed.

Brault was sixty-one years old with over thirty years of experience in the branch. He was familiar with the workings of the department but he could not be expected to inject energy and new ideas. The problem was compounded by the fact that many of the architects and engineers on staff were of the same generation; some had been recruited in the early 1900s.[68] By the late 1940s the branch was eager to recruit new staff to meet the increasing volume of work but most young architects were not interested in government work. Not only did civil service salaries for architects continue to fall compared to those in the private sector,[69] but, as a 1947 memo pointed out:

> At the present time there are few outstanding architects who have had professional experience outside the Department of Public Works. This has not enhanced the reputation of the Department, and has resulted, in many cases, in younger architects refusing to accept employment in the Department where the reputation for design is lacking.[70]

The situation was not helped by Alphonse Fournier, the minister of public works from 1942 to 1953, who did little to defend the reputation of the department. Fournier seems to have accepted his department's poor performance, and explained that he could not change the mentality of his staff, many of whom had come in at an early age and were now set in their ways.[71]

The real crisis facing the Department of Public Works and the Chief Architect's Branch was one of organization. The administrative structure within the department had not changed significantly since its formation in the 1860s and 1870s. In 1871 the Chief Architect's Branch had been given responsibility for the design, construction, maintenance, and repair of all federal buildings under the jurisdiction of the Department of Public Works. As the volume of construction and the size of the federal building inventory increased, the branch responded by taking on new staff in Ottawa, hiring resident architects in various regional centres, and contracting more and more of the work to private architects. Other departments eased the burden on the branch by setting up their own in-house engineering and architectural services. The erosion of the department's mandate as the central construction agency to the federal government, which had begun in the 1880s with the establishment of independent building services within the Penitentiaries Branch and the Department of Militia and Defence, gained momentum during World War II. In 1952 the Senate Committee on Finance reported that more than half the federal construction expenditure were being spent outside of the Department of Public Works.[72]

By 1953 the federal government's need for new buildings had far exceeded the production capacity of the Chief Architect's Branch. Many major projects that had been identified in the postwar period – with architects appointed and estimates submitted to Parliament – had become mired in the overburdened public works bureaucracy.[73] Within the Chief Architect's Branch the staff was clearly overwhelmed by the administrative detail not only of managing the department's public building projects but also of overseeing its property management and maintenance program.[74] (For example, by the 1940s there were over 2,000 cleaning staff in Ottawa alone.) By 1953 it was widely acknowledged throughout government that the Department of Public Works, including the Chief Archi-

tect's Branch, was in need of radical reform and of an infusion of new people with new ideas.

Conclusion

War and reconstruction brought transition and crisis to the Department of Public Works and the Chief Architect's Branch. During the war the department had languished, busying itself with the mundane work generated by the war effort. As the pace of construction picked up in the postwar era, the Chief Architect's Branch was able to regain ground as an important centre of federal construction but, as government expanded and as the nation entered into a period of rapid growth, it quickly became apparent that the Department of Public Works was not sufficiently equipped to meet demands placed upon it.

Despite these problems, the postwar era cannot be described as a period of stagnation. Projects such as the new National Capital Plan by Jacques Gréber and buildings such as the National Printing Bureau in Hull were significant accomplishments. Generally, the public buildings designed during these years depict Canadian architecture at a crossroads. Unlike other periods of building, when dominant architectural themes or styles can be identified, federal architecture in the 1940s and early 1950s varied considerably, ranging from designs still tied to historical traditions to those that broke completely from the past and explored the materials and structural language of modernism. In the next decade this architectural dichotomy between tradition and modernism, past and future, would cease to be an issue as Canadian architects and the Canadian people enthusiastically embraced the modern aesthetic and the modern ethic to the exclusion of all others.

CHAPTER EIGHT

Into the Modern Era, 1953–1967

The year 1953 marked the beginning of a new era in government building in Canada. Under the direction of dynamic new leadership, the Department of Public Works was completely reorganized. New staff was recruited and new administrative systems were developed, enabling the department to respond to the pent-up demand for more and bigger government buildings. Throughout the 1950s the Chief Architect's Branch, reconstituted as the Building Construction Branch, was able to sustain a level of construction that had no close equivalent in the history of the department. Between 1927 and 1939 the Chief Architect's Branch constructed more than three hundred new buildings; by the late 1950s the Building Construction Branch had close to that number of buildings under contract in a single year. The growth in bureaucracy that had been noted in the late 1940s and early 1950s continued its upward spiral, and the business of constructing larger, more modern office buildings throughout the federal system remained the central preoccupation of the Department of Public Works. Federal development in the North, the expansion of facilities for the Royal Canadian Mounted Police, the construction of new research laboratories for government research programs, and the reform and expansion of the Canadian penitentiary system in the 1960s all generated new work for the department. The buildings constructed during the fifteen years from 1953 to 1967 represented the last significant outward expansion of the network of federal public buildings that had begun in 1867.

The reorganization of the department coincided with the rise of the Modern movement in Canada. Although postwar architecture in Canada cannot be described in terms of a single cohesive movement, by 1953 a new generation of architects, who championed the modernist ideology of the European and U.S. avant-garde, dominated the Canadian architectural scene. Federal buildings of the 1950s and 1960s mirror the complex nature of modern architecture in Canada, but it is the International style of the Bauhaus, characterized by its simple cubic volumes and transparent curtain walls, that epitomizes this period of construction. The rejection of the historical traditions and the belief that new technologies and machine-made materials provide the tools to design better buildings and better, more humane communities, complemented a widespread sense of optimism and the conviction that new technology would provide the basis for building a better and more prosperous nation.

The Building Construction Branch would sustain high construction volumes throughout the 1960s and into the 1970s, but by the early 1960s new architectural influences and political pressures gradually began to reshape and redefine the federal building program. The functionalist principles of the International style had been exploited and abused by speculative builders in the 1950s who had used inexpensive man-made materials and industrial design standards to create an increasingly bleak and banal urban landscape. As a result, Canadian architects began in the 1960s to explore once again purely aesthetic values of form, texture, and composition to create a more varied, dynamic, and expressive architecture. The political and economic climate was also changing. The optimism of the 1950s gave way to a more cautious political outlook in the face of slowed economic growth, rising unemployment rates, growing regional disparities, and the uncertainty brought on by the election of four short-lived minority governments between 1962 and 1968. While the demand for government building remained high, there was increasing pressure to cut construction costs and to streamline the building process.

Reshaping the Department of Public Works, 1953

In August 1953 a Liberal government under Prime Minister Louis St Laurent was re-elected for a fifth consecutive term after he convinced the country that his party alone had the experience and the know-how to guide the nation to greater wealth and prosperity. This claim seemed to be confirmed by a healthy economic outlook, following several years of sustained growth and prosperity throughout the nation. The 'baby boom' was on and immigration was on the rise, producing the first substantial growth in population since the early part of the century. Unemployment levels were down to less than 3 per cent, and investment, the Gross National Product, and personal incomes had doubled since 1939.[1] Economic prosperity meant rising revenues for the federal government. This money was, in turn, reinvested in expanded social programs, in the rearmament and expansion of the Canadian armed forces in response to the Cold War, and in expensive public works such as the Trans-Canada Highway, the St Lawrence Seaway, and later the Trans-Canada Pipeline.

Many new government buildings had also been promised during the election campaign of 1953 but it was widely acknowledged that the Department of Public Works was not capable in its present state of delivering on those promises. For this reason the whole department was targeted for major reforms.[2] Alphonse Fournier, who had served as the minister from 1942 to 1953, was moved to the Department of Justice, and the task of rebuilding Public Works was given to Robert Winters, a young and energetic politician from Nova Scotia. Major-General H.A. Young was appointed the new deputy minister. Both were well suited to the task. Winters, a protégé of the powerful C.D. Howe, was well connected in government and he had already demonstrated his energy and political acumen, first as minister of reconstruction and supply, and later as minister of natural resources and national development. He was an engineer by training, with a degree from the prestigious Massachusetts Institute of Technology. His presence alone did much to restore the credibility of the department. As a 1953 article on Winters in *Maclean's* stated: 'Normally the Minister of Public Works knows a great deal about politics. Now for the first time in human memory, he knows something about public works.'[3] H.A. Young, who had served as quartermaster general of the Canadian Army, as vice-president of the Central Mortgage and Housing Corporation, and as Winters' deputy minister of resources and development, was an experienced administrator with a reputation for ruthless efficiency.[4] Young expressed some reluctance to take on a department that had such a poor reputation, but he was assured by the prime minister that he would be given a free hand to carry out the first major overhaul of the department since 1879.[5]

Within a few months of their arrival, Winters and Young had developed a new organizational structure. The first step was to divide the Chief Architect's Branch into two new branches. The Property and Building Management Branch became responsible for managing and maintaining buildings, and the Building Construction Branch, headed by a chief architect, became responsible for design and construction. Within the Building Construction Branch, four new divisions or working units were created to decentralize authority and to free the chief architect from some of the details of project development.[6] The Requirements Division was responsible for defining the needs of clients and for developing preliminary designs. If a project was to be completed by the department, the Preliminary Design Section within the Requirements Division would prepare sketch elevations. A project was then handed to the Plans and Specifications Division, which prepared working drawings and specifications. The Contracts Division worked on the estimates and administered contracts for in-house projects. If a project was contracted to a private architect, preliminary plans were – in theory – drawn up by the architect; many complained that in practice the department often submitted one of its own designs to guide the architect in the work.

The role of the district offices was also rationalized and strengthened. Eleven districts were identified and all the regional staff members were brought together in offices in each district. These regional offices were responsible for the project management of buildings designed within the department and for overseeing projects under contract to private architects. Although the offices still reported to the chief architect, they were given much greater autonomy to authorize spending. They also carried out some design work for small projects. It was a system whereby the design and construction process was defined as a series of clearly differentiated steps that were taken by specialized branches, each with their own internal hierarchies and chains of command. It was a system that enabled the Building Construction Branch to more than double its volume of construction in just a few years.[7]

Staffing was the key to making the system work. Throughout the department Winters and Young carried out an extensive cull of the old administrative staff, retiring or transferring many employees, and aggressively recruited new ones. In the Building Construction Branch, E.A. Gardner had been appointed acting chief architect following J.-C.-B. Brault's retirement in 1952. Gardner had served as Brault's assistant from 1947, but unlike many of his predecessors he had come to the post with a fairly diverse professional background. A graduate of the McGill School of Architecture, Gardner maintained a private practice in Ottawa in the 1930s before accepting a job in 1940 with the National Defence Works Directorate to design buildings for the Navy and the Army. There he developed an expertise in hospital design, and in 1946 he was transferred to the Chief Architect's Branch to supervise the construction of hospitals for the Department of Veterans Affairs and the Indian Health Services.[8] Gardner, who was not part of the old department establishment, obviously met with the approval of Winters and Young, and in 1953 they confirmed him in the position as chief architect.

Recruiting new staff for the Building Construction Branch was not as easy. Canadian architects were not interested in a career in government when there were so many, more desirable job opportunities in the private sector. In order to fill the many vacancies in the branch, Gardner began a recruiting drive in Europe, where the levels of unemployment in the profession were still high. The Preliminary Design Section in the Requirements Division was clearly a product of this effort. Of the eleven architects in the section by 1956, only two were Canadian-born. The others were a multi-national mix of Hungarian, Lithuanian, Polish, Ukrainian, English, and one American.[9] But despite the aggressive hiring campaign, it was not until the late 1950s that the branch was able to fill all its vacancies.

Modernism as Public Policy

The reform of the department coincided with the rise of the Modern movement in Canadian architecture.[10] The idea of modernity was not new to Canadian architecture, but in the 1950s its meaning was redefined. In the 1930s and 1940s modernism was not incompatible with tradition; most Canadian architects understood it as a purifying aesthetic that would rid architecture of its archaic historicism and return it to a simpler, purer, and more rational approach to design, but it was seen as an architecture that still retained a sense of continuity with the past. By the late 1940s a new generation of architects and educators had emerged that embraced the revolutionary ideology of the radical European and U.S. modernists. As expressed in 1955 by Toronto architect John C. Parkin, one of the leading exponents of the Modern movement in Canada:

> I think we can safely say that the battle between modern and tradition . . . has swung indisputably in favour of modern. Canadians, conservative by habit and inclination, have fallen victims to the present trend. Granted there are mopping up skirmishes here and there, nonetheless, we have evidence in every field of the construction industry that the Canadian people like ornament-free, glass-walled, efficient-looking (and efficient-acting) buildings of modern architecture.[11]

In a sense, Parkin was rewriting the past. In the rhetoric of the 1950s, the history of Canadian architecture of the interwar period was reinterpreted as the long struggle and eventual triumph of modernism over the reactionary forces of tradition.

The Modern movement in Canada in the 1950s was most strongly influenced by the functionalist ideology and architectural minimalism of the German Bauhaus school, which had been imported into the United States during the war and which is commonly referred to as the International style. By the mid-1950s architects and architectural firms such as John B. Parkin Associates in Toronto, Green, Blankstein and Russell in Winnipeg, and Sharp, Thompson, Berwick and Pratt in Vancouver emerged as leaders of modern architecture in Canada. Although each developed a distinctive style and drew upon different architectural sources, their buildings were characterized by the 'ornament-free, glass-walled, efficient-looking (and efficient-acting) buildings' associated with the International style. The strength of the Modern movement was also reinforced by reforms at several schools of architecture. John Bland at McGill and J.H.G. Russell at the University of Manitoba were both leading figures in the Modern movement in Canada and both introduced a curriculum strongly influenced by the Bauhaus model.[12] As will be seen, not all Canadian architects embraced International modernism with the same rigour, but widespread acceptance of the architectural and ideological correctness of modern architecture demanded that all architects conform to some extent to its vocabulary.

The new architecture meshed perfectly with the general climate of optimism that prevailed during the 1950s. Government and business believed that the application of modern principles of public administration, economic management, and technological advancement would lead to ever better and more prosperous communities. Architects of the postwar generation were energized by a similar sense of mission and by a conviction that they too had the tools and knowledge to build better, more efficient, and more humane cities. For example, Raymond Affleck, a student at McGill in the 1940s, said he entered practice in 1949 with the assurance that he could change the world with glass and metal.[13] The architect's sense of power was reinforced by the seemingly unlimited opportunities to apply this knowledge in building new office towers, government buildings, schools, hospitals, and residential and commercial developments.

In the 1950s the idea of modernity was synonymous with progress, and advocates of modern architecture could be found beyond the architectural profession, even within the realm of public policy. The issue of modern architecture was first raised in relation to federal buildings in the report of the Royal Commission on National Development in the Arts, Letters and Sciences – better known as the Massey Commission – that was tabled in 1951.[14] The commission's mandate was to examine ways to promote Canadian culture and science in all fields, including architecture and town planning. In its report, the quality of federal architecture was criticized as being dominated by the 'cult of the extinct' and for its tendency toward imitative and derivative styles.[15] The old arguments resurfaced: that the design of federal buildings should not be left to civil servants and instead should be turned over to private architects. National competitions should be held for major public buildings to 'avoid the mediocrity which so easily besets government architecture.'[16] While the Massey Commission was critical of the past and not entirely clear on the future, it did suggest that architects look to the possibilities of 'the new engineering architecture.'[17] This point of view also found its way into the House of Commons. In 1955 a member of Parliament advised the minister of public works: 'there is no necessity for carrying on . . . the massive stone type of construction we see evidenced in public buildings'; he believed it was more important that 'the buildings we construct . . . are in conformity with the new trend in Canadian architecture.'[18]

Federal Architecture in the International Style

Between the fall of 1953 and 1955 the new administration of the Department of Public Works laid out a program of federal building that would occupy the Building Construction Branch for the next decade. Buildings in more traditional styles, such as the East and West Memorial Buildings and the Printing Bureau in Hull, were still under construction during this period, but all new designs reflected the influence of modern architecture. Two of the earliest and most important projects of this period, which epitomized the new federal image, were the customs house in Vancouver and the General Post Office in Winnipeg, both begun in the fall of 1953 (Figures 8.1 and 8.2).[19]

The two buildings are erudite essays of the International style. The designs of both are defined by an asymmetrical massing of distinct building volumes that correspond to a functional unit. The Winnipeg General Post Office is composed of two separate elements: a ten-storey office block, which contains the post office and general office space, and a three-storey block behind it, which houses the postal terminal. In the latter, industrial standards of construction were followed, with high ceilings and a steel and reinforced-concrete slab construction. It was designed to withstand the weight of the heavy mail sorting equipment and also to support a helicopter landing-pad on the roof. The Vancouver Customs House followed a more compact design that featured two intersecting volumes in which the two-storey long room cut through the vertical slab of a nine-storey office block.[20] Both buildings were enclosed by a glass curtain wall, which gave them a light, transparent quality. On the Winnipeg General Post Office the exterior is controlled by the simple, two-dimensional structural grid that is stripped of any applied ornamentation. The grid also defined the exterior of the Vancouver Customs House but here it provided the framework for a more complex and dynamic play of void and solid in which large expanses of glass contrasted with the horizontal and vertical planes of polished stone. The glass-walled stairwell, which revealed an interior staircase, was a motif closely associated with the architecture of the Bauhaus.

The Winnipeg General Post Office most clearly illustrates the fluid, unstructured definition of space that was characteristic of the International style. The main entrance is set behind the outer row of piers so that one enters into the structural frame before entering through the thin, diaphanous sheet of glass that separates the interior from the exterior. The organization of the interior is radically different from federal buildings of the past (Figure 8.3). The hierarchical sequencing of spaces – usually defined by the vestibule, the elevator or entrance hall, and the main post office lobby – was eliminated in favour of a completely open floor plan broken up into zones of activity. The elevator banks and mechanical services form an island in the middle of this space, and a sliding, open-framed, stainless steel gate was installed between the entrance lobby area and the post office area. In this way, the post office could be closed to the public without interrupting the overall spatial unity. The Winnipeg Gen-

8.1. Vancouver Customs House, Granville Street, Vancouver, British Columbia, 1953–5, in 1955. Designed by C.B.K. Van Norman. Demolished in 1992. (NA, PA-185826)

8.2. General Post Office, Winnipeg, Manitoba, 1953–7. Designed by Green, Blankstein and Russell. (J. Wright, Parks Canada, 1992)

eral Post Office is still occupied by the federal government but the Vancouver Customs House was demolished in 1992.

The William Lyon Mackenzie Building in Toronto was the largest building project to be undertaken by the Building Construction Branch (Figure 8.4).[21] Planning began in the mid-1950s, the contract was signed in 1957, and the building was completed in 1961. It stands on Adelaide Street at the head of Toronto Street on the site of the Toronto Post Office of 1871–4 (see Figure 1.3), which was demolished to make way for the new building. One member of Parliament lamented the loss of this 'fine old post office,' but the demands of progress clearly had priority over any sentimental desire to preserve relics from the past.[22] The new building established a very different relationship with its surroundings. The old post office had formed the centre-piece of a cohesive urban grouping composed of buildings that were of different periods and styles but that were compatible in scale and materials. The William Lyon Mackenzie Building makes no attempt to exploit the compositional potential of the site. As seen from the bottom of Toronto Street, it presents itself as an implacable wall of glass and steel. The architecture of the International style, which regarded the past as irrelevant and aesthetically and philosophically flawed, was not noted for its sensitivity to the existing urban fabric (Figure 8.5).

Designed by the Toronto firm of Shore and Moffat, the design is similar in many respects to the Winnipeg General Post Office. The ground plan forms a simple rectangular base for a more complex and asymmetrical massing composed of three distinct building units of four, twelve, and sixteen storeys. The characteristic curtain wall, with its regular grid pattern, is also evident in this building but, unlike the Vancouver and Winnipeg buildings, colour plays an important part in the design. The metal panels below the windows are tinted a bright turquoise, which contrasts with the slate grey colour of the anodized aluminum sheathing. An open-air square or garden at the centre of the complex was an innovative feature in federal design and would lead to the enclosed atrium buildings that dominated federal architecture of the 1970s and 1980s.

The influence of the International style was equally evident in smaller federal buildings. Two of the best examples of this type are the Town of Mount Royal Post Office (1954–5) in Quebec, by Jean Michaud and R.T. Affleck, and the Truro Federal Building (1956–7) in Nova Scotia, by Vincent Rother in association with Robert E. Cassidy of Truro (Figures 8.6 and 8.7).[23] Rectangular in form and plan, the exterior elevations are dominated by the clearly defined structural bays that are infilled by large sheets of glass. The basic plan of the two buildings, which consists of a post office flanked by an entrance lobby on one side and a night lobby with its private mail boxes on the other, was dictated by the Building Construction Branch, but in both cases the architects gave it a modern interpretation. The spaces are defined by simple planes of brick that intersect with large panes of glass, and so the traditional distinction between load-bearing walls and transparent glass is blurred. Generally, interior furnishings were supplied by the Department of Public Works, but in the case of the Mount Royal Post Office the patterned brickwork in the main entrance lobby and many of the furnishings, including the light, welded-steel writing-tables, were designed by one of the young associates in the firm.[24] The Mount Royal Post Office received a Massey medal for architecture in 1961.

During the 1950s and early 1960s a number of very good examples of the International style were built for the Department of Public Works. However, the experimentation with new materials and new technologies, which was central to the new architecture, sometimes clashed with the inherently cautious and conservative management practices within the federal government. In the case of the William Lyon Mackenzie Building, the success of its design depended on the development of a reliable, durable, and weather-resistant window system, and the architects worked closely with a window manufacturing company and with experts from the United States to develop a design specifically for it. This cooperative arrangement, however, conflicted with departmental regulations stating that architects were not allowed to name specific manufacturers in their specifications. The district architect in Toronto, who represented the department on the project, suggested that a standard off-the-shelf window be used. In explaining his position to the chief architect, he wrote: 'While

8.3. Main postal lobby, Winnipeg General Post Office. The metal gate can be seen on the lower left. (H. Kalen Photographs, 1959)

8.4. William Lyon Mackenzie Building, Toronto, Ontario, 1957–61. Designed by Shore and Moffat. (NA, PA-800448)

I am in agreement that our designs and thinking should keep pace with modern trends, I feel we should be governed by proven methods of construction.'[25] Shore and Moffat won the argument but other firms were not as successful.

In 1956 John B. Parkin Associates contracted to design a one-storey post office in the model residential community of Don Mills in the north end of Toronto. The original plans called for floor-to-ceiling plate-glass windows set in a steel frame, but the district office architect insisted that the amount of glass and the size of the individual panes be reduced. He also wanted the window sills to be raised from floor level to desk height for reasons of safety, maintenance, and heat loss.[26] The original design was in fact very similar to the Truro Federal Building and the Town of Mount Royal Post Office, which were allowed to be constructed without any loss of their architectural integrity. However, the reorganization had given district architectural offices far more independence, resulting in some inconsistencies in policy throughout the system.

The National Library and National Archives Building: Architectural Alternatives

The buildings discussed so far represent the most orthodox expressions of the International style, but federal buildings of the period, like Canadian architecture in general, did not always conform to Bauhaus principles of design. Modern architecture was not a cohesive movement. In Europe between the wars it assumed many different forms, from the organic, sculptural architecture of the German and Dutch expressionists, to the architecture of the Scandinavian countries that was characterized by freer planning and a taste for the colours and textures of traditional and natural building materials. In the United States it was exemplified by the distinctive work of Frank Lloyd Wright and the Prairie school. For the average Canadian architect, the various manifestations of modernism offered a wide vocabulary of forms that could be applied to buildings with varying degrees of success depending on the skill of the architect. There were also many Canadian architects, particularly those who had entered professional practice in the 1920s and 1930s, who could not accept the architectural polemics espoused by men like John C. Parkin. These architects worked within the modernist idiom but retained qualities of design rooted in their own architectural traditions and personal experience.

The National Library of Canada and the Public Archives of Canada (now the National Archives of Canada) Building in Ottawa provides the best and most notable example of the evolutionary modernism in federal architecture (Figure 8.8). The National Library of Canada was established in 1953 in response to recommendations of the Massey Commission, and a few years later the Toronto firm of Mathers and Haldenby was appointed to design a structure to house the new institution. The start of construction was delayed until 1962 and the building was finally opened to the public in 1967.[27] The National Library and National Archives Building is composed of three overlapping but distinct building volumes. A four-storey, U-shaped block for offices and principal working areas is wrapped around a taller central block, which contains the main public areas on the first three floors and the book stacks and records storage areas above. An auditorium forms a separate unit on the west side of the building. The exterior is sheathed in Canadian granite to harmonize with the nearby Supreme Court Building. The geometric simplicity of the massing and the extensive use of glass set in a regular grid pattern reflects the influence of the International style, but the symmetrical plan with two projecting pavilions on either side of the main entrance imparts a sense of formality and order that refers back to the classical tradition. In contrast to the diaphanous, two-dimensional surfaces characteristic of Bauhaus modernism, the windows are pushed back into their stone frames, giving the wall a more substantial, three-dimensional appearance. The central block, with its small rectangular windows that punctuate the stone, assumes an almost bunker-like solidity.

The survival of a more formal architectural tradition is also apparent in the organization of the interior spaces. In contrast to the free unstructured spaces in the Winnipeg General Post Office, the plan of the National Library and National Archives Building is defined as a hierarchy of spaces. The main entrance and public foyer form the central axis and lead off

8.5. William Lyon Mackenzie Building as seen from the bottom of Toronto Street. (J. Wright, Parks Canada, 1992)

8.6. Mount Royal Post Office, Town of Mount Royal, Quebec, 1954–5. Architects: Jean Michaud and R.T. Affleck. (J. Wright, Parks Canada, 1991)

8.7. Federal Building, Truro, Nova Scotia, 1956–7. Designed by Vincent Rother in association with Robert E. Cassidy in 1956. (NA, PA-185805)

8.8. National Library and Public Archives Building, Ottawa, Ontario, 1967. Designed by Mathers and Haldenby in 1955. (M. Trépanier, Parks Canada, 1993)

into two secondary axes to a reading room at one end and the auditorium at the other. A similar arrangement is found on the second floor, with the reference and catalogue room over the main entrance and a library reading room to the rear. At the same time the interior plan strives for clean, uncluttered spaces that are filled with natural light. The public spaces retain an element of formal grandeur; they are beautifully finished with high-quality materials and craftsmanship, soft blond-coloured wood, polished marble floors, and bronze detailing in the staircase and door frames (Figure 8.9). Large murals by some of Canada's well-known artists decorate the main reading rooms. To many architects of the period, this building would have been chastised for its architectural and ideological impurities, but today the value and legitimacy of historical traditions are once again acknowledged in architecture. The design achieves a successful synthesis of some of the best qualities of modernism within a continuing tradition of monumental public architecture.

The Dilemma of Ottawa

The National Library and National Archives was the last major building to be initiated in central Ottawa until the mid-1960s. Several others had been identified but all failed to get beyond the planning stages. The grand schemes for the central core presented in the Gréber plan were considered by many to be dated and outmoded almost as soon as the report had been tabled. The Massey Commission expressed strong reservations about the plan, which it felt was only substituting the romanticism of the Château Laurier with the architecture of Greece and Rome.[28] The East and West Memorial Buildings and the Printing Bureau in Hull were the only major projects to be constructed according to Gréber's plan, and the Memorial Buildings in particular were severely ridiculed in modernist circles for their overt historicism.[29] On the other hand, there remained a strong sense among the public, the politicians, and many architects that modern architecture, with its roots in industrial design, failed to satisfy the popular perception of an important public building.

This lack of consensus explains the fate of a national competition in 1953 for the design of a new building for the National Gallery of Canada.

The winning design by Green, Blankstein and Russell of Winnipeg was a rigorous and uncompromising expression of the International style. It was highly praised by some segments of the architectural community, but others had difficulty accepting such an austere design as a suitable home for an important national institution.[30] Another national competition and numerous planning studies would follow before Moshe Safdie was finally given the commission to design the National Gallery of Canada, completed in 1989.

The idea that a major public building should be imbued with the dignity of state was deeply ingrained. As late as 1967 the architects for the new External Affairs building in Ottawa – now known as the Lester B. Pearson Building – ran into resistance from Minister of External Affairs Paul Martin, who disliked the low, terraced design with which he was presented. He expressed a preference for something more like the National Research Council Building across the street, which had been designed in a Beaux-Arts style in the early 1930s.[31] By this time, however, the issue of defining a consistent architectural image for the national capital no longer seemed relevant. Instead, it appears that high-profile projects in the national capital were viewed as opportunities to showcase the work of some of the best, most respected architects in the country.

During the 1950s and early 1960s the Department of Public Works dealt with the dilemma of building in the central core by avoiding it. Most new construction during this period took place in the satellite developments, where a more practical and economical approach to government building could be applied. Tunney's Pasture and the National Research Council complex on Montreal Road were expanded, and new areas were opened up. Confederation Heights, located in the southwest of the city, was the site of new headquarters for the Post Office, the Department of Public Works, and Communications Research (Figure 8.10).[32] A testing laboratory for Public Works and a central heating plant were also erected on the site. The Post Office Building, named for Sir Alexander Campbell, was designed by Shore and Moffat of Toronto. Like the Winnipeg General Post Office, it features a tall office tower in front and a lower workshop building behind. The Sir Charles Tupper Building, located across the street, was built as the new headquarters of the Department of Public

8.9. Main Reference Room, National Library of Canada, Mural by Alfred Pellan. (NA, C-50886)

Works (Figure 8.11). In contrast to the compact plan and simple geometric volumes of the post office, this building is a low rambling structure consisting of a complex composition of intersecting blocks that stretch out into the landscape and are staggered down the slope of the hill. The use of tinted enamelled panels under the windows and the *brise-soleil* on the windows facing south were recurring features of the period. Both the Sir Alex ander Campbell and the Sir Charles Tupper buildings were constructed under very tight budgets, which dictated the use of brick facing and the installation of serviceable but economical government office interiors.

Setting gave the buildings at Confederation Heights their distinctive character. Most of the federal buildings discussed so far are situated in confined urban lots, surrounded by a jumble of architectural styles and building types. At Confederation Heights the buildings stand as isolated objects on a green tableau of lawn and trees intersected by major traffic arteries. By today's standards, the site may be seen as a sterile balance of architecture and landscape that contradicts the current concept of the city as a constantly changing organic whole made up of interrelated spaces and functions arranged on human scale, but it illustrates an important phase in the history of urban planning. Based on three basic elements – highrise construction, low-density development, and fast, efficient automobile transportation – it provides a small and very contained illustration of an approach to urban design that was conceptualized in the writings of Le Corbusier in the 1910s, and which was realized on a large scale in the development of Brasília as the modern capital of Brazil in the 1950s.

Government of Canada Buildings in the 1950s and 1960s

Most federal buildings in the 1950s and 1960s did not approach the scale or design quality evident in many of the projects discussed above. As always, small and mid-sized government office buildings, which were now generally referred to as 'Government of Canada Buildings' or GOCBs, were the mainstay of the Building Construction Branch. By the

8.10. Birds-eye view of Confederation Heights, Ottawa, Ontario. The Sir Alexander Campbell Building for the Post Office Department (architects: Shore and Moffat) is on the left; the Sir Charles Tupper Building for the Department of Public Works is on the right. (*Public Works In Canada* 5, no. 3 [March 1957]:33)

8.11. Sir Charles Tupper Building, Ottawa, Ontario, 1957–61. Designed by Hazelgrove, Lithwick and Lambert. (J. Wright, Parks Canada, 1992)

1950s many of the older federal buildings, which had been designed to house a post office on the ground floor and perhaps a customs office above, could no longer accommodate all the required government services. The enthusiasm for modern architecture also led to the perception that older government buildings were old-fashioned and outmoded in appearance and that they did not reflect the government's modern and progressive self-image. The Massey Commission went as far as to state that 'our older post offices can only be described as sordid.'[33] During this period many older federal government buildings were, in the parlance of the federal bureaucracy transferred to Crown Assets Disposal. Many nineteenth- and early twentieth-century government buildings were demolished, but, fortunately, many others were rescued by communities that still regarded them as valuable assets. Many found new life as town halls, court-houses, libraries, and office buildings.

The GOCBs of the 1950s and 1960s exhibit a variety of design solutions. The federal building in Sudbury, Ontario, is a good regional adaptation of the International style (Figure 8.12). The post office building in St John's, Newfoundland, conforms to a more conservative design type, similar to those established in the late 1940s and early 1950s (Figure 8.13).[34] The federal building in Brockville, Ontario, cannot be described as being in the International style but it represents a good example of regional design that effectively combines modern elements with an appreciation of local materials evident in the use of textured rubble limestone walls (Figure 8.14).

The most common and ubiquitous pattern for this period is illustrated by the federal building in Arvida, Quebec (Figure 8.15). While accurate figures have not been compiled, variations of this basic design type probably account for more than half of the urban public building construction in Canada between 1953 and 1963. Built to accommodate the post office, the Department of Public Works, the Unemployment Insurance Commission, as well as a caretaker's apartment, it is a two-storey building with a reinforced concrete foundation and a steel-frame superstructure. The exterior walls are faced with brick, enamelled-metal panels, and aluminum window sashes and railings. Its simple rectangular plan is

8.12. Federal Building, Sudbury, Ontario, 1955–8. Architects: Fabro and Townend. (NA, PA-185820)

8.13. Post Office Building, St John's, Newfoundland, 1959. Architects: D.A. Weber and C.A. Fowler. (Public Works and Government Services Canada. Heritage Recording and Technical Data Services, 1993)

masked by the asymmetrical composition of the façade, which is defined by a solid brick 'feature wall' to one side juxtaposed by a large expanse of glass curtain wall on the other. The walls and roof are defined as thin slabs that project out from the front façade to form an overhang to reduce the amount of direct sunlight on the interior. The use of the glass-fronted stairwell, a feature seen on the Vancouver Customs House, adds a dynamic diagonal line to the design. Typically, the building was built slightly back from the street to set it apart from the other, often similar, commercial structures that surrounded it.

Variations on this theme were built in hundreds of towns and cities across the country. The Arvida building was designed by the Building Construction Branch, but many others were contracted to private consultants. The Government of Canada Building in Sarnia, Ontario, which adopts a very similar formula but on a larger scale, was designed by Riddle, Connor and Associates (Figure 8.16). The practice of using larger numbers of private consultants resulted in some diversity in the character and quality of the designs, but these differences were much less apparent than might be expected. Working for the federal government imposed considerable restraints and limitations on the freedom of architects to develop individual solutions. The preliminary planning process that was set up in 1953, whereby staff from the Requirements Division worked with the client department to develop a basic plan and program, often meant that commissioned architects were given a 'suggested' plan as a guide for development of the design.[35] The architects could try to resist the system and develop something original, but, as the Toronto firm of John B. Parkin Associates discovered in its project for the Don Mills Post Office, the effort was sometimes more trouble than it was worth. It was easier to give the client, in this case the Department of Public Works, what it wanted, standard designs that used proven materials and familiar modes of construction.[36]

Mass Production in Post Office Construction

Small post offices had always played an important part in the activities of

8.14. Federal Building, Brockville, Ontario, 1962–4. Architects: Drever and Smith. (NA, PA-185810)

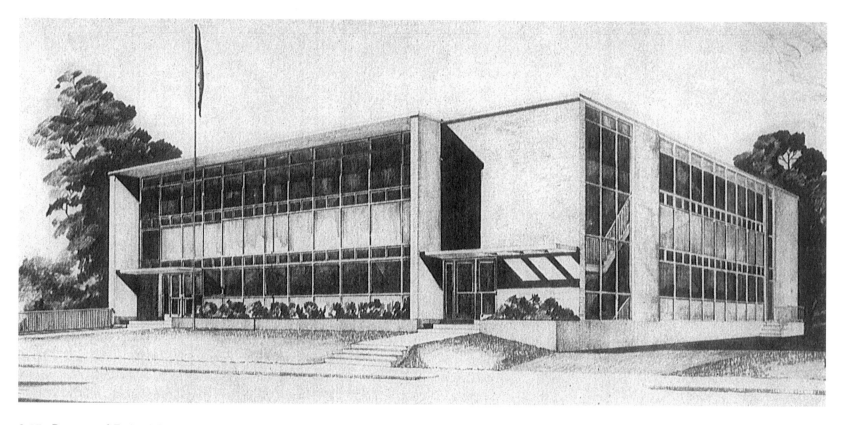

8.15. Drawing of Federal Building, Arvida, Quebec, 1955–6. Designed by the Building Construction Branch. (*Public Works in Canada* 3, no. 10 [Oct. 1955]:41)

8.16. Government of Canada Building, Sarnia, Ontario, 1956–60. Architects: Riddle, Connor and Associates. (University of Calgary, Canadian Architectural Archives, Panda Collection)

the Building Construction Branch, but in the mid-1950s and 1960s new government policies prompted a building boom of unprecedented scale for this level of facility. During the late 1940s and early 1950s relatively few were erected because the efforts of an understaffed department were focused on the more pressing large-scale projects. The increase in staff in the mid-1950s coincided with a gradual increase in the number of post offices that were constructed. In 1957 the Liberal government launched a new program of 'winter works' designed to provide employment over the traditionally lean winter months. Once again the small post office provided a useful but relatively inexpensive vehicle for distributing economic benefits widely. Between 1957 and the program's demise in 1967 approximately 750 were constructed across the country.[37]

The winter works construction program represented the final phase in the outward expansion of a network of federal buildings that had begun in 1867. At the same time the department showed the first signs of unburdening itself of the increasingly unwieldy real estate empire. Most of these post offices were built for communities that, prior to the establishment of new guidelines in 1957, had been considered too small to justify the expense of a separate building; many others were built to replace older buildings that were too big and too expensive to operate.[38] The imposing public buildings of the late nineteenth and early twentieth centuries, with their characteristic corner tower, were often replaced by these small and inconspicuous structures.[39]

The typical small federal post office of this period ranged from 800 to 2,500 square feet and was expected to cost approximately $25,000 or less. Most had only one room, although a few slightly larger ones included additional space for other government departments. They were usually one storey in height with a flat roof and a wood-frame or masonry (usually cinder block) structure. Most were sheathed in brick and only a few were built entirely of wood. The main entrance was slightly off-centre, with a mailbox and night lobby containing private boxes to one side, and with the post office lobby to the other. A row of large windows with transom lights above them was set within a frame of wood sashes and plywood panels. The main façade was either recessed slightly and sheltered by the overhanging roof or by a simple porch supported by tubular steel posts. Almost all were set back from the sidewalk, providing a small patch of lawn where a flag-pole and perhaps a sign could be raised (Figure 8.17).

In 1964 the standard design was revised and improved under the direction of James A. Langford, who became chief architect in 1963. An internal competition was established for all employees in the department for a standard 800-square foot post office. The winning proposal, known as the SP-800, was a significant improvement on the old design (Figure 8.18). Its post-and-beam construction, so familiar to suburban residential development across the country, consisted of widely spaced uprights supporting laminated wood beams that spanned the building from front to back. It was a simple and compact yet pleasing design that was inexpensive to build. The use of standardized and modular building components made it faster to erect, and easier and less expensive to alter. The 'feature wall,' which was often extended out beyond the building envelope, was intended to provide an opportunity to introduce local materials or design motifs characteristic of the community or region. The chief architect had intended this design to be a limited edition, to be replaced after a few years by something new.[40] Unfortunately, it proved to be too successful, and the same plan was used with little variation until the winter works program ended in 1967.

Other Clients: The RCMP and Scientific Research

A series of standard plans was also developed for the Royal Canadian Mounted Police.[41] The RCMP building in Moncton, a simple two-storey brick block punctuated by continuous rows of sash windows on either side of a central entrance, is an example of the headquarters for a division or subdivision (Figure 8.19). The branch also developed standard plans for small detachment buildings, which combined a residence with an office and a lock-up. Several different types were developed; one was based on plans borrowed from the Central Mortgage and Housing Corporation, and another was designed by the Building Construction Branch. Both drew upon residential models. The buildings designed for the RCMP were rather dull and prosaic, but the client was quite satisfied. The RCMP, like the Department of Militia and Defence in the early 1900s, placed little value on architectural invention. They wanted buildings that were clean, comfortable, efficient, and, most importantly, economical.

The expansion of the national network of research centres that had begun in the 1940s continued unabated throughout the 1950s and 1960s. The National Research Council and the Department of Agriculture remained the principal clients, but other departments and agencies, such as the Department of Fisheries and Oceans and the Pulp and Paper Institute of Canada, were also building new laboratories. Most of the work generated by these programs was very conventional, showing no substantial change from the design types developed in the 1940s and early 1950s. The Fisheries Research Board Station on the University of British Columbia campus, designed by Thompson, Berwick and Pratt of Vancouver, was one exception (Figures 8.20 and 8.21). One of three research buildings on the campus designed by the firm, it was distinguished from the typical government research facility by the clear separation of the laboratory from the administrative functions.[42] The larger block housed a fish cannery, a cold storage facilities, a workshop, and various laboratories. The smaller administrative block housed the offices of the International North Pacific Fisheries Commission, a lounge, and a lecture room. The two units were linked by an overhead walkway. The clarity of the construction and the simplicity of the geometry was characteristic of the work of Thompson, Berwick and Pratt, who were leaders of the Modern movement on the west coast.

Building in the North: The New Frontier

Building in the North provided the Building Construction Branch with some of its most exciting challenges, and its work, particularly in the harsh conditions of the Arctic, was a source of pride for the branch.[43] The federal government had been building in the Yukon and the Northwest Territories since the turn of the century, but, with the exception of the brief

8.17. Standard Post Office, Ponteix, Saskatchewan, *ca.* 1957–8. Designed by the Building Construction Branch. (J. Wright, Parks Canada, 1992)

8.18. An example of an SP-800 at Brechin, Ontario. Designed by the Building Construction Branch. (J. Wright, Parks Canada, 1993)

but intense period of development in Dawson during the gold-rush, the demands of the North had only a marginal impact upon the activities of the Department of Public Works. Prior to World War II the federal presence in the North was almost exclusively represented by the RCMP, whose primary function was to assert Canadian sovereignty. In the 1920s the Chief Architect's Branch had occasionally been called upon to design and arrange the shipment of prefabricated barrack buildings to new posts, but neither the RCMP nor the Chief Architect's Branch gave serious consideration to the unique problems of building in the Arctic. Much of what was erected in the early years was unsuited to the harsh climate.[44]

After the war, northern development emerged as a government priority. No longer a vast wilderness of undetermined value, the North was seen as the new frontier; its wealth of natural resources would bring greater prosperity and enable the nation to push the boundaries of modern industrial society even into the High Arctic.[45] Its mineral and hydroelectric potential promised new sources of wealth to Canadian and international resource industries. The postwar development boom was triggered to a large extent by the onset of the Cold War and the recognition of the strategic importance of the North as the first line of defence against a Soviet invasion over the polar cap. The establishment of three different systems of manned and unmanned radar stations – the Pinetree Line, the Mid-Canada Line, and the Distant Early Warning (DEW) Line – brought new wealth and established lines of supply and communication that were funded by both the Canadian and the U.S. governments.

Throughout the 1950s and 1960s the federal government and the Department of Public Works continued to build schools, hospitals, and other government buildings in such established centres as Whitehorse, Yellowknife, and Fort Smith, but they also began to lay out new model communities that boasted many of the amenities found in modern Canadian cities in the south. Inuvik, which was begun in 1955, and an expansion of Frobisher Bay (now Iqaluit), which was planned in 1963 but never completed, illustrate well the federal government's vision of the North and its changing shape from the mid-1950s to the early 1960s. Inuvik was intended to replace the nearby community of Aklavik as the administrative and research centre for the Mackenzie District.[46] The new townsite was selected in 1953 and construction began two years later. The town consisted of government offices with a post office and territorial liquor store, the RCMP barracks, a twenty-room school, an eighty-bed hospital, residential accommodation for a population of 1,700, a central heating plant, twenty miles of road, and an airport (Figure 8.22).[47] Some of the building plans were prepared by the Calgary firm of Rule, Wynn and Rule; others were prepared by the staff of the Building Construction Branch.[48]

Cold, permafrost, the short building season, the absence of local building supplies, and the difficulty of shipping materials into the area demanded innovative approaches to construction, meticulous planning, and accurate scheduling of the work. Like the earlier generation of buildings at Dawson, those at Inuvik were constructed on wooden piles. At Inuvik the piles were creosoted and steam-jetted into the permafrost, where they were left for a year to freeze.[49] The next spring pre-cut building materials were transported by road to Great Slave Lake and shipped by barge to the townsite. Under these conditions only light wooden buildings of the simplest design were practical, and the two-storey wood-frame and plywood buildings with a low-pitched or flat roof that were constructed at Inuvik were typical of federal buildings in the North in the 1950s. The first floors were usually raised about three to five feet above ground level to provide insulated air space between the building and the cold ground. An important innovation at Inuvik was the 'utilidor,' an above-ground conduit that enclosed all the community utilities – steam heat from a central heating plant, electricity, water, and sewage. The town was fully occupied in 1961.

The vision of the North as the new frontier that could be conquered and subdued by modern technology and industry reached a peak of enthusiasm in 1958. The Conservative Party, under the leadership of John Diefenbaker, had just won a federal election. Its 'Road to Resources' campaign had promised a new age of prosperity that would be fuelled by northern development. A flagship of their northern policy was a $75-million plan for a modern Arctic city at Frobisher Bay on Baffin Island, which was flourishing with the presence of a U.S. Strategic Air Command

8.19. Standard RCMP district headquarters. The Moncton RCMP building is seen in the top left. Designed by the Building Construction Branch. (*RCMP Quarterly* 5, no. 4 [April 1957]:26)

8.20. Fisheries Research Board Station, Vancouver, British Columbia, 1957–60. Architects: Thompson, Berwick and Pratt. (J. Wright, Parks Canada, 1993)

(SAC) base.[50] In 1958 an interdepartmental committee was formed to define requirements, and the following year a team of architectural and engineering consultants was assembled to prepare a more detailed proposal.[51] One year later the team unveiled a futuristic vision consisting of twelve silo-like apartment buildings surrounding a plastic dome that would enclose a shopping centre, schools, churches, a fire hall, administrative offices, a community hall, a bank, a restaurant, a funeral home, a liquor store, and parks and gardens with a fountain (Figures 8.23 and 8.24). Other service buildings would be located outside this central grouping. Heat and electricity would be provided by a nuclear power station. The plain functional character of the buildings at Inuvik was to be replaced by the construction of these strikingly modern twelve-storey apartment blocks featuring elevators, large plate-glass windows, and even small balconies off each apartment. The interior of the central dome, where temperatures would be maintained at a constant 70°F and where ladies could stroll in the mall in high-heeled shoes with their baskets of groceries, was a direct transplant of suburban Toronto or Vancouver to the High Arctic.

By the 1960s the defence strategy of the United States changed with the development of long-range missiles and bombers that could refuel in the air. The U.S. air bases in the Arctic became obsolete and in 1963–4 the SAC bases at Frobisher Bay and Churchill, Manitoba, were closed. The departure of the U.S. military and the declining strategic importance of the North meant that the construction of such a sophisticated and expensive development no longer seemed necessary or viable. Frobisher Bay would remain the main administrative centre for the eastern Arctic but subsequent government construction would assume a more realistic scale. The futuristic vision of the early 1960s gave way to the more mundane but necessary business of constructing schools, hospitals, and RCMP detachments in the North.

Correctional Institutions

In the late 1890s the Penitentiaries Branch of the Department of Justice had wrested control of the construction and maintenance of federal prisons

8.21. Bird's-eye view of the Fisheries Research Board Station (lower left corner). The Forest Products Laboratory, also designed *ca.* 1955 by Thompson, Berwick and Pratt in a similar manner, can be seen in the centre of the photograph. (University of British Columbia Library, Special Collections)

8.22. Federal Housing Units, Inuvik, N.W.T., 1955, in 1958. (Northwest Territories Archives, Watt Collection, N90-0005:308)

from the Chief Architect's Branch. This arrangement survived until 1961, when penitentiary construction was transferred back to the Department of Public Works as part of a general government policy to centralize all federal construction services under one department. The move also coincided with sweeping reforms of the Canadian correctional system and the beginning of a ten-year building program that would increase the number of federal prisons from nine to thirty-four.[52] At the peak of construction in the mid-1960s penitentiaries accounted for over 40 per cent of the work carried out under the direction of the Building Construction Branch.

The new correctional institutions reflected new approaches to penal reform. The inadequacies of the Canadian penitentiary system had been the subject of discussion since the 1930s but little progress was made until the 1950s. In 1958 a federal-provincial conference was held on the state of Canadian prisons. As a result of this meeting the Department of Justice established a Correctional Planning Committee, headed by A.J. MacLeod, with a mandate to develop a plan to reform the federal penitentiary service according to modern correctional principles. In the past, penitentiaries had been designed to punish offenders and to modify their behaviour through confinement, isolation, and forced labour. Modern correctional institutions were developed according to two main factors: the goal of rehabilitation by retraining and counselling, and the importance of having different types of institutions and programs that were designed to meet the needs of different types of offenders. The committee's report, submitted in 1959, recommended that five separate regions be established in Canada, each with a full range of correctional facilities: a reception and classification centre where the needs and the security risk of an offender would be assessed; minimum-, medium-, and maximum-security institutions; and specialized detention centres for youths and drug offenders. Priority was given to medium-security institutions, three of which were designed for young delinquents and one for drug offenders. On the recommendation of officials within the Canadian Corrections Service, the well-known U.S. firm of Hellmuth, Obata and Kassabaum was commissioned to develop a basic design and construction concept.

In the late 1950s this firm had built a penitentiary at Marion, Illinois, which was seen as an appropriate model.[53] Although the plan and layout of the building in Marion was very different from those that were eventually built in Canada, all were similar in their use of a modular approach to construction, which consisted of pre-cast concrete panels set into a structure composed of pre-cast concrete posts and beams. A new design unit was created within the Building Construction Branch to supervise the work, and the individual projects were contracted out to Canadian architects who adapted the basic concept to specific requirements.[54] By 1963 construction had begun on a Narcotic Addicts' Treatment Institution at Matsqui, British Columbia, and a Youth Offenders' Institution at Cowansville, Quebec. Plans for three other medium-security institutions for young offenders were developed for Springhill, Nova Scotia, Warkworth, Ontario, and Drumheller, Alberta, by 1964.[55] Standard plans for a maximum-security facility and for a reception centre were also developed between 1964 and 1967, but construction on this part of the program did not begin in earnest until the end of the decade.

The institution at Cowansville was the first to be constructed under the program (Figures 8.25 and 8.26).[56] Unlike the fortress-like buildings of the past, the complex adopted an informal, less authoritarian plan. The buildings were organized into four main groupings: an administrative centre and a building for receiving visitors, a service centre with dining hall, school, chapel, gymnasium, and laundry, a special treatment centre with a hospital and reception centre, and the living centre consisting of four separate dormitory buildings. Each unit housed 108 inmates organized into sixteen-room living units. Movement between each of the areas was controlled by a system of covered corridors that were enclosed on each side by concrete grills. Concrete grills were also installed over all the windows, and a high, wire-mesh fence surrounded the property.

The buildings were constructed of standardized pre-cast, reinforced-concrete beams and posts that were infilled with pre-cast concrete panels. The other medium-security institutions, would vary in layout and plan but all were based on a reconfiguration of this basic construction unit. The modular approach was intended to streamline the design and con-

8.23. Proposal for town of 5,000 at Frobisher Bay (Iqaluit), Baffin Island. Project team: Dickinson and Associates, Toronto; Rounthwaite and Fairfield. Plans prepared in 1959. (*Public Works in Canada 7*, no. 10 [October 1959]:29)

8.24. Interior of mall, Frobisher Bay. (*Public Works in Canada 7*, no. 10 [October 1959]:30)

8.25. Youth Offenders' Institution, Cowansville, Quebec, 1962–6. Architect: P.O. Trépanier. Based on standard program developed by Hellmuth, Obata and Kassabaum. (Kenneth McReynolds, *Physical Components of Correctional Goals* [Ottawa: Information Canada 1972])

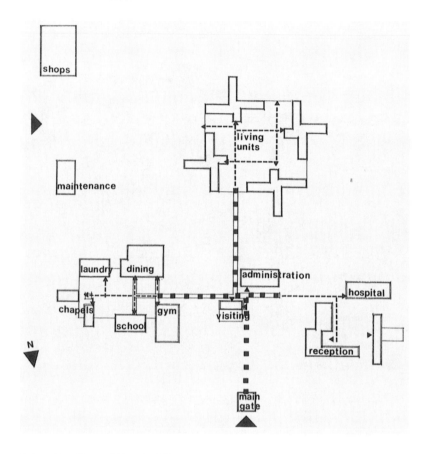

8.26. Site Plan of Youth Offenders' Institution, Cowansville. (Kenneth McReynolds, *Physical Components of Correctional Goals* [Ottawa: Information Canada 1972])

struction phase but the innovative nature of the system occasionally created its own problems. For example, the contractors responsible for the Springhill facilities were unfamiliar with pre-cast concrete construction, and many delays were incurred while they tried to fathom how to put the building together.[57]

Changing Conditions in Government Building, 1964 – 1967

During the years from 1964 to 1967 the Department of Public Works and the Building Construction Branch were buffeted by a number of conflicting and contradictory forces. In some ways, the quality of federal design was never higher. The coming centennial celebration in 1967 was being marked by the construction of a number of important public buildings and cultural institutions that showcased the work of some of Canada's best architects. New policies, intended to encourage better and more innovative standards of design, were also initiated in the mid-1960s. But at the same time, pressure was mounting to control the costs for construction in the face of rising expenditures for the expensive new social programs that were being implemented under a Liberal minority government. Generous budgets could be found for a few high-profile projects, but elsewhere the Treasury Board, the powerful overseer of all government spending, was forcing the Department of Public Works to develop cheaper and more efficient ways of providing basic office accommodation.

The 1960s was also a period of organizational flux. In 1960 the Diefenbaker government had established the Royal Commission on Government Organization to examine all government departments.[58] The Glassco Commission, as it was commonly known, pointed to the proliferation of separate construction branches outside the Department of Public Works that now controlled over 60 per cent of the total spending for federal construction. Once again, it was recommended that the Department of Public Works should assume responsibility for all the architectural and engineering services within the federal system.[59] It was also suggested that the department act solely as a service agency, responding to the needs of other government departments rather than initiating projects. In response to the report of the Glassco Commission, the construction of penitentiaries and foreign embassies was transferred to the department in 1961, but attempts at further centralization were stalled by the refusal of the larger departments – in particular the Department of Transport and the Department of National Defence – to relinquish autonomy over their own programs.[60]

In 1963 the Department of Public Works underwent another internal restructuring that was designed to create what was described as a centrally controlled, decentralized organization. Federal buildings were broken down into five categories of design – office buildings, laboratories, penitentiaries, northern construction, and special projects. Five teams were established in Ottawa to provide design expertise for each type. The teams were responsible for operations research, establishing general standards, programming construction projects, and establishing design review criteria. A Client Department Division, a Consulting Services Division, and an Administration Services section were also created to provide liaison services, specialized technical support, and administrative services to the regions. The regional offices, which operated as semi-autonomous agencies, were responsible for tendering contracts, the supervision of private consultants, and the administration of contracts. Under the new regime very little new design work was carried out by departmental staff. As noted above, some standard plans were developed in-house, but most other buildings were contracted to outside architects.[61]

The reorganization of the Building Construction Branch coincided with the appointment of James A. Langford as chief architect.[62] At the age of thirty-five, Langford was by far the youngest ever appointed; he was also the first since E.L. Horwood (1914–18) to be hired from outside the federal government. But in many respects Langford conformed to the typical professional profile of a chief architect: as the former deputy minister of public works for the Province of Saskatchewan, he was very familiar with the business of administering a design and construction agency within a government bureaucracy. Langford was a youthful outsider who came to the position with a determination to raise the quality of federal buildings across the country. He claimed that the typical federal building provided good, serviceable accommodation, but that the designs

tended to be repetitive and that contract architects were never given enough lattitude to develop new ideas and new solutions. He felt that the department should assume the role of a knowledgable client and work with the architect on behalf of the future tenants to develop the best possible plan.[63] To indicate the new emphasis on design quality, he initiated design awards for buildings constructed for the Department of Public Works.[64]

Langford also set up a fine arts program that allocated a percentage of the construction costs to works of art. The mural in the lobby of the Ottawa headquarters of the Department of Agriculture is a notable product of this program (Figure 8.27). Created by Vancouver artist Takao Tanabe, it is an abstract composition executed in soft earthy colours that harmonize beautifully with the light and airy entrance foyer of the building, which was completed in the 1960s. The project was an artistic success but it also revealed the difficulties inherent in such a program. Although the minister of agriculture had agreed to the idea of a mural, he had envisioned something along the lines of a modern-day 'Gleaners'; Tanabe's modern composition did not please him at all. The mural was completed as proposed but the Department of Agriculture would never again participate in the program.[65] Using federal buildings as a vehicle for displaying and supporting the work of Canadian artists was an innovative idea but it was fraught with many pitfalls. Departments were reluctant to increase the cost of buildings by such frills, particularly if they might not like what they paid for. It also left the government open to criticism from the public as to what constitutes good art and whether public funds should be spent on such extravagances.

The pattern of government spending on federal building within the Department of Public Works reflected changing needs and priorities. By the mid-1960s the demand for a typical federal public building, containing a post office and other government services, was declining. Other specialized buildings such as penitentiaries and research institutions, accounted for a much larger percentage of the government's construction budget.[66] Federal architecture in this period also reflected new trends in design. The functionalist principles of the International style had been exploited in the hands of many developers as a licence to

8.27. Mural by Takao Tanabe in the lobby of the Sir John Carling Building, Ottawa, Ontario. (M. Trépanier, Parks Canada, 1994)

produce sterile glass boxes built of cheap materials. In the 1960s Canadian architects sought to redefine and rethink modern architecture in terms of humanistic rather than mechanistic values. In formal terms, the pristine cubic volumes and the slick, translucent surfaces associated with the International style were being supplanted by an architecture of textured surfaces and complex compositions composed of varied and irregular masses.

The National Arts Centre, Ottawa

The new trend could be detected at all levels of building, but the federal building project that epitomizes the architectural aesthetics of the 1960s is the National Arts Centre in Ottawa (Figure 8.28).[67] The federal government had been considering the idea of a large auditorium and convention centre on Confederation Square since 1961. In 1963 the National Capital Arts Alliance, a group of fifty-five arts groups in the Ottawa region, put forward a recommendation to build an arts centre that would serve as a showcase for the performing arts both in the national capital and throughout Canada. With the centennial of Confederation just three years away, the proposal was approved and the secretary of state was given responsibility for the project. G. Hamilton Southam was appointed to coordinate the project, and a number of subcommittees, made up of representatives from the performing arts community, were created to advise on building requirements. The Montreal firm of Affleck, Desbarats, Dimakopoulos, Lebensold, Sise was selected to prepare the plans. As the architects of the Place des Arts in Montreal, the Queen Elizabeth Theatre in Vancouver, and the Centennial Centre in Charlottetown, the firm had considerable experience in the field.

The National Arts Centre in Ottawa was a major architectural and cultural achievement for the federal government. As completed in 1969, it featured a 2,300-seat hall for opera, an 800-seat theatre, a smaller studio for experimental productions, and a salon for chamber music recitals. The exterior design is conceived as a series of terraces that hug the slope leading down to the Rideau Canal. Three strong masses, corresponding to the three main theatres, project above the low-lying profile of the terraces. In contrast to the regular geometry of the International style, the design adopts the triangle as its basic module that is repeated, multiplied, and expanded throughout the building. The overall composition, which incorporates a variety of irregular masses, assumes an organic quality, so that the compositional complexity is constantly shifting as one moves around the building. Although the exterior is sheathed entirely in an exposed aggregate concrete, the architects treated the surface in a variety of contrasting textures to give the building the sense of fortress-like solidity and rugged massing that defined the brutalist aesthetic of the 1960s in Canada.

In addition, the National Arts Centre had a liberating effect on architecture in the national capital. Although it was part of a larger plan for the redevelopment of downtown Ottawa, the architects were given the freedom to develop a unique design.[68] Rather than try to define a stylistic theme that would shape all federal development according to a single image, the National Arts Centre introduced the idea that important federal buildings could serve as a showcase for the best in Canadian architecture. Such subsequent projects as the National Gallery of Canada and the Canadian Museum of Civilization were manifestations of this same attitude.

The National Arts Centre also left the federal government with a huge financial hangover. The steering committee clearly intended to create a notable architectural and cultural landmark and no one involved in the project was able or willing to dampen the general spirit of enthusiasm. In 1965 the project had been estimated at about $20 million;[69] when the building was at last opened in 1969 the final bill was $46.4 million. The National Arts Centre seemed to confirm in the minds of many politicians and bureaucrats that good architecture was expensive to build, and their experience with this project fuelled a growing climate of restraint in government building.

'Chevrolets – not Cadillacs': The General-Purpose Office Building

As millions of dollars were being spent on the National Arts Centre and

8.28. National Arts Centre, Ottawa, Ontario, 1965–8. Architects: Affleck, Desbarats, Dimakopoulos, Lebensold, Sise. (Public Works and Government Services Canada, Heritage Recording and Technical Data Services, 1993)

even more federal money was being pumped into the development of the Expo 67 site in Montreal, the Building Construction Branch was developing new guidelines for government office accommodation based on commercial standards. This idea had been born during World War I with the construction of the Hunter Building in Ottawa, but at that time the approach was seen as a temporary, stopgap measure. In the 1960s the new standards would dictate most of what was built in Ottawa.

The rigour with which the government, and in particular the Treasury Board, imposed cost-cutting measures on government buildings was a reflection of the new priorities in spending.[70] In the face of slowed economic growth, rising unemployment rates, and growing regional disparities, the Liberal minority government under the leadership of Lester B. Pearson entered into a number of expensive cost-sharing arrangements with the provinces to implement a national health care program, job training programs, generous funding to post-secondary education, and an improved Canada Pension Plan. Spending on public works remained relatively stable but the rising demand for office space, particularly in Ottawa, forced the Department of Public Works to find cheaper ways of meeting the need. These financial pressures and their impact on design can be traced through three major office buildings in Ottawa that were constructed in the 1960s.

The Brooke Claxton Building at Tunney's Pasture was a forerunner of the general-purpose office building (Figure 8.29).[71] Completed in 1964, it was planned as a monolithic tower with a single service core, a configuration that provided the most space at the lowest cost. It also adopted a basic structural module that was defined on the exterior by the single window unit. All structural and finishing details throughout the building were based on this module. This approach cut costs and streamlined the production process. The Brooke Claxton Building was, however, built for a specific tenant, and the quality of the exterior materials was comparatively high: it featured a light grey granite facing on the structural piers and a polished black granite base. The building also included specialized spaces, such an oak-panelled boardroom on the ground floor and a recessed terrace on the sixteenth for the minister's offices. Although radically different in scale and materials from the two- and three-storey

8.29. Brooke Claxton Building, Tunney's Pasture, Ottawa, Ontario 1961–4. Architects: Balharrie, Helmer, Greenspoon, Freedlander, Dunne. (J. Wright, Parks Canada, 1993)

buildings that had previously defined the campus-like environment, it was situated at the head of the central boulevard and served as a focal point to the complex.

The pressure to reduce costs mounted through the mid-1960s. The largest office complex to be erected during these years was the Department of National Defence Headquarters in Ottawa, which was designed by the Toronto firm of John B. Parkin Associates (Figure 8.30). It consists of two towers that are linked by a lower horizontal block, and is faced with sand-coloured, pre-cast concrete panels. The deeply recessed windows give the façade a sculptural, three-dimensional appearance characteristic of the period. Because of its proximity to the Parliament Buildings, the National Defence Headquarters was freed from some of the financial restrictions placed on other projects, but the dialogue between the architect and the Department of Public Works provides a revealing case study of the government's overriding concern with budgets.

The planning process was marked by constant tension between the architects and the department (with the Treasury Board watching in the background) as to what constituted acceptable standards in design and construction. The original proposal, which included a number of innovative features, such as an arched-span structural system that allowed for more widely spaced piers, was estimated at approximately $30 per square foot. The Department of Public Works, as directed by the Treasury Board, insisted that the cost be reduced to no more than $20 to $25 per square foot, and suggested that the architects adopt a cheaper flat-plate structure, lower the ceiling heights, reduce the amount of exterior glass, cut back on the air-conditioning system, and use less expensive finishing materials for the public spaces. To illustrate what the department wanted, the architects were given a tour of some recently constructed commercial-grade buildings in Ottawa. Representatives of the Parkin firm subsequently described these buildings as cheaply built, with minimum quality materials and mechanical systems, and featuring constricted public spaces.[72] Department officials countered criticisms with the statement that what the government wanted was 'a Chevrolet – not a Cadillac.'[73]

The debate over cost and features continued until fall 1967, when the contract with the architects came very close to being cancelled. The Treasury Board Advisory Committee on Accommodations had received a proposal from Robert Campeau, a major developer of commercial and residential buildings in Ottawa, who offered to take over the project. Campeau proposed to construct a building according to his own plans, which would then be leased back to the government for a number of years. At the end of the lease agreement, the building would become the property of the federal government – a 'rent-to-own' arrangement on a grand scale. According to John C. Parkin, who was given the opportunity to review the project for the minister, Campeau had reduced the cost by proposing a single tower that would be sheathed in a cheaper black and aluminum curtain wall and that would have far less window area. The building would also be serviced by only one elevator bank and would not differentiate between public spaces and general-purpose office space.[74] Parkin defended his design and the higher cost on the grounds that it was an important part of the redevelopment of Confederation Square and the parliamentary precinct. The materials and fragmented massing he proposed were designed to harmonize with the scale, colour, and romantic profile of the older buildings around Parliament Hill. Parkin won the argument and kept the contract after he made some further compromises, but Campeau's lease-back scheme would resurface in the 1970s.

While the Department of National Defence Headquarters was under construction, the Department of Public Works was working on its own solution to the rising cost of government building. It was called the General-Purpose Office Building (Figure 8.31).[75] The prototype, which was to be located in Tunney's Pasture, was designed by architect Ronald Ogilvie who had considerable experience designing commercial-grade space. Like the Brooke Claxton Building, the General-Purpose Office Building was a monolithic block sheathed in pre-cast concrete panels with a single service core. It adopted a flat-plate construction on a five-foot modular system with a standard structural grid of twenty-feet square. It had also been planned without a specific occupant in mind. This eliminated the client department from the planning process and it also avoided the problems of dealing with individual departments which often entered

8.30. Department of National Defence Headquarters, Ottawa, Ontario, 1969–74. Designed by John B. Parkin Associates. (M. Trépanier, Parks Canada, 1994)

8.31. Prototype design of a General-Purpose Office Building, 1967–9. Architect: Ronald Ogilvie. Designed *ca.* 1967. The building is now known as the R.H. Coats Building. (J.E. Wilkins, 'Production of a Prototype,' *Dispatch*, no. 1 [1968]:3)

into the process with special needs and expected additional features. The contract bids all came in at about the $20-per-square-foot target; at a time when the government was still reeling over the staggering cost overruns for the National Arts Centre, the project was hailed as a major success. The government's first general-purpose office building is now known as the R.H. Coats Building and its offspring can be found throughout the national capital region.

Conclusion

During the 1950s and 1960s the Department of Public Works produced some outstanding architectural works that mirrored the evolution of Canadian architecture in general. Buildings such as the Vancouver Customs House, the Winnipeg General Post Office, and the William Lyon Mackenzie Building in Toronto redefined the federal image in terms of International modernism and established a vocabulary of design that set the pattern of building for the next decade. By the mid-1960s federal building was beginning to see the influence of new approaches to modernism that were characterized by a freer hand in form, composition, and materials. This shift was expressed most eloquently in the design for the National Arts Centre in Ottawa. At the same time, the expansion of the federal government's involvement in other areas – scientific research, culture, northern development, and penitentiary services – began to claim an increasing proportion of the federal construction budget.

The federal building program of the 1950s and 1960s marked the last and most significant expansion of the vast real estate empire that had been created and managed by the Department of Public Works. The volume of building carried out during these years had no close equivalent in the history of the department. More importantly, buildings constructed during these years reflected the changing nature of the place of government in Canadian society. The unprecedented expansion of government into all aspects of Canadian life created a demand for millions of square feet of additional office space across the country. Previous generations of urban public buildings, which had been designed to house a post office and one or two additional departments, were quickly rendered obsolete. In their place the government erected hundreds of lean and efficient-looking glass-walled cubes to accommodate the dozens of government agencies and departments that had been instituted in the flush of post-war social democracy. These buildings also reflected a changing attitude towards the nature of a public building in Canada. The steel and glass structures built by the federal government were becoming indistinguishable from the office buildings of any commercial or institutional enterprise. The archi-

tecture of the federal government was assuming a new corporate identity that seemed to speak less of the dignity and formality of the state and more of a new image of government built on principles of lean and efficient public administration. At a time when government had permeated so many aspects of Canadian life, the need to create artificial architectural symbols of the federal presence no longer seemed appropriate.

Epilogue

By 1967 the vast real estate empire that had been built up over the previous one hundred years was entering into its last significant phase of expansion. The continued growth of the civil service sustained high construction volumes in Ottawa through to the 1980s. At one end of the architectural spectrum, projects such as Arthur Erickson's mirrored-glass addition to the Bank of Canada, Moshe Safdie's National Gallery of Canada, and Douglas Cardinal's Museum of Civilization continued the trend established by the National Arts Centre to use major government commissions as an opportunity to showcase the work of some of Canada's best architects. At the other end of the spectrum, the Department of Public Works oversaw the construction of acres upon acres of open office space contained in massive government office complexes (most of them on the Quebec side of the Ottawa River) that seemed to suggest the lean, efficient corporate identity of the modern civil service.

Outside Ottawa the process of decentralization and the establishment of large, semi-autonomous bureaucracies in regional centres after 1967 resulted in a demand for a new kind of government office building. This was the era of the atrium building, which was often characterized by an irregular massing of building volumes defined horizontally by a series of staggered, horizontal tiers. In buildings such as the Complexe Guy-Favreau in Montreal, the Joseph Shepard Building in North York, and the Harry Hays Building in Calgary, government agencies that provide direct service to the public – Unemployment Insurance Commission, Revenue Canada, Armed Forces Recruitment Centres, Department of Health and Welfare – were often located in shop-front offices situated around a central atrium. It was a spatial configuration that created an internal public square that operated as a one-stop shopping mall of government services.

The building program that had been laid out in the early 1960s for the Canadian Corrections Service continued into the 1970s. Many new scientific research facilities were also constructed during these years. But, in other more traditional areas of government construction the demand for building was in decline. The boom of the 1950s and 1960s had sated the government's need for the typical Government of Canada Building that in the past had represented the core of the work of the Department of Public Works. New projects were confined to the construction of a few large mail-processing plants and some small government buildings and post offices located in the growing suburban and dormitory communities around major urban centres.

The federal government continues to construct new buildings to meet new requirements and new priorities, but it is no longer expansionary. Although changes in technology, cuts in spending, transfers of programs to the provinces and regions, and the amalgamation of some departments and services have created a demand for new facilities in some areas, they have also rendered many government structures obsolete or surplus to government needs. Perhaps the most significant change in the federal building program was the creation of Canada Post in 1981. As a crown corporation, Canada Post is responsible for its own buildings, and under new, cost-saving policies it has radically altered the public image of the post office. Postal services, which are often contracted out to local businesses, can now be found at the back of the local drug store or in small booths located in shopping malls. No longer an imposing edifice imbued with the dignity and power of the state, the new public face of the post office is that of a low-cost operation devoted to lean, efficient, user-friendly service to the public. In the wake of this policy, the small urban post office is becoming an anachronism.

In the past the management and maintenance of federal buildings was dictated primarily by functional requirements. Buildings were disposed of when they were no longer needed, either through demolition or by sale on the open market. During the 1950s and 1960s the Department of Public Works carried out an extensive cull of its pre-World War I buildings, often replacing them with much smaller one-storey post offices or government buildings that were cheap to build and less expensive to maintain. Buildings that were retained were often altered and refurbished to meet current standards of construction, accommodation, or access, with little or no attempt to respect the character of the original design.

It is only in the past two decades that the federal government has begun to recognize the value of its building inventory, not simply as a real property asset but also as an historical and cultural resource. In the 1970s the Department of Public Works began work on several architectural conservation projects. One of the first and most important was the painstaking restoration of the East Block of the Parliament Buildings, but it was been followed by others. Perhaps the most innovative effort of the 1980s was the Sinclair Centre in Vancouver, designed by the Vancouver firm of Richard Henriquez. This compact group of early federal buildings, including the main post office of 1905–10, a 1911 customs examining warehouse, a 1909 commercial building, and a government office building of the 1930s, was preserved on the exterior while the central core of the complex was completely reconfigured into a multi-level shopping arcade with government offices on the upper floors.

These projects were highly successful but they represented isolated incidents. By the early 1980s the federal government recognized the need to develop more comprehensive policies and administrative mechanisms to ensure that the older federal stock of buildings was being managed responsibly and sensitively. In 1982 the Cabinet gave its approval to the Federal Heritage Building Policy for all government buildings that were forty or more years old. Its aim was to develop criteria for evaluating and identifying buildings of heritage value and to advise and assist custodial departments on how to manage them appropriately.

The effectiveness of the policy will be tested as pressures mount to cut spending and to reduce the size of the federal building inventory wherever possible. It will also have to contend with unprecedented numbers of buildings. Today, it is estimated that the federal government owns approximately 65,000 buildings across the country, the majority of them constructed after 1950. Many of these buildings, which are now reaching forty years of age, are in need of upgrading or are no longer required. Already some that were constructed in the building boom of the 1950s have been torn down, the most notable being the Vancouver Customs House built in 1953–5. Others, including the massive William Lyon Mackenzie Building in Toronto, are being considered for disposal.

One hundred and fifty years of architecture by the Department of Public Works has left an indelible mark on the character of the Canadian landscape. Structures such as the Parliament Buildings in Ottawa, the early Fuller post offices, the 1935 dominion building in Hamilton, the 1957 William Lyon Mackenzie Building in Toronto, and the National Arts Centre in Ottawa represent outstanding examples of the architecture of their period. Others, perhaps not as well known for the merits of their design, constitute important historical resources that illustrate the changing role of the federal government in Canadian society. The surviving buildings at Grosse Île, which recall its one-hundred-year history as a quarantine station, are now being developed as part of a national historic park to commemorate and interpret the immigrant experience in Canada. The modest wood-frame buildings that were built in the last quarter of the nineteenth century at Fort Battleford in Saskatchewan are preserved to mark the beginning of the process of annexation of the lands and peoples of the Prairies into the political and social structure of what is now Canada.

The majority of buildings, however, cannot lay claim to national historical or architectural importance. Thousands of government buildings – post offices, customs houses, Government of Canada Buildings, drills halls – derive value within the context of their own communities. By their scale, central location, and quality of construction and design, these buildings represent important visual landmarks within the urban landscape. The presence of a federal building also held considerable importance to a community as a symbol of the stability and viability of that community. The fact that so many have found new uses as town halls, museums, libraries, community centres, and commercial or office buildings is an indication of their importance to their communities.

The buildings that remain under federal ownership will require new approaches to management. The goal of the federal heritage policy is not simply to select one or two of the most outstanding examples and to preserve them as architectural period pieces, nor is its aim to preserve them all at any expense. Custodial departments must be able to adapt their buildings to meet new requirements and new uses. Buildings that no longer have a use cannot be kept indefinitely. Within this framework, however, there is a need to accept heritage value – along with cost and efficiency – as a key factor in determining how they will be managed, maintained, or even disposed of. There is a need to establish guidelines that encourage departments to carry out alterations in a manner that respects the original character of a building or to implement policies that give priority to proposals for renovation or adaptive reuse, either within the government or outside it, over proposals to demolish.

Over the course of a century, the Government of Canada and the Department of Public Works created a real estate empire that was shaped by operational, political, and economic needs and goals. In doing so, it also created a valuable cultural resource that tells a history – in stone, brick, wood, steel, and glass – of the federal presence in communities. These buildings are a familiar part of the everyday experience of all Canadians; they represent an essential ingredient in defining a distinctly Canadian sense of place.

Notes

INTRODUCTION

1 Douglas Owram, *Building for Canadians: A History of the Department of Public Works, 1840–1960* (Ottawa: Department of Public Works 1979), and Margaret Archibald, *By Federal Design: The Chief Architect's Branch of the Department of Public Works, 1881–1914* (Ottawa: Environment Canada 1983).

2 Queen's University Archives, Adam Shortt Papers, letter from the Civil Service Commission to J.B. Hunter, deputy minister of the Department of Public Works (hereafter cited as DPW), 12 October 1914.

3 James A. Langford, interview with author, 15 June 1992.

4 'A Competent Chief Architect and Representative Government Buildings the Most Pressing Need in Canada's Advancement,' *Construction* 5, no. 1:43–4.

5 Sandra Gwyn, 'Why Ottawa Is Afraid of Art,' *Canadian Art* 19 (May–June 1962):210.

CHAPTER ONE

1 Canada, *Statutes of Canada*, 'An Act Respecting the Public Works of Canada,' assented 21 December 1867.

2 For a history of the Board of Works (renamed the Department of Public Works in 1859), see Owram, *Building for Canadians*, and J.E. Hodgetts, *Pioneer Public Service: An Administrative History of the United Canadas, 1841–1867* (Toronto: University of Toronto Press 1955).

3 Owram, *Building for Canadians*, 119.

4 K.M. Cameron, *Public Works in Canada under the Direction of the Department of Public Works* (Ottawa: J.O. Patenaude 1939), 63. A complete inventory of the buildings acquired from the United Canadas is printed in DPW, *General Report of the Commissioner of Public Works, 1867* (Ottawa 1868), app. 23. An account of those buildings transferred back to the provinces appears in DPW, *Report of the Minister of Public Works, 1867–1868* (Ottawa 1869), 44–8.

5 Architectural History Branch, 'Parliament Buildings, Ottawa, Ontario: Building Report 86–52,' Federal Heritage Buildings Review Office (hereafter cited as FHBRO) (Ottawa: Environment Canada 1986). This report consists of five separate studies of the Parliamentary Library, the East and West Blocks, the new Centre Block, and the Parliament Hill grounds. See also National Film Board of Canada (hereafter cited as NFB), *Stones of History: Canada's Houses of Parliament* (Ottawa: Queen's Printer 1967); Carolyn A. Young, *The Glory of Ottawa: Canada's First Parliament Building* (Montreal and Kingston: McGill-Queen's University Press 1995).

6 Architectural History Branch, 'Parliament Buildings'; NFB, *Stones of History*. A detailed account of the scandal and charges of mismanagement can be found in C. Cameron, *Charles Baillairgé: Architect and Engineer* (Montreal and Kingston: McGill-Queen's University Press, 1989), 94–106.

7 A. Désilets, *Hector-Louis Langevin: un père de la Confédération canadienne (1826–1906)*, Les Cahiers d'Histoire 14 (Québec: Les Presses de l'Université Laval 1969). See also B. Fraser, 'The Political Career of Sir Hector Louis Langevin,' *Canadian Historical Review* 42 (June 1961):93–132. For a study of Langevin's contribution to the Department of Public Works during this period, see Owram, *Building for Canadians*, chap. 6.

8 National Archives of Canada (hereafter cited as NA), MG26A, Macdonald Papers, LB, 18, vol. 18:687, letter from Macdonald to Lord Monck, 11 October 1872.

9 Owram, *Building for Canadians*, 141.

10 Canada, House of Commons, *Debates*, 7 May 1886, 1163.

11 Rubidge retired on 1 July 1871. NA, RG2, ser. 1, vol. 48, Privy Council Minutes, 29 June 1871. Scott had already been hired as architect on 24 May 1971. NA, RG2, Order in Council no. 1020, 24 May 1871. On 17 February 1872, Scott was named chief architect. NA, RG2, Order in Council no. 131, 17 February 1872.

12 For a detailed study of the early organization and administration of the Chief Architect's Branch, see Archibald, *By Federal Design*.

13 NA, RG2, Order in Council no. 1020, 24 May 1871.

14 NA, RG11, vol. 445, subj. 1103, memo from Langevin to the Privy Council, 28 June 1871.

15 J. Wright, 'Thomas Seaton Scott: The Architect versus the Administrator,' *Journal of Canadian Art History* 6, no. 2 (1982):202–19. See also *Dictionary of Canadian Biography* (Toronto: University of Toronto Press 1990), vol. 12, s.v. 'Thomas Seaton Scott.'

16 During the 1850s and 1860s Scott designed a few houses for middle-class clients in Montreal and about five Anglican parish churches in Quebec and eastern Ontario. In the 1850s he was also identified as supervising architect for a number of small railway stations along the Grand Trunk Railway in Quebec. Wright, 'Thomas Seaton Scott,' 202–5.

17 In government appointments at this time the role of politics and patronage cannot be dismissed. According to Scott's obituary he was persuaded to come to Ottawa by George-Étienne Cartier. 'Mr. T.S. Scott's Death,' *Journal* (Ottawa), 17 June 1895. Both Cartier and Langevin were closely associated with the Grand Trunk Railway and Scott may well have been known to them through this connection. Inevitably patronage and knowing the right people played a part in his selection, but, as with all professional appointments, it was also in the government's interests to hire someone capable of doing the job well.

18 L. Wodehouse, 'Alfred B. Mullett and his French Style Government Buildings,' *Journal of the Society of Architectural Historians* 31, no. 1 (March 1972):22–37. See also L. Craig et al., *The Federal Presence: Architecture, Politics and Symbols in United States Government Buildings* (Cambridge, Mass.: MIT Press 1978), 155–62.

19 NA, RG11, vol. 309:941–5, letter from Drewe to the Department of Public Works, Toronto, 4 March 1870.

20 NA, RG11, vol. 313:62–3, letter from Rubidge to Langley, 7 November 1870.

Because the Mullett plans have disappeared, it is impossible to determine who was responsible for the final design, but the similarities between the Langley drawings and a building such as the New York Post Office and Courthouse (1869–75) suggest that Mullett strongly influenced the design of the building. Langley's influence, however, cannot be dismissed as he had already shown himself to be conversant with this new architectural fashion. In 1868 Langley designed the new residence of the lieutenant-governor of Ontario, one of the earliest and most elegant examples of the Second Empire style in residential design.

21 For a general study of the influence of the Second Empire style in Canada, see C. Cameron and J. Wright, 'Second Empire Style in Canadian Architecture,' in *Canadian Historic Sites: Occasional Papers in History and Archaeology*, no. 24 (Ottawa: Parks Canada 1980).

22 A description of the interior appeared in DPW, *Report of the Minister of Public Works, 1872–1873* (Ottawa 1874), app. 18:124–5.

23 Ibid.

24 NA, RG11, vol. 653, letter from Scott, 16 September 1871.

25 C.P. Mulvany, *Toronto: Past and Present* (Toronto: W.E. Caiger 1884), 51.

26 For a general history of the Department of Customs and Excise, see D. MacIntosh, *The Collectors: A History of the Department of Customs and Excise* (Toronto: NC Press 1984).

27 The Montreal Examining Warehouse (1874–7) was designed by Bourgeau and Leprohon of Montreal. The Toronto Examining Warehouse (1873–5) was designed by William Irving.

28 The Conservative government was defeated in the wake of the Pacific scandal, in which the Conservative Party was found to have accepted substantial donations for their 1872 election from men who were subsequently granted the charter to build a transcontinental railway. P.B. Waite, *Canada, 1874–1896: Arduous Destiny* (Toronto: McClelland and Stewart 1971), chap. 2.

29 Owram, *Building for Canadians*, 128.

30 NA, MG26A, Macdonald Papers, vol. 226:96802, letter from Langevin to Macdonald, 15 April 1872.

31 Waite concisely analysed the ambiguous and ambivalent relationship between government and patronage: 'Governments were not always enthusiastic dispensers of patronage, but their supporters expected it and insisted upon it . . . The worst side of patronage is the obvious one. But it kept the party together; it created and sustained party loyalty; it was the reward for the otherwise unrewardable party services. Government enterprises were therefore notoriously inefficient. Patronage inevitably involved the use of local as against outside talent.' *Canada, 1874–1896*, 55. For a discussion of the role of patronage in the federal bureaucracy, see J.E.

Hodgetts et al., *The Biography of an Institution: The Civil Service Commission of Canada, 1908–1967* (Montreal and Kingston: McGill-Queen's University Press 1972), 9–23.

32 The federal buildings at Guelph, Ontario (1876–8), and at St-Jean, Quebec (1877–80), were typical of this period of design. In Manitoba, which had achieved limited provincial status in 1870, the federal government constructed at Winnipeg three very modest mansard buildings (a post office and savings bank, a customs house, and a land titles office) between 1873 and 1875.

33 DPW, *Report of the Minister of Public Works, 1876–1877* (Ottawa 1878), 129. See also R.A. Preston, *Canada's RMC: A History of the Royal Military College* (Toronto: University of Toronto Press 1969), 60.

34 The dome of the library was supported by thirty-two iron ribs prefabricated in England with a patent plaster infill. DPW, *Report of the Minister of Public Works, 1867* (Ottawa 1868), 97–8.

35 In Architectural History Branch, 'Parliament Buildings,' see the section on the Parliament Hill grounds by S. Coutts. See also J. Adell, 'The Retaining Walls, Parliament Hill,' FHBRO (Ottawa: Environment Canada 1990).

36 G.K. Hughes, *Music of the Eye: Architectural Drawings of Canada's First City: 1822–1914* (Saint John: New Brunswick Museum and Royal Architectural Institute of Canada 1991), 74–7.

37 District engineers reporting to the department's Engineering Branch were placed in British Columbia and Prince Edward Island in the 1870s. In British Columbia the Chief Architect's Branch also used B.W. Pearse to design or supervise construction of public buildings or both. Although he does not appear to have been on staff, he seems to have acted as branch agent in Victoria. Archibald, *By Federal Design*, 29.

38 J.P.M. Lecourt first appeared as resident architect in Winnipeg in 1874. DPW, *Report of the Minister of Public Works, 1873–1874* (Ottawa 1875), app. 19:29.

39 The Department of Justice also owned the Kingston Penitentiary, which was transferred from the Board of Works, and the St-Vincent-de-Paul Penitentiary at Montreal, which was purchased in 1872. For discussions on nineteenth-century penitentiary design in Canada, see D. Johnson, 'Penitentiary Design in Canada before 1950: A Synopsis,' in Agenda Paper, (Ottawa: Environment Canada, Historic Sites and Monuments Board of Canada February 1990), and C.J. Taylor, 'The Kingston Penitentiary and Moral Architecture,' in *Lawful Authority: Readings in the History of Criminal Justice in Canada*, R.C. Macleod, ed. (Toronto: Copp Clark Pitman 1988).

40 Unpublished documents in the Department of Justice indicate that the designs of both the Stony Mountain and the New Westminster penitentiaries were associated with Thomas Painter, the chief trades instructor and sometime architect of the Kingston Penitentiary during the 1860s, or with James Adams, who would later become the chief engineer of Kingston Penitentiary and architect to the Penitentiaries Branch in the 1880s. Johnson, 'Penitentiary Design,' 40, n. 26.

41 Archibald, *By Federal Design*, 24.

42 The section on drill halls in Canada has been largely drawn from J. Adell, 'Architecture of the Drill Hall in Canada, 1863–1939,' Agenda Paper (Ottawa: Environment Canada, Historic Sites and Monuments Board of Canada June 1989), 14–17.

43 Adell, 'Architecture of the Drill Hall,' 8–9.

44 The other two were built in Toronto and London. The Toronto Drill Hall was built in 1876–7 by the local militia unit with a grant from the city. The London Drill Hall was built in 1876 by the Department of Militia and Defence. Adell, 'Architecture of the Drill Hall,' 15.

45 DPW, *Report of the Minister of Public Works, 1879* (Ottawa 1880), app. 3:11.

46 DPW, *Report of the Minister of Public Works, 1867–1868* (Ottawa 1869), 47.

47 N. Anick, 'Thematic Study: Immigration to Canada, 1814–1914,' Agenda Paper 1984-30 (Ottawa: Environment Canada, Historic Sites and Monuments Board of Canada 1984). See also N. Anick, 'Grosse Île and Partridge Island Quarantine Stations,' Agenda Paper 1983-9 (Ottawa: Environment Canada, Historic Sites and Monuments Board of Canada 1983), 275–302. For a detailed history of Grosse Île and the surviving buildings on the site, see a report by Histoire et Archéologie, Bureau régional de Québec, 'Grosse Île: Rapport Environnement 90-031,' (Environnement Canada, Bureau d'évaluation des édifices fédéraux du patrimoine 1990).

48 DPW, *Report of the Minister of Public Works, 1867* (Ottawa 1868).

49 DPW, *Report of the Minister of Public Works, 1872–1873* (Ottawa 1874), 133.

50 Histoire et Archéologie, 'Grosse Île,' 20–5.

51 DPW, *Report of the Minister of Public Works, 1880–1881* (Ottawa 1882), 24. See also Histoire et Archéologie, 'Grosse Île,' 5–7.

52 According to the annual reports of the minister of public works from 1870 to 1881, immigrant sheds were erected in Toronto (1870), Kingston (1872), Quebec (1872), Montreal (1872), Sherbrooke (1872), and London (1873), and an immigration hospital was built in Winnipeg in 1880.

53 Canada, Department of Marine and Fisheries, *Report of the Minister of Marine and Fisheries, 1872–1873* (Ottawa 1874), xi–xiv. For a report on pre-Confederation marine hospitals, see M. Coleman, 'Marine Hospital, Douglastown, New Brunswick,' Agenda Paper 1989-36 (Ottawa, Environment Canada, Historic Sites and Monuments Board of Canada 1989).

54 DPW, *Report of the Minister of Public Works*, 1872–81. The marine hospital at Lunenburg is described in DPW, *Report of the Minister of Public Works, 1878–1879* (Ottawa 1880), app. 3:17.

55 For general readings on the early history of the North-West Territories, see G. Friesen, *The Canadian Prairies: A History* (Toronto: University of Toronto Press 1984), and R.D. Francis and H. Palmer, eds., *The Prairie West: Historical Readings* (Edmonton: Pica Pica Press 1985), in particular, D. Swainson, 'Canada Annexes the West: Colonial Status Confirmed,' reprinted from *Federalism in Canada and Australia: The Early Years* (Waterloo: University of Waterloo Press 1978). See also R.C. Macleod, 'Canadianizing the West: The North-West Mounted Police as Agents of the National Policy, 1873–1905'; and P. Voisey, 'The Urbanization of the Canadian Prairies, 1871–1916.'

56 Swainson, 'Canada Annexes the West.'

57 DPW, *Report of the Minister of Public Works, 1876–1877* (Ottawa 1878), 77–8.

58 J. de Jonge, 'Five Buildings, Fort Battleford National Historic Park, Battleford, Saskatchewan: Building Report 89-10,' FHBRO (Ottawa: Environment Canada, 1989). See also W. Hildebrant, *Fort Battleford: A Cultural History*, 2 vols., Microfiche Report Series no. 376 (Ottawa: Environment Canada 1988).

59 Archibald, *By Federal Design*, 5.

CHAPTER TWO

1 David Ewart, chief architect from 1897 to 1914, and Fuller's son, T.W. Fuller, chief achitect from 1927 to 1936, both worked for Thomas Fuller.

2 A comprehensive list of the buildings constructed under Thomas Fuller was prepared by C.A. Thomas, 'Dominion Architecture: Fuller's Canadian Post Offices, 1881–1896,' (MA thesis, University of Toronto 1978), 5 and app. B. This thesis is invaluable as a source on Fuller's career and his work at the Department of Public Works. Other useful sources on Fuller's work include R. Rostecki and L. Maitland, 'Post Offices by Thomas Fuller, 1881–1896,' Agenda Paper (Ottawa: Environment Canada, Historic Sites and Monuments Board of Canada 1982). According to Rostecki and Maitland, construction costs for these buildings usually ranged from $7,000 to $50,000 for medium to small communities with populations of less than 10,000.

3 In 1878–9, $367,415 was spent on the construction of new public buildings. Over the next ten years the amount rose steadily to a high in 1888–9 of $1,072,312. DPW, *Report of the Minister of Public Works, 1888–1889* (Ottawa 1890), app. 1:9. After 1889 expenditures fell to around $500,000 on new construction. The lowest expenditure, $294,471, was recorded in 1896–7, the year

following the federal election and the defeat of the Conservative government. DPW, *Report of the Minister of Pubic Works, 1896–1897* (Ottawa 1898) app. 1:7.

4 For a more detailed account of the department's reorganization, see Owram, *Building for Canadians*, 139–41.

5 Ibid., 140.

6 The statistics are based on accounts published annually in DPW, *Report of the Minister of Public Works*, 1880–96. As spending fell in the 1890s, this dropped to around 35 per cent.

7 Following the 1878 election the Department of Public Works was taken over by Charles Tupper and Langevin was named postmaster general. In 1879 Tupper assumed control of the new Department of Railways and Canals and Langevin returned to public works. Although the portfolio no longer commanded the same political influence, Langevin wanted the appointment. With the death of George-Étienne Cartier in 1873, Langevin, as Macdonald's senior Quebec minister and his second-in-command, exercised considerable power and influence. Public works was considered an ideal portfolio for patronage, particularly in the older, established provinces of Ontario and Quebec where most of its budget was spent. Owram, *Building for Canadians*, 140.

8 Waite, *Canada, 1874–1896*, 103. As a result of this new tariff, customs revenues increased from $12.9 million in 1878 to $18.4 million in 1880.

9 NA, RG2, ser. 2, Report of the Privy Council, no. 1273, 7 September 1881, memorandum from Langevin to the Privy Council requesting that it accept Scott's resignation after a three-month leave of absence due to ill health. That request was modified a month later when Langevin asked that Scott's resignation be withdrawn. Instead, he was to be granted retirement with a pension though he was only fifty-five. NA, RG2, Report to Privy Council, AE9616, 28 October 1881.

10 *Free Press* (Ottawa), 7 August 1891, 2.

11 NA, RG11, vol. 591:3–9, 'Memo as to Increases to Salaries of Employees at Headquarters,' 20 January 1875. This document identified Ewart as the highest paid architectural draughtsman. He was first appointed on 16 May 1871.

12 Samuel Keefer (1811–90) was a well-known engineer who served as deputy commissioner of public works from 1857 to 1864. In this capacity he was the senior civil servant in charge of construction of the Parliament Buildings and he worked closely with Fuller. Keefer resigned in 1864 after taking much of the blame for the mismanagement of the project. While he never completely recovered professionally from the scandal, throughout his life he maintained good contacts with the Conservative Party and with John A. Macdonald in particular. In 1880 Macdonald selected Keefer as one of three commissioners to investigate the Liberal govern-

ment's administration of the Canadian Pacific Railway. *Dictionary of Canadian Biography, 1881–1890* (Toronto: University of Toronto Press 1982), vol. 11, s.v. 'Samuel Keefer.'

13 NA, MG26A, Macdonald Papers, vol. 226:97108, letter to Keefer from Fuller, Glen Falls, N.Y., 5 October 1881.

14 NA, MG26A, Macdonald Papers, vol. 226:97106, letter from Keefer to Macdonald, 13 October 1881.

15 This summary of Fuller's early career is based on research in Thomas, 'Dominion Architecture,' chap. 3.

16 The state capitol project in Albany is described in Thomas, 'Dominion Architecture,' 73–80.

17 In 1883 the office employed fourteen architects. By 1897 they were called architectural draughtsmen and, despite a marked increase in the volume of work, the number had only increased by three. Archibald, *By Federal Design*, 6.

18 General sources on Victorian architecture in Britain include M. Brooks, *John Ruskin and Victorian Architecture* (London: Thames and Hudson 1987), R. Dixon and S. Muthesius, *Victorian Architecture* (London: Thames and Hudson 1978), J. Gloag, *Victorian Taste: Some Social Aspects of Architecture and Industrial Design from 1820–1900* (London: A. and C. Black 1962), M. Girouard, *Sweetness and Light: The Queen Anne Movement, 1860–1900* (Oxford: Clarendon Press 1977); H.R. Hitchcock, *Architecture: Nineteenth and Twentieth Centuries* (Harmondsworth, Middlesex: Penguin Books 1958), and H.R. Hitchcock, *Early Victorian Architecture in Britain* (New York: Da Capo Press 1972).

19 Secondary sources on the Langevin Block include I. Douall, 'Langevin Block, Ottawa, Ontario: Building Report 87-40,' see also Waite, *Canada, 1874–1896*, 233–4; and Owram, *Building for Canadians*, 156–65.

20 Doull, 'Langevin Block,' 184–9.

21 DPW, *Report of the Minister of Public Works, 1883–1884* (Ottawa 1884), 48–9.

22 Doull, 'Langevin Block,' 189–90.

23 Canada, House of Commons, *Debates*, 1883, 908; and W. Eggleston, *The Queen's Choice: A Story of Canada's Capital* (Ottawa: Queen's Printer 1961), 144, 160.

24 The McGreevy scandal and the scandal surrounding the Langevin Building are discussed in Waite, *Canada, 1874–1896*, 218–20, 231–4, and Owram, *Building for Canadians*, 160–5.

25 Canada, House of Commons, *Sessional Papers*, 'Report of the Royal Commission Appointed to Inquire into Certain Matters Relating to the Civil Service of Canada, 1892,' no. 16c (Ottawa 1892).

26 After Fuller left Canada in 1867 his work was dominated by the classical styles. The state capitol in Albany was designed in a Second Empire style and his design for the San Francisco Town Hall and Law Courts (1871) was in a grandiose Italian classical style. See Thomas, 'Dominion Architecture,' 73–80.

27 DPW, *Report of the Minister of Public Works, 1882–1883* (Ottawa 1884), app. 2:27.

28 Other buildings of this type included the public building in New Glasgow, Nova Scotia (1882–7), the public building in Newcastle, New Brunswick (1884–6), and the public building in Charlottetown, Prince Edward Island (1885–7).

29 While it is difficult to compare costs of buildings because of such variables as the costs for a site, the transport of materials, and labour, the amount spent on the Newcastle Public Building was listed as $42,000, while that for the post office in St Stephen, New Brunswick, which was almost the same size, was listed at $22,500. A list of construction costs is found in Thomas, 'Dominion Architecture,' app. B.

30 For a general survey on the Arts and Crafts movement in Britain, see P. Davey, *Architecture of the Arts and Crafts Movement* (New York: Rizzoli 1980).

31 The Baddeck Post Office is now owned by the Victoria County Museum and Archives. It was recently used as a library, but because of structural problems the building has been vacated and is being stabilized until funds are raised for repairs. D. MacAulay, telephone conversation with the author, Baddeck, N.S., 16 December 1991. A public building in Montague, P.E.I., was constructed of brick in a style similar to that of the Baddeck building, with wide, round-arched windows, an irregular disposition of windows, and a steeply pitched gable roof with simple gabled dormers. DPW, *Report of the Minister of Public Works, 1885–1886* (Ottawa 1887), app. 2:25.

32 Thomas, 'Dominion Architecture,' 108–10; Rostecki and Maitland, 'Post Offices by Thomas Fuller, 1881–1896,' 72–3; and DPW, *Report of the Minister of Public Works, 1886–1887* (Ottawa 1888), 31.

33 Thomas, 'Dominion Architecture,' 108–10.

34 The Summerside Public Building was one of three government buildings built in Prince Edward Island during this period. The construction of all three (the others were a post office in Montague and a public building in Charlottetown) was supervised by David Stirling of the firm Stirling and W.C. Harris. While these two architects were not on the payroll of the Chief Architect's Branch, they appear to have been resident representatives. Similar arrangements seem to have been set up in other provinces. For example, D.E. Dunham and G.E. Fairweather, who had received federal government contracts in the late 1870s, supervised the construction of several buildings in New Brunswick. Although these architects may have had some influence on design, in all cases credit for the drawings was given to the branch in Ottawa.

35 In 1881 the Department of Public Works assumed responsibility for hiring and supervising maintenance staff. Owram, *Building for Canadians*, 150.

36 The post office in Winnipeg (1884–6), built at the beginning of Fuller's term, was a curious expression of High Victorian classicism executed in polychromatic brickwork. The Victoria Public Building (1894–7) was based on a reworking of the Langevin Building design.

37 The Vancouver Post Office was constructed in 1890–4 and the Calgary and Lethbridge public buildings were constructed in 1893–5.

38 This section on armouries and drills hall is based on a manuscript report by J. Adell, 'Architecture of the Drill Hall in Canada, 1863–1939,' Agenda Paper (Ottawa: Environment Canada, Historic Sites and Monuments Board of Canada June 1989), 14–27.

39 The Department of Militia and Defence built drill halls in Hamilton, Victoria, and Quebec. The drill hall at Quebec was commissioned to the architect Eugène Taché.

40 Henry James was trained in England as a civil engineer and worked for the Great Western Railway before emigrating in the 1870s. In 1878 he was hired as an engineer with the Chief Architect's Branch in Ottawa. He died in 1893. Adell, 'Architecture of the Drill Hall,' 20–1.

41 The Toronto and Halifax armouries were among the few buildings with large uninterrupted interior spaces at the time they were built. The Toronto Drill Hall spanned 125 feet and the Halifax building 110 feet. Both were constructed using triangular steel Fink trusses. It was the first time these all-metal trusses were used in Canadian construction and, once introduced, the Fink truss was used by the federal government for almost all its larger drill halls until 1914. Adell, 'Architecture of the Drill Hall,' 22.

42 A general source on the early history of the North-West Territories is R.D. Francis and H. Palmer, eds., *The Prairie West: Historical Readings* (Edmonton: Pica Pica Press 1985). In this volume, see D. Swainson, 'Canada Annexes the West: Colonial Status Confirmed,' reprinted from *Federalism in Canada and Australia: The Early Years* (Waterloo: University of Waterloo Press 1978); and K. Norrie, 'The National Policy and the Rate of Prairie Settlement,' 237–53, reprinted from *Journal of Canadian Studies* 14 (Fall 1979):63–76. See also G. Friesen, *The Canadian Prairies: A History* (Toronto: University of Toronto Press 1984), chap. 8.

43 J.W. Brennan, *Regina: An Illustrated History* (Toronto: James Lorimer and the Canadian Museum of Civilization 1989), 12–14. A post office, land titles building, and court-house were also built in the 1880s, but all have disappeared.

44 Remark made by N. Flood Davin, member of Parliament for Assiniboia West, in

D.H. Bocking, ed., *Saskatchewan: A Pictorial History* (Saskatoon: Western Producer Prairie Books 1979), 87.

45 Brennan, *Regina: An Illustrated History*, 12. A detailed narrative account is also found in P. Berton, *The Last Spike: The Great Railway, 1881–1885* (Toronto: McClelland and Stewart 1971), 113–22.

46 E.C. Morgan, *North-West Mounted Police, 1873–1883*, Manuscript Report Series no. 113 (Ottawa: Parks Canada 1970), 87–9. A study of some of the early buildings of the North-West Mounted Police barracks known as the RCMP Depot was prepared by I.J. Saunders, 'Eleven Early Buildings at the RCMP Depot, Regina, Saskatchewan: Building Report 86-22,' FHBRO (Ottawa: Environment Canada 1986).

47 Canada, Royal North-West Mounted Police, *Report of the Commissioner of the North-West Mounted Police, 1888* (Ottawa 1889), 16.

48 Ibid., 12.

49 G.E. Mills et al., 'Early Court Houses of the Old Territorial North-West and the Prairie Provinces,' in *Early Canadian Courthouses*, M. Carter, ed. (Ottawa: Environment Canada, 1983), 130–6.

50 Regina (1886), Prince Albert (1886), Calgary (1888), Moosomin (1890), Moose Jaw (1893), Lethbridge (1892–4), Wolseley (1894), Regina (1894–5), Medicine Hat (1899), and Fort Macleod (1902). The Regina Court-house, a two-storey brick building, replaced an earlier frame building. Other court-houses of the period were also constructed of brick or stone but they were usually smaller than it in scale. The Lethbridge court facilities were housed with the post office and customs offices in a three-storey brick building, constructed in 1892–3.

51 Secondary sources on Native education policy and industrial schools are Friesen, *The Canadian Prairies*, 157–61; J. Gresko, 'White Rites and Native Rites: Indian Education Policy and Native Response,' in *Western Canada: Past and Present* (Calgary: University of Calgary and McClelland and Stewart West 1975), 163–82; D. Johnson, 'Indian Schools in Canada including Red Bank Day School, Red Bank Reserve, New Brunswick,' Agenda Paper (Ottawa: Environment Canada, Historic Sites and Monuments Board of Canada 1988); J.J. Kennedy, 'Qu'Appelle Industrial School; White 'Rites' for the Indians of the old North-West,' MA thesis, Carleton University 1970; and J.L. Tobias, 'Protection, Civilization, Assimilation: An Outline History of Canada's Indian Policy,' *Western Canadian Journal of Anthropology* 6 (1976):13–30.

52 Canada, Department of the Interior, *Report on Industrial Schools for Indians and Half-Breeds, to the Right Honourable, the Minister of the Interior*, prepared by N.F. Davin (Ottawa 1879) (printed copy held in NA).

53 DPW, *Report of the Minister of Public Works, 1888–1889* (Ottawa 1890), app. 2:38. See also NA, RG11, vol. 3911, Plans and Specifications for Saint Paul's School, and *The Changing Scene: A History of West St Paul* (Winnipeg: West St. Paul Centennial Committee 1989), 65–8.

54 For a study of Canadian schools, see 'Historic Schools of Canada,' 4 vols., Agenda Paper (Ottawa: Environment Canada, Historic Sites and Monuments Board of Canada 1987). For classroom size, see 1:52–89.

55 N. Anick, 'Thematic Study: Immigration to Canada, 1814–1914,' Agenda Paper 1984-30 (Ottawa: Environment Canada, Historic Sites and Monuments Board of Canada 1984).

56 Located first at Albert Head on Vancouver Island, it was moved in 1893 to William Head.

57 Histoire et Archéologie, Bureau régional de Québec, 'Grosse Île: Rapport 90-3,' FHBRO (Ottawa: Environment Canada, 1990), pt. 3 (1881–1900), 18–22. Plans for the first-class detention building at Grosse Île are found in NA, National Map Collection (hereafter NMC), RG11M, acc. 77803/39, item 229.

58 Plans for the third-class detention buildings at William Head are found in NA, NMC, RG11M, acc. 77803/30, items 231 and 232.

59 L. Noppen et al., *Québec: Trois siècles d'architecture* (Quebec: Éditions Libre Expression 1979), 311. The plans and specifications are found in NA, RG11, vol. 3917, Plans and Specifications, November 1886.

60 *Leader* (Regina), 9 February 1886, quoted in *Regina Before Yesterday: A Visual History, 1882–1945* (Regina: 75th Anniversary Board, Historical Committee 1978), 46.

61 M. Archibald, 'The Establishment of the Experimental Farms Branch, 1886,' Agenda Paper 1981-57 (Ottawa: Environment Canada, Historic Sites and Monuments Board of Canada 1981).

62 J. Adell, 'Main Dairy Barn, Central Experimental Farm Ottawa: Building Report 86-69,' FHBRO (Ottawa: Environment Canada 1986).

63 The branch also designed three more modest shingle-style residences for senior staff at the farm. Similar residences were built for the superintendents at the branch farm in Brandon, Manitoba, in 1889 (plans in NA, NMC, RG11M, NMC 0045754), and for the superintendent of the farm at Agassiz, British Columbia, in 1891 (plans in NA, RG11, vol. 3913, Plans and Specifications).

64 J. Adell, 'McNeely Residence, Central Experimental Farm, Ottawa, Ontario: Building Report 86-67,' FHBRO (Ottawa: Environment Canada 1986).

65 Histoire et Archéologie, Bureau régional de Québec, 'Grosse Île, Rapport 90-3,' 23–8. Two similar buildings – one for the superintendent and the other for the farm manager – were constructed at the experimental farm at Indian Head, Saskatchewan in 1888–9.

66 *Canadian Architect and Builder* 2, no. 12 (December 1889): 142.

67 G.F. Stalker, 'The Buildings of the Dominion,' *Canadian Architect and Builder* 7, no. 1 (January 1894):14; and 7, no. 9 (September 1894):113.

68 Stalker, 'The Buildings of the Dominion,' 7, no. 1:14.

CHAPTER THREE

1 In 1897–98 the budget for new construction remained relatively small (about $400,000), but it began to increase by the turn of the century. By 1904 the budget for new construction had risen to $2.5 million. A recession at the end of the decade caused a slight slow-down in spending but it quickly resumed when Robert Borden's new Conservative government took power in 1911. The largest annual budget from 1896 to 1914 for new construction is recorded in 1913–14, when $10,018,188 was spent. DPW, *Report of the Minister of Public Works*, 1897–1914.

2 For a general historical survey of the period, see R.C. Brown and R. Cook, *Canada 1896–1921: A Nation Transformed* (Toronto: McClelland and Stewart 1974).

3 On 1 October 1896 Thomas Fuller retired from public service. DPW, *Report of the Minister of Public Works, 1897–1898* (Ottawa 1899), 2. At 73 his retirement was long overdue, but his departure within a few months of a Liberal victory suggests that it was motivated, at least in part, by political factors. He had been brought to Ottawa by a Conservative government and had administered a program that had been criticized by the Liberals for its corruption, inefficiency, and extravagance.

4 In 1907 the Commission to Enquire into and Report upon the Operation of the Civil Service Act and Kindred Legislation was set up by the Liberal government. In 1911 the Commission to Enquire into All Matters Connected with or Affecting the Administration of the Various Departments of the Government and the Conduct of Public Business Therein was established. The latter employed George Murray, a senior British civil servant, to prepare its report. J.E. Hogdetts et al., *The Biography of an Institution: The Civil Service Commission of Canada, 1908–1967* (Montreal and Kingston: McGill-Queen's University Press 1972), chaps. 1 and 2. See also Brown and Cook, *Canada, 1896–1921*, 192–4; and R.C. Brown, *Robert Laird Borden: A Biography* (Toronto: Macmillan of Canada 1975), 1:211–14.

5 As Laurier's senior Quebec politician, Tarte had considerable power and he assumed an active role in the administration of the department. He had, however, taken on the assignment with the belief that the department had grown large and

inefficient. He immediately cut positions and reduced expenditures. Owram, *Building for Canadians*, 168–9. Under Rogers, the department thrived; he was one of Borden's most powerful and competent ministers. Budgets increased to their highest levels despite slowed economic growth, and a number of major projects, such as the massive redevelopment for central Ottawa, were initiated. Other ministers included James Sutherland, 1902–5, Charles S. Hyman, 1905–7, William Pugsley, 1907–11, and F.D. Monk, 1911–12.

6 According to the *Civil Service List* of 1905 (Ottawa 1905), 174, Gobeil was appointed deputy minister on 1 January 1891.

7 NA, MG26G, Laurier Papers, letter from Cartwright to Laurier, 27 July 1907, quoted in Owram, *Building for Canadians*, 187.

8 Canada, House of Commons, *Debates*, 20 April 1920, quoted in Owram, *Building for Canadians*, 214.

9 NA, RG11, vol. 3102, Estimates of Canada for the fiscal year ending 30 June 1904, s.v. 'Civil Government.'

10 At the time Hunter was one of the two youngest deputy ministers in Ottawa. The other was William Lyon Mackenzie King, who had also joined the civil service in 1900.

11 C.G.D. Roberts, *A Standard Dictionary of Canadian Biography: The Canadian Who Was Who* (Toronto: Trans-Canada Press 1934), 180; 'Former Chief Architect Dies,' *Journal* (Ottawa), 8 June 1921; and R. Hunter, 'The Ottawa Buildings of David Ewart,' research paper, Carleton University, May 1979.

12 NA, RG11, vol. 3132, Estimates of Canada for the fiscal year ending 31 March 1912. The majority of the staff were identified as architectural draughtsmen, but this appears to have been the general title given to those engaged in building design and construction. The Chief Architect's Branch also included a number of clerical and other support staff.

13 As a result of the Civil Service Act of 1908 many temporary architectural staff were reclassified as permanent public servants. The permanent staff of the Department of Public Works grew from twenty-seven in 1905 to 234 in 1908. Owram, *Building for Canadians*, 187.

14 According to the testimony of Deputy Minister Antoine Gobeil before the 1907 Commission on the Civil Service, some of the architects and engineers in the department had been hired with degrees or diplomas from McGill University, the University of Toronto, the Royal Military College, or the école Polytechnique in Montreal. Canada, House of Commons, *Sessional Papers*, 1907–8, 'Report of the Civil Service Commissioners,' no. 29a (Ottawa: Kings's Printer 1908), 1104. For a detailed study of the Chief Architect's Branch and the staff in the early 1900s, see Archibald, *By Federal Design*, 5–21.

15 Richard C. Wright served as chief architect from 1914 to 1927, T.W. Fuller from 1927 to 1936, and C.S. Sutherland from 1936 to 1946. J.-C.-G. Brault was hired in 1914 or 1915 and served as chief architect from 1946 to 1952.

16 Information provided by D. Johnson. Canada, Department of Justice, *Report of the Minister of Justice*, 1897–1906.

17 For a history of the architecture of the Canadian Parks Service, see E. Mills, 'Rustic Building Programs in Canada's National Parks, 1887–1950,' Agenda Paper (Ottawa: Environment Canada, Historic Sites and Monuments Board of Canada 1992).

18 The earliest example of the Edwardian Baroque style in federal building was a Customs House in Halifax, which was begun in 1902. NA, RG11, vol. 3090, Estimates of Canada for fiscal year ending 30 June 1902, 15. The Halifax Customs House was located at the corner of Water Street, George Street, and Market Lane. It was demolished in the 1930s to make way for the new dominion building, which was built under the Public Works Construction Act of 1934.

19 E. Mills, 'Block 15, Granville Street, Vancouver, British Columbia: Building Reports 83-24, 25, 26, 27,' FHBRO (Ottawa: Environment Canada 1983).

20 For a study of the Arts and Crafts movement in Britain, see P. Davey, *Architecture of the Arts and Crafts Movement* (New York: Rizzoli 1980).

21 Sources on Edwardian architecture include A.S. Gray, *Edwardian Architecture: A Biographical Dictionary* (Iowa City: University of Iowa Press 1986); R. MacLeod, *Style and Society: Architectural Ideology in Britain, 1835–1914* (London: RIBA Publications 1971), 84–105; A. Service, ed., *Edwardian Architecture and Its Origins* (London: Architectural Press 1975); and 'London 1900,' *Architectural Design* 48, nos. 5–6 (1978).

22 For this period in Canadian architecture, see K. Crossman, *Architecture in Transition: From Art to Practice, 1885–1906* (Montreal and Kingston: McGill-Queen's University Press 1987), chap. 6; G. Hunt, *John M. Lyle: Toward a Canadian Architecture*, exhibition catalogue (Kingston: Agnes Etherington Arts Centre, 1982); G. Simmins, *Ontario Association of Architects: A Centennial History, 1889–1989* (Toronto: Ontario Association of Architects 1989), chap. 3; and *The Architecture of Edward and W.S. Maxwell* (Montreal: Montreal Museum of Fine Arts 1991).

23 Ewart accompanied W.S. Fielding to examine the Royal Mint and museums in England, Edinburgh, and Paris. *Canadian Architect and Builder* 14, no. 6 (June 1901):124. The trip is also referred to in DPW, *Report of the Minister of Public Works, 1900–1901* (Ottawa 1902), 9.

24 One of the most notable examples of a public building in the Edwardian Baroque style during this period was William Young's design for the War Office in White

hall (1898–1907). It would have been well advanced when Ewart visited London in 1901, and the parallels with the Vancouver Post Office are notable. The rusticated base, the row of Ionic columns, and the domed corner towers are features that could have been inspired by the War Office. The building is illustrated in Service, *Edwardian Architecture*, 306.

25 The R.V. Winch Building and the Bank of Commerce were begun in 1906. These were followed by the Bauer Building (now Pemberton Building) of 1910 and the Rogers Building of 1911–12. Subsequent buildings included the Royal Bank, the Bank of Nova Scotia, and the Merchant's Bank. See Mills, 'Block 15, Granville Street,' 106–7. Today the Vancouver Post Office is part of a larger complex of federally owned buildings known as the Sinclair Centre. In 1981–6 it was converted into a multi-level shopping mall with offices on the upper floors. The exterior of the original building has been well preserved; it still exerts a commanding presence on the downtown area.

26 Crossman, *Architecture in Transition*, chap. 5. Articles on the use and technology of steel construction appeared frequently in the Canadian architectural press of the period. An article entitled 'Some Observations on Fireproof Buildings in New York,' *Canadian Architect and Builder* 6, no. 3 (1893): 36–8, shows a familiarity with various forms of steel construction, including the independent steel frame. The earliest independent steel frame building in Canada was probably the Robert Simpson Store in Toronto (1895). Crossman, *Architecture in Transition*, 68.

27 According to the *Province* (Vancouver), 13 June 1909, the Vancouver Post Office was credited with opening a new era in construction through the use of steel-ribbed design.

28 See, for example, the public buildings in Regina (1906–8), Edmonton (1907, demolished), Brantford (1913–15), and Lethbridge (1912). Scaled-down versions of this type were also built in Carman, Manitoba (1914), and Dartmouth, Nova Scotia (1914).

29 C.A. Hale, 'Postal Station "A," 126–40 Prince William Street, Saint John, New Brunswick: Building Report 83-59,' FHBRO (Ottawa: Environment Canada 1983).

30 C.A. Hale, 'Postal Station "A," Fredericton, New Brunswick: Building Report 83-28,' FHBRO (Ottawa: Environment Canada 1983). A domed clock tower was planned but never built. In keeping with Beaux-Arts principles of symmetry, it was to be located above the main entrance.

31 See, for example, the public buildings in Fort William (now Thunder Bay), Ontario, and in Moncton, New Brunswick, which were built in the 1930s. See also Chapter 6.

32 The Humboldt Public Building was designated a National Historic Site in 1977.

G. Utas and J. Wright, 'Post Office, Humboldt, Saskatchewan,' Agenda Paper (Ottawa: Environment Canada, Historic Sites and Monuments Board of Canada 1976). The Federal Heritage Buildings Review Office has completed several architectural and historical evaluations of other buildings of this type. See E. Mills, 'Federal Building, Battleford, Saskatchewan: Building Report 83-03'; J. Adell, 'Old Post Offices in Seaforth, Harriston, Milverton, Palmerston and Tilbury, Ontario: Building Reports 87-01, 02, 03, 04, 30'; and B. Dewalt, 'Federal Building, Melfort, Saskatchewan: Building Report 87-121,' FHBRO (Ottawa: Environment Canada 1983 and 1987).

33 Similar post offices were built at Tignish in Prince Edward Island, at Saint John (Fairville), Hartland, Grand Falls, and Hampton in New Brunswick, at Louiseville, Matane, and Lac Mégantic in Quebec, at Grimsby, Tilbury, Mount Forest, Dresden, Kemptville, and Athens in Ontario, and at Morden in Manitoba.

34 The Campbellton Public Building was almost identical to the 1900 public building in Picton, Ontario.

35 D. Johnson, 'Federal Building, Newmarket, Ontario: Building Report 83-71,' FHBRO (Ottawa: Environment Canada 1983).

36 The Post Office Department was always very enthusiastic about the idea of building post offices according to standard plans. In 1916 the assistant secretary to the Post Office urged the chief architect to press on the idea. He wrote, 'Of course, someday, when standard buildings are adopted, all such questions [about existing accommodation] will be unnecessary, as we shall know at once, not only what each building may look like but what it contains. May that happy day soon arrive.' NA, RG11, vol. 2711, File no. 2556-20-A, letter from Graham Moon to E.L. Horwood, 12 August 1916.

37 Between 1901 and 1916 the number of incorporated cities in the Prairie provinces rose from three to seventeen towns from twenty-five to 150, and villages from fifty-seven to 423. These new communities typically began with a train station and a grain elevator; basic consumer services, such as a general store, a hardware store and perhaps a bank, were then added. P. Voisey, 'Urbanization of the Canadian Prairies, 1871–1916,' *Histoire Sociale/Social History* 8 (May 1975):77–101; see also A.F.J. Artibise, 'The Urban West: The Evolution of Prairie Towns and Cities to 1930,' *Prairie Forum* 4 (1979):237–62.

38 DPW, *Report of the Minister of Public Works, 1898–1899* (Ottawa 1900), 2.

39 See, for example, 'Government Architecture,' *Canadian Architect and Builder* 15, no. 12 (December 1902):142; and 'A Competent Chief Architect and Representative Government Buildings the Most Pressing Need in Canada's Advancement,' *Construction* 5, no. 1 (December 1911):43–4.

40 D. Hevenor Smith, *The Office of the Supervising Architect of the Treasury: Its His-*

tory, Activities and Organization (Baltimore: Johns Hopkins Press 1923), 16–29; and L. Craig et al., *The Federal Presence: Architecture, Politics and Symbols in United States Government Buildings* (Cambridge Mass.: MIT Press 1978), 202–3.

41 The issue of who should design federal buildings was just as contentious in the United States. After the Tarnsey Act was revoked in 1912, it was replaced by the Public Buildings Act of 1913, which allowed for the employment of private architects on large projects. As in Canada, however, such legislation was opposed by the bureaucracy, in this case the Treasury Department, which preferred to keep control of designing and supervising construction. The arguments were the same as in Canada – efficiency, economy, and consistency in quality versus excellence in design. Smith, *The Office of the Supervising Architect*, 15–18 and 28–38.

42 Simmins, *Ontario Association of Architects*, chap. 5, and Crossman, *Architecture in Transition*, chap. 1.

43 Frank Darling and John A. Pearson had established themselves early as leading practitioners of the grand classical style through their branch bank designs for the Canadian Bank of Commerce. Usually a contract such as the one in Winnipeg would have gone to a local firm, but in 1903 Darling and Pearson had opened up a branch office there to capitalize on the building boom that was under way. For this reason they were eligible for the Winnipeg contract. R. Rostecki and C. Cameron, 'Canadian Imperial Bank of Commerce, Winnipeg, Manitoba,' Agenda Paper 1976-06 (Ottawa: Environment Canada, Historic Sites and Monuments Board of Canada 1976).

44 Construction costs for these buildings can be found in the 'Accountant's Report,' in DPW, *Report of the Minister of Public Works*, 1904–10. The Vancouver Post office, with 76,320 square feet, cost $448,128, while the Winnipeg Post Office, with 83,616 square feet, cost $746,934. Part of the difference in cost can be explained through the Winnipeg costs including the 5 per cent architect's fee, whereas costs for professional services for the Vancouver building were buried in civil service salaries. But this single variable cannot explain the 60 per cent cost differential.

45 N. Clerk, 'Édifice fédéral, Collingwood, Ontario: Rapport 83-48,' FHBRO (Ottawa: Environnement Canada 1983).

46 'There is a very clever man, an architect in our town, who has done some good work. I would like to have him show what he can do.' NA, RG11, vol. 3942, letter from Currie to Monk, minister of public works, n.d., in Estimates of Canada for the fiscal year 1913–14, 723–5.

47 Generally a public building of this scale for a community of the size of Collingwood received a budget ranging from $50,000 to $100,000. The Collingwood Public Building cost approximately $144,000.

48 M. Birkhans, 'Francis C. Sullivan, Architect,' *RAIC Journal* 39, no. 3 (March 1962):32–6.

49 J.W.L. Wright, *Customs and Excise in Canada: A History* (Ottawa: Queen's Printer 1964), 23.

50 Customs examining warehouses were built in Vancouver (1911–13), Calgary (1914), Edmonton and Winnipeg (1911), Port Arthur (1914–16), Ottawa (1913–16), and Montreal (1912–14). All were four- or five-storey, brick blocks with rusticated stone bases and modest classical detail. A smaller, two-storey customs examining warehouse was constructed in Fort William, Ontario, in 1913. See N. Clerk, 'Revenue Canada Building, Thunder Bay, Ontario: Building Report 89-149,' FHBRO (Ottawa: Environment Canada 1989); Mills, 'Block 15, Granville Street'; and R. Hunter, 'Connaught Building, Ottawa: Building Report 87-39,' FHBRO (Ottawa: Environment Canada 1987).

51 NA, RG11, vol. 3148, Estimates of Canada for the fiscal year ending 31 March 1914. The Department of Public Works holds the building plans (Plan H-59A) at the Heritage Plan Room.

52 D. Morton, *A Military History of Canada* (Edmonton: Hurtig Publishers 1985), 111; C. Miller, 'Sir Frederick William Borden and Military Reform, 1896–1911,' *Canadian Historical Review* 50, no. 3 (September 1969):265–84; and J. Adell, 'Architecture of the Drill Hall in Canada, 1863–1939,' Agenda Paper (Ottawa: Environment Canada, Historic Sites and Monuments Board of Canada, June 1989), 28–33.

53 NA, RG9, 11A2, vol. 28, item 4, Report of the Militia Council, 1909.

54 This type of militia building is examined in D. Johnson, 'Military Stores Building, Ottawa, Ontario: Building Report 83-56,' FHBRO (Ottawa: Environment Canada 1983).

55 In a June 1909 letter the Militia Council included guidelines to reduce construction costs by eliminating superfluous ornament and developing standard designs. NA, RG9, 11A2, Report of the Militia Council, 1909, item 791.

56 NA, RG9, 11A2, Report of the Militia Council, 1910, vol. 29.

57 Adell, 'Architecture of the Drill Hall,' 35–8.

58 The drill hall at Trois-Rivières is also an example of a Class B facility. Built for small urban centres, this type was smaller than the Class A facilities, which were intended for use as battalion headquarters in large cities. Adell, 'Architecture of the Drill Hall,' 30–1.

59 Archibald, *By Federal Design*, 25.

60 I.J. Saunders, 'Mewata Armoury, Calgary, Alberta: Building Report 83-82,' FHBRO (Ottawa: Environment Canada 1983). See also M. Cullen, 'Prince of

Wales Armoury, Edmonton, Alberta,' Agenda Paper 1987–12 (Ottawa: Environment Canada, Historic Sites and Monuments Board of Canada June 1987).

61 R. Whitaker, *Canadian Immigration Policy since Confederation*, Canada's Ethnic Groups Booklets, no. 15 (Toronto: Canadian Historical Association 1991):6–8. According to Whitaker, Sifton undertook an administrative overhaul of the immigration system in order to have the branch operate in a more business-like manner.

62 The Department of the Interior stated, 'There is no immigrant settler accommodation east of the prairie provinces. At Halifax, Saint John, Quebec and Montreal, we have immigration buildings where persons detained for any reason were given accommodation . . . In Western Canada we have . . . quite a number of immigration halls which . . . were erected to meet the needs of a rush of settlers into a new district where there was no hotel or other accommodation.' Canada, Department of the Interior, *Annual Report of the Department of the Interior, 1906–1907* (Ottawa 1908), pt. 2:88.

63 The Vancouver Immigration Hall (1914–15) has been demolished. Building plans are held at the NA, NMC, RG11M, acc. 79003/44, item 552-591.

64 By the twentieth century many of these buildings would have been designed and constructed with little input from the Chief Architect's Branch in Ottawa. A resident public works officer was assigned to Grosse Île as a works manager. He probably would have had some buildings constructed under contract with a local builder. For a comprehensive study of the extant buildings at Grosse Île, see Histoire et Archéologie, Bureau régionale de Québec, 'Grosse Île, Quebec: Rapport 90-031,' FHBRO (Ottawa: Environment Canada 1990).

65 The Department of Marine and Fisheries had been using reinforced concrete construction in some of their lighthouses since 1906. M. Cullen, 'Long Point Lightstation, Lake Erie, Ontario: Building Report 86-77,' FHBRO (Ottawa: Environment Canada 1986). A contemporary example of reinforced concrete construction by the Department of Public Works was the 1913–14 Gonzales Observatory in Victoria. This building was designed in close cooperation with the Dominion Meteorological Service (part of the Department of Marine and Fisheries). E. Mills, 'Gonzales Observatory, Victoria, British Columbia: Building Report 83-60,' FHBRO (Ottawa: Environment Canada 1983).

66 Like many North-West Mounted Police posts, it was constructed by the police using local labour. B. Dewalt, 'NWMP Buildings, Dawson, Yukon Territory: Building Reports 87-68, 69, 72,' FHBRO (Ottawa: Environment Canada 1987).

67 NA, RG11, vol. 1268, file 199967, letter from Sifton to Tarte, 2 February 1899.

68 Charleson's main preoccupation was the construction of the Yukon telegraph. M.

Archibald, 'A Structural History of the Administration Building, Dawson, Yukon Territory,' Manuscript Report Series no. 217 (Ottawa: Parks Canada 1977), 10.

69 For a comprehensive history of this building, see Archibald, 'A Structural History.'

70 According to an inventory of the public buildings constructed by the Department of Public Works under David Ewart, of the 206 buildings that were built, 141 survive today. Fifty-seven are still owned by the federal government; the remainder are owned by municipal governments or have private owners. M. Trépanier, 'Public Buildings by David Ewart, 1897–1914' (1990), manuscript on file at the Architectural History Branch of Environment Canada in Ottawa.

CHAPTER FOUR

1 H. Fisher, *The Dominion Government and the Municipality of Ottawa* (Ottawa 1918), cited in J.H. Taylor, *Ottawa: An Illustrated History* (Toronto: James Lorimer and the Canadian Museum of Civilization 1986).

2 At the Liberal convention in 1893 Laurier was quoted as saying, 'and when the day comes, as it will by and by, it shall be my pleasure and that of my colleagues, I am sure, to make the City of Ottawa the centre of the intellectual development of this country, and the Washington of the North.' From W. Eggleston, *The Queen's Choice: A Story of Canada's Capital* (Ottawa: Queen's Printer 1961), 154.

3 Between 1900 and 1911 the civil service tripled in size and it more than doubled again by 1920. Taylor, *Ottawa: An Illustrated History*, 120.

4 Brown and Cook, *Canada, 1896–1921*, 28–9.

5 These nationalistic sentiments as articulated by architects were not confined to Ottawa or the federal government. By the late nineteenth century, Canadian architects were expressing the need to develop forms that were rooted in Canadian culture and traditions. Themes such as responsiveness to climate, use of local materials, and revival of Quebec and colonial vernacular buildings were identified as potential reference points for developing a distinctly Canadian architecture. But these references could not be applied to building in Ottawa, which required a language of architecture suitable to important public buildings and one that would express Canada's inherent cultural diversity or duality. K. Crossman, *Architecture in Transition: From Art to Practice, 1885–1906* (Montreal and Kingston: McGill-Queen's University Press 1987), chaps. 7–9. Nor were these nationalistic sentiments restricted to Canada. For example, the Arts and Crafts movement in Britain was an architectural manifestation of the nationalistic perspective. Not a revivalist movement, it advocated instead a new approach to architecture that was rooted in the vernacular building traditions of pre-industrial, pre-classical Britain.

P. Davey, *Architecture of the Arts and Crafts Movement* (New York: Rizzoli 1980).

6 *Canada: Painted by T. Mower Martin, Described by Wilfred Campbell, LL.D* (London: A. and C. Black 1906), 104–5, in W.E. deVilliers-Westfall, 'The Dominion of the Lord: An Introduction to the Cultural History of Protestant Ontario in the Victorian Period,' *Queen's Quarterly* 83 (1976): 47–70.

7 Much has been written about the evolution of town planning in the nineteenth and twentieth centuries. For general studies on the history of town planning in Europe and North America, see M. Simpson, *Thomas Adams and the Modern Planning Movement, Britain, Canada and the United States, 1900–1940* (London: Mansell 1985); A. Sutcliffe, *Toward the Planned City: Germany, Britain, the United States and France, 1790–1914* (Oxford: Basil Blackwell 1981); and W.H. Wilson, *The City Beautiful Movement* (Baltimore: Johns Hopkins University Press 1989). For studies of the emergence of town planning in Canada, see T.I. Gunton, 'The Ideas and Policies of the Canadian Planning Profession,' and O. Saarinen, 'The Influence of Thomas Adams and the British New Towns Movement in the Planning of Canadian Resources Communities,' in A.F.J. Artibise and G.A. Stelter, eds., *The Usable Urban Past: Planning and Politics in the Modern Canadian City* (Toronto: McClelland and Stewart 1979); W. Van Nus, 'The City Beautiful Thought in Canada, 1893–1930,' in A.F.J. Artibise and G.A. Stelter, eds., *The Canadian City: Essays in Urban History* (Toronto: McClelland and Stewart 1977); and M. Simpson, 'Thomas Adams in Canada, 1914–1930,' *Urban History Review* 11, no. 2 (October 1982):1–16.

8 Sutcliffe, *Toward the Planned City*, 97–8; and Wilson, *The City Beautiful Movement*, chap. 3.

9 Eggleston, *The Queen's Choice*, 155–61.

10 F.G. Todd, 'Preliminary Report to the Ottawa Improvement Commission,' Canada, House of Commons, *Sessional Papers*, 1911–12, no. 51a (Ottawa 1912), 20–37.

11 Todd, 'Preliminary Report,' 21.

12 DPW, *Report of the Minister of Public Works, 1900–1901* (Ottawa 1902), 9.

13 The Dominion Observatory featured a rusticated Nepean sandstone similar to the Parliament Buildings, though the architecture was predominantly Romanesque, with the characteristic round-arched openings with squat Romanesque columns.

14 The preliminary design was similar to that of the completed building but featured pointed-arched windows throughout and a rose window over the main entrance. A Second Empire version was prepared by A.A. Linnell of the Department of Mines. The plans are now in the National Archives. For a history of the museum, see G.

Simmins, 'The Victoria Museum in Ottawa: David Ewart and the Architecture of Gothic Nationalism,' research paper, University of Toronto, 1980.

15 NA, RG11, vol. 2922, docket 5805, letter from Hunter, deputy minister of public works, 1934.

16 The Archives Building was commissioned to the local firm of Band, Burritt, Meredith and Ewart, but it also conformed to the Tudor Gothic theme. For a history of the Archives Building, see K. MacFarlane, 'Former Dominion Archives, Ottawa, Ontario: Building Report 86-87,' FHBRO (Ottawa: Environment Canada, 1986). For a history of the Royal Mint, see M. de Caraffe and J. Wright, 'Royal Canadian Mint, Ottawa, Ontario: Building Report 86-04,' FHBRO (Ottawa, Environment Canada 1986). For a comprehensive history of Ewart's Ottawa buildings, see R. Hunter, 'The Ottawa Buildings of David Ewart,' research paper, Carleton University, May 1979.

17 Sources on the architecture of the Victoria Memorial Museum include S. Coutts, 'Victoria Memorial Museum, Ottawa: Building Report 85-86,' FHBRO (Ottawa: Environment Canada 1985); G. Simmins, 'The Victoria Museum,' and C.J. Taylor, 'Some Early Ottawa Buildings,' Manuscript Report Series no. 268 (Ottawa: Parks Canada 1975).

18 NA, RG11, vol. 2950, 5370-1-A, 'General Conditions for the Guidance in Preparing the Competitive Designs for the Proposed New Departmental and Justice Buildings' (Ottawa 1906). For correspondence relating to the competition, see NA, RG11, vol. 4239, file 1298-1. For a detailed published account of the competition, see Crossman, *Architecture in Transition*, 137–42. The decision to hold an open competition may have been made because the Chief Architect's Branch was already overburdened, but it was also partly the result of forceful lobbying by the Ottawa-based Royal Architectural Institute of Canada.

19 *Canadian Architect and Builder* 20, no. 9 (September 1907), supp.; no. 10 (October 1907), supp.; no. 11 (November 1907), 15–20. Twenty-nine submissions were received by 1 July 1907. Darling and Pearson of Toronto, Saxe and Macdonald of Montreal, and Vallance and Brown of Montreal were runners-up. Two other proposals, by Sproatt and Rolph of Toronto and James Foulis of Ottawa, were published in *Canadian Architect and Builder* 20, no. 11 (November 1907):15–20, and no. 12 (December 1907):15–19.

20 Crossman, *Architecture in Transition*, 140–1.

21 A short history of the Maxwell firm has been published in R.M. Pepall, *La Construction d'un musée des beaux-arts: Building a Beaux-Arts Museum* (Montreal: Le Musée des Beaux-Arts 1986), 87–8. See also *The Architecture of Edward and W.S. Maxwell* (Montreal: Montreal Museum of Fine Arts 1991), 167–9.

22 Canada, House of Commons, *Sessional Papers*, 'Report of the Correspondence of the Ottawa Improvement Commission Relating to the Improvement and Beautifying of Ottawa,' no. 57a (Ottawa 1912).

23 R. Hunter, 'Connaught Building, Ottawa, Ontario: Building Report 87-39,' FHBRO (Ottawa: Environment Canada 1987).

24 For example, see 'Proposed Departmental Building – A Gross Breach of Faith with Architectural Profession,' and 'A Competent Chief Architect and Representative Government Buildings the Most Pressing Need in Canada's Advancement,' in *Construction* 3, no. 6 (May 1910):72, and 5, no. 1 (December 1911):44.

25 Many of these letters and petitions were published in Canada, House of Commons, *Sessional Papers*, no. 57a (Ottawa 1912).

26 NA, RG11, vol. 3144, letter from Hunter, deputy minister of public works, December 1911, 7.

27 For correspondence on the Wellington Street competition, see NA, RG11, vols. 2950–1.

28 In May 1912 Frederick Todd was commissioned to prepare a general plan for the development of a new federal precinct on the north side of Wellington Street. His proposal, submitted in July 1912, consisted of two ranges of buildings on either side of a wide east–west mall centred on the Mackenzie Tower of the West Block. The most prominent feature was to be the Courts Building set back at the cliff edge and fronted by an open green or square leading to Wellington Street. A prominent tower would terminate the east–west vista at the west end of the site and a secondary tower would be placed on the building situated at the corner of Wellington and Bank streets. Todd's proposal did not include architectural elevations, though he did reiterate his earlier recommendation that 'the general style should not differ very materially from the style of the parliament building, but a somewhat more severe gothic, better adapted to office purposes, can probably be used.' NA, RG11, vol. 2950, file 5084-1, letter from Todd to Hunter, deputy minister of public works, 8 July 1912.

29 NA, RG11, vol. 2951, file 5084-1, letter to Lord Strathcona, Canadian high commissioner, to the minister of public works, 9 May 1912.

30 In his autobiography, Mawson assumed that he had lost the appointment to Chicago architect Edward Bennett, but according to departmental correspondence his name was first discussed in the context of the 1913 Wellington Street competition. He also said that the Royal Institute of British Architects had recommended another landscape architect (perhaps White), but behind-the-scenes manoeuvring by Lord Strathcona and the Canadian Pacific Railway are a more likely explanation for Mawson's rejection and the rather curious and inappropriate appointment of

White. T.H. Mawson, *The Life and Times of an English Landscape Architect* (London: Richards Press 1927), 187.

31 Edward White (1873–1952) served as president of the Institute of Landscape Architects from 1931 to 1933. D. Ottewill, *The Edwardian Garden* (New Haven: Yale University Press 1989), 55, 216n68, 216n69.

32 Aston Webb (1849–1930) maintained one of the largest architectural firms in England at the time. He was knighted in 1904. A.S. Gray, *Edwardian Architecture: A Biographical Dictionary* (Iowa City: University of Iowa Press 1986), 374–8.

33 NA, RG11, vol. 2950, file 5084-1, 'New Government Buildings, City of Ottawa,' 6 November 1912.

34 NA, RG11, vol. 2951, 'General Plan for Competitive Designs New Departmental Buildings and Courts Building, Canada,' 1913.

35 NA, RG11, vol. 2951, file 5370-1-B, 'Submissions for Competition,' n.d.

36 NA, RG11 vol. 2951, file 5370-1-A, memo to Hunter from Russell and Collcutt, 9 July 1913. The Board of Assessors was made up of Thomas Edward Collcutt of the Royal Institute of British Architects, J.H.G. Russell of the Royal Architectural Institute of Canada, and J.-O. Marchand, representing the Government of Canada.

37 Given the grand scale of the scheme, it is not surprising that an article in a British journal misunderstood the nature of the project and referred to the published plans as 'the new Parliament Buildings, City of Ottawa,' *Builder*, May 1913.

38 'Ottawa Has Great Possibilities from Viewpoint of Mr. Mawson, Town Planner,' *Citizen* (Ottawa), 30 April 1913.

39 The Board of Assessors first met on 30 June 1913. The order in council for the establishment of the Federal Plan Commission was passed on 13 September 1913. The commission was chaired by Herbert S. Holt, a Montreal businessman. The other commissioners were Toronto architect Frank Darling, Alexandre Lacoste, and R. Home-Smith, as well as the mayors of Hull and Ottawa. The selection of the six finalists for the Wellington Street competition was made 9 April 1914, but by that time the report of the Federal Plan Commission was well under way.

40 Frank Darling was the only member of the commission who was a professional architect.

41 Edward H. Bennett (1874–1954) was an Englishman trained at the École des Beaux-Arts in Paris. He then moved to the United States and established himself as a urban planner of the City Beautiful school. He worked with Daniel Burnham on plans for San Francisco in 1904–5 and for Chicago in 1906–9. Bennett remained as consultant to the Chicago Plan Commission from 1910 to 1930. During his career he was involved in the design of more than forty urban schemes.

Macmillan Encyclopedia of Architects (London: The Free Press 1982), s.v. 'E.H. Bennett.'

42 *Report of the Federal Plan Commission on the General Plan for the Cities of Ottawa and Hull* (Ottawa 1916). Half the cost was to be met by the federal government and half by the municipalities. Secondary sources on the Federal Plan Commission include, Eggleston, *The Queen's Choice*, 167–9; T. Regehr, 'A Capitalist Plans the Capital,' paper presented to the annual conference of the Canadian Historical Association, Ottawa, 1982; and C.A. Thomas, 'Washington of the North: Canada, The City Beautiful and the Planning of Ottawa, 1899–1915,' paper presented to the annual conference of the Society of Architectural Historians, Washington, D.C., 1986.

43 *Report of the Federal Plan Commission*, 110.

44 Ibid., 110–11.

45 Rhodri Windsor-Liscombe, 'Nationalism or Cultural Imperialism: The Chateau Style in Canada,' *Architectural History* 36 (1993):127–44. This article provides an excellent analysis of the British, and particularly Scottish, influences on the Château style in Canada, a close relationship that owes much to the strong cultural ties between Scotland and Canada in the late nineteenth and early twentieth centuries.

46 Harold D. Kalman, *The Railway Hotels and the Development of the Chateau Style in Canada* (Victoria: University of Victoria, Maltwood Museum 1968).

47 By 1919 the Chief Architect's Branch had nine proposals for the government centre: two preliminary proposals dating from 1912 (by Frederick Todd and by White and Webb); the six proposals that resulted from the 1913 competition; and the report of the Federal Plan Commission. Initially the committee considered three different approaches to developing detailed plans for individual buildings: it could pay off the six architectural firms and hold another open competition; it could invite architects who had demonstrated an ability to work in the Château style to prepare sketch plans while the Chief Architect's Branch would prepare contract drawings; or the Department of Public Works could take over the entire project. NA, RG11, vol. 2950, file 5084-1, memo from Hunter, deputy minister of public works, 23 August 1919.

48 For an examination of the role of Thomas Adams (1871–1940) in the development of town planning in Canada, see Saarinen, 'The Influence of Thomas Adams,' 268–72; Simpson, 'Thomas Adams in Canada,' 1–16; and Simpson, *Thomas Adams*, chaps. 3, 4, and 5.

49 Adams was not an architect or an urban designer but he had designed a few townsites and residential areas in Canada. In Ottawa he was responsible for the layout of Lindenlea, which he proposed as a model residential suburb. In all his designs his aesthetic orientation was to the informality of the picturesque and the British landscape tradition.

50 'Former Chief Architect Dies,' *Evening Journal* (Ottawa), 8 June 1921.

51 The plan was accompanied by a detailed description prepared by Wright and Adams and submitted to David Ewart. NA, RG11, vol. 2950, file 5084-1, letter from Wright and Adams to Ewart, 10 December 1920.

52 The sum of $500,000 for the construction of the new departmental buildings was allocated in 1923 but never spent. NA, RG11, vol. 2911, file 5509-2-A, memorandum from Hunter, deputy minister of public works, to O'Brien, 10 January 1923.

53 For a list of the members of the project team, see NA, RG11, vol. 2911, file 5509-2-A, memorandum from Fuller, chief architect, 1 May 1928.

54 NA, RG11, vol. 2950, file 5084–1, memorandum from Hunter, deputy minister of Public Works, to Wright, chief architect, 30 March 1920.

55 'Building Adds Beauty and Dignity to the Capital,' *Morning Citizen* (Ottawa), 28 February 1927. Sources on the Confederation Building include I. Doull, 'Confederation Building, Justice Building, Justice Annex, Supreme Court of Canada, Ottawa: Building Reports 87-34 to 87-37,' FHBRO (Ottawa: Environment Canada 1987), and J. Wright, 'Building in the Bureaucracy: The Architecture of the Department of Public Works, 1927–1939,' MA thesis, Queen's University, 1988.

56 NA, RG11, vol. 2911, file 5509-2A, memorandum on a petition presented to the Dominion Government by the Royal Architectural Institute of Canada, 16 February 1928.

57 NA, RG11, vol. 2911, file 5509-2A, letter from Craig, architect, to the minister of public works, 6 June 1928.

58 Plans for two new departmental buildings in Ottawa are dated November 1937. DPW, Plan Room, files 148 and 149.

59 Eggleston, *The Queen's Choice*, 173.

60 On 24 April 1927 the prime minister gave a speech in the House of Commons on the need for a strengthened Federal District Commission. See Canada, House of Commons, *Debates*, 24 April 1928, 2311–21.

61 Eggleston, *The Queen's Choice*, 183–4.

62 NA, RG11, vol. 2716, file 5370-4A, report by Gréber, city planner and architect, 7 February 1938.

63 NA, RG11, vol. 4156, file 12503-3-A, letter from Noffke to Sutherland, 9 May 1938. According to this letter, both Noffke and Gréber wanted to use a light-coloured stone.

64 For a detailed discussion of government buildings of this period, see Chapter 6.

65 Gréber played a key role in the development of both buildings. In the case of Postal Station B, Noffke submitted his final plans with this note attached: 'the elevations have been drawn strictly on suggested and appointed lines by Mr. Jacques Gréber, architect and consulting town planner.' NA, RG11, vol. 4156, file 12503-3-A, letter from Noffke to Sutherland, chief architect, 11 April 1938. Noffke's first proposal consisted of a flat roof with carved figures below the cornice line.

66 In his diaries King described his reaction to Cormier's first proposal. He thought that the design, which he compared both to a factory and to contemporary architecture in Moscow, was too modern. He wanted something that was more traditional, like the Confederation Building, but in the end a compromise was worked out. The Château roof was incorporated into the design, but King still felt some disappointment that the building had 'something of a modernistic note.' Mackenzie King diaries, 14 July 1938, cited in M. O'Malley, 'Mackenzie King Dreamed of the Most Beautiful Capital in the World,' *Canadian Heritage* 12, no. 1 (February–March 1986):35–7.

67 Noulan Cauchon, town planner for the city of Ottawa, had definite ideas of how the city should develop. In 1910 he prepared his own master plan for the city, which was endorsed by Ottawa City Council. In 1921 he was appointed chairman of the city's planning council. See Taylor, *Ottawa: An Illustrated History*, 146–8.

CHAPTER FIVE

1 Architectural History Branch, 'Centre Block, Parliament Buildings,' in 'Parliament Buildings, Ottawa, Ontario: Building Report 86-52,' FHBRO (Ottawa: Environment Canada 1986); Owram, Building for Canadians, 199–204; NFB, *Stones of History*; Eggleston, *The Queen's Choice*; and W.D. Cromarty, 'Ottawa and the Parliament Buildings,' *Construction* 17, no. 5 (May 1924):141–71. Additional research on the building was compiled by S. Coutts, in an unpublished report on the Parliament Buildings for Canadian Parks Service in 1988.

2 Owram, *Building for Canadians*, 202.

3 By 1916 the House of Commons and the Senate had outgrown the original buildings. There was a demand for more office space, and occupants complained about the poor heating and ventilation. NFB, *Stones of History*.

4 The joint parliamentary committee recommended that an additional storey be added, but 'without a change in the general character and style of architecture.' NFB, *Stones of History*.

5 Wallace sandstone was used for courts, air towers, light wells, chimneys, and penthouses. This material was not used on the original building. NFB, *Stones of History*.

6 Pearson argued that the red stone did not harmonize with the design: 'Gothic architecture symbolizes strength. It should give a suggestion of solidity. To add anything of a nature extraneous to the suggestion of massiveness, defeats its purpose. The red arch does not harmonize with the setting. Instead of beholding the wall surface the eye is caught and held by the red. This gives an uneven tone. There is nothing restful about it. The new building on the other hand gives a feeling of repose.' NA, RG11, vol. 2666, file 1575, unidentified newspaper clipping, 'Robbed of red, we get yellow.'

7 M. Brosseau, 'Gothic Revival in Canadian Architecture,' in *Canadian Historic Sites: Occasional Papers in Archaeology and History*, no. 25 (Ottawa: Parks Canada 1980).

8 Sources on military hospitals include J.H.W. Bower, 'Canada's War Hospital Development,' *Construction* 13, no. 3 (March 1920):87–98, 101–2; W.L. Symons, 'Canada's Military Hospitals,' *Construction* 13, no. 3 (March 1920):71–83; D. Morton and G. Wright, *Winning the Second Battle: 1915–1930* (Toronto: University of Toronto Press 1987); Military Hospitals Commission, *Report of the Military Hospitals Commission* (Ottawa 1917); Department of Soldiers' Civil Re-establishment, *Canada's Work for Disabled Soldiers* (Ottawa [1919]).

9 Prior to World War I, W.L. Symons practised in Toronto with the firm Symons and Rae. L. Maitland, 'The Design of Tuberculosis Sanatoria in the Late Nineteenth Century in Canada,' Society for the Study of Architecture in Canada, *Bulletin* 14, no. 1 (March 1989):13.

10 Morton and Wright, *Winning the Second Battle*, 88–92.

11 Much of the design work had been completed before the transfer to the Department of Public Works. For example, plans for a military convalescent hospital in Winnipeg, dating from March 1917 (prior to the transfer to Public Works), were signed by Symons as chief architect to the Military Hospitals Commission. These buildings show that the established design formula in plan, construction type, and exterior design were defined prior to the involvement of the Chief Architect's Branch. NA, NMC, RG11M, Manitoba Military Convalescent Home, Winnipeg, 21 March 1917, NMC 0047627. While on staff at Public Works, Symons's name always appeared next to that of the chief architect's on all plans, indicating his equal status.

12 J.D. Thompson and G. Goldin, *The Hospital: A Social and Architectural History* (New Haven: Yale University Press 1975), 126–39.

13 The practical and medical advantages of temporary field hospitals were first recognized during the Crimean War. Isambard Brunel designed prefabricated ward pavilions that were transportable and cheaply constructed of wood and tin for the British Army in 1858. This development came too late to have much impact on

the high mortality rate in British field hospitals, but the benefits of such buildings became clear during the American Civil War. Ibid., 153–65.

14 Bower, 'Canada's War Hospital Development,' 87.

15 Ibid., 88–9.

16 For a description of the process, see Symons, 'Canada's Military Hospitals,' 71–3.

17 The plans for the hospital at Grosse Île are held at the NA, NMC 90768. Work on the foundation began in 1913, but war brought the project to a halt.

18 Symons, 'Canada's Military Hospitals,' 79.

19 Other large military hospitals included the Westminster Hospital near London, Ontario, Tuxedo Park near Winnipeg, and Shaughnessy Hospital in Vancouver.

20 A permanent site for the Orthopaedic Hospital was secured in 1918 when seven acres of land with buildings were bought from the National Cash Register Company on Christie Street in Toronto. Morton and Wright, *Winning the Second Battle*, 88. For a description of the London Psychopathic Hospital, see Symons, 'Canada's Military Hospitals,' 77–8. See also DPW, *Report of the Minister of Public Works, 1920–1921* (Ottawa 1922), 20.

21 Maitland, 'The Design of Tuberculosis Sanatoria,' 5–13.

22 The argument was made in Department of Soldiers' Civil Re-establishment, *Canada's Work for Disabled Soldiers*, 20.

23 According to DPW, *Report of the Minister of Public Works, 1915–1916* (Ottawa 1917), 71, the government rented nineteen buildings in the city at an annual cost of $411,847. Construction costs for the Hunter Building were $1.5 million, which meant that the government could amortize the building in three years.

24 NA, RG11, vol. 319, letter from Hunter to Carvell, 29 January 1918, in Owram, *Building for Canadians*, 196.

25 NA, RG11, vol. 319, letter from Wright to Hunter, 16 May 1916, in Owram, *Building for Canadians*, 196.

26 Sources on the Hunter Building include 'New Government Offices, Ottawa, Ontario,' *Construction* 13, no. 1 (January 1920):3–6; 'Government Office Building, Ottawa,' *Construction* 11, no. 10 (October 1918):331; 'Chief Architect's Report,' in DPW, *Report of the Minister of Public Works, 1918–1919* (Ottawa 1920),18; and Owram, *Building for Canadians*, 195–6.

27 Canada, House of Commons, *Debates*, 5 May 1919, 2507.

28 For an examination of the corporate, technological, economic, and aesthetic forces that influenced demands for modern office buildings in the United States, see E. Shultz and W. Simmons, *Offices in the Sky* (Indianapolis: Bobbs-Merrill 1956); and R.A.M. Stern, G. Gilmartin, and T. Mellins, *New York 1930: Architecture and Urbanism Between the Two World Wars* (New York: Rizzoli 1987), 513–16. A 1924 issue of *Architectural Forum* was dedicated to the question of office plan-

ning; the articles, written by leading American authorities in this highly specialized field, provide a good survey of the state of office planning just after the completion of the Hunter Building. H. Wiley Corbett, 'The Planning of Office Buildings'; C.T. Coley, 'Office Buildings, Past, Present and Future'; and L.J. Sheridan, 'Economic Factors of the Office Building Project,' *Architectural Forum* 41, no. 3 (September 1924).

29 The relationship between the development of large corporations and large commercial office space is examined in Shultz and Simmons, *Offices in the Sky*. Other studies on this phenomenon include G. Gad and D. Holdsworth, 'Building for City, Region, and Nation,' in *Forging a Consensus: Historical Essays on Toronto*, ed. V.L. Russell (Toronto: University of Toronto Press 1984); and L. Dick, *The Confederation Life Building: Early Skyscraper Architecture and White Collar Work in Winnipeg*, Microfiche Report Series no. 304 (Ottawa: Environment Canada 1987).

30 Changes in the structure of bureaucracy in the early twentieth century are examined in J.E. Hodgetts, *The Canadian Public Service: A Physiology of Government, 1867–1970* (Toronto: University of Toronto Press 1973).

31 J.H. Thompson and A. Seager, *Canada, 1922–1939: Decades of Discord* (Toronto: McClelland and Stewart, 1985), 23–6, 77.

32 J.H. King had been borrowed from the government of British Columbia where he had been the provincial minister of public works. Spending figures are taken from DPW, *Report of the Minister of Public Works*, 1921–3. People in the industry urged that construction begin again. See 'Delayed Public Buildings,' *Construction* 14, no. 3 (March 1921):91.

33 Thompson and Seager, *Canada, 1922–1939*, 97–9. In the 1921 census, 369 towns reported populations of between one and 5,000. About a hundred of them lost population during the 1920s, while forty-four of them grew by only 5 per cent or less. According to Thompson and Seager, the decline in small urban centres was linked to the advent of the mail-order houses and to the ease of car travel, which together undermined the role of many smaller communities as local trading and commercial centres.

34 The shortage of centralized federal office space in Toronto was noted in a 1921 article in *Construction*, which pointed out that the Customs Department in Toronto was forced to house its offices 'in several scattered buildings with nothing which resembles a cohesive working plan or proper co-ordination as regards services and administration.' 'Delayed Public Buildings,' *Construction* 14, no. 3 (March 1921):91.

35 Around 1919 Ewart was appointed to serve on the sub-committee formed to direct the development of the Federal Plan Commission, and in 1915 he served as a

departmental representative on the parliamentary committee that was formed to oversee the design and construction of the Centre Block.

36 Queen's University Archives, Adam Shortt Papers, letter to Hunter from Shortt, chairman of the Civil Service Commission, 12 October 1914. Shortt argued the need for a chief architect of exceptional architectural skills who could design public buildings that would raise the artistic standards of the nation. He described Horwood as 'an architect . . . of only fair average standard,' whose work 'has been quite commonplace.' Horwood was appointed to the post despite this strong protest.

37 Richard C. Wright (1862–1927) was the son of John Wright of the architectural firm Wright and Durand in London, Ontario. He served his apprenticeship under George Durand and then worked in the office of Clarence Luce in New York. He left the private sector in 1906 to take up the post of assistant chief architect. *Canadian Architect and Builder* 19, no. 12 (December 1906):xi.

38 One potential candidate for an architectural position in Ottawa pointed out that the salary was less than that of a non-professional employed in the Cape Breton railway yards. For an examination of the plight of the professional in the federal public service, see J. Swettenham and D. Kealy, *Serving the State: A History of the Professional Institute of the Public Service of Canada, 1920–1970,* (Ottawa: Le Droit 1970), 8.

39 See, for example, W.L. Sommerville, 'Government Architectural Departments,' *Construction* 14, no. 4 (April 1921):104–5. Sommerville took the standard line that government architectural departments were staffed by architects who were either young and inexperienced or lacked the talent to survive the competition in the private sector.

40 This same design was used on the post office at Stellarton, Nova Scotia.

41 The Markham Post Office (1908) was one of the earliest examples of a one-storey brick post office. It was demolished in 1970.

42 J. Adell, 'Architecture of the Drill Hall in Canada, 1863–1939,' Agenda Paper (Ottawa: Environment Canada, Historic Sites and Monuments Board of Canada 1989).

43 In 1920–1 the Chief Architect's Branch designed four stables at the Fairmont Barracks in Vancouver. They were concrete and frame buildings sheathed in a rough siding and they housed 140 horses. 'Chief Architect's Report,' in DPW, *Report of the Minister of Public Works, 1920–1921* (Ottawa 1922), 19. The most interesting project was the establishment of the first RCMP post on Ellesmere Island in the High Arctic (see Chapter 8). For a description of these buildings, see 'Chief Architect's Report,' in DPW, *Report of the Minister of Public Works, 1921–1922* (Ottawa 1923), 18.

44 The Department of Immigration and Colonization was established in 1917. De-partment of Immigration and Colonization, *Report of the Minister of Immigration and Colonization, 1917–1918* (Ottawa 1919), 5.

45 Between 1900 and 1920, 3.4 million immigrants entered Canada. Between 1920 and 1940 only 1.4 million entered the country.

46 Plans were also prepared for a larger convalescent home at William Head, but the project was cancelled. They, too, adopted a Tudor Gothic style.

47 J. Dicken McGinnis, 'From Health to Welfare: Federal Government Policies Regarding Standards of Public Health for Canadians, 1919–1945,' PhD thesis, University of Alberta, 1980.

48 Histoire et Archéologie, Bureau régional de Québec, 'Grosse Île: Rapport 90-031,' FHBRO, pt. 5 (1920 à nos jours) (Ottawa: Environment Canada 1990).

49 Grosse Île was taken over by the Department of Agriculture, to be used as an animal quarantine station. Partridge Island was scaled down in 1938 and closed in 1942. H.E. Wright, 'Partridge Island: Rediscovering the Irish Connection,' in *The Irish in Atlantic Canada* (Fredericton: New Ireland Press 1991), 127–49; and 'An Assessment of Partridge Island and its Relation to the Immigration Theme' (1983), manuscript on file, Atlantic Regional Office, Parks Canada, Halifax.

50 'Cereal Building No. 76, Central Experimental Farm, Ottawa,' evaluation report prepared by Architectural History Branch and Engineering and Architecture, Parks Canada 1983. For a shorter version of this report, see J. Wright, 'Cereal Building, Central Experimental Farm, Ottawa, Ontario: Building Report 84-04,' FHBRO (Ottawa: Environment Canada 1984).

51 K. MacFarlane, 'Building No. 74 (Botanical Laboratory), Central Experimental Farm, Ottawa: Building Report 87-57,' FHBRO (Ottawa: Environment Canada 1987).

52 For the history and architecture of the Animal Diseases Research Institute in Hull, see J. Harris, 'Former Animal Diseases Research Institute, Hull, Quebec: Building Report 85-50,' FHBRO (Ottawa: Environment Canada 1985).

CHAPTER SIX

1 'Government Resuming Building Programme,' *Construction* 20, no. 5 (May 1927): 138.

2 Thompson and Seager, *Canada, 1922–1939,* 77–85.

3 This chapter is based on 'Building in the Bureaucracy: The Architecture of the Department of Public Works, 1927–1939,' the author's MA thesis, Queen's University, 1988.

4 Owram, *Building for Canadians,* 81. By 1927 the staff had been reduced by six

architects and one draughtsman. Almost all those who remained had been hired prior to 1918. These statistics on the branch staff are based on information found in *Civil Service List*, 1918 (Ottawa 1919), s.v. 'Department of Public Works,' and in NA, RG11, vol. 3221, Estimates of Canada for the fiscal year ending 31 March 1929.

5 The richest source of primary documentation on Fuller's career is found in his personnel file compiled by the Civil Service Commission, in NA, RG32, vol. 542, s.v. 'Thomas W. Fuller.' Much of the material has been published in Archibald, *By Federal Design*, 14–15. See also M. Archibald, *Thomas W. Fuller (1865–1951): A Preliminary Study*, Research Bulletin no. 105 (Ottawa: Parks Canada 1978), and Wright, 'Building in the Bureaucracy,' 17–22.

6 Fuller had an unusually diverse and interesting career within the branch. As mentioned earlier, he had been sent to Dawson City in 1899 to serve as resident architect during its boom period. Soon after his return to Ottawa in 1901, he became the architect specializing in drill halls and armouries just as the Department of Militia and Defence was beginning an extensive building program.

7 A more detailed account of their training and working environment is found in Wright, 'Building in the Bureaucracy,' chap. 1. A useful primary resource on the roles and responsibilities of architects within the branch can be found in NA, RG33/15 (papers of the Royal Commission on Technical and Professional Services 1930).

8 A drawing of the Calgary Public Building dated 1919 and signed B.A. Dore is held in the photography collection of the National Archives of Canada (DPW 1979-140, box 4339.) The building was constructed in 1930–2. No longer under federal ownership, the building has been completely renovated and it now houses part of the Calgary Centre for the Performing Arts.

9 D. Johnson, 'Dominion Building, Toronto, Ontario: Building Report 83-31,' FHBRO, (Ottawa: Environment Canada 1983).

10 G. Hunt, *John M. Lyle: Toward a Canadian Architecture*, exhibition catalogue (Kingston: Agnes Etherington Art Centre 1982), 83. According to Lyle's plan, Union Station was to form the terminus of a new style 'Federal Avenue,' which would extend through to Queen Street.

11 P.E. Nobbs, 'Recent Architecture in Canada,' Royal Architectural Institute of Canada, *Journal* 13, no. 9 (September 1936):171.

12 The building was extensively remodelled in the 1970s and early 1980s. Fortunately its heritage value and its importance to the streetscape were recognized: the exterior was restored and new thermal pane windows that retained the look of the originals were installed. The long room was also restored but the rest of the building, which was described as a maze of dark dingy offices, was gutted and modern

open office space was installed. Paul Harasti, Public Works Canada, conversation with the author, Toronto, 23 February 1993.

13 C.A. Hale, 'Federal Building, Moncton, New Brunswick: Building Report 84-35,' FHBRO (Ottawa: Environment Canada 1984), and J. Doherty, 'Federal Building, Thunder Bay, Ontario: Building Report 88-50,' FHBRO (Ottawa: Environment Canada 1988).

14 The Parry Sound Public Building was originally planned as a two-storey structure. A third storey was added at the last minute when the militia requested additional space in the building. NA, RG11, vol. 3233, Estimates of Canada, 1930–31, 318–22. See also J. Wright, 'Parry Sound Federal Building, Parry Sound, Ontario: Building Report 85-32,' FHBRO (Ottawa: Environment Canada 1985).

15 Construction costs ranged from a low of $14,000 to a high of $26,000. Information taken from DPW estimates for 1927–39 in NA, RG11.

16 Ibid. The amounts given are for construction costs alone.

17 NA, RG11, vol. 2712, file 2556-20D, memo to the chief architect from Hunter, 27 October 1938.

18 M. de Caraffe and J. Wright, 'Federal Building, Montreal, Quebec: Building Report 83-29,' FHBRO (Ottawa: Environment Canada 1984). Straight-line sorting methods had already been introduced at Postal Station A in Toronto, but this post office was located in one wing of Toronto Union Station and the design was determined to a large extent by Lyle's Beaux-Arts design.

19 Previously goods and people entered the country by train or boat; the main customs ports were located in urban centres near the train station or port terminals. Controls at highway crossings were very lax. Usually, customs officials assigned to monitor the border maintained an office in the nearest town, making it quite a simple matter to enter and leave the country illegally.

20 In 1926 the government established a special customs inquiry, which led to the dismissal of some employees and the establishment of tighter controls at border crossings. D. MacIntosh, *The Collectors: A History of the Department of Customs and Excise* (Toronto: NC Press 1984), 57.

21 For a discussion on the evolution of customs and immigration border-crossing stations in the 1930s, see E. Mills, 'Pacific Highway Custom and Immigration Building, Surrey, B.C.: Building Report 84-36,' FHBRO (Ottawa: Environment Canada 1984).

22 Examples of this type were found at St Croix, Clair, and Forest City in New Brunswick, Emerson in Manitoba, and Coutts and Carway in Alberta. These have all disappeared.

23 This argument was used in justifying the new customs buildings at Huntingdon,

British Columbia. NA, RG11, vol. 3256, Estimates of Canada, 1934–5, 210–11.

24 The Department of Mines had established a research branch in 1909, but the facilities remained small until the 1930s when it entered of period of rapid expansion that would culminate in the massive development on Booth Street in the late 1950s. The buildings constructed during the 1930s include the Ore Dressing Lab in 1932, the Fuel Testing Lab in 1927–29, with additions in 1937, and the Industrial Minerals Lab in 1939. S. Ricketts, 'Four Structures of the Energy, Mines and Resources Complex, Ottawa, Ontario: Building Report 86-61,' FHBRO (Ottawa: Environment Canada 1986).

25 Sources on buildings for the National Research Council include Sinaiticus, 'The National Research Council Building, Ottawa,' *Construction* 25, no. 8 (August 1932):172–8; and 'Research and Progress: Hand in Hand,' *Contract Record and Engineering Review* 46 (23 August 1932):857–78. See also M. Coleman, 'National Research Council Building, Ottawa, Ontario: Building Report 87-42,' FHBRO (Ottawa: Environment Canada, 1987).

26 E.A. Arthur, 'A Review of the RAIC Exhibition,' Royal Architectural Institute of Canada, *Journal* 9, no. 10 (December 1932):261.

27 A.E. Safarian, *The Canadian Economy in the Great Depression* (Toronto: McClelland and Stewart 1970), 135. A headline announced: 'Construction Holds Up Well,' *Contract Record and Engineering Review* 44 (31 December 1930): 1590–7. According to the *Toronto Globe* (12 February 1935), by 1933 unemployment levels in the construction industry had risen to 67 per cent.

28 The principal sources used to describe the economy and politics of the Depression are Safarian, *The Canadian Economy*, chaps. 3–5; J. Struthers, *No Fault of Their Own: Unemployment and the Canadian Welfare State, 1914–1941* (Toronto: University of Toronto Press 1983), chaps. 3–4; and Thompson and Seager, *Canada, 1922–1939*, chaps. 9–11.

29 For further information on the Public Works Administration, in particular its building program, see L. Craig et al., *The Federal Presence: Architecture, Politics and Symbols in United States Government Buildings* (Cambridge, Mass.: MIT Press 1978), 281–327. See also C.W. Short and R. Stanley-Brown, *Public Buildings: A Survey of Architectural Projects Constructed by Federal and Other Governmental Bodies Between the Years 1933 and 1939* (Washington 1939).

30 Numerous articles appeared in construction trade journals. 'Public Works Construction Programme Needed to Overcome Depression,' Royal Architectural Institute of Canada, *Journal* 10, no. 7 (July 1933):125; 'Public Works in the New Deal,' Ibid., 10, no. 11 (November 1933):187; W.D. Black, 'Construction: the Joint in the Armour of Depressions,' *Construction* 27, no. 1 (January–February

1934):9–14. The government was also inundated with letters from professional organizations and construction lobby groups. The letters sent to the Department of Public Works are found in NA, RG11, vol. 2761, file 3194-13, pt. D.

31 Struthers, *No Fault of Their Own*, 105–19.

32 Canada, *Statutes of Canada*, 'An Act to Provide for the Construction and Improvement of Certain Public Works and Undertakings Throughout Canada,' 24–25, Geo. V, chap. 59, pp. 1349–54, assented 3 July 1934.

33 The deputy minister of public works first requested the chief architect to draw up a list of recommended sites in August 1933. NA, MG26K, Bennett Papers, file P-350-1933, p. 35438, memo from the deputy minister to Fuller, August 1933.

34 One member of Parliament noted that of the $19.5 million public building budget, $14.6 million was allocated to Conservative ridings. Canada, House of Commons, *Debates*, 1934, p. 4301. See also NA, RG11, vol. 3256, Estimates for the Public Works Construction Act, 1934. In Calgary West the projects included a new aerodrome and RCAF barracks, and a retaining wall along the Bow River.

35 As pointed out by one member of Parliament, the $40 million allocation was fairly modest compared to the U.S. program and it barely compensated for the money that had not been spent over the previous three years. Canada, House of Commons, *Debates*, 1934, 4418, comment made by J. Vallance, member of Parliament for South Battleford.

36 NA, RG11, vol. 2712, 'Temporary Employees at Ottawa Under Public Works Construction Act, 1934,' 29 November 1934, hiring lists.

37 NA, RG11, vol. 2911, file 5509-2a, 'Petition to the Dominion Government from the Royal Architectural Institute of Canada,' 16 February 1928.

38 These criticisms have been drawn from the many letters to the department arguing for more contracts to private architects. Many can be found in NA, RG11, vol. 2711, file 2556-208, and vol. 2911, file 5509-2A, 2B; see also 'Editorial,' Royal Architectural Institute of Canada, *Journal* 6, no. 10 (October 1929):351; and 'Should Architects in Private Practice Be Employed on Public Buildings?' Royal Architectural Institute of Canada, *Journal* 6, no. 10 (October 1929):51.

39 NA, RG11, vol. 2712, 'Public Works Construction Act, 1934: List of Outside Architects,' 29 November 1934. Many more architects would be engaged in the succeeding years.

40 NA, MG26K, Bennett Papers, file U-125M, pp. 499919–20, letter to Stewart from Sullivan, 25 July 1934.

41 P.E. Nobbs, 'Present Tendencies Affecting Architecture in Canada, Part II,' Royal Architectural Institute of Canada, *Journal* 7, no. 9 (September 1930):314.

42 Sources on Art Deco include E. Weber, *Art Deco in North America* (London: Bison 1985); N. Messler, *The Art Deco Skyscraper* (Frankfurt am Main and Bern: Peter

Lang 1983); and R.A.M. Stern, G. Gilmartin and T. Mellins, *New York 1930: Architecture and Urbanism Between the Two World Wars* (New York: Rizzoli 1987). For a study of Art Deco in Britain, see 'Britain in the 1930s,' *Architectural Design* 49, nos. 11 and 12 (1979).

43 Sources on Canadian architecture in the 1930s include Hunt, *John Lyle*; S. Wagg, *Ernest Isobel Barott, Architect: An Introduction*, exhibition catalogue (Montreal: Canadian Centre for Architecture 1985); and I. Gournay, ed., *Ernest Cormier and the Université de Montréal* (Montreal: Canadian Centre for Architecture, 1990).

44 'Dominion Public Building, Winnipeg,' Royal Architectural Institute of Canada, *Journal* 15, no. 6 (June 1938):148.

45 'Dominion Building Halifax,' *Engineering and Contract Record* 51 (2 July 1937):26–9. An account of the construction of this building was related to the author by W.C. Jarvis, an architect for the Chief Architect's Branch in the 1930s (interview 14 June 1980). Originally J.L. Kingston was commissioned to prepare the plans. His proposal, a curious-looking, multi-storeyed brick building in a vaguely Georgian style, clearly did not meet the approval of the department. It was withdrawn, but not before a sketch elevation was published in *Engineering and Contract Record in 1935* 49, no. 3 (March 1935):219. A copy of the plan is found in NA, PA 124521.

46 Known as the Kane system, it was developed by K.C. Kane of the Dominion Bridge Company of Canada. It consisted of a light structural frame composed of latticed steel beams and trusses that were welded together to form an independent, self-supporting framework designed to carry the construction load of the building. This light frame was then encased in concrete to provide the additional strength necessary to carry the live load. According to advocates of the Kane system, it was cheaper than a standard steel frame. In addition, the use of welded steel elements meant a quieter construction site, and because the formwork for the concrete could be suspended from the steel frame, pouring concrete was faster and required less wood. It was said to use only Canadian-made steel components, which might explain the government's willingness to experiment. The Kane system was employed on a few commercial and institutional buildings in Montreal, including the Montreal Postal Terminal, but its advantages must have been a little overstated because the Halifax building appears to be the last in which it was used. Sources on the Kane system include 'A Building with an Unusual Structural Problem: Montreal Neurological Institute,' *Engineering and Contract Record* 48 (November 1934):992–6; 'Completely Welded Steelwork and Concrete Frame: Canadian General Electric Company,' *Contract Record and Engineering Review* 46 (17 February 1932):1436–41; and G. Wallace, 'Current Trends in Structural Design,' *Contract Record and Engineering Review* 46 (28 December 1932):1431–3. The deci-

sion to use the Kane system on the Halifax building is referred to in NA, RG11, vol. 4130, memorandum to the deputy minister from Fuller, 25 April 1934.

47 On 30 March 1937 Max Downing wrote to the chief architect advocating the use of monolithic concrete because of its low cost and low maintenance (NA, RG11, vol. 4105, file 684-1-C). Articles on this construction technique began to appear in Canadian journals in the mid-1930s. See, for example, A.J. Boase, 'Trends in Application of Concrete to Building Construction,' *Engineering and Contract Record* 48 (26 December 1934):1084–5, and 'Construction Feature of New Administration Building for Ontario Hydro Electric Power Commission,' *Engineering and Contract Record* 49 (10 July 1935):1092–3.

48 'Postal Station K, Toronto, Ontario,' Royal Architectural Institute of Canada, *Journal* 14, no. 9 (September 1937):182–3. Postal Station K received an honourable mention in the public buildings section of the Royal Architectural Institute of Canada annual awards. See 'Awards at the Eighth Annual Exhibition RAIC,' Royal Architectural Institute of Canada, *Journal* 16, no. 3 (March 1939):55.

49 N. Clerk, 'City Delivery Building, Toronto, Ontario: Building Report 83-08,' FHBRO (Ottawa: Environment Canada 1983).

50 C.A. Hale, 'Dominion Public Building, Amherst, Nova Scotia: Building Report 83-40,' FHBRO (Ottawa: Environment Canada 1983).

51 The earliest example was the post office in St-Romuald, Quebec (1929–30). Other similar examples in Quebec were constructed at Pointe Claire, Thurso, and Cabano. French-style buildings were also developed for the museum and office buildings located at two national historic parks that had French associations, Louisbourg in Nova Scotia and Fort Beauséjour in New Brunswick. Although constructed under the direction of the Department of Public Works, the plans of these later buildings were prepared by the Architecture and Engineering Branch of the Canadian Parks Service.

52 NA, RG11 vol. 3712, memorandum from Fuller to Cardin, 21 March 1936.

53 Situated on a rise of land and at the head of a Y-junction of two commercial streets, this building forms a community focal point despite its small scale. Although no longer owned by the federal government, it remains an important landmark in the community as the current Okanagan Regional Library. J. Harris, 'Public Building, Salmon Arm, British Columbia: Building Report 84-45,' FHBRO (Ottawa: Environment Canada Ottawa, 1984).

54 NA, RG11, vol. 3264, Public Works estimates, 1936–7, cites a memorandum from the chief architect, 2 December 1931.

55 N Division was established in 1920 when the headquarters of the RCMP was moved from Regina to Ottawa. According to the annual reports of the Department of Public Works, a storage and training building (1939–40), stables (1939), a

laboratory (1938) and a hangar (1938) were constructed at N Division. See also I.J. Saunders, 'Royal Canadian Mounted Police Barracks ('N' Division), Ottawa, Ontario: Building Report 84-53,' FHBRO (Ottawa: Environment Canada 1984); and S. Coutts, 'RCMP Stable, "N" Division, Ottawa, Ontario: Building Report 84-52,' FHBRO (Ottawa: Environment Canada 1984).

56 J. Adell, 'Architecture of the Drill Hall in Canada, 1863–1939,' Agenda Paper (Ottawa: Environment Canada, Historic Sites and Monuments Board of Canada 1989), 42–8.

CHAPTER SEVEN

1 Sources on the wartime activities of the NRC include W. Eggleston, *National Research in Canada: The NRC, 1916–1966* (Toronto: Clarke, Irwin 1978), chaps. 6–10. See also National Research Council (hereafter cited as NRC), *Annual Report of the National Research Council, 1942–1943* (Ottawa 1944), 7.

2 It was pointed out that if Britain's aeronautical laboratory was destroyed, the Ottawa laboratory would be the only remaining facility within the Commonwealth. Eggleston, *The NRC*, 139.

3 A list of the buildings on the site in 1948 appeared in NRC, *National Research in Review, 1949* (Ottawa 1949). It included the Aerodynamics Building, Hydraulics Laboratory and Model Testing Basin, Model Workshop, Structures Laboratory, Gasoline and Oil Laboratory, Engine Laboratory, and Central Heating Plant. A description of the buildings constructed during this period can be found in DPW, *Report of the Minister of Public Works*, 1939–45. See also H.G. Hughes, 'Division of Mechanical Engineering of the National Research Council,' Royal Architectural Institute of Canada, *Journal* 23, no. 5 (May 1946):105–15. Hughes, was born in 1902, received his architectural training at the School of Architecture at McGill, worked for various Montreal architects, and began a private practice in Ottawa in 1932. From 1941 he served with the Royal Canadian Engineers, and after the war he joined the Hospital Design Division of the Department of National Health and Welfare.

4 John Bland, architect, telephone conversation author, Ste-Anne-de-Bellevue, Quebec, 16 November 1992.

5 Eggleston, *The NRC*, 111.

6 Hughes, 'Division of Mechanical Engineering,' 105–6.

7 P. Mayrand and J. Bland, *Three Centuries of Architecture in Canada* (Montreal: Federal Publications Service 1971), 109.

8 Designs in the modern style were most commonly found in residential design, apartment buildings, and some commercial buildings, in particular those buildings associated with new technology, such as gas stations, bus terminals, movie theatres, and radio stations.

9 This reorganization brought almost all federal health programs, including quarantine stations and the two lazarettos, marine hospital services, and the food and drug laboratories of the Department of Trade and Commerce, into one department, that of Pensions and National Health. The only health service to stay outside the program was the Indian Health Services, which remained part of the Department of Mines and Resources until 1945, when it too became part of the renamed Department of National Health and Welfare.

10 See W.R. Feasy, *Official History of the Canadian Army Medical Services, 1939–1945: Organization and Campaigns* (Ottawa: Queen's Printer 1956), 42, 62–70. See also G.H. Agnew, *Canadian Hospitals, 1920–1970: A Dramatic Half Century* (Toronto: University of Toronto Press 1974), 55–6.

11 A description of the veterans' hospital in Victoria is found in 'Victoria Veterans' Hospital,' *Canadian Hospital* 24, no. 11 (November 1947):40–1.

12 T.B. McBain, 'Pension Hospitals Being Expanded to Meet Anticipated War Needs,' and 'New Veterans' Health and Occupational Center,' *Canadian Hospital* 21, no. 3 (March 1944):40–1, and 25, no. 4 (April 1948):31–2.

13 Department of Veterans Affairs, *Report of the Work of the Department of Veterans Affairs for the Year Ending 31 March 1950* (Ottawa 1951), 35. See also Feasy, *Official History of the Canadian Army Medical Services*, 67.

14 One of the first architects to work for the Department of Veterans Affairs was E.A. Gardner, who would become the new chief architect of the Department of Public Works in 1952. According to Gardner, he did much of the preliminary design and planning work. The project was then handed over to the Chief Architect's Branch, which supervised the construction. It is not clear whether contract architects were given more independence in the design. NA, Sound Archives, C 42467, acc. 1984-459. E.A. Gardner, former chief architect, interview with J. Wright.

15 An entire issue of Royal Architectural Institute of Canada, *Journal* 26, no. 10 (October 1949) is devoted to an account of Sunnybrook Hospital. Articles include H.L. Allward, 'The Planning of Sunnybrook Hospital' (313–22), and C.D. Carruthers, 'Structural Features' (340–51).

16 For a study of the development in hospital design in the first half of the twentieth century, see Agnew, *Canadian Hospitals*, 179–95, and J.D. Thompson and G. Goldin, *The Hospital: A Social and Architectural History* (New Haven: Yale University Press 1975), 187–201.

17 The modern hospital had to provide space for radiology, pathology, and pharmaceutical services. Out-patient services were also much expanded. Growth in these areas meant that by the end of the war approximately 50 per cent of a hospital's

floor space was taken up by these support services. See P. Vivian, 'Panel Discussion on Hospital Building,' Royal Architectural Institute of Canada, *Journal* 25, no. 9 (September 1948):289–92.

18 A recent article on the evolution of the university hospital in the United States in the 1920s and 1930s and its influence on Cormier's design for the Université de Montréal provides historical context relevant to the development of Sunnybrook Hospital. See I. Gournay, 'L'architecture hospitalo-universitaire,' *Journal of Canadian Art History* 13, no. 2, and 14, no. 1 (1990–1):26–43.

19 Agnew, *Canadian Hospitals*, 183. In Canada a very similar type of configuration appeared much earlier in Cormier's design for the Université de Montréal, which was developed around 1927 but was not completed until the 1940s and in which Cormier planned to incorporate a teaching hospital. Cormier was strongly influenced by the Medical School and Hospital at the University of Rochester (*ca.* 1923), which features a series of wings projecting at right angles from the perpendicular spine of the building. See Gournay, 'L'architecture hospitalo-universitaire.'

20 Shaughnessy Hospital in Vancouver was expanded in 1947 with the construction of a new chest unit and in the late 1950s with a large new wing designed by Mercer and Mercer. Other new facilities included the Hôpital des Anciens Combattants of 1953–4 in Ste-Foy, Quebec (the architects were Robert Blatter, Fernand Caron, Roland Dupéré, and Charles A. Jean) and the Department of Veterans Affairs hospital at Ste-Anne-de-Bellevue, built in the 1970s.

21 Owram, *Building for Canadians*, 251. Most of the buildings constructed for the Department of National Defence were located at the Canadian naval bases at Halifax in Nova Scotia and at Esquimalt and Comox in British Columbia. Sources on the construction programs during this period include I. Doull, 'CFB Esquimalt-Dockyard, Esquimalt, British Columbia: Building Report 89-202,' FHBRO (Ottawa: Environment Canada, 1989), 2 vols., and I. Doull, 'CFB Esquimalt-Naden, Esquimalt British Columbia: Building Report 89-204,' FHBRO (Ottawa: Environment Canada 1989).

22 Between 1939 and 1945 the civil service grew more than it had in the previous seventy-five years. In 1938 there were 44,000 civil servants; by 1945 that number had grown to 140,000. Owram, *Building for Canadians*, 256.

23 I. Doull, 'Confederation Building, Justice Building, Justice Annex, Supreme Court of Canada, Ottawa, Ontario: Building Reports 87-34 to 87-37,' FHBRO (Ottawa: Environment Canada 1987) includes an evaluation of the Justice Annex, which was built in 1942 and is the last surviving example of wartime temporary building in Ottawa. See also I. Doull, 'Beaver Barracks, Metcalfe Street, Ottawa: Building Report 90-325,' FHBRO (Ottawa: Environment Canada 1990), on a temporary building constructed by the Department of National Defence. (At the time of writing, the Beaver Barracks is still standing, but its demolition is imminent.)

24 General sources on the federal government's reconstruction program include R. Bothwell, I. Drummond, and J. English, *Canada Since 1945* (Toronto: University of Toronto Press 1981), 45–83; R. Bothwell and W. Kilbourn, *C.D. Howe: A Biography* (Toronto: McClelland and Stewart 1979), chap. 12; D. Creighton, *The Forked Road: Canada, 1939–1957* (Toronto: McClelland and Stewart 1976); and J.L. Granatstein, *The Ottawa Men: The Civil Service Manadarins, 1935–1957* (Toronto: Oxford University Press 1982), 161–8.

25 In 1926 the Department of Public Works accounted for 4.91 per cent of government expenditures; by 1945 it accounted for only 0.35 per cent. Owram, *Building for Canadians*, 264–5.

26 Owram, *Building for Canadians*, 258–61.

27 The annual reports of the Chief Architect's Branch identify sixty-seven additions to federal buildings between 1945 and 1951. DPW, *Report of the minister of public works*, 1945–52.

28 E. Tumak, 'Arthur Meighen Building, Toronto: Building Report 92-18,' FHBRO (Ottawa: Environment Canada 1992), and 'Postal Station "B," Montreal,' *Canadian Builder* 1, no. 5 (November–December 1951), 20–1.

29 NA, RG11, vol. 4139, file 11753-6, Public works estimates, 1948–9.

30 NA, RG11, vol. 3298, Public works estimates, 1948–9, pp. 79–82.

31 E. Mills, 'Federal Building, Victoria, British Columbia: Building Report 91-208,' FHBRO (Ottawa: Environment Canada 1992).

32 Other examples of this type of standard post office have been evaluated in F. Graham, 'Post Office, Chapleau, Ontario; Government of Canada Building, Geraldton, Ontario; Federal Building, Little Current, Ontario: Building Reports 89-152, 90-147, 90-148,' FHBRO (Ottawa: Environment Canada, Ottawa 1991).

33 Canada, House of Commons, *Debates*, 28 June 1951, 4827. E.G. Hansell, member of Parliament for MacLeod, to Alphonse Fournier, minister of public works.

34 Research and evaluation reports on these buildings include R. Hunter, 'Customs and Immigration Stations at St-Théophile, Quebec and St-Bernard-de-Lacolle, Quebec: Building Reports 89-131 and 89:133,' FHBRO (Ottawa: Environment Canada 1989); S. Ricketts, 'Customs and Immigration Border Station, St-Bernard-de-Lacolle, Quebec: Building Report 89-131,' FHBRO (Ottawa: Environment Canada 1989); and G. Fulton, 'Border Crossing Facilities at Andover, N.B.; Stanhope, Quebec; Emerson East, Manitoba; Boissevain, Manitoba; Carway, Alberta; Douglas, British Columbia; Kingsgate, British Columbia; Osoyoos, British

Columbia: Building Reports 91-94 to 91-101,' FHBRO (Ottawa: Environment Canada 1991).

35 The Federal District Commission was now made up of the minister of public works, two members from the City of Ottawa, one from the City of Hull and twelve other people from across Canada, including two from the Engineering Institute of Canada, two from the Royal Architectural Institute of Canada, and one from the Canadian Institute of Town Planners.

36 As discussed in Chapter 4, Gréber had been in Ottawa in the late 1930s to advise on specific issues related to the development of Confederation Square and some of the new buildings along Wellington Street. His work had been cut short by the outbreak of war. Gréber's appointment was a blow to Canadian architects and town planners, and many letters of protest were sent to Ottawa. In the end a compromise was worked out and some Canadian professionals, who had been recommended by the Royal Architectural Institute of Canada, were engaged on the project.

37 J.W. Pickersgill and D.F. Forster, *The Mackenzie King Record, 1947–1948*, vol. 4 (Toronto: University of Toronto Press 1970), 322.

38 National Capital Planning Service, *Plan for the National Capital: General Report* (hereafter cited as the *Gréber Report*) (Ottawa 1950). Sources on the development of the Federal District Commission and, later, the National Capital Commission after the war include Eggleston, *The Queen's Choice*, 183–201; 'Plan for the National Capital,' Royal Architectural Institute of Canada, *Journal* 26, no. 12 (December 1949):397–421; and H. Kennedy et al., 'The Federal District Commission,' Royal Architectural Institute of Canada, *Journal* 32, no. 11 (November 1955):429–41. See also the annual reports of the Federal District Commission.

39 *Gréber Report*, 91.

40 *Gréber Report*, 92.

41 *Gréber Report*, 253–6.

42 J. Mattie, 'West Memorial Building, Ottawa: Building Report 92-01,' FHBRO (Ottawa: Environment Canada 1992).

43 *Federal District Commission*, Annual Report, 1948, 8–10. For a general analysis of Cormier's work see I. Gournay, ed., *Ernest Cormier and the Université de Montréal* (Montreal: Canadian Centre for Architecture 1990). See also *Journal of Canadian Art History* 13–14, nos. 1 and 2 (1990–1); the entire issue is devoted to the work of Cormier.

44 Cormier's drawings also show a large plaza (which would have accentuated the sense of civic grandeur) in front of the building. It was never completed.

45 G. Cherry, ed., *Shaping the Urban World* (London: Mansell 1980), 123. The 1944 Greater London Plan also introduced the idea of a green belt as a mean of containing suburban growth. A.M. Edwards, *The Design of Surburbia: A Critical Study in Environmental History* (London: Pembridge Press 1981), 151–52.

46 Cherry, *Shaping the Urban World*, 70–2, 109.

47 The Dominion Experimental Farm and the NRC Montreal Road campus were both earlier examples of government development outside the central core, but in both cases the suburban locations were called for by their functions, which were incompatible with an urban setting.

48 The Dominion Bureau of Statistics building was followed soon after by a power plant (1950–1), by architects Ross, Patterson, Townshend and Fish; a storage building (1950–1); a virus laboratory (1953–5), a hygiene laboratory (1953–57), and a food and drug laboratory (1953–4) by architects Marani and Morris; and an archives storage building (1953–4). Several other buildings, dating from the 1960s, 1970s, and 1980s, did not adhere to the formula established in the 1950s.

49 F.R. Hayes, *The Chaining of Prometheus: Evolution of a Power Structure for Canadian Science* (Toronto: University of Toronto Press 1973), 3.

50 Bothwell and Kilbourn, *C.D. Howe*, 182.

51 Canada, Department of Agriculture, *Canada Agriculture: The First 100 Years* (Ottawa 1967), 35–6, 45.

52 By 1953 Science Service Branch laboratories for the Department of Agriculture had been constructed at Kentville, Nova Scotia (1950–1), Charlottetown (1951–2), Ste-Anne-de-la-Pocatière, Quebec (1951–2); St-Jean, Quebec (1951–2), Fredericton (1952–3); Belleville, Ontario (1952–3), and the University of Western Ontario, London (1952–3). Smaller laboratories were also built at Sault Ste Marie and Chatham in Ontario, Indian Head and Swift Current in Saskatchewan, and Lennoxville in Quebec.

53 The Department of Fisheries and Oceans maintained research stations at Nanaimo, British Columbia, and at Halifax.

54 DPW, *Report of the Minister of Public Works for the Fiscal Year Ended 31 March 1955* (Ottawa 1956), 32.

55 Architectural History Branch, 'Institute for Environmental Chemistry Laboratories (Building M-12) and Institute of Research in Construction (Building M-20), National Research Council, Ottawa, Ontario: Building Report 90-245,' FHBRO (Ottawa: Environment Canada 1991).

56 B. Beaghan, historian, Royal Canadian Mounted Police, conversation with author, Ottawa, 30 November 1992.

57 The staff architect, A.B. Wright, was sent to Newfoundland in 1949 to coordinate the work of the Chief Architect's Branch in the province. Owram, *Building for Canadians*, 272.

58 Agnew, *Canadian Hospitals*, 53–5. G.J. Wherrett, *The Miracle of the Empty Beds: A History of Tuberculosis in Canada* (Toronto: University of Toronto Press 1977), chap. 7.

59 Wherrett, *The Miracle of the Empty Beds*, 52.

60 Department of National Health and Welfare, *Report of the Minister of Health and Welfare, 1949* (Ottawa 1950), 105.

61 M.E. Armstrong-Reynolds, 'Former Moose Factory Indian Hospital, Moose Factory, Ontario: Building Report 88-120,' FHBRO (Ottawa: Environment Canada 1988). See also M. Armstrong-Reynolds, 'Former Indian Hospital, Sioux Lookout, Ontario: Building Report 88-121,' FHBRO (Ottawa: Environment Canada 1988).

62 After the war the Department of National Health and Wealth managed a grants program for new hospital construction in Canada. Much of the work of the Hospital Design Division consisted of reviewing applications for grants, developing model plans, and defining basic hospital design standards, as well as developing preliminary plans for hospitals built for the department.

63 A first-hand assessment of the department in the early 1950s was later written by Major-General H.A. Young, who was appointed deputy minister in 1953 with a mandate to carry out an extensive reorganization of the department. NA, MG31, E8, H.A. Young Papers, 'Review of the Department of Public Works, Aug. 1962.' The tired state of the Chief Architect's Branch and its inability to cope with the increasing volumes of work was confirmed by E.A. Gardner, who took over as assistant chief architect in 1952 and who became chief architect soon after. NA, Sound Archives, C 42467, acc. 1984-459, Interview J. Wright with E.A. Gardner, former chief architect. See also Owram, *Building for Canadians*, 280–1.

64 Owram, *Building for Canadians*, 260.

65 According to Brault's personnel file he had completed two years of architectural study at Cornell University and in 1913 successfully passed by correspondence exams that made him an associate of the Royal Institute of British Architects. He came to Ottawa with letters of recommendation from three of the most successful Montreal firms – Edward and William Maxwell, Ross and Macfarlane, and Ernest I. Barott – though the nature of his jobs at these firms was not stated. He was first listed as a member of the Chief Architect's Branch in 1915 and he progressed steadily through the system. NA, RG32, Public Service Commission, Historical Series, s.v. 'J.C.G. Brault.'

66 NA, RG32, vol. 27, memo from G.T. Jackson to D.R. Turnball, Civil Service Commission, 22 August 1947.

67 NA, RG32, vol. 27, memo from the director of personnel, Civil Service Commission, 11 August 1947.

68 NA, RG32, vol. 27, memorandum to Mr Nelson, 26 August 1947, regarding architects on the staff at the Chief Architect's Branch. This memorandum identifies thirteen architects working in the branch, of whom six had been hired prior to 1918.

69 Owram, *Building for Canadians*, 277. By 1950 engineering graduate could expect to earn $3,650 per year in government service, $4,250 in teaching, and $9,300 in the private sector.

70 NA, RG32, vol. 27, memo from G.T. Jackson to D.R. Turnball, Civil Service Commission, 22 August 1947.

71 Owram, *Building for Canadians*, 283.

72 The fragmentation of federal construction services was considered highly inefficient. Owram, *Building for Canadians*, 285.

73 For example, in 1949 architects were appointed for major public buildings in Vancouver and Winnipeg but construction did not begin until the mid-1950s.

74 NA, MG31, E8, H.A. Young Papers, 'Review of the Department of Public Works, August 1962.'

CHAPTER EIGHT

1 R. Bothwell, I. Drummond, and J. English, *Canada Since 1945* (Toronto: University of Toronto Press, 1981), 139–44; Bothwell and Kilbourn, *C.D. Howe: A Biography*, 261; and Creighton, *The Forked Road*, 243.

2 For a general discussion of the reorganization of the department, see Owram, *Building for Canadians*, 275–302. For a personal account, see NA, MG31, E8, H.A. Young Papers, 'Review of the Department of Public Works, Aug. 1962.'

3 The article, published in November 1953, was quoted by a member of Parliament in Canada, House of Commons, *Debates*, 9 April 1954, 3946.

4 H.A. Young was born in Winnipeg in 1898. Prior to his appointment as deputy minister of resources and development, he was appointed vice-president of the Central Mortgage and Housing Corporation. He remained the deputy minister of public works until 1963.

5 NA, MG31, E8, H.A. Young Papers, 'Review of the Department of Public Works, August 1962.'

6 C. Hicks, 'Preliminary Design Division,' *Dispatch* (Winter 1956–7): 2–3. The new divisions were created in March 1955. C. Hicks, 'PWD Building Designers Average $1 Million of Work Each Week,' *Public Works in Canada* 5, no. 6 (June 1957): 10.

7 In the fiscal year 1950–1 the budget for public buildings was $51.9 million. In 1958–9 the budget had risen to $116.2 million. (Figures taken from DPW, *Re-*

port of the Minister of Public Works, 1950–1, 1958–9.) Other sources on the construction volumes of the Department of Public Works during this period include H.C. Green, 'DPW Construction Planning,' *Engineering and Contract Record* 71, no. 1 (January 1958): 102–4; and H.A. Young, 'New Look in Federal Public Works,' *Public Works in Canada* 10, no. 6 (June 1962): 10–13.

8 Much of the biographical information on E.A. Gardner is based on an interview conducted in 1980. A tape of the interview is held by NA, Sound Archives, C 42467, acc. 1984-459, E.A. Gardner, former chief architect, interview with J. Wright. See also 'Appointment,' Royal Architectural Institute of Canada, *Journal* 29, no. 5 (May 1952):157. Born in 1902, Gardner was educated at McGill and graduated in 1927. As a student he worked during the summer in the office of J.A. Ewart and with the firm of Richards and Abra. After graduation he worked with Cecil Burgess, entering into partnership in 1930. Private commissions disappeared during the war, and in 1940 Gardner took his first job with the federal government.

9 Hicks, 'Preliminary Design Division,' 3.

10 Much has been written in the past decade on post-war architecture in Canada. Recent general surveys of this period include G. Baird and G. Kapelos, 'Northern Polarities: Architecture in Canada Since 1950,' in *O Kanada* (an exhibition catalogue for Akademie der Kunste, Berlin), (Ottawa: Canada Council 1982); C. Bergeron, *Architecture du XXième siècle au Québec* (Quebec: Méridien and Musée de la Civilisation 1989); Bureau of Architecture and Urbanism, *Toronto Modern: Architecture 1945–1965* (Toronto: Coach House Press 1987); E.S. Sanderson, 'Canada,' and C. Bergeron, 'Developments in Canadian Architecture,' in *International Handbook of Contemporary Developments in Architecture*, ed. W. Sanderson (Westport, Conn.: Greenwood Press 1981); G. Simmins, *Ontario Association of Architects: A Centennial History, 1889–1989* (Toronto: Ontario Association of Architects 1989), chap. 6; and L. Whiteson, *Modern Canadian Architecture* (Edmonton: Hurtig 1983).

11 J.C. Parkin, 'Anarchy in Architecture,' *Saturday Night*, 25 June 1955:7.

12 John Bland was named director of the McGill School of Architecture in 1941. For a description of the reform of the school curriculum at McGill, see Bergeron, *Architecture du XXième siècle*, 146–7.

13 Quoted from Bergeron, *Architecture du XXième siecle*, 146.

14 'Architecture and Town Planning,' in *Report of the Royal Commission on National Development in the Arts, Letters and Sciences, 1949–1951* (hereafter cited as the *Massey Report*) (Ottawa 1951), 216–20. To assist the commission, representatives of each of the areas under study were appointed and were asked to prepare a supplementary report. Eric Arthur of Toronto prepared an essay on 'Architecture,' and

Gérard Morisset of Québec wrote on 'Les arts dans la Province de Québec.' Both essays are published in Royal Commission Studies, *A Selection of Essays Prepared for the Royal Commission on National Development in the Arts, Letters and Sciences* (Ottawa 1951).

15 *Massey Report*, 218.

16 Ibid., 220.

17 Ibid., 218.

18 J.B. Hamilton, member of Parliament for York West, in Canada, House of Commons, *Debates*, 1 July 1955, 5581. Hamilton went on to suggest that these 'newer men' should be given an opportunity to work for the department.

19 It is interesting to note that the architects for both projects were first appointed in 1949, but there is no indication that the designs date from that period. The Vancouver Customs House was originally identified in 1945 and 1948 as a four-storey building but, like many projects of the period, it had to be expanded to accommodate a much larger civil service. Construction contracts were not signed until late 1954, which would suggest that the drawings were being prepared over the course of the year. Sources on the Vancouver Customs House include 'Largest Concrete Structure Completed,' *Public Works in Canada* 3, no. 3 (March 1955):22. On the Winnipeg building, see 'General Post Office and Terminal Building, Winnipeg, Manitoba,' Royal Architectural Institute of Canada, *Journal* 36, no. 2 (February 1959):33–7.

20 It was constructed of reinforced concrete, probably in response to the shortage of steel at the time. At its completion it was considered the largest concrete structure ever built in Canada.

21 'Federal Building, Adelaide Street, Toronto,' Royal Architectural Institute of Canada, *Journal* 33, no. 5 (May 1956):178. The project files for this building are found in NA, RG11, vols. 4943–5, file 746-652.

22 R.H. Small, in Canada, House of Commons, *Debates*, 19 July 1955, 6393.

23 'Post Office, Mount Royal,' *Canadian Architect* 1, no. 3, (March 1956):29–32. 'Truro Building to Follow Ultra Modern Design,' *Public Works in Canada* 4, no. 7 (July 1956):45.

24 The young associate was Guy Desbarets. This project marked the beginning of Desbarets' long association with the Department of Public Works. In the Trudeau era Desbarets was named associate deputy minister of design.

25 NA, RG11, vol. 4943, file 746-652, letter from District Architect D.G. Creba to E.A. Gardner, 12 December 1956.

26 University of Calgary, Canadian Architectural Archives, Parkin/NORR Collection, 1A/75.01, letter from D.G. Creba to Project Architect George Eber (Parkin Associates), 9 January 1957. The project was clearly not a happy experience for either

Parkin or the district office. At one point the district architect wrote to Parkin regarding the most recent revision submitted by his firm: 'The drawings and specifications, taken as a whole are more than a disappointment and this Department is deeply concerned that you have completely ignored a certain amount of the comments and amendments.' Letter to John B. Parkin Associates from District Architect Creba, 18 February 1957.

27 Sources on the design of the National Library include 'The National Library and Archives Building, Ottawa, Ontario,' Royal Architectural Institute of Canada, *Journal* 32, no. 8, (August 1955):303–5; and 'Handsome Modern Structure to House National Library,' *Dispatch* (Spring 1962):8, 28.

28 *Massey Report*, 220.

29 Desbarets criticized the design of the East and West Memorial Buildings: 'The purpose of the Department of Veterans' Affairs Building is that of a government office building ... Why, then, is Ottawa being fortified with twin castle and colonnade in between? Why should an office building ... be planned on a quadrangle, so as to condemn thousands of secretaries to stare at each other across a masonry pit for half of their lives?' G. Desbarets, 'Letter to the Editor,' Royal Architectural Institute of Canada, *Journal* 28, no. 1 (January 1951):20–1.

30 'National Gallery Competition,' Royal Architectural Institute of Canada, *Journal* 31, no. 4 (April 1953):104–17. See also R. Cawker and W. Bernstein, *Contemporary Canadian Architecture: The Mainstream and Beyond* (Toronto: Fitzhenry and Whiteside 1988), 21. Designs were also prepared for a National Museum of History by the Vancouver firm of Thompson, Berwick and Pratt, but it was never completed. Sketches of the building were published in *Canadian Architect* 10, no. 9 (September 1965):52.

31 Langford claims he was aware of Martin's conservative tastes and invited Prime Minister Lester B. Pearson to the presentation. Pearson, who was known to be more receptive to modern architecture, coaxed Martin to accept the proposal, stating that 'we old fellows have to move with the times.' James A. Langford, interview with author, 15 June 1992.

32 '$15 Million Ottawa Project,' *Public Works in Canada* 5, no. 3 (March 1957):33. In the late 1960s the development was expanded with the construction of a new Taxation Data Centre for Revenue Canada, and also of the CBC headquarters, a building project that fell under the direct responsibility of the CBC.

33 *Massey Report*, 217.

34 Another very similar but smaller building was erected in St John's. Known as the Sir Humphrey Gilbert Building, it was built for the Customs and Excise Branch in 1957–9. Both St John's buildings were designed by the Montreal firm of Lawson and Betts in association with A.J.C. Paine.

35 J. Kettle, 'Five Years of DPW,' *Canadian Architect* 5, no. 12 (December 1960):66. According to the article, two-thirds of the federal government's building construction budget was allocated to projects going to private consultants.

36 The limitations imposed on the architects' freedom were criticized in 1957 by J. Kettle in 'Federal Architecture,' *Canadian Architect* 2, no. 4 (April 1957):18–24. This process was also described by the succeeding chief architect, James A. Langford, in an interview, 15 June 1992.

37 DPW, *Report of the Minister of Public Works*, 1957–67. In later years the reports no longer provide information on individual projects, only a final total. In the early 1960s the numbers ranged from fifty-eight to ninety-four in one year.

38 Canada, House of Commons, *Debates*, 9 April 1954, 3971. Previously government guidelines dictated that annual revenues of at least $10,000 had to be generated in order to justify the expense of constructing a purpose-built post office, but in 1957 that figure was lowered to $3,000 per year in order to create a larger pool of eligible communities for the program. See 'Design and the Small Post Office,' *Dispatch* (Fall 1964):1–4.

39 The clearest illustration of the diminishing profile of the public building in smaller communities can be seen in the town of Almonte, Ontario. The original post office, which was built in 1888 under the direction of Thomas Fuller, is a visually dynamic and physically imposing structure that sits on a rise of land and dominates the main commercial streetscape. In the 1970s Public Works Canada sold the old building and replaced it with a small, one-storey, standard brick post office that sits at the bottom of the hill, a relatively minor, inconspicuous feature on the street. Fortunately, the old Almonte Public Building was saved from demolition and it is now privately owned and used for office space.

40 James A. Langford, interview with author, 15 June 1992.

41 The *RCMP Quarterly*, which was published by the force throughout the 1950s, regularly featured information and illustrations of new buildings under construction. In particular, see the following articles: 'Some Aspects of the Building Construction Program of the Force,' 22, no. 3 (January 1957):207–13; 'Standard Detachment Quarters,' 22, no. 3 (January 1957):200–1; and 'RCMP Building Program,' 5, no. 4 (April 1957):25–7.

42 *Canadian Architect* 10, no. 8 (August 1965):10. The other two buildings designed by Thompson, Berwick and Pratt for the federal government on the University of British Columbia campus are the Power Service Building (1959) and the Forest Products Laboratory (*ca.* 1955).

43 During interviews, both of the chief architects who served during the 1950s and 1960s identified northern projects as among their most notable achievements.

44 J. de Jonge, 'Building on the Frontier: The Mounted Police in the Canadian

North,' paper presented to the Society for the Study of Architecture in Canada, Edmonton, June 1990.

45 For a general history of the North, see M. Zaslow, *The Northward Expansion of Canada, 1914–1967* (Toronto: McClelland and Stewart 1988), 306–28.

46 See Ibid., 319–20; and P.F. Cooper, 'Application of Modern Technology in an Arctic Environment,' *Polar Record* 14, no. 89 (1968):144.

47 G.B. Pritchard, 'New Inuvik Townsite Thrives 150 Miles Inside the Arctic Circle,' *Dispatch* (Winter 1961):1–3. Pritchard was the first chief of the Northern Construction Division within the Building Construction Branch. E.A. Gardner, chief architect from 1952 to 1963, also described the Inuvik project during an interview with the author (NA, Sound Archives, C 42467, acc. 1984–459, E.A. Gardner, former Chief Architect, interview with J. Wright, *ca.* 1985). See also 'Northern Construction,' *Public Works in Canada* 6, no. 11 (November 1958):31–2.

48 The plans for some of the Inuvik buildings are held in the University of Calgary, Canadian Architectural Archives, 254A/91.01, projects 5701, 5703 and 5704. They include a single-staff residence, a fire hall, and an RCMP building.

49 'Northern Construction,' *Public Works in Canada* 6, no. 11 (November 1958):31–2.

50 Zaslow, *The Northward Expansion*, 332–3.

51 The team included Peter Dickinson and Associates, architects, Toronto; Rounthwaite and Fairfield, architects, Toronto; W. Sefton and Associates, Ltd., structural engineers, Toronto; Brais, Frignon and Hanley, mechanical and electrical engineers, Montreal; and C.E. Gravel, civil engineer, Montreal. Sources on the plans for Frobisher Bay include 'Planned Northern Community Enclosed in Plastic Bubble,' *Public Works in Canada* 7, no. 10 (October 1959):29–30; Zaslow, *The Northward Expansion*, 343.

52 Sources on the reform of the Canadian penitentiary system in the 1960s include D. Fulton, 'Recent and Proposed Developments in Federal Corrections Canada,' *Canadian Journal of Corrections* 2, no. 1 (January 1960):2–13; D. Fulton, 'Recent Developments in Canada's Correctional Services,' *Canadian Journal of Corrections* 3, no. 3 (July 1961):269–70; 'Canadian Penitentiary Services,' *Canadian Journal of Corrections* 7 (1965):254–67; J.E. Gardner, 'The Canadian Penitentiary Ten-Year Plan,' *Canadian Journal of Corrections* (1969):271–81; and O. Carrigan, *Crime and Punishment in Canada: A History* (Toronto: McClelland and Stewart 1991), 371–4. See also Canada, Solicitor General, *Annual Report of the Commissioners of Penitentiaries*, –7.

53 See W.D. Hunt, *Encyclopedia of American Architects* (New York: McGraw-Hill 1980), 424; and 'Maximum Security Institution, Federal Penitentiary, Marion,

Illinois,' *Architectural Record* 126 (September 1959):226–30. For a detailed description of the Cowansville institution, see G. de Gennaro, *Prison Architecture: An International Survey of Representative Closed Institutions and Analysis of Current Trends in Prison Design* (London: Architectural Press 1975).

54 James A. Langford, interview with author, 15 June 1992.

55 DPW, *Report of the Minister of Public Works, 1962–1963* (Ottawa: 1963), 28–30; and DPW, *Report of the Minister of Public Works, 1963–1964* (Ottawa: 1964), 43–4.

56 K. McReynolds, *Physical Components of Correctional Goals* (Ottawa: Information Canada 1972), 15–20.

57 James A. Langford, interview with author, 15 June 1992.

58 Sources on the Glassco Commission include 'Supporting Services for Government,' in *Report of the Royal Commission on Government Organization* (Ottawa: Queen's Printer 1962), 2:25–7, 41–8, 65–6; Hodgetts, *The Canadian Public Service*, 25, 121–2, 172; and Owram, *Building for Canadians*, 300–2.

59 Royal Commission on Government Organization, *Supporting Services for Government*, 2: 41. The percentage of federal construction expenditure administered by the department had held steady at 40 per cent.

60 In fact, it was not until 1989 that the architecture and engineering services of Transport Canada and the Canadian Parks Service were transferred to the Department of Public Works. The Department of National Defence still maintains in 1996 its own construction branch. After 1961 the Building Construction Branch was responsible for the construction of foreign embassies; several were designed and built on contract in Australia, Brazil, West Germany, India, Pakistan, Poland, and Turkey. These buildings have not been included in the study because it was not possible to visit the sites.

61 The reorganization is described in DPW, *Report of the Minister of Public Works for 1963–1964* (Ottawa 1964).

62 His predecessor, E.A. Gardner, had suffered a heart attack in 1962 and was transferred to the less strenuous position of special adviser to the deputy minister of public works. Langford was interviewed for the job in 1962 but because of difficulties in approving the appointment he did not assume his duties until April 1963.

63 Much of the information on James A. Langford's career in the department is based on a interview with Mr Langford by the author on 15 June 1992. See also 'Appointment of Chief Architect of Federal Department of Public Works,' *RAIC Journal* 40, no. 1 (January 1963):11.

64 'Department of Public Works Design Awards for Architecture,' *RAIC Journal* 42, no. 9 (September 1965):69. The winners of the first awards were Shore and Mof-

fat for the Sir Alexander Campbell Building in Ottawa; Gardner, Thornton and Gathe for St Mary's Indian Residential School in Mission City, British Columbia, and Thompson, Berwick and Pratt for the Fisheries Research Board Station and the Agriculture Laboratory building in Vancouver.

65 James A. Langford, interview with the author, 15 June 1992.

66 By 1964, 55 per cent of the budget of the Building Construction Branch was being spent on laboratories and penitentiaries. Only 17 per cent was spent on federal public buildings, and this amount was spread out over two hundred different contracts. The rest of the budget was spent on special projects (such as the National Library and National Archives) and on northern construction. DPW, *Report of the Minister of Public Works, 1963–1964* (Ottawa 1964), 41.

67 'National Arts Centre, Ottawa,' *Canadian Architect* 14, no. 7 (July 1969):30–79.

68 The National Arts Centre was part of a general redevelopment of the Confederation Square and canal area that had been prompted by the removal in 1966, at last, of the railway station and train yards to the suburban fringe. In 1961 John B. Parkin Associates had been engaged to develop an overall plan for the development of the areas, to include a conference centre or auditorium, a new museum, a new hotel complex, and parks. Much of what was proposed was never completed, but the success of the National Arts Centre gave the federal government a fresh perspective on the problem of building in the heart of the national capital. Documentation on the project is held at the University of Calgary, Canadian Architectural Archives, Parkin/NORR Collection, 110A/81.14, project 6214. This file contains the correspondence and plans for the redevelopment of downtown Ottawa between 1961 and 1964.

69 '$20 Million Dollar Centre,' *Financial Post* 39 (29 May 1965): 61.

70 For a general discussion of the economic and social programs initiated under the Pearson government, see J.L. Granatstein et al., *Nation: Canada Since Confederation* (Toronto: McGraw-Hill 1990), 455–516.

71 'Brooke Claxton Building,' *Dispatch* (Winter 1964):4–7.

72 The debate on the costs continued over several months. It can be followed in the voluminous project files held by the Canadian Architectural Archives at the University of Calgary; the best summary is in a report of an interview between Parkin and the DPW dated 27 October 1966 in Parkin/NORR Collection, 110A/8.14, project 6549, box 125, file DPW 2. To assist the architects, the Department of Public Works supplied them with a report entitled 'Multi-purpose Office Buildings Cost Study,' dated February 1966, which also includes a survey of a number of government office buildings and the cost per square foot. The William Lyon Mackenzie Building in Toronto was estimated at $20.60 per square foot, while the Sir Alexander Campbell Building on Confederation Heights was estimated at $14.60 per square foot. The latter was identified as the guide for future building.

73 University of Calgary, Canadian Architectural Archives, Parkin/NORR Collection, 110A/81.14, project 6549, box 123, letter to Parkin Associates from the Department of Public Works, 2 November 1966.

74 Ibid., box 125, file DPW 4, letter to Lucien Lalonde, minister of public works from John C. Parkin, 20 September 1967.

75 J.E. Wilkins, 'Production of a Prototype,' *Dispatch*, no. 1 (1968):2–5.

Bibliography

MANUSCRIPT SOURCES

Department of Public Works

Collection of Architectural Drawings

National Archives of Canada

R.B. Bennett Papers
Department of Public Works Records
William Lyon Mackenzie King Papers
Sir John A. Macdonald Papers
National Map Collection, Department of Public Works
Public Service Commission, Historical Files
Royal Commission on Technical and Professional Services, 1930
Sound Archives, 'Interview with Mr. E.A. Gardner, former Chief Architect, 1980'
H.A. Young Papers

University of Calgary, Canadian Architectural Archives

Parkin/NORR Collection
Wynn, Rule and Wynn Collection

GOVERNMENT DOCUMENTS

Department of Agriculture, *Canada Agriculture: The First 100 Years*. Ottawa: 1967.

Federal Plan Commission. *Report of the Federal Plan Commission on the General Plan for the Cities of Ottawa and Hull*. Ottawa 1916.
Department of Health and Welfare. *Report of the Minister of Health and Welfare, 1949*. Ottawa 1950.
House of Commons. *Debates*. Ottawa 1867–1967.
– *Sessional Papers*, 'Preliminary Report to the Ottawa Improvement Commission.' Prepared by F.G. Todd. Ottawa 1903.
– *Sessional Papers*, 'Report of the Civil Service Commissioners,' no. 29a. Ottawa 1908.
– *Sessional Papers*, 'Report of the Correspondence of the Ottawa Improvement Commission Relating to the Improvement and Beautification of Ottawa,' no. 57a. Ottawa 1912.
– *Sessional Papers*, 'Report of the Royal Commission Appointed to Inquire into Certain Matters Relating to the Civil Service of Canada,' no. 16C. Ottawa 1892.
Department of Immigration and Colonization. *Report of the Minister of Immigration and Colonization, 1917–1918*. Ottawa 1919.
Department of the Interior. *Annual Report of the Minister of the Interior, 1906–1907*. Ottawa 1908.
– *Report on Industrial Schools for Indians and Half-Breeds, to the Right Honourable, the Minister of the Interior*. Prepared by N.F. Davin. Ottawa 1879.
Department of Justice. *Report of the Minister of Justice*, Ottawa 1898–1907.
Department of Marine and Fisheries. *Report of the Department of Marine and Fisheries, 1872–1873*. Ottawa 1874.
Military Hospitals Commission. *Report of the Military Hospitals Commission*. Ottawa 1917.

National Capital Commission. *Annual Report of the National Capital Commission*. (Title varies.) Ottawa 1901–67.

National Capital Planning Service. *Plan for the National Capital: General Report*. Ottawa 1950.

National Research Council. *Annual Report of the National Research Council*. Ottawa 1940–3.

– *National Research in Review, 1949*. Ottawa 1949.

North-West Mounted Police. *Report of the Commissioner of North-West Mounted Police, 1888*. Ottawa 1889.

Department of Public Works. *Dispatch*. Ottawa 1954–68.

– *Report of the Minister of Public Works*. (Title varies.) Ottawa 1867–1967.

Royal Canadian Mounted Police. *RCMP Quarterly*. Ottawa 1951–7.

Report of the Royal Commission on Government Organization. Ottawa 1962.

Report of the Royal Commission on National Development in the Arts, Letters and Sciences, 1949–1951. Ottawa 1951.

Department of Soldiers' Civil Re-establishment. *Canada's Work for Disabled Soldiers*. Ottawa [1919].

Solicitor General. *Annual Report of the Commissioners of Penitentiaries*, Ottawa 1962–67.

Statutes of Canada. 'An Act Respecting the Public Works of Canada.' Assented 21 December 1867.

– 'An Act to Provide for the Construction and Improvement of Certain Public Works and Undertakings Throughout Canada (Public Works Construction Act).' Assented 3 July 1934.

Department of Veterans Affairs. *Report of the Work of the Department of Veterans Affairs, 1950*. Ottawa 1951.

PERIODICALS

Architecture Canada, 1966–7.

Canadian Architect, 1955–69.

Canadian Architect and Builder, 1888–1908.

Canadian Hospital, 1939–50.

Canadian Journal of Corrections, 1960–9.

Construction, 1907–34.

Contract Record, 1908–12.

Contract Record and Engineering Review, 1912–33.

Engineering and Contract Record, 1933–9.

Journal RAIC, 1963–6.

Public Works in Canada, 1953–64.

RAIC Journal, 1959–63.

Royal Architectural Institute of Canada, *Journal*, 1924–59.

BOOKS AND ARTICLES

Agnew, G.H. *Canadian Hospitals, 1920–1970: A Dramatic Half Century*. Toronto: University of Toronto Press 1974.

Archibald, M. *By Federal Design: The Chief Architect's Branch of the Department of Public Works, 1881–1914*. Ottawa: Environment Canada 1983.

The Architecture of Edward and W.S. Maxwell. Montreal: Montreal Museum of Fine Arts 1991.

Artibise, A.F.J. 'The Urban West: The Evolution of Prairie Towns and Cities to 1930.' *Prairie Forum* 4 (1979):237–62.

Artibise, A.F.J., and G.A. Stelter, eds. *The Canadian City: Essays in Urban History*. Toronto: McClelland and Stewart 1977.

– *The Usable Urban Past: Planning and Politics in the Modern Canadian City*. Toronto: McClelland and Stewart 1979.

Baird, G., and G. Kapelos. 'Northern Polarities: Architecture in Canada Since 1950.' *O Kanada*, Exhibition Catalogue for Akademie der Kunste, Berlin. Ottawa: Canada Council 1982.

Bergeron, C. *Architecture du XXième siècle au Quebec*. Quebec: Méridien and Musée de la Civilisation 1989.

Berton, P. *The Last Spike: The Great Railway, 1881–1885*. Toronto: McClelland and Stewart 1971.

Birkhans, M. 'Francis C. Sullivan, Architect.' Royal Architectural Institute of Canada, *Journal* 39, no. 3 (March 1962):32–6.

Bocking, D.H., ed. *Saskatchewan: A Pictorial History*. Saskatoon: Western Producer Prairie Books 1979.

Bothwell, R., I. Drummond, and J. English. *Canada Since 1945*. Toronto: University of Toronto Press 1981.

Bothwell, R., and W. Kilbourn. *C.D. Howe: A Biography*. Toronto: McClelland and Stewart 1979.

Brennan, J.W. *Regina: An Illustrated History*. Toronto: James Lorimer and the Canadian Museum of Civilization 1989.

'Britain in the 1930s.' *Architectural Design* 49, nos. 11 and 12 (1979).

Brooks, M.W. *John Ruskin and Victorian Architecture*. London: Thames and Hudson 1987.

Brosseau, M. 'Gothic Revival in Canadian Architecture,' *Canadian Historic Sites, Occasional Papers in Archaeology and History*, no. 25. Ottawa: Parks Canada 1980.

Brown, R. Craig. *Robert Laird Borden: A Biography*. Toronto: Macmillan of Canada 1975.

Brown, R. Craig, and R. Cook. *Canada, 1896–1921: A Nation Transformed*. Toronto: McClelland and Stewart 1974.

Bureau of Architecture and Urbanism. *Toronto Modern: Architecture 1945–1965*. Toronto: Coach House Press, 1987.

Cameron, C. *Charles Baillairgé: Architect and Engineer*. Montreal and Kingston: McGill-Queen's University Press 1989.

Cameron, C., and J. Wright. 'Second Empire Style in Canadian Architecture.' *Canadian Historic Sites: Occasional Papers in Archaeology and History*, no. 24. Ottawa: Parks Canada 1980.

Cameron, K.M. *Public Works in Canada under the Direction of the Department of Public Works*. Ottawa: J.O. Patenaude 1939.

Carrigan, O. *Crime and Punishment in Canada: A History*. Toronto: McClelland and Stewart 1991.

Carter, M., et al. *Early Canadian Courthouses*. Ottawa: Environment Canada 1983.

Cawker, R., and W. Bernstein. *Contemporary Canadian Architecture: The Mainstream and Beyond*. Toronto: Fitzhenry and Whiteside 1988.

Cherry, G., ed. *Shaping the Urban World*. London: Mansell 1980.

Cooper, P.F. 'Application of Modern Technology in an Arctic Environment.' *Polar Record* 14, no. 89 (1968):144.

Craig, L., et al. *The Federal Presence: Architecture, Politics and Symbols in United States Government Buildings*. Cambridge, Mass.: MIT Press 1978.

Creighton, D. *The Forked Road: Canada, 1939–1957*. Toronto: McClelland and Stewart 1976.

Crossman, K. *Architecture in Transition: From Art to Practice, 1885–1906*. Montreal and Kingston: McGill-Queen's University Press 1987.

Davey, P. *Architecture of the Arts and Crafts Movement*. New York: Rizzoli 1980.

de Gennaro, G. *Prison Architecture: An International Survey of Representative Closed Institutions and Analysis of Current Trends in Prison Design*. London: Architectural Press 1975.

de Jonge, J. 'Building on the Frontier: The Mounted Police in the Canadian North.' Paper presented to the Society for the Study of Architecture in Canada, Edmonton, June 1990.

Désilets, A. *Hector-Louis Langevin: Un père de la Confédération canadienne (1826–1906)*. Les cahiers d'histoire 14. Quebec: Les Presses de l'Université Laval, 1969.

deVilliers-Westfall, W.E. 'The Dominion of the Lord: An Introduction to the Cultural History of Protestant Ontario in the Victorian Period.' *Queen's Quarterly* 83 (1976):47–70.

Dicken McGinnis, J.P. 'From Health to Welfare: Federal Government Policies Regarding Standards of Public Health for Canadians, 1919–1945. PhD thesis, University of Alberta 1980.

Dixon, R., and S. Muthesius. *Victorian Architecture*. London: Thames and Hudson 1978.

Edwards, A.M. *The Design of Suburbia: A Critical Study in Environmental History*. London: Pembridge Press 1981.

Eggleston, W. *The Queen's Choice: A Story of Canada's Capital*. Ottawa: Queen's Printer 1961.

– *National Research in Canada: The NRC, 1916–1966*. Toronto: Clarke, Irwin 1978.

Feasy, W.R. *Official History of the Canadian Army Medical Services, 1939–1945: Organization and Campaigns*. Ottawa: Queen's Printer 1956.

Fraser, B. 'The Political Career of Sir Hector Louis Langevin.' *Canadian Historical Review* 42 (June 1961):93–132.

Friesen, G. *The Canadian Prairies: A History*. Toronto: University of Toronto Press 1984.

Gad, G., and D. Holdsworth. 'Building for City, Region, and Nation.' *Forging a Consensus: Historical Essays on Toronto*, V.L. Russell, ed. Toronto: University of Toronto Press 1984.

Girouard, M. *Sweetness and Light: The Queen Anne Movement, 1860–1900*. Oxford: Clarendon Press 1977.

Gloag, J. *Victorian Taste: Some Social Aspects of Architecture and Industrial Design from 1820–1900*. London: A and C. Black 1962.

Gournay, I., ed. *Ernest Cormier and the Université de Montréal*. Montreal: Canadian Centre for Architecture 1990.

Granatstein, J.L. *The Ottawa Men: The Civil Service Mandarins, 1935–1957*. Toronto: Oxford University Press 1982.

Granatstein, J.L., et al. *Nation: Canada Since Confederation*. Toronto: McGraw-Hill 1990.

Gray, A.S. *Edwardian Architecture: A Biographical Dictionary*. Iowa City: University of Iowa Press 1986.

Gresko, J. 'White Rights and Native Rites: Indian Education Policy and Native Response.' *Western Canada: Past and Present*. A.W. Rasporich, ed. Calgary: University of Calgary and McClelland and Stewart West 1975.

Gywn, Sandra. 'Why Ottawa Is Afraid of Art.' *Canadian Art* 19 (May–June 1962): 210–13.

Hayes, F.R. *The Chaining of Prometheus: Evolution of a Power Structure for Canadian Science*. Toronto: University of Toronto Press 1973.

Hitchcock, H.R. *Architecture: Nineteenth and Twentieth Centuries*. Harmondsworth, Middlesex: Penguin Books 1958.

– *Early Victorian Architecture in Britain*. New York: Da Capo Press 1972.

Hodgetts, J.E. *Pioneer Public Service: An Administrative History of the United Canadas, 1841–1867*. Toronto: University of Toronto Press 1955.

– *The Canadian Public Service: A Physiology of Government, 1867–1970*. Toronto: University of Toronto Press 1973.

Hodgets, J.E., et al. *The Biography of an Institution: The Civil Service Commission of Canada, 1908–1967*. Montreal and Kingston: McGill-Queen's University Press 1972.

Hughes, G.K. *Music of the Eye: Architectural Drawings of Canada's First City: 1822–1914*. Saint John: New Brunswick Museum and Royal Architectural Institute of Canada 1991.

Hunt, G. *John M. Lyle: Toward a Canadian Architecture*. Exhibition catalogue. Kingston: Agnes Etherington Arts Centre 1982.

Hunter, R. 'The Ottawa Buildings of David Ewart.' Research paper, Carleton University May 1979.

Jordy, W.H. *American Buildings and Their Architects: The Impact of European Modernism in the Mid-Twentieth Century*. Garden City, N.Y.: Doubleday 1972.

Journal of Canadian Art History 13–14, nos. 1 and 2 (1990–1). Issue devoted to the work of Ernest Cormier.

Kalman, Harold D. *Railway Hotels and the Development of the Chateau style in Canada*. Studies in Architectural History. No. 1. Victoria: University of Victoria 1968.

– *A History of Canadian Architecture*. Toronto and London: Oxford University Press, 1994. 2 vols.

Kennedy, J.J. 'Qu'Appelle Industrial School: White 'Rites' for the Indians of the Old North-West.' MA thesis, Carleton University, 1970.

'London 1900.' *Architectural Design* 48, no. 5–6 (1978).

MacIntosh, D. *The Collectors: A History of the Department of Customs and Excise*. Toronto: NC Press 1984.

MacLeod, R. *Style and Society: Architectural Ideology in Britain, 1835–1914*. London: RIBA Publications 1971.

Maitland, L. 'The Design of Tuberculosis Sanatoria in the Late Nineteenth Century in Canada.' Society for the Study of Architecture in Canada, *Bulletin* 14, no. 1 (March 1989):5–13.

Mawson, T.H. *The Life and Times of an English Landscape Architect*. London: Richards Press 1927.

Mayrand, P., and J. Bland. *Three Centuries of Architecture in Canada*. Montreal: Federal Publications Service 1971.

McReynolds, K. *Physical Components of Correctional Goals*. Ottawa: Information Canada 1972.

Messler, N. *The Art Deco Skyscraper*. Frankfurt am Main, Bern: Peter Lang 1983.

Miller, C. 'Sir Frederick Wallace Borden and Military Reform, 1896–1922.' *Canadian Historical Review* 50, no. 3 (September 1969):265–84.

Morton, D. *A Military History of Canada*. Edmonton: Hurtig Publishers 1985.

Morton, D., and G. Wright. *Winning the Second Battle: 1915–1930*. Toronto: University of Toronto Press 1987.

National Film Board of Canada. *Stones of History: Canada's Houses of Parliament*. Ottawa: Queen's Printer 1967.

Noppen, L., et al. *Québec: Trois siècles d'architecture*. Quebec: Éditions Libre Expression, 1979.

Norrie, K. 'The National Policy and the Rate of Prairie Settlement.' *Journal of Canadian Studies* 14 (Fall 1979):63–76.

O'Malley, M. 'Mackenzie King Dreamed of the Most Beautiful Capital in the World.' *Canadian Heritage* 12, no. 1 (February–March 1986):35–7.

Owram, D. *Building for Canadians: A History of the Department of Public Works, 1840–1960*. Ottawa: Department of Public Works 1979.

Pepall, R.M. *La Construction d'un musée des beaux-arts: Building a Beaux-Arts Museum*. Montreal: Le Musée des Beaux-Arts 1986.

Pickersgill, J.W., and D.F. Forster. *The Mackenzie King Record*. 4 vols. Toronto: University of Toronto Press 1970.

Preston, R.A. *Canada's RMC: A History of the Royal Military College*. Toronto: University of Toronto Press 1969.

Safarian, A.E. *The Canadian Economy in the Great Depression*. Toronto: McClelland and Stewart 1970.

Sanderson, W., ed. *International Handbook of Contemporary Developments in Architecture*. Westport, Conn.: Greenwood Press 1981.

Service, A., ed. *Edwardian Architecture and Its Origins*. London: Architectural Press 1975.

Short, C.W., and R. Stanley-Brown. *Public Buildings: A Survey of Architectural Projects Constructed by Federal and Other Governmental Bodies Between the Years 1933 and 1939*. Washington 1939.

Shultz, E., and W. Simmons. *Offices in the Sky*. Indianapolis: Bobbs-Merrill 1956.

Simmins, G. 'The Victoria Museum in Ottawa: David Ewart and the Architecture of Gothic Nationalism.' Research paper, University of Toronto 1980.

– *Ontario Association of Architects: A Centennial History, 1889–1989*. Toronto: Ontario Association of Architects, 1989.

Simpson, M. 'Thomas Adams in Canada, 1914–1930.' *Urban History Review* 11, no. 2 (October 1982):1–16.

– *Thomas Adams and the Modern Planning Movement, Britain, Canada and the United States, 1900–1940*. London: Mansell 1985.

Smith, D. Hevenor. *The Office of the Supervising Architect of the Treasury: Its History, Activities and Organization*. Baltimore: Johns Hopkins Press 1923.

Stern, R.A.M., G. Gilmartin, and T. Mellins. *New York 1930: Architecture and Urbanism between the Two World Wars*. New York: Rizzoli 1987.

Struthers, J. *No Fault of Their Own: Unemployment and the Canadian Welfare State, 1914–1941*. Toronto: University of Toronto Press 1983.

Sutcliffe, A. *Toward the Planned City: Germany, Britain, the United States and France, 1790–1914*. Oxford: Basil Blackwell 1981.

Swainson, D. 'Canada Annexes the West: Colonial Status Confirmed,' in *Federalism in Canada and Australia: The Early Years*. Waterloo: University of Waterloo Press 1978.

Swettenham, J., and D. Kealy. *Serving the State: A History of the Professional Institute of the Public Service of Canada, 1920–1970*. Ottawa: Le Droit 1970.

Taylor, C.J. 'The Kingston Penitentiary and Moral Architecture,' in *Lawful Authority: Readings in the History of Criminal Justice in Canada*, R.C. Macleod, ed. Toronto: Copp Clark Pitman 1988.

Taylor, J.H. *Ottawa: An Illustrated History*. Toronto: James Lorimer and the Canadian Museum of Civilization 1986.

Thomas, C.A. 'Dominion Architecture: Fuller's Canadian Post Offices, 1881–1896.' M.A. thesis, University of Toronto 1978.

Thompson, J.D., and G. Goldin. *The Hospital: A Social and Architectural History*. New Haven: Yale University Press 1975.

Thompson, J.H., and A. Seager. *Canada, 1922–1939: Decades of Discord*. Toronto: McClelland and Stewart 1985.

Tobias, J.L. 'Protection, Civilization, Assimilation: An Outline History of Canada's Indian Policy.' *Western Canadian Journal of Anthropology* 6 (1976):13–30.

Voisey, P. 'Urbanization of the Canadian Prairies, 1871–1916.' *Histoire Sociale/Social History* 8 (May 1975):77–101.

Wagg, S. *Ernest Isobel Barott, Architect: An Introduction*. Exhibition catalogue. Montreal: Canadian Centre for Architecture 1985.

Waite, P.B. *Canada, 1874–1896: Arduous Destiny*. Toronto: McClelland and Stewart 1971.

Weber, E. *Art Deco in North America*. London: Bison 1985

Wherrett, G.J. *The Miracle of the Empty Beds: A History of Tuberculosis in Canada*. Toronto: University of Toronto Press 1977.

Whitaker, R. *Canadian Immigration Policy since Confederation*. Canada's Ethnic Groups Booklets, no. 15. Toronto: Canadian Historical Association 1991.

Whiteson, L. *Modern Canadian Architecture*. Edmonton: Hurtig 1983.

Wilson, W.H. *The City Beautiful Movement*. Baltimore: Johns Hopkins University Press 1989.

Windsor-Liscombe, Rhodri. 'Nationalism or Cultural Imperialism?: The Chateau Style in Canada.' *Architectural History* 36 (1993):127–44.

Wodehouse, L. 'Alfred B. Mullett and His French Style Government Buildings.' *Journal of the Society of Architectural Historians* 31, no. 1 (March 1972):22–37.

Wright, H.E. 'Partridge Island: Rediscovering the Irish Connection,' in *The Irish in Atlantic Canada*. Fredericton: New Ireland Press 1991.

Wright, J. 'Thomas Seaton Scott: The Architect versus the Administrator.' *Journal of Canadian Art History* 6, no. 2 (1982):212–19.

–'Building in the Bureaucracy: The Architecture of the Department of Public Works, 1927–1939.' M.A. thesis, Queen's University 1988.

Wright, J.W.L. *Customs and Excise in Canada: A History*. Ottawa: Queen's Printer 1964.

Young, Carolyn A. *The Glory of Ottawa: Canada's First Parliament Buildings*. Montreal and Kingston: McGill-Queen's University Press 1995.

Zaslow, M. *The Northward Expansion of Canada, 1914–1967*. Toronto: McClelland and Stewart 1988.

PARKS CANADA, DEPARTMENT OF CANADIAN HERITAGE

Manuscript Reports

Adell, J. 'Architecture of the Drill Hall in Canada, 1863–1939.' Agenda Paper. Historic Sites and Monuments Board of Canada, Environment Canada 1989.

Anick, N. 'Thematic Study: Immigration to Canada, 1814–1914.' Agenda Paper 1984-30. Historic Sites and Monuments Board of Canada, Environment Canada 1984.

Archibald, M. *A Structural History of the Administration Building, Dawson, Yukon Territory*. Manuscript Report Series no. 217. National Historic Parks and Sites Branch, Parks Canada 1977.

– *Thomas W. Fuller (1865–1951): A Preliminary Study*. Research Bulletin no. 105. Ottawa: Parks Canada 1978.

– 'The Establishment of the Experimental Farms Branch, 1886.' Agenda Paper

1981-57. Historic Sites and Monuments Board of Canada, Environment Canada 1981.

Atlantic Regional Office, Canadian Parks Service. 'An Assessment of Partridge Island and its Relation to the Immigration Theme.' Manuscript on file. Atlantic Regional Office, Canadian Parks Service, Halifax 1983.

Coleman, M. 'Marine Hospital, Douglastown, New Brunswick.' Agenda Paper 1989-36. Historic Sites and Monuments Board of Canada, Environment Canada 1989.

Cullen, M. 'Prince of Wales Armoury, Edmonton, Alberta.' Agenda Paper 1987-12. Historic Sites and Monuments Board of Canada, Environment Canada 1987.

Dick, L. *The Confederation Life Building: Early Skyscraper Architecture and White Collar Work in Winnipeg.* Microfiche Report Series no. 304. Ottawa: Environment Canada 1987.

Hildebrant, W. *Fort Battleford: A Cultural History.* 2 vols. Microfiche Report Series no. 376. Ottawa: Environment Canada 1988.

'Historic Schools of Canada.' 4 vols. Agenda Paper. Historic Sites and Monuments Board of Canada, Environment Canada 1987.

Johnson, D. 'Indian Schools in Canada including Red Bank Day School, Red Bank Reserve, New Brunswick.' Agenda Paper. Historic Sites and Monuments Board of Canada, Environment Canada 1988.

– 'Penitentiary Design in Canada before 1950.' Agenda Paper. Historic Sites and Monuments Board of Canada, Environment Canada 1990.

Mills, E. 'Rustic Building Programs in Canada's National Parks, 1887–1950.' Agenda Paper. Historic Sites and Monuments Board of Canada, Environment Canada 1992.

Morgan, E.C. *North-West Mounted Police, 1873–1883.* Manuscript Report Series no. 113. National Historic Parks and Sites Branch, Parks Canada 1970.

Rostecki, R., and C. Cameron. 'Canadian Imperial Bank of Commerce, Winnipeg, Manitoba.' Agenda Paper 1976-06. Historic Sites and Monuments Board of Canada, Environment Canada 1976.

Rostecki, R., and L. Maitland. 'Post Offices by Thomas Fuller, 1881–1896.' Agenda Paper. Historic Sites and Monuments Board of Canada, Environment Canada 1982.

Taylor, C.J. *Some Early Ottawa Buildings.* Manuscript Report Series no. 268. National Historic Parks and Sites Branch, Parks Canada 1975.

Trepanier, M. 'Public Buildings by David Ewart, 1897–1914.' Manuscript on file. Architectural History Branch, Environment Canada 1990.

Utas, G., and J. Wright. 'Post Office, Humboldt, Saskatchewan.' Agenda Paper. Historic Sites and Monuments Board of Canada, Environment Canada 1976.

Federal Heritage Buildings Review Office: Building Reports

Adell, J. 'McNeely Residence, Central Experimental Farm, Ottawa, Ontario: Building Report 86-67.'

– 'Main Dairy Barn, Central Experimental Farm, Ottawa, Ontario: Building Report 86-69.'

– 'Old Post Offices in Seaforth, Harriston, Milverton, Palmerston and Tilbury, Ontario: Building Reports 87-01, 02, 03, 04, 30.'

Architectural History Branch. 'Parliament Buildings, Ottawa, Ontario: Building Report 86-52.'

– 'Institute for Environmental Chemistry Laboratories (Building M-12) and Institute of Research in Construction (Building M-20), National Research Council, Ottawa, Ontario: Building Report 90-245.'

Armstrong-Reynolds, M. 'Former Moose Factory Indian Hospital, Moose Factory, Ontario: Building Report 88-120.'

– 'Former Indian Hospital, Sioux Lookout, Ontario: Building Report 88-121.'

Clerk, N. 'City Delivery Building, Toronto, Ontario: Building Report 83-08.'

– 'Édifice féderale, Collingwood, Ontario: Rapport 83-48.'

– 'Revenue Canada Building, Thunder Bay, Ontario: Building Report 89-149.'

Coleman, M. 'National Research Council Building, Ottawa, Ontario: Building Report 87-42.'

Coutts, S. 'RCMP Stable, 'N' Division, Ottawa, Ontario: Building Report 84-52.'

– 'Victoria Memorial Museum, Ottawa, Ontario: Building Report 85-86.'

Cullen, M. 'Long Point Lightstation, Lake Erie, Ontario: Building Report 86-77.'

de Caraffe, M., and J. Wright. 'Federal Building Montreal, Quebec: Building Report 83-29.'

– 'Royal Canadian Mint, Ottawa, Ontario: Building Report 86-04.'

de Jonge, J. 'Five Buildings, Fort Battleford National Historic Park, Battleford, Saskatchewan: Building Report 89-10.'

Dewalt, B. 'NWMP Buildings, Dawson, Yukon Territory: Building Reports 87-68, 69, 72.'

– 'Federal Building, Melfort, Saskatchewan: Building Report 87-121.'

Doherty, J. 'Federal Building, Thunder Bay, Ontario: Building Report 88-50.'

Doull, I. 'Confederation Building, Justice Building, Justice Annex, Supreme Court of Canada, Ottawa, Ontario: Building Reports 87-34 to 87-37.'

– 'Langevin Block, Ottawa, Ontario: Building Report 87-40.'

– 'CFB Esquimalt-Dockyard, Esquimalt, British Columbia: Building Report 89-202.' 2 vols.

– 'CFB Esquimalt-Naden, Esquimalt, British Columbia: Building Report 89-204.'

– 'Beaver Barracks, Metcalfe Street, Ottawa, Ontario: Building Report 90-325.'

Fulton, G. 'Border Crossing Facilities at Andover, New Brunswick; Stanhope, Quebec; Emerson East, Manitoba; Boissevain, Manitoba; Carway, Alberta; Douglas, British Columbia; Kingsgate, British Columbia; Osoyoos, British Columbia: Building Reports 91-94 to 91-101.'

Graham, F. 'Post Office, Chapleau, Ontario; Government of Canada Building, Geraldton, Ontario; Federal Building, Little Current, Ontario: Building Reports 89-152, 90-147, 90-148.'

Hale, C.A. 'Postal Station "A," Fredricton, New Brunswick: Building Report 83-28.'

– 'Postal Station "A," 126–40 Prince William Street, Saint John, New Brunswick: Building Report 83-59.'

Hale, C.A. 'Federal Building, Moncton, New Brunswick: Building Report 84-35.'

Harris, J. 'Public Building, Salmon Arm, British Columbia: Building Report 84-45.'

– 'Former Animal Diseases Research Institute, Hull, Quebec: Building Report 85-50.'

Histoire et Archéologie, Bureau régional de Québec. 'Grosse île: Rapport 90-031.' 1990.

Hunter, R. 'Connaught Building, Ottawa, Ontario: Building Report 87-39.'

– 'Customs and Immigration Stations at St. Théophile, Quebec, and St. Bernard de Lacolle, Quebec: Building Reports 89-131 and 89:133.'

Johnson D. 'Dominion Building, Toronto, Ontario: Building Report 83-31.'

– 'Military Stores Building, Ottawa, Ontario: Building Report 83-56.'

– 'Federal Building, Newmarket, Ontario: Building Report 83-71.'

MacFarlane, K. 'Former Dominion Archives, Ottawa, Ontario: Building Report 86-87.'

– 'Building No. 74 (Botanical Laboratory), Central Experimental Farm, Ottawa, Ontario: Building Report 87-57.'

Mattie, J. 'West Memorial Building, Ottawa, Ontario: Building Report 92-01.'

Mills, E. 'Federal Building, Battleford, Saskatchewan: Building Report 83-03.'

– 'Block 15, Granville Street, Vancouver, British Columbia: Building Reports 83-24, 25, 26, 27.'

– 'Gonzales Observatory, Victoria, British Columbia: Building Report 83-60.'

– 'Pacific Highway Custom and Immigration Building, Surrey, British Columbia: Building Report 84-36.'

– 'Federal Building, Victoria, British Columbia: Building Report 91-208.'

Ricketts, S. 'Four Structures of the Energy Mines and Resources Complex, Ottawa, Ontario: Building Report 86-61.'

– 'Customs and Immigration Border Station, St. Bernard de Lacolle, Quebec: Building Report 89-131.'

Saunders, I.J. 'Mewata Armoury, Calgary, Alberta: Building Report 83-82.'

– 'Royal Canadian Mounted Police Barracks ("N" Division), Ottawa, Ontario: Building Report 84-53.'

– 'Eleven Early Buildings at the RCMP Depot, Regina, Saskatchewan: Building Report 86-22.'

Tumak, E. 'Arthur Meighen Building, Toronto, Ontario: Building Report 92-18.'

Wright, J. 'Cereal Building, Central Experimental Farm, Ottawa, Ontario: Building Report 84-04.'

– 'Parry Sound Federal Building, Parry Sound, Ontario: Building Report 85-32.'

Index

Page numbers in italics refer to illustrations.